I became an uncle! Not just an old guy the kids call uncle, but a real one! I have a niece! Think of Itachi from Sarada's perspective.

—Kenji Taira, 2016

Chibi Sasuke's Sharingan Legend

SHONEN JUMP MANGA EDITION

VOLUME 2

STORY AND ART BY KENJI TAIRA

Translation: Amanda Haley
Touch-Up Art & Lettering: Thea Willis, Snir Aharon
Design: Yukiko Whitley
Editor: Alexis Kirsch

UCHIHA SASUKE NO SHARIN GANDEN © 2014 by Masashi Kishimoto, Kenji Taira
All rights reserved.
First published in Japan in 2014 by SHUEISHA Inc., Tokyo.
English translation rights arranged by SHUEISHA Inc.

The stories, characters and incidents mentioned in
this publication are entirely fictional.

No portion of this book may be reproduced or transmitted in any form or by any
means without written permission from the copyright holders.

Printed in the U.S.A.

Published by VIZ Media, LLC
P.O. Box 77010
San Francisco, CA 94107

10 9 8 7 6 5 4 3 2 1
First printing, January 2018

viz.com

shonenjump.com

PARENTAL ADVISORY
NARUTO: CHIBI SASUKE'S SHARINGAN LEGEND
is rated T for Teen and is recommended for ages 13
and up. This volume contains fantasy violence.

ratings.viz.com

NARUTO

Chibi Sasuke's Sharingan Legend

TWO-MAN CELL!!

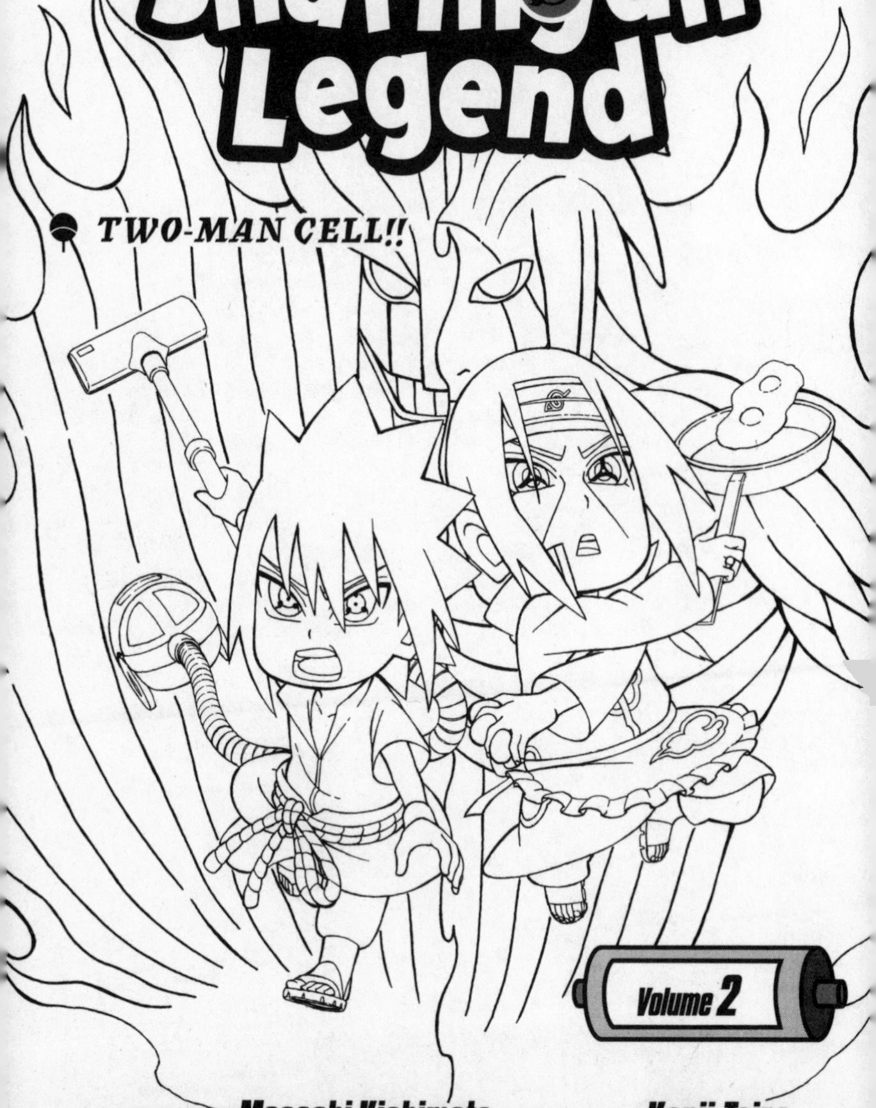

Volume 2

Based on Naruto by **Masashi Kishimoto** - Story and Art by **Kenji Taira**

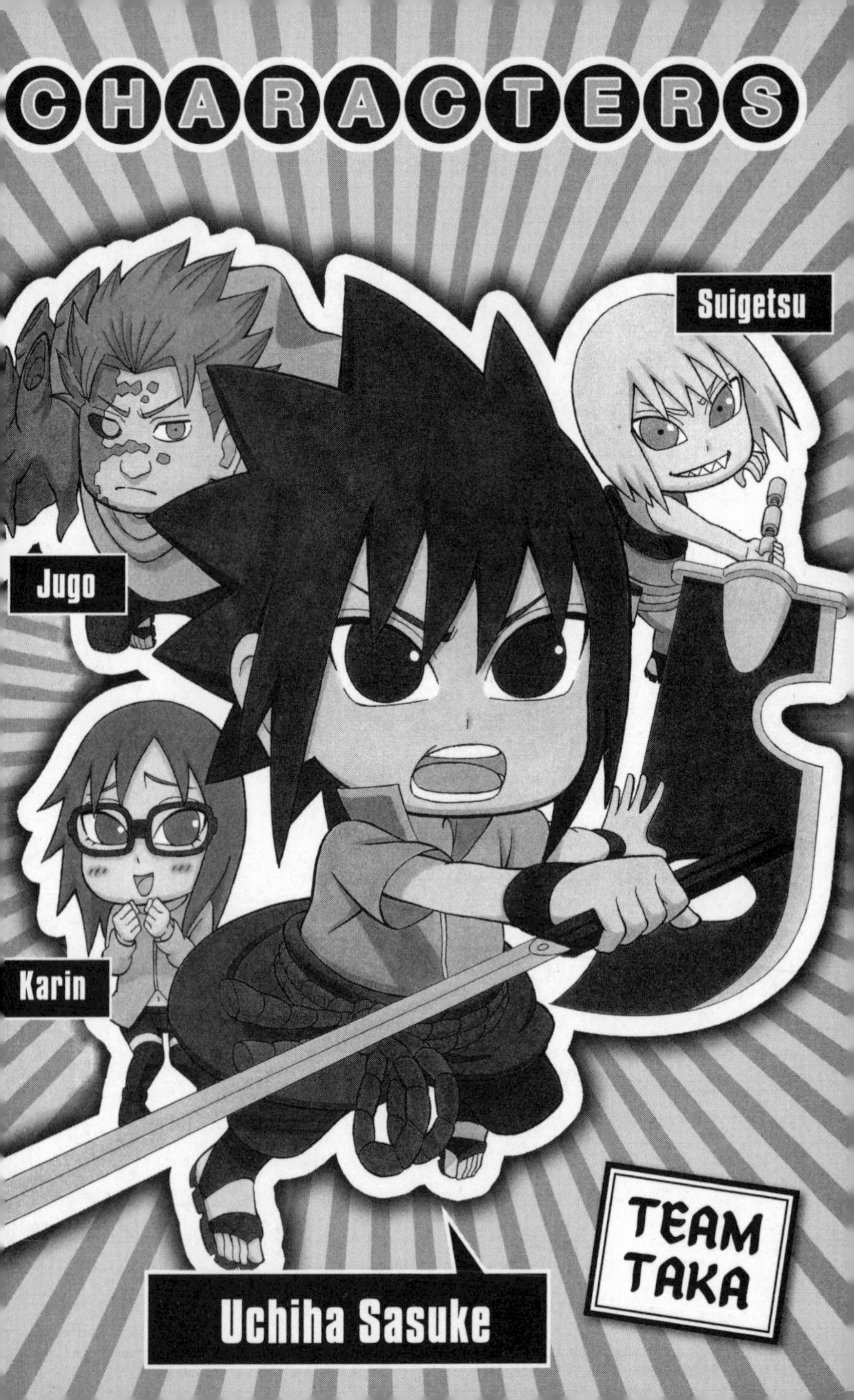
CHARACTERS
Suigetsu
Jugo
Karin
TEAM TAKA
Uchiha Sasuke

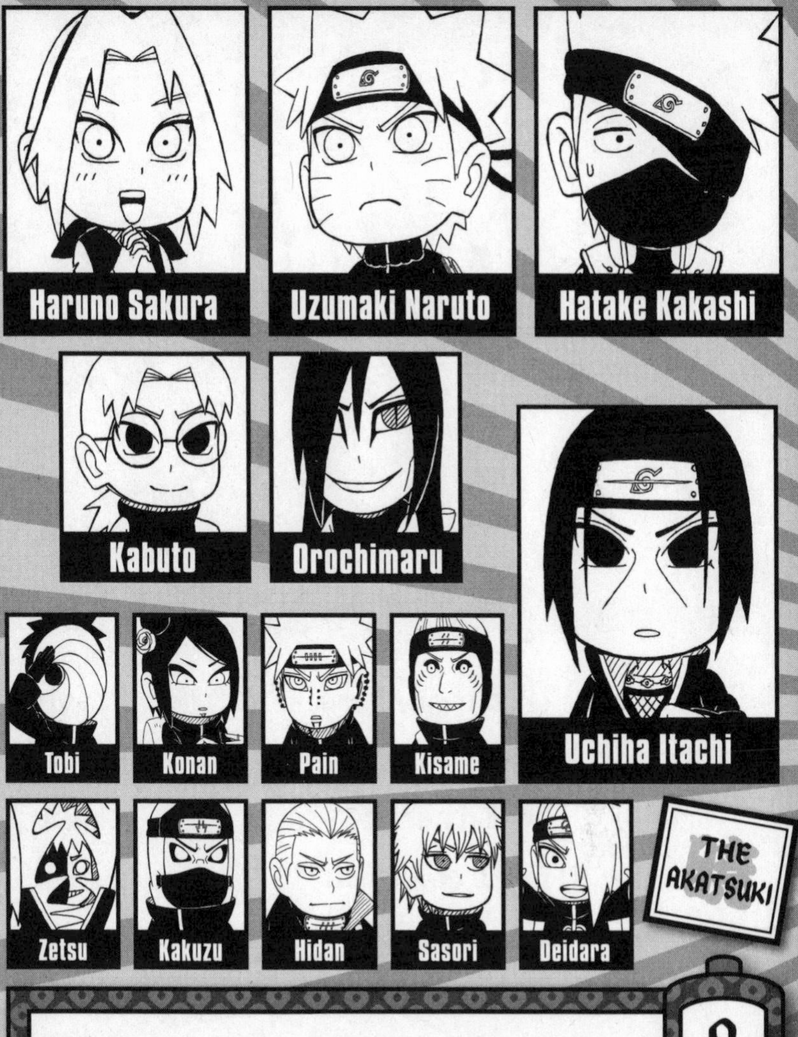
Hatake Kakashi
Uzumaki Naruto
Haruno Sakura
Uchiha Itachi
Orochimaru
Kabuto
Kisame
Pain
Konan
Tobi
THE AKATSUKI
Deidara
Sasori
Hidan
Kakuzu
Zetsu

OUR STORY

Uchiha Sasuke was once a ninja of Konohagakure Village, until he parted ways with Naruto, Sakura and the others. Now he travels as a rogue shinobi with Suigetsu, Karin and Jugo. Together, they are Team Taka. Sasuke devotes every day to the search for his big brother, Itachi. Will he ever make it to his objective? Either way, Sasuke's long journey is bound to be eventful!

NARUTO Chibi Sasuke's Sharingan Legend

VOL. 2
TWO-MAN CELL!!

CONTENTS

Chapter 6: Team Taka's Summer Vacation!! 7

Chapter 7: Summer Festival!! 22

Chapter 8: Orochimaru!! 39

Chapter 9: Signs of Autumn!! 60

Chapter 10: The Akatsuki's Winter Vacation!! 70

Chapter 11: Sasuke VS.XXX!! 99

Chapter 12: Uchiha Sasuko!! 114

Chapter 13: Two-Man Cell!! 125

Chapter 14: The Great Detective Sasuke!! 140

Special: Mini Manga 150

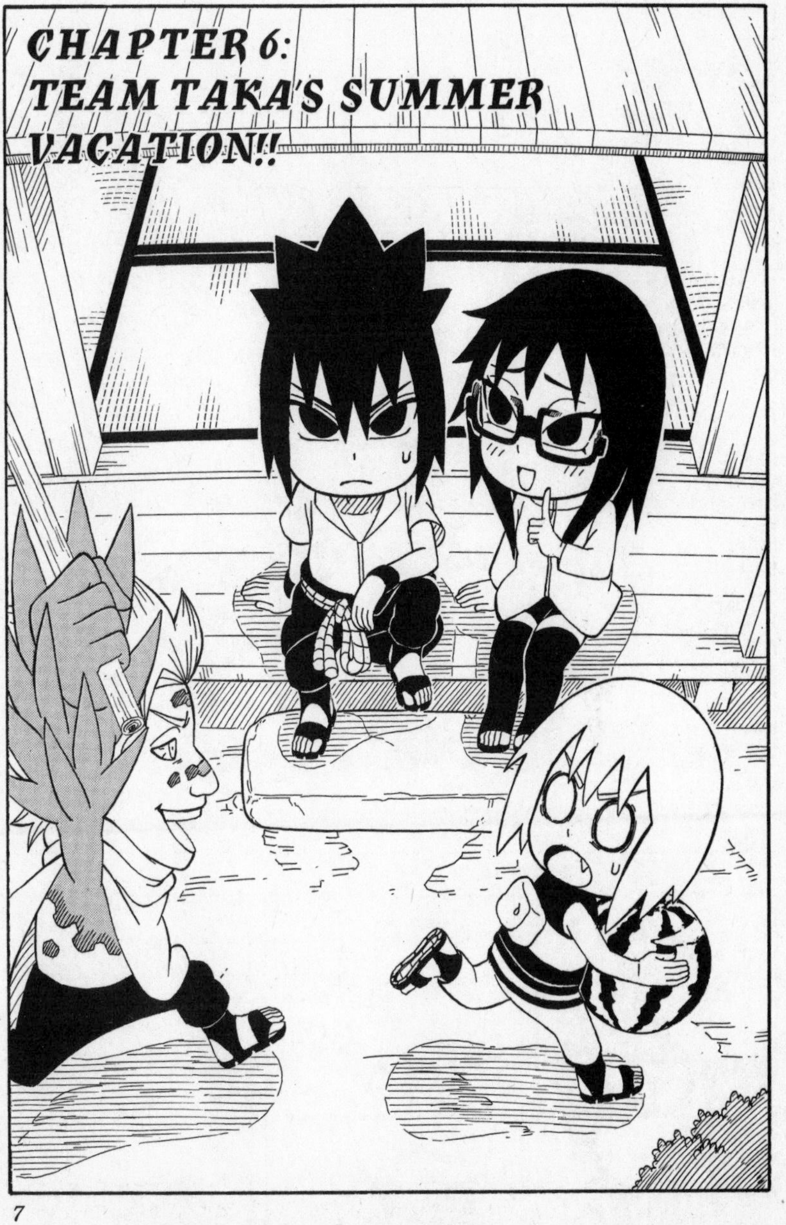
CHAPTER 6:
TEAM TAKA'S SUMMER VACATION!!

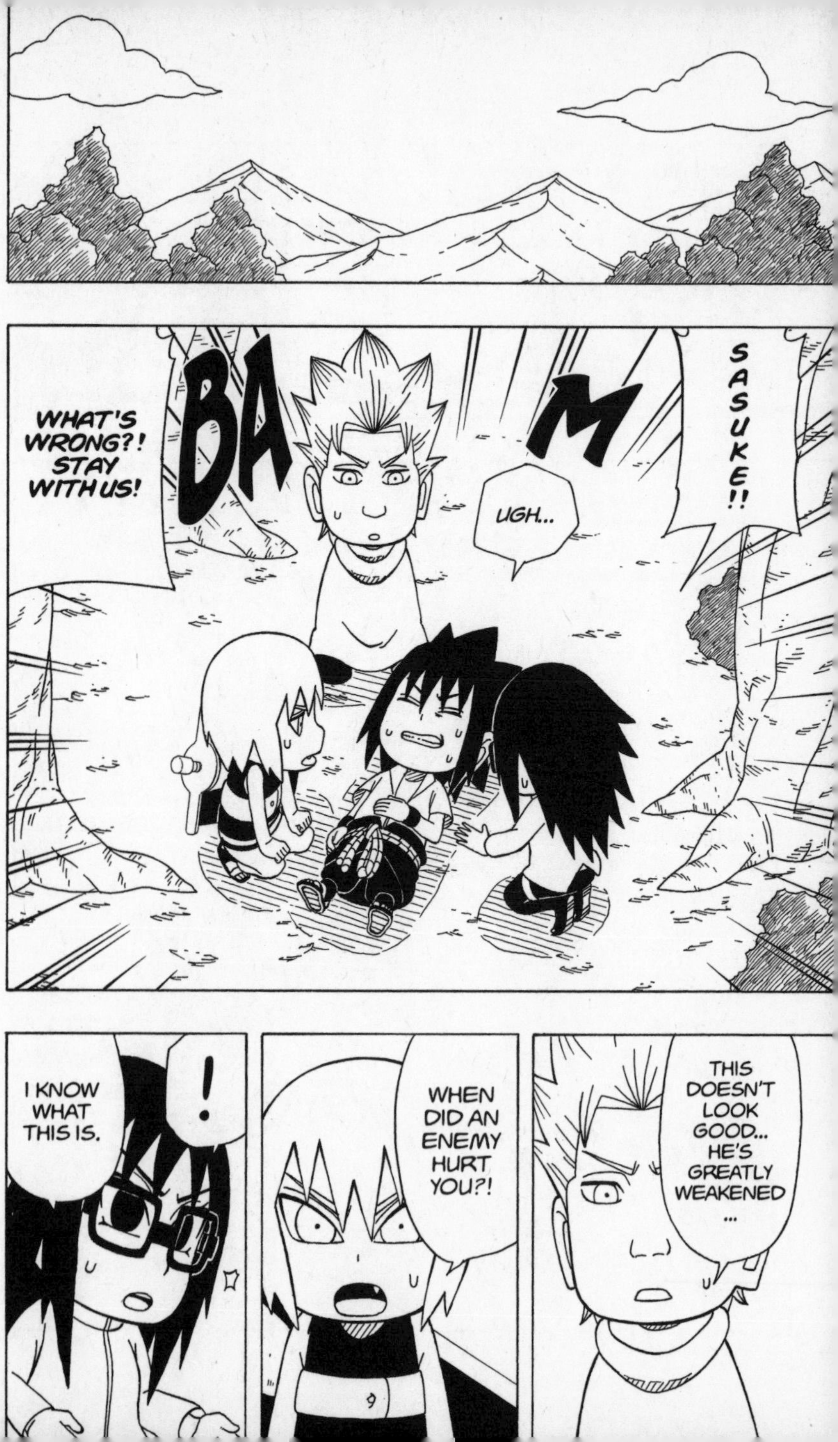
SASUKE!!
BAM
UGH...
WHAT'S WRONG?! STAY WITH US!
THIS DOESN'T LOOK GOOD... HE'S GREATLY WEAKENED...
WHEN DID AN ENEMY HURT YOU?!
!
I KNOW WHAT THIS IS.

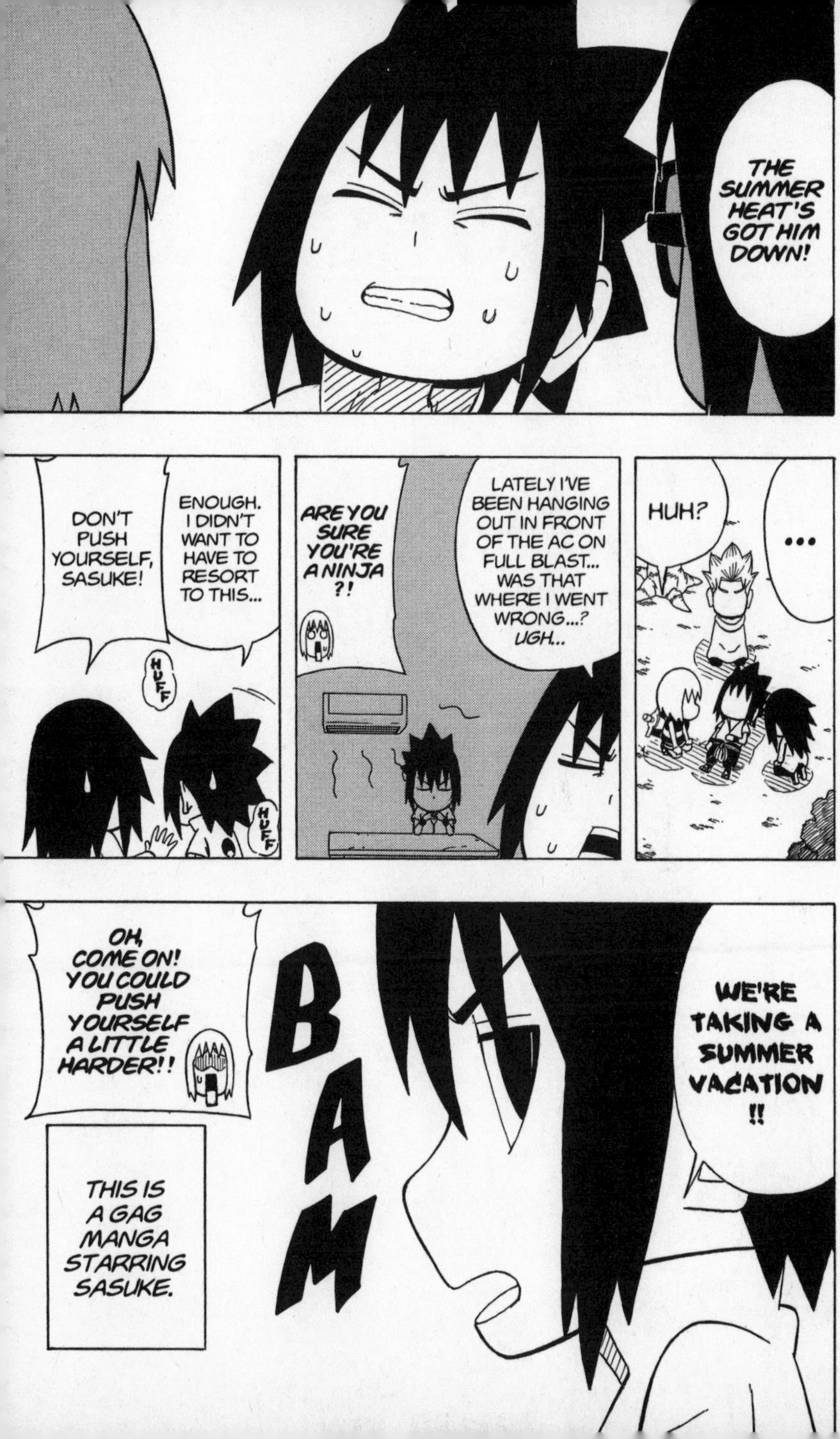
THE SUMMER HEAT'S GOT HIM DOWN!
...
HUH?
LATELY I'VE BEEN HANGING OUT IN FRONT OF THE AC ON FULL BLAST... WAS THAT WHERE I WENT WRONG...? UGH...
ARE YOU SURE YOU'RE A NINJA?!
ENOUGH. I DIDN'T WANT TO HAVE TO RESORT TO THIS...
DON'T PUSH YOURSELF, SASUKE!
HUFF
HUFF
WE'RE TAKING A SUMMER VACATION!!
BAM
OH, COME ON! YOU COULD PUSH YOURSELF A LITTLE HARDER!!
THIS IS A GAG MANGA STARRING SASUKE.

THE POOL

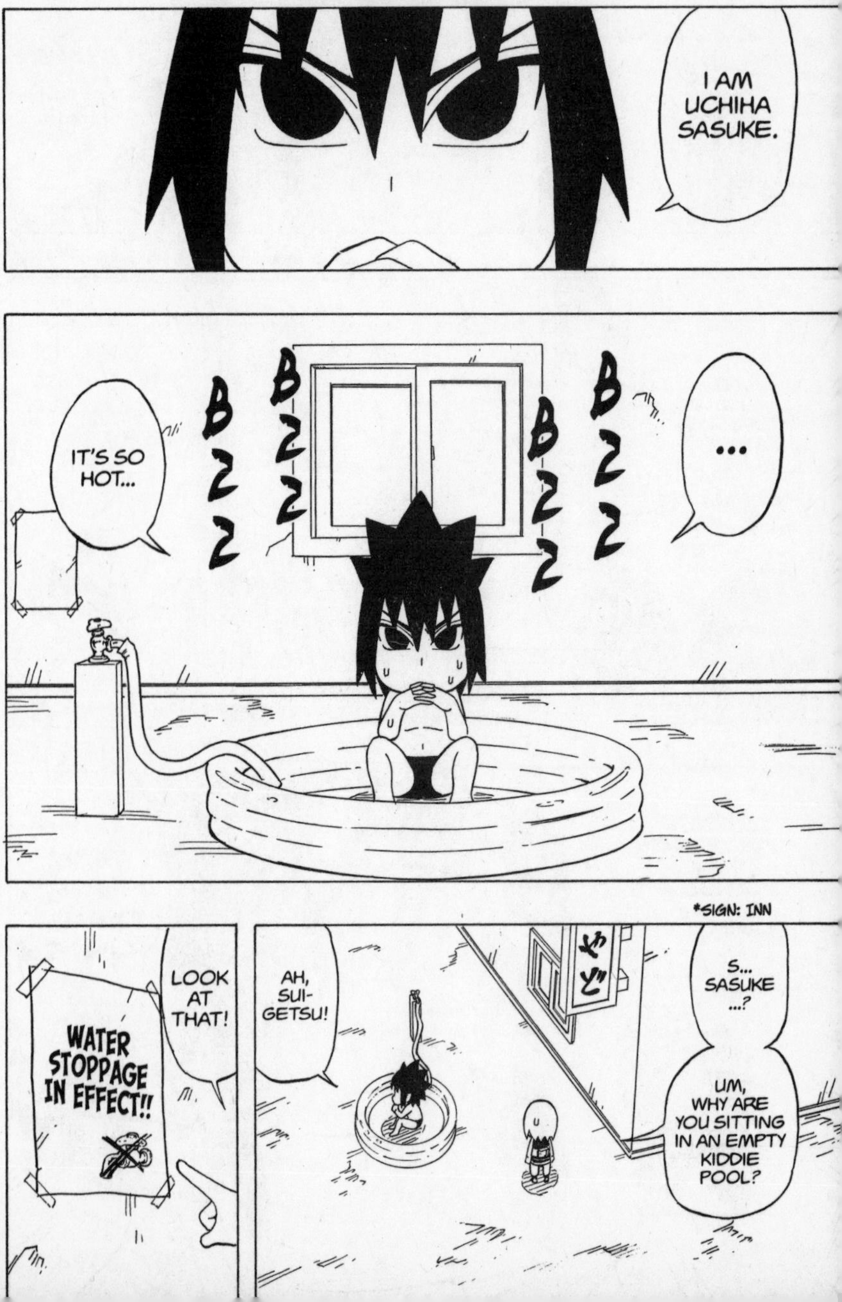
I AM UCHIHA SASUKE.
...
BZZZ
BZZZ
BZZZ
BZZZ
IT'S SO HOT...
*SIGN: INN
やど
S... SASUKE ...?
UM, WHY ARE YOU SITTING IN AN EMPTY KIDDIE POOL?
AH, SUI-GETSU!
LOOK AT THAT!
WATER STOPPAGE IN EFFECT!!

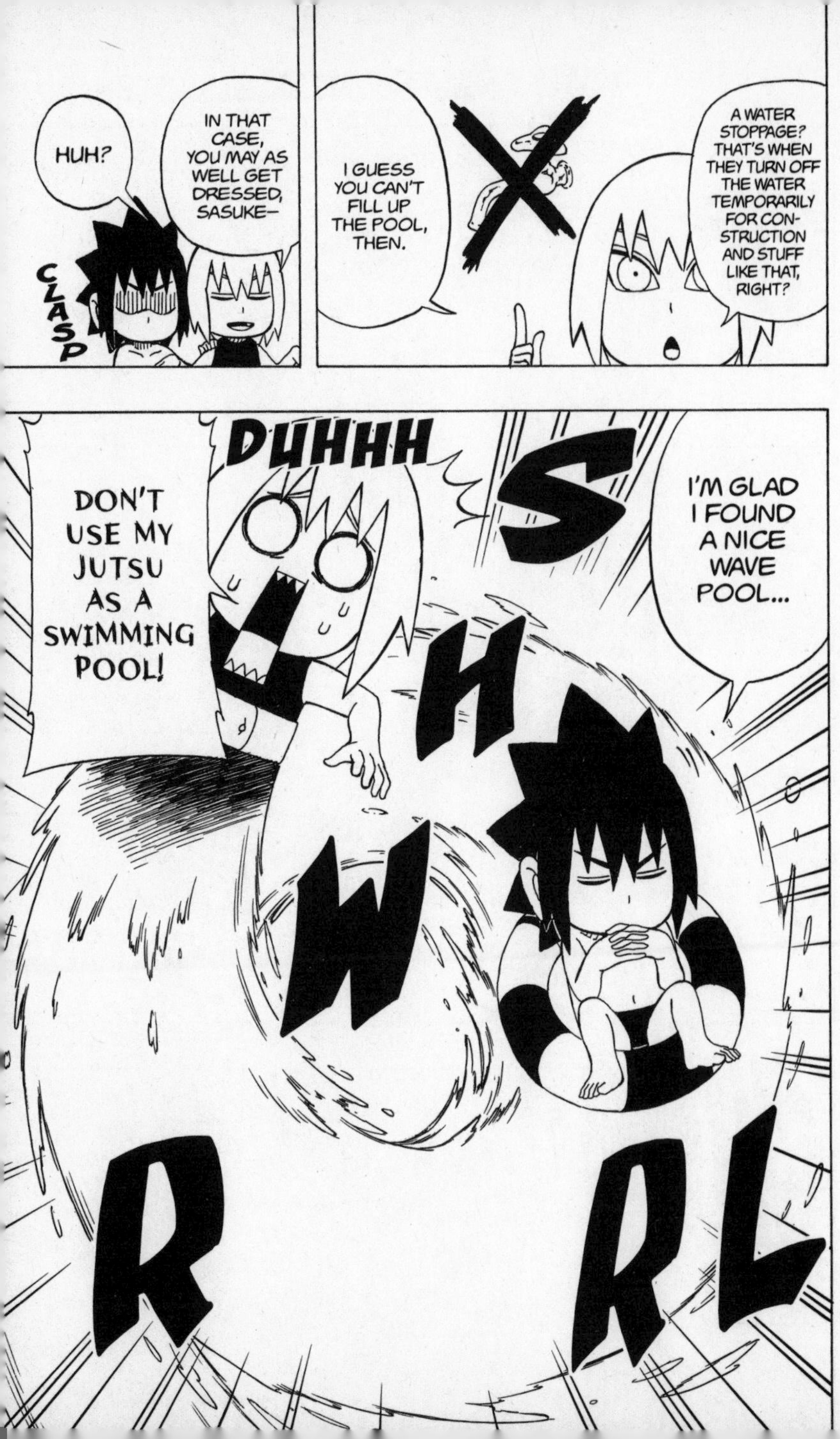
A WATER STOPPAGE? THAT'S WHEN THEY TURN OFF THE WATER TEMPORARILY FOR CON-STRUCTION AND STUFF LIKE THAT, RIGHT?
I GUESS YOU CAN'T FILL UP THE POOL, THEN.
IN THAT CASE, YOU MAY AS WELL GET DRESSED, SASUKE—
HUH?
CLASP
I'M GLAD I FOUND A NICE WAVE POOL...
SHWRRL
DUHHH
DON'T USE MY JUTSU AS A SWIMMING POOL!

NAGASHI SOMEN

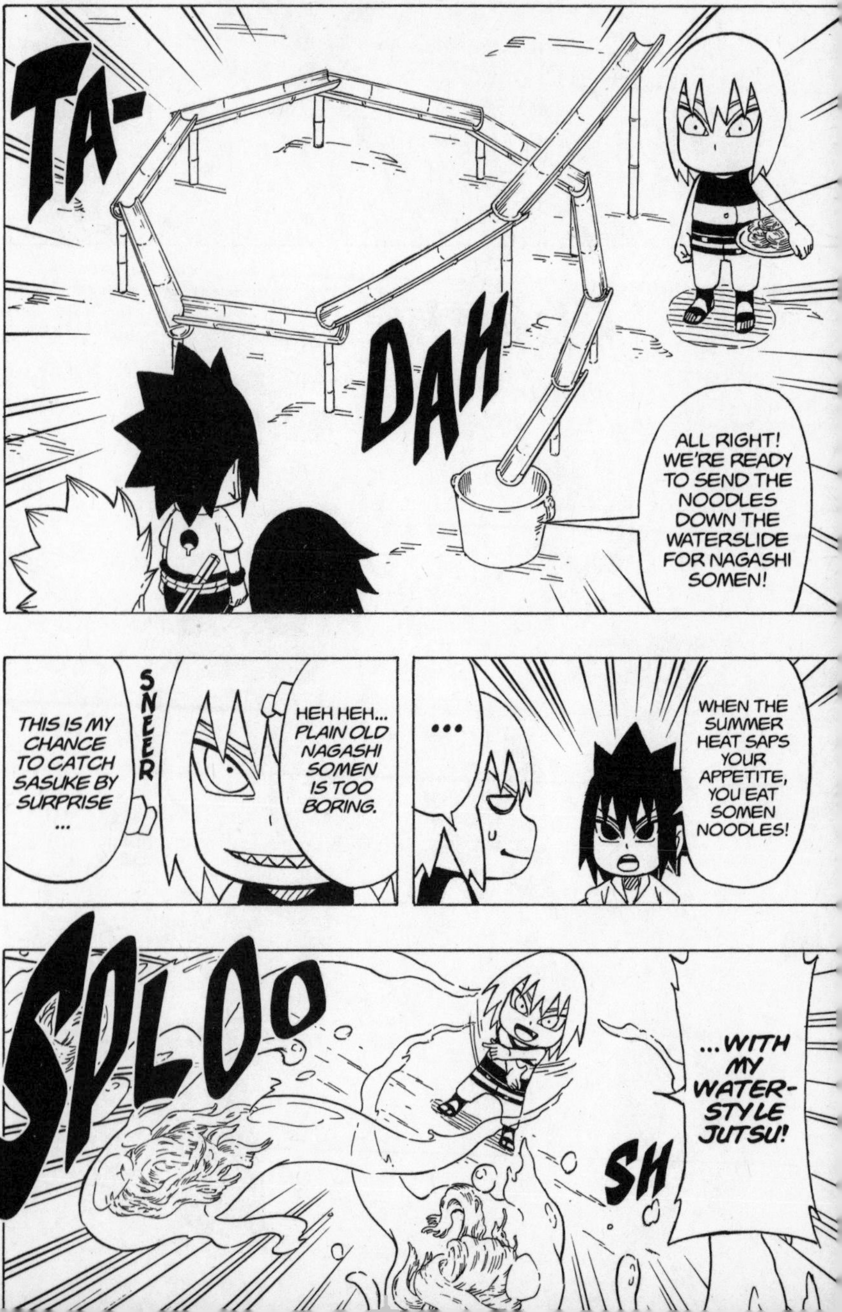
TA-
DAH
ALL RIGHT! WE'RE READY TO SEND THE NOODLES DOWN THE WATERSLIDE FOR NAGASHI SOMEN!
WHEN THE SUMMER HEAT SAPS YOUR APPETITE, YOU EAT SOMEN NOODLES!
...
HEH HEH... PLAIN OLD NAGASHI SOMEN IS TOO BORING.
SNEER
THIS IS MY CHANCE TO CATCH SASUKE BY SURPRISE ...
...WITH MY WATER-STYLE JUTSU!
SH
SPLOO

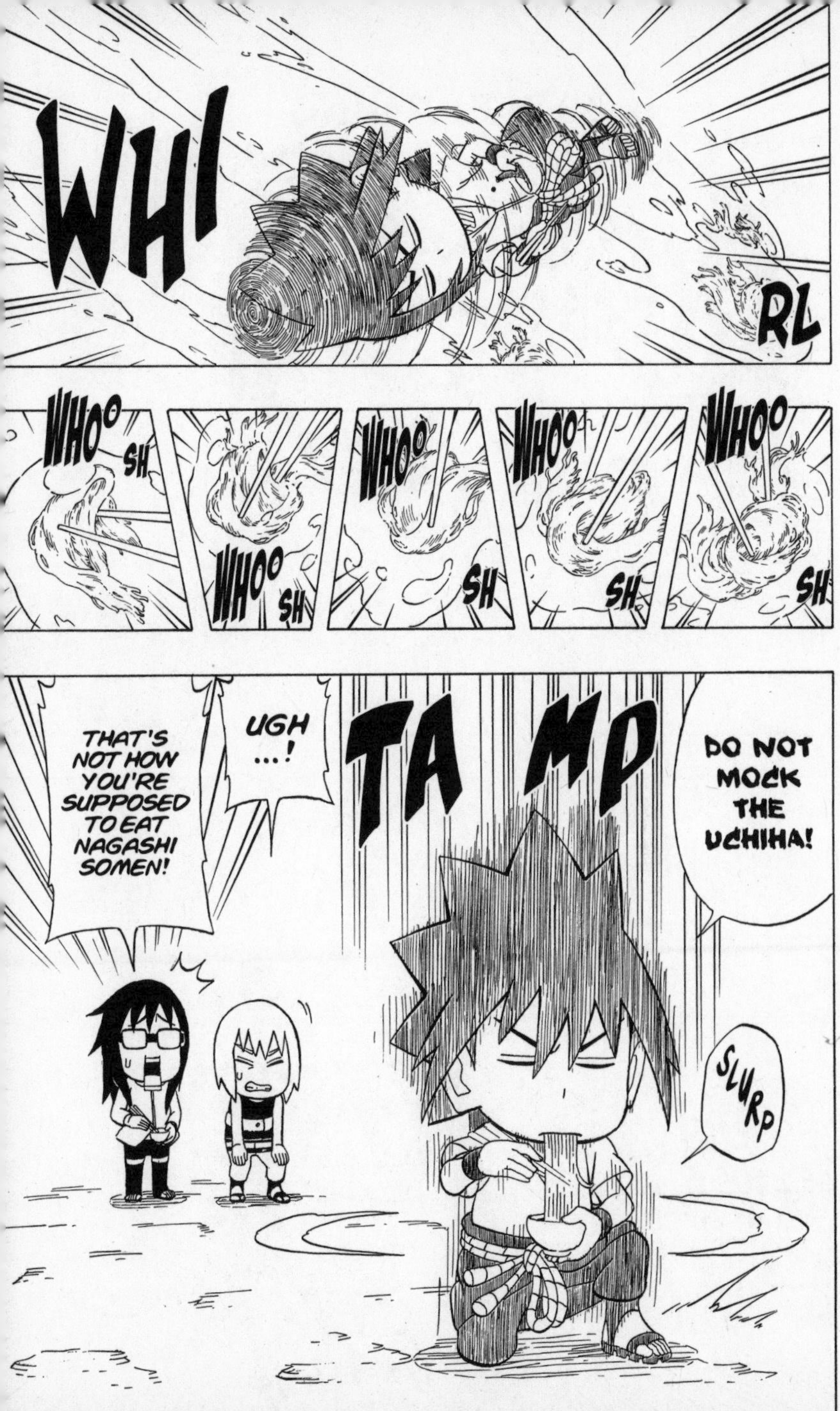
WHI
RL
WHOOSH
WHOOSH
WHOOSH
WHOOSH
WHOOSH
DO NOT MOCK THE UCHIHA!
TAMP
SLURP
UGH ...!
THAT'S NOT HOW YOU'RE SUPPOSED TO EAT NAGASHI SOMEN!

SUNTANNING

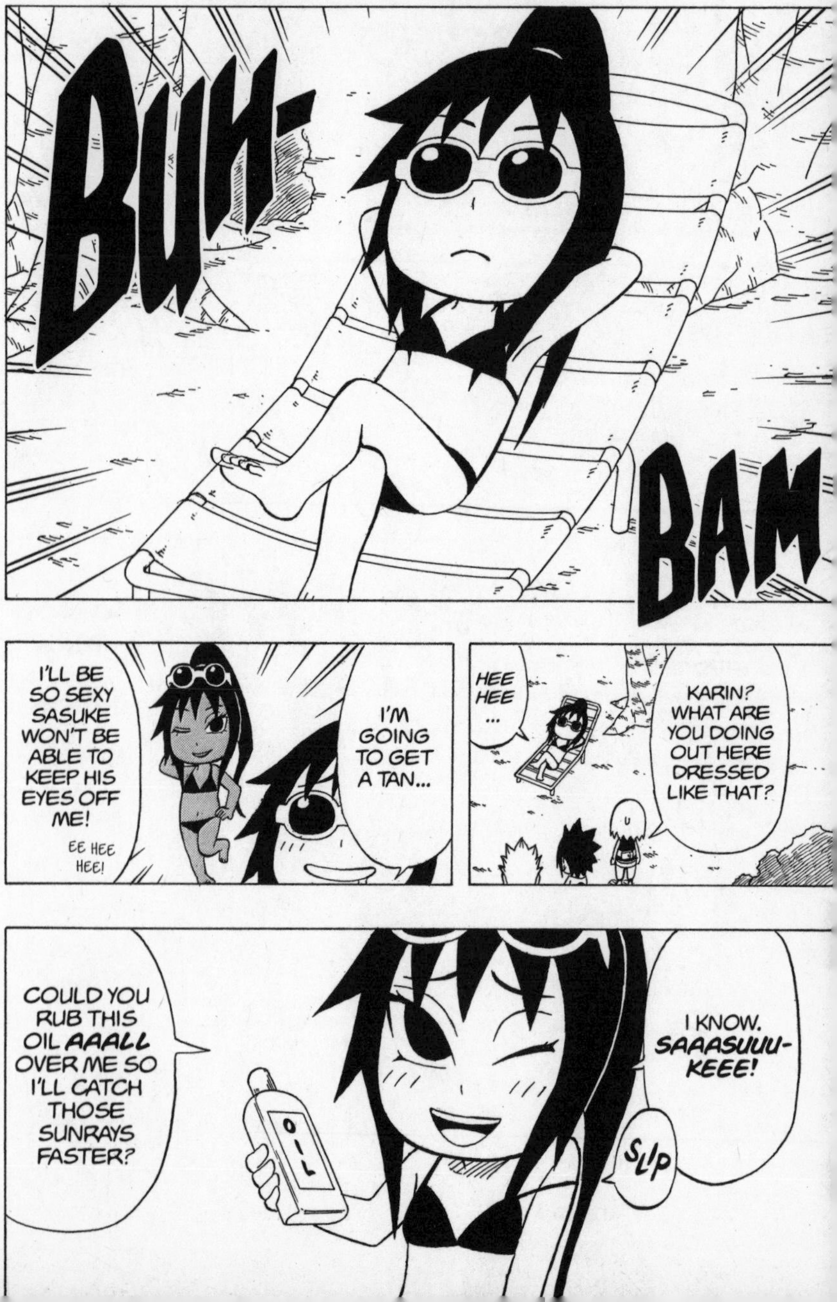
BUH-BAM
KARIN? WHAT ARE YOU DOING OUT HERE DRESSED LIKE THAT?
HEE HEE ...
I'M GOING TO GET A TAN...
I'LL BE SO SEXY SASUKE WON'T BE ABLE TO KEEP HIS EYES OFF ME!
EE HEE HEE!
I KNOW. SAAASUUU-KEEE!
SLIP
COULD YOU RUB THIS OIL AAALL OVER ME SO I'LL CATCH THOSE SUNRAYS FASTER?
OIL

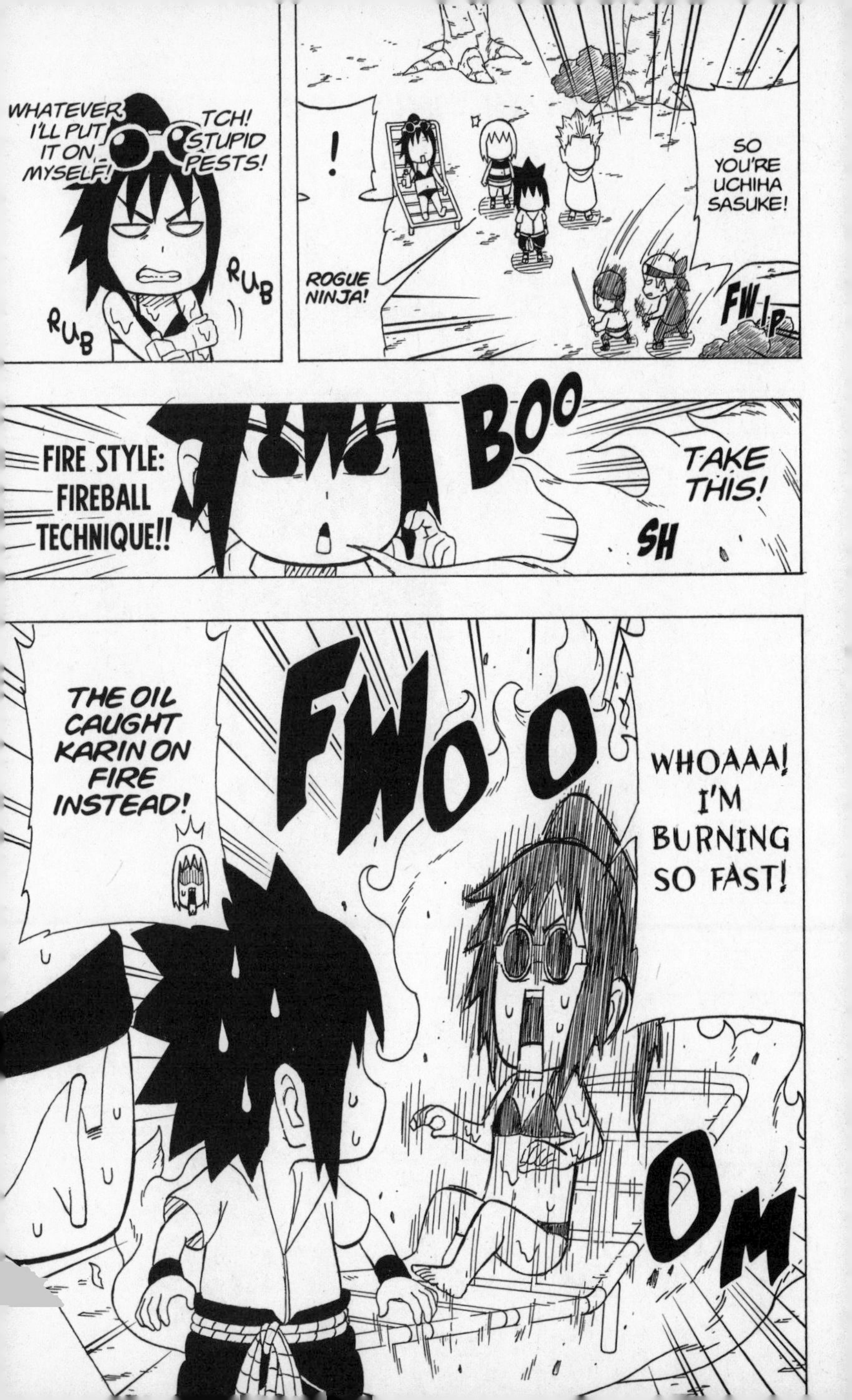
SO YOU'RE UCHIHA SASUKE!
FWIP
!
ROGUE NINJA!
TCH! STUPID PESTS!
WHATEVER. I'LL PUT IT ON MYSELF!
RUB
RUB
TAKE THIS!
SH
BOO
FIRE STYLE: FIREBALL TECHNIQUE!!
WHOAAA! I'M BURNING SO FAST!
FWOOOM
THE OIL CAUGHT KARIN ON FIRE INSTEAD!

SHAVE ICE

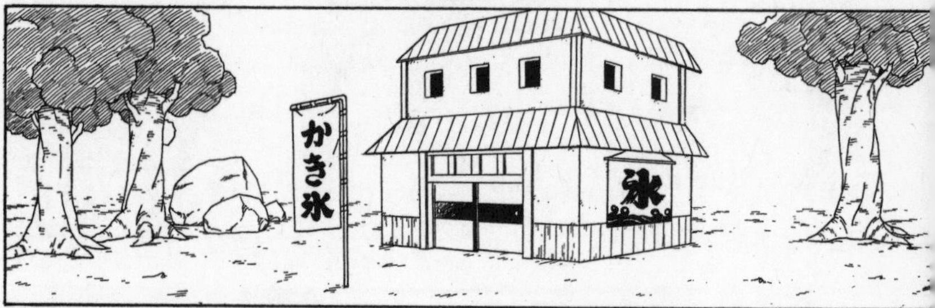
かき氷
氷

*SIGN (LEFT): SHAVE ICE, SIGN (RIGHT): ICE

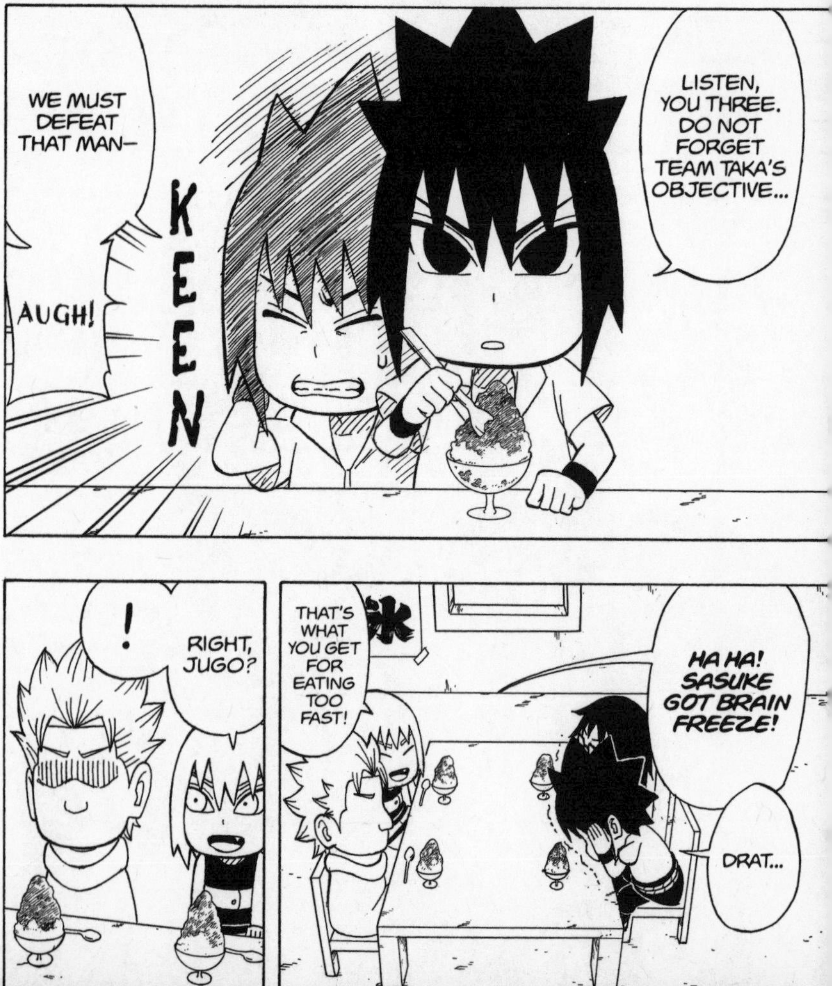
LISTEN, YOU THREE. DO NOT FORGET TEAM TAKA'S OBJECTIVE...
WE MUST DEFEAT THAT MAN—
KEEN
AUGH!
HA HA! SASUKE GOT BRAIN FREEZE!
THAT'S WHAT YOU GET FOR EATING TOO FAST!
DRAT...
!
RIGHT, JUGO?

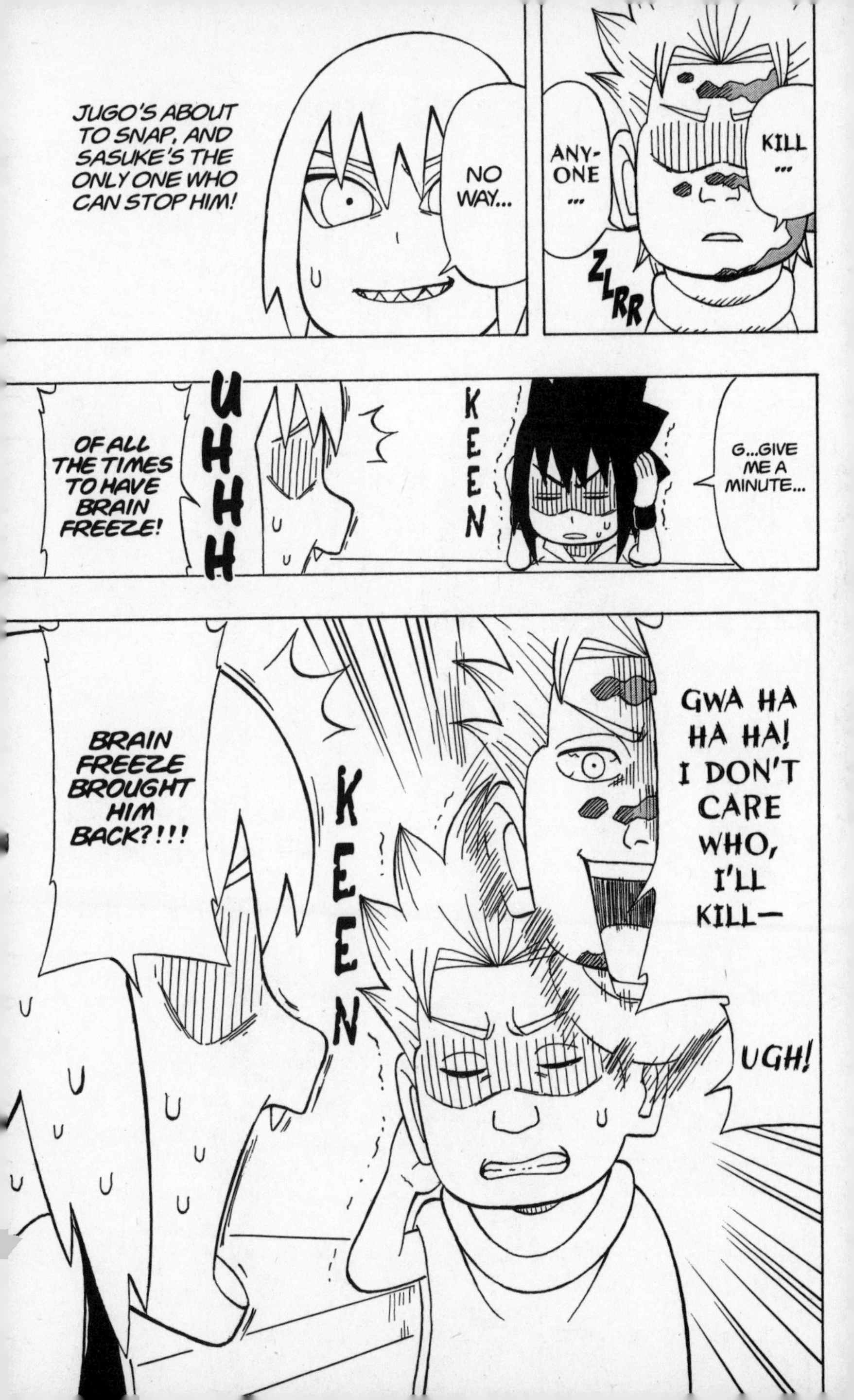
ANY-ONE ...
KILL ...
ZLRR
NO WAY...
JUGO'S ABOUT TO SNAP, AND SASUKE'S THE ONLY ONE WHO CAN STOP HIM!
G...GIVE ME A MINUTE...
KEEN
UHHHH
OF ALL THE TIMES TO HAVE BRAIN FREEZE!
GWA HA HA HA! I DON'T CARE WHO, I'LL KILL—
UGH!
KEEN
BRAIN FREEZE BROUGHT HIM BACK?!!!

TEAM TAKA VS. THE HEAT!!

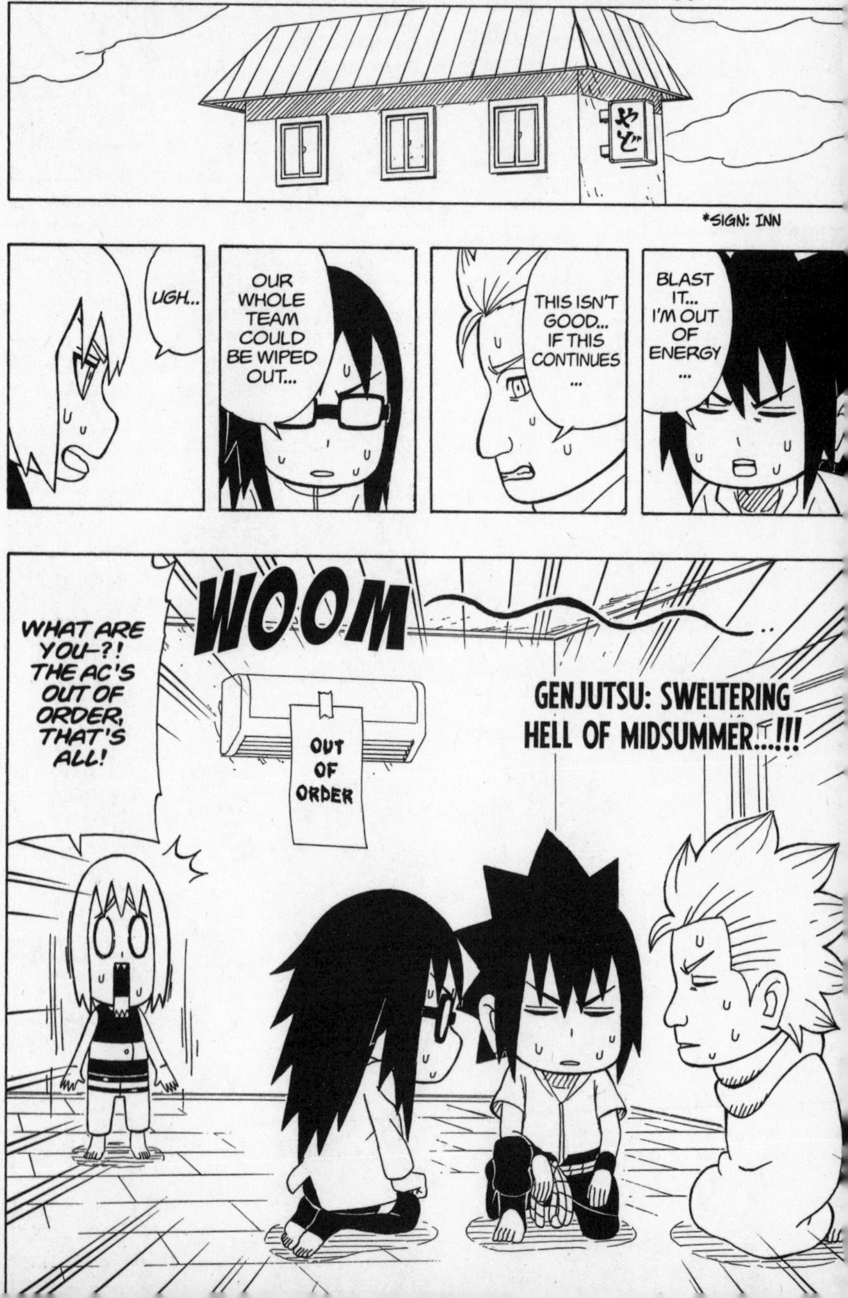
やど
*SIGN: INN
BLAST IT... I'M OUT OF ENERGY...
THIS ISN'T GOOD... IF THIS CONTINUES...
OUR WHOLE TEAM COULD BE WIPED OUT...
UGH...
WOOM
GENJUTSU: SWELTERING HELL OF MIDSUMMER...!!!
OUT OF ORDER
WHAT ARE YOU-?! THE AC'S OUT OF ORDER, THAT'S ALL!

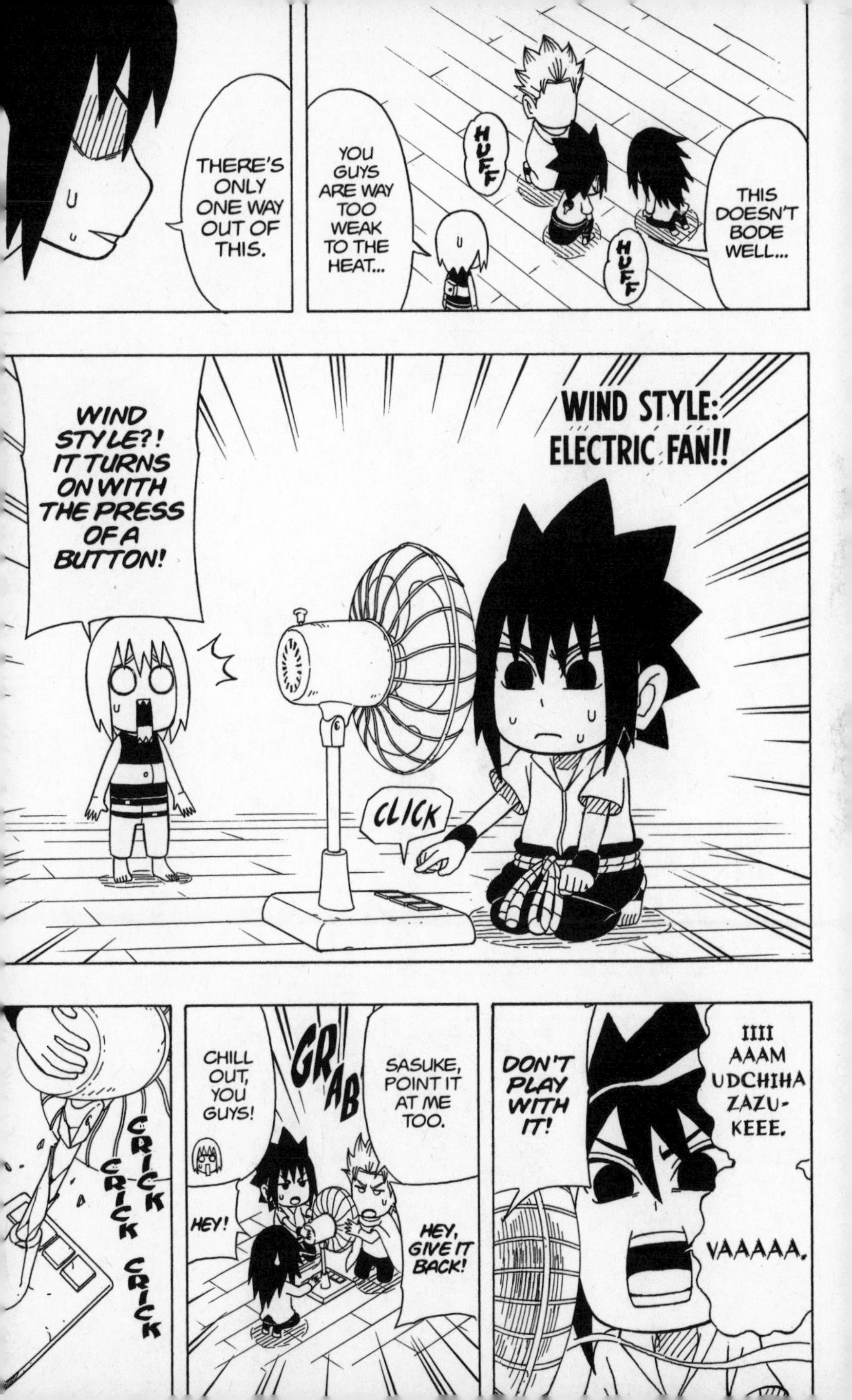
THIS DOESN'T BODE WELL...
HUFF
HUFF
YOU GUYS ARE WAY TOO WEAK TO THE HEAT...
THERE'S ONLY ONE WAY OUT OF THIS.
WIND STYLE: ELECTRIC FAN!!
WIND STYLE?! IT TURNS ON WITH THE PRESS OF A BUTTON!
CLICK
IIII AAAM UDCHIHA ZAZU-KEEE.
DON'T PLAY WITH IT!
VAAAAA.
SASUKE, POINT IT AT ME TOO.
GRAB
CHILL OUT, YOU GUYS!
HEY!
HEY, GIVE IT BACK!
CRICK CRICK
CRICK CRICK

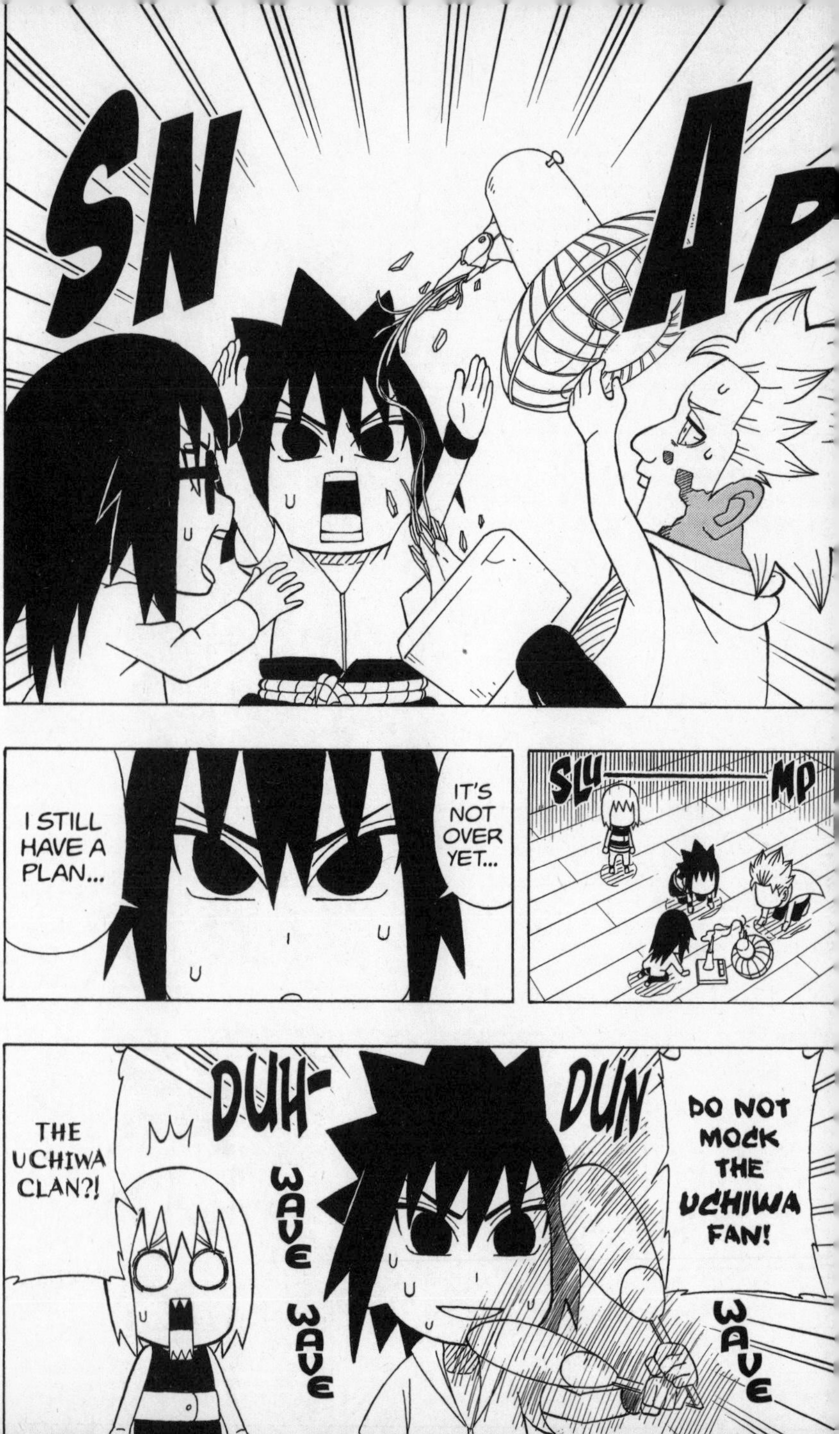
SNAP
SLU———MP
IT'S NOT OVER YET...
I STILL HAVE A PLAN...
DUH-DUN
DO NOT MOCK THE UCHIWA FAN!
WAVE
WAVE WAVE
THE UCHIWA CLAN?!

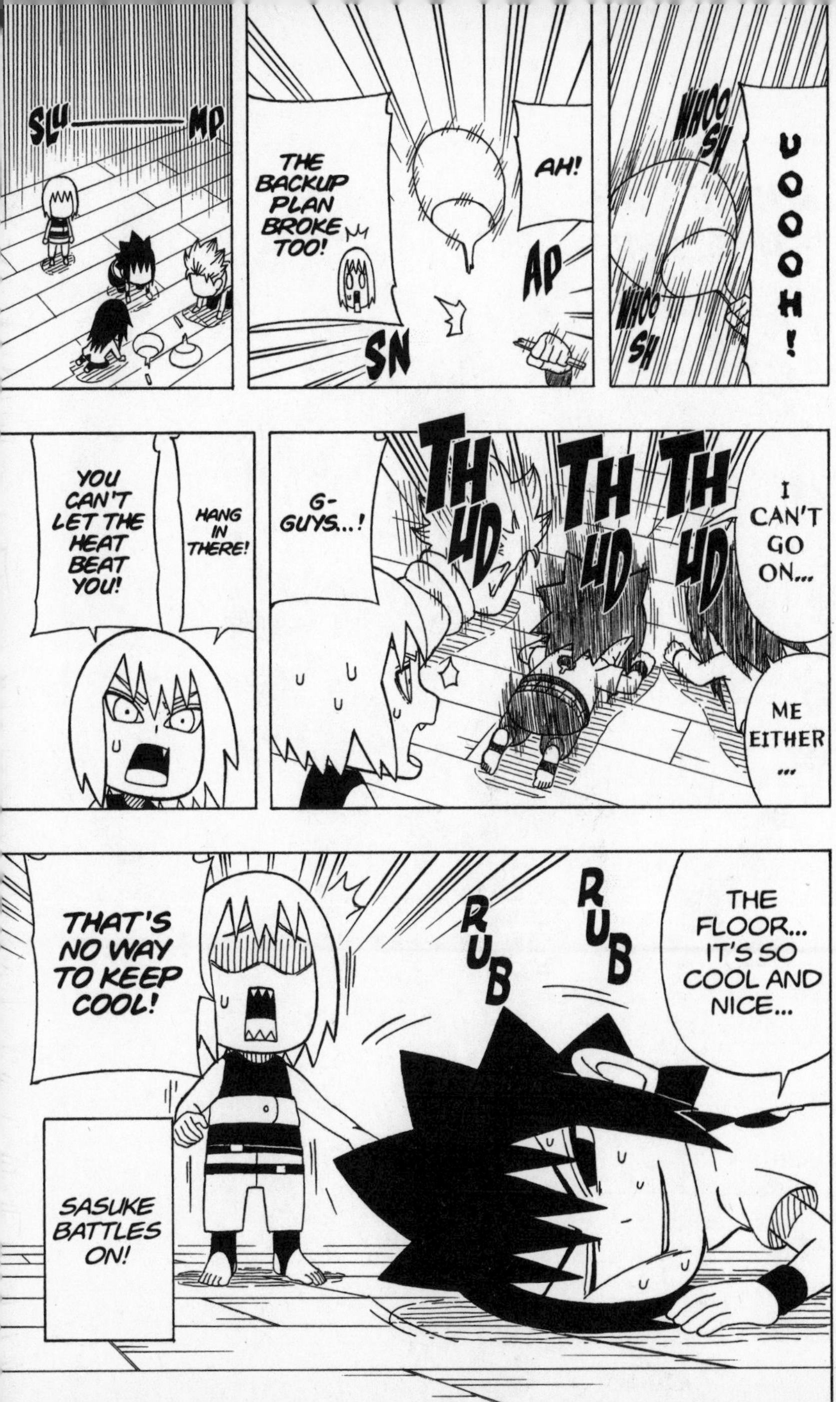
UOOOOH!
WHOOSH
WHOOSH
AH!
THE BACKUP PLAN BROKE TOO!
SNAP
SLU———MP
I CAN'T GO ON...
ME EITHER...
THUD
THUD
THUD
G-GUYS...!
HANG IN THERE!
YOU CAN'T LET THE HEAT BEAT YOU!
THE FLOOR... IT'S SO COOL AND NICE...
RUB
RUB
THAT'S NO WAY TO KEEP COOL!
SASUKE BATTLES ON!

CHAPTER 7: SUMMER FESTIVAL!!

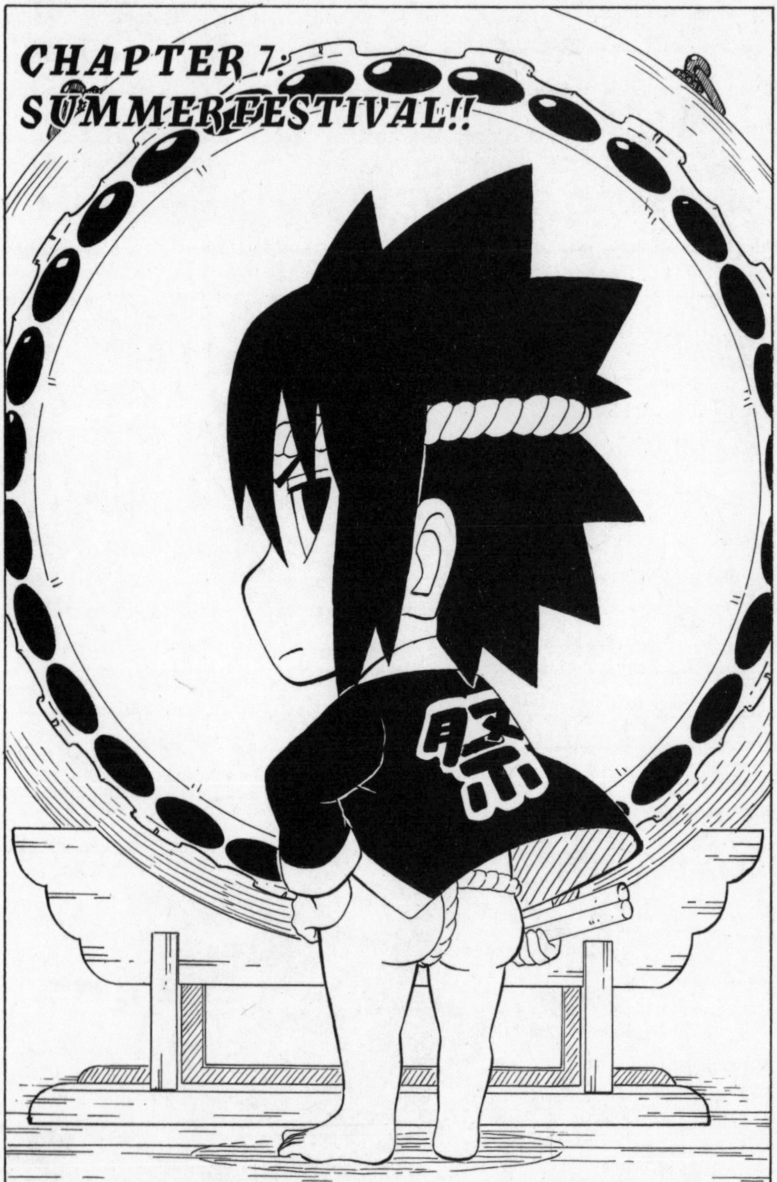
祭

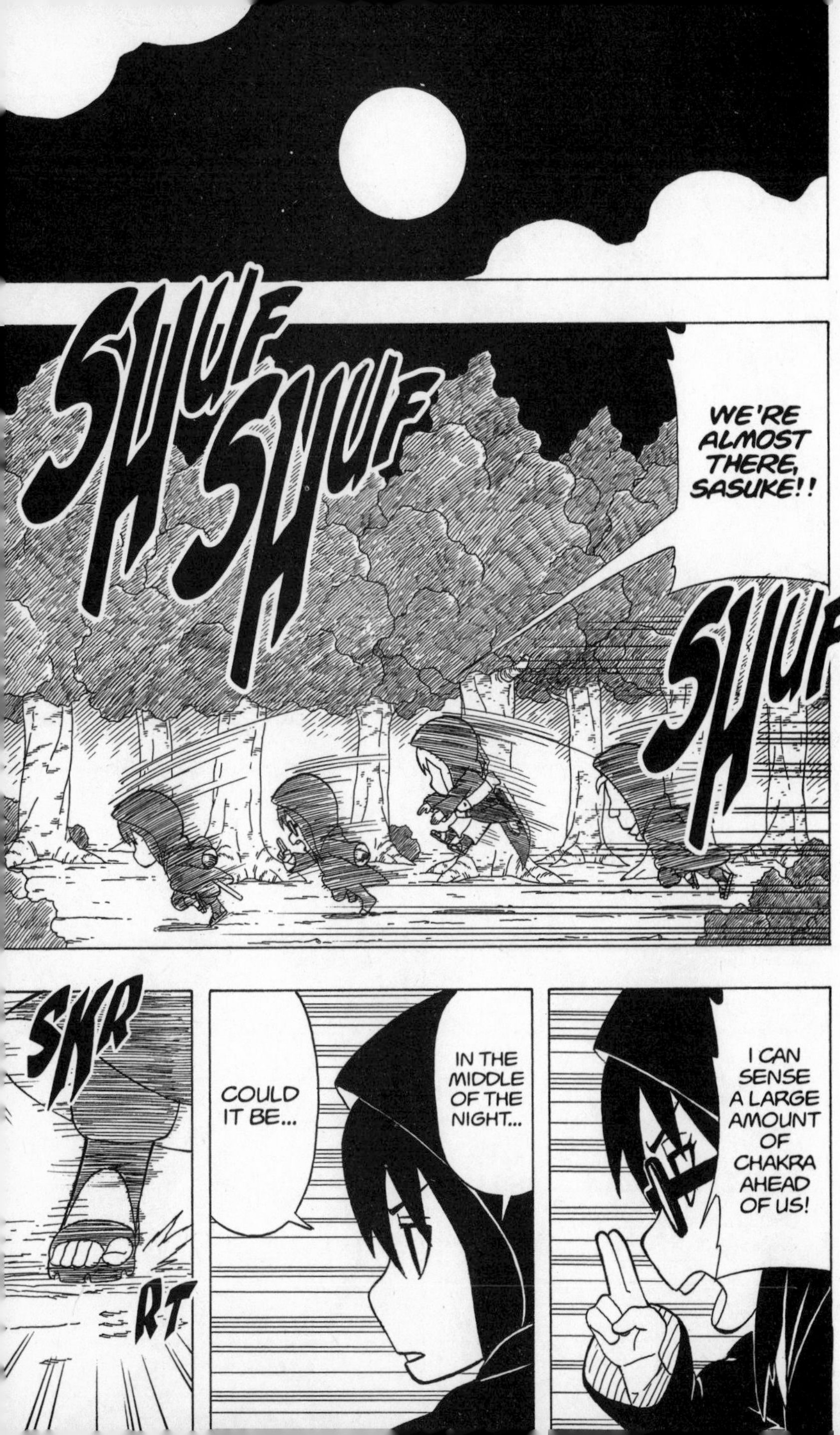
WE'RE ALMOST THERE, SASUKE!!
SHUF
SHUF SHUF
I CAN SENSE A LARGE AMOUNT OF CHAKRA AHEAD OF US!
IN THE MIDDLE OF THE NIGHT...
COULD IT BE...
SKRRT

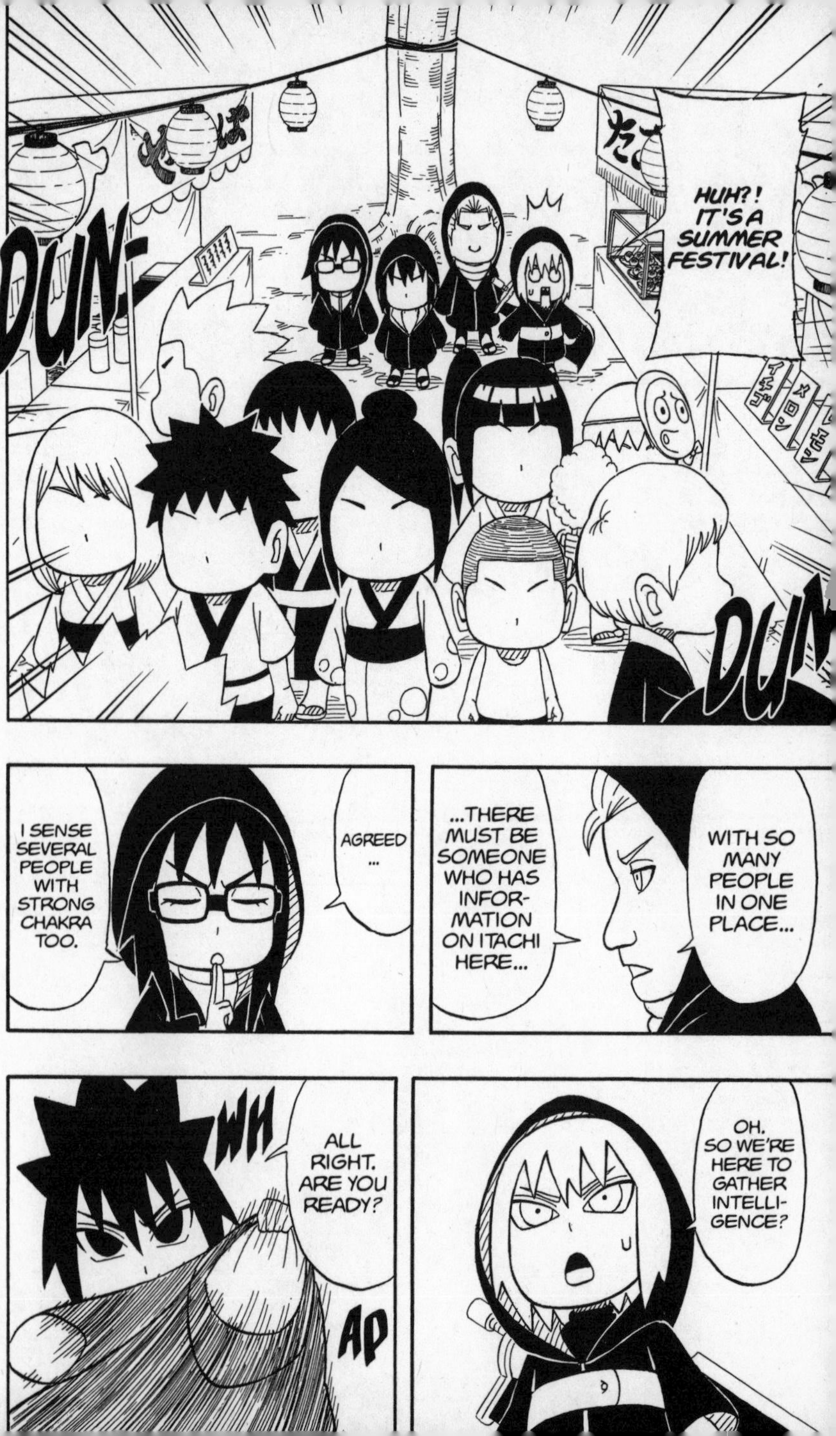
HUH?! IT'S A SUMMER FESTIVAL!
DUN
DUN-
WITH SO MANY PEOPLE IN ONE PLACE...
...THERE MUST BE SOMEONE WHO HAS INFORMATION ON ITACHI HERE...
AGREED ...
I SENSE SEVERAL PEOPLE WITH STRONG CHAKRA TOO.
OH. SO WE'RE HERE TO GATHER INTELLIGENCE?
ALL RIGHT. ARE YOU READY?
WH
AP

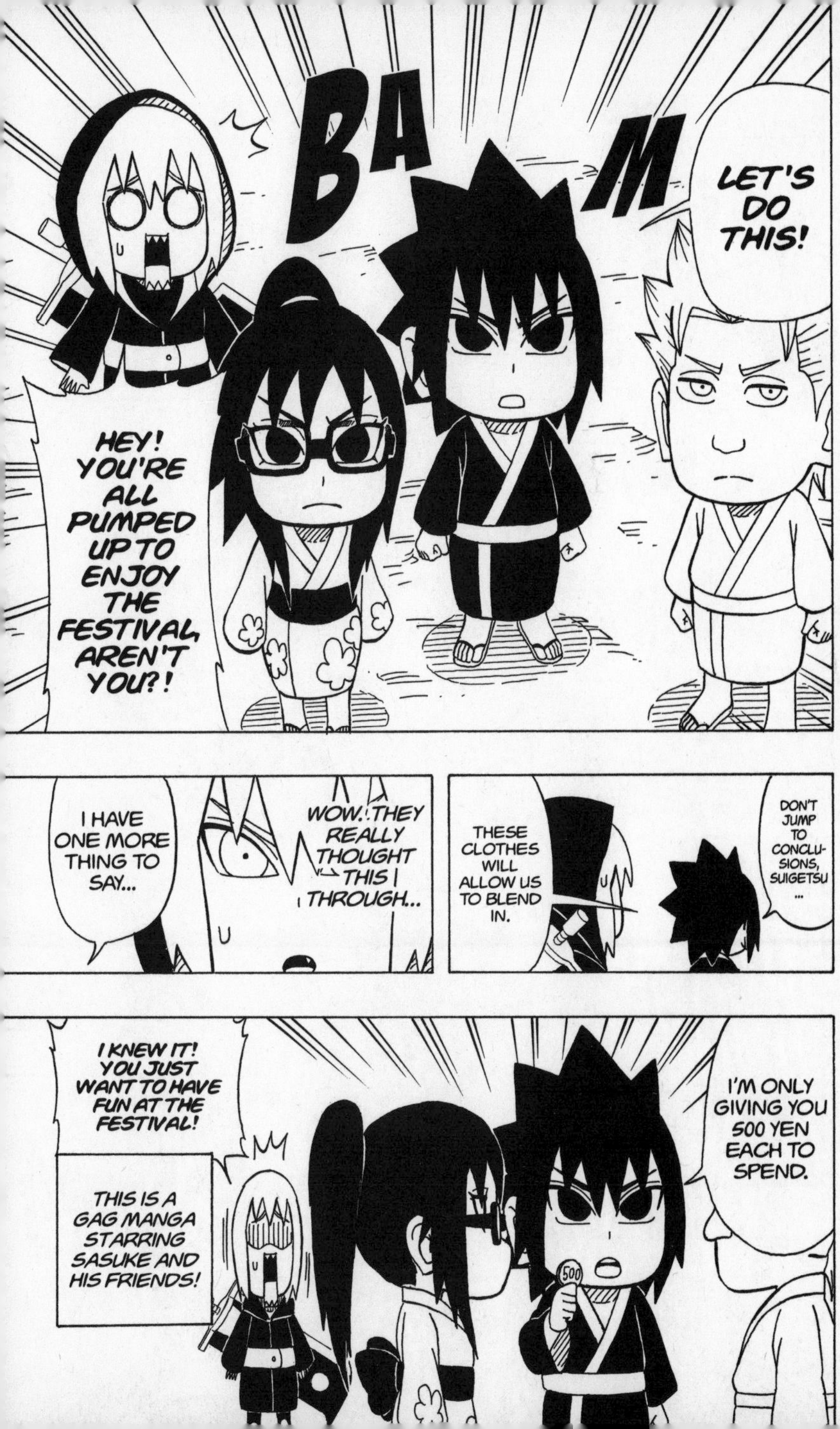
LET'S DO THIS!
BAM
HEY! YOU'RE ALL PUMPED UP TO ENJOY THE FESTIVAL, AREN'T YOU?!
DON'T JUMP TO CONCLUSIONS, SUIGETSU...
THESE CLOTHES WILL ALLOW US TO BLEND IN.
WOW... THEY REALLY THOUGHT THIS THROUGH...
I HAVE ONE MORE THING TO SAY...
I'M ONLY GIVING YOU 500 YEN EACH TO SPEND.
500
I KNEW IT! YOU JUST WANT TO HAVE FUN AT THE FESTIVAL!
THIS IS A GAG MANGA STARRING SASUKE AND HIS FRIENDS!

THE KUSANAGI BLADE

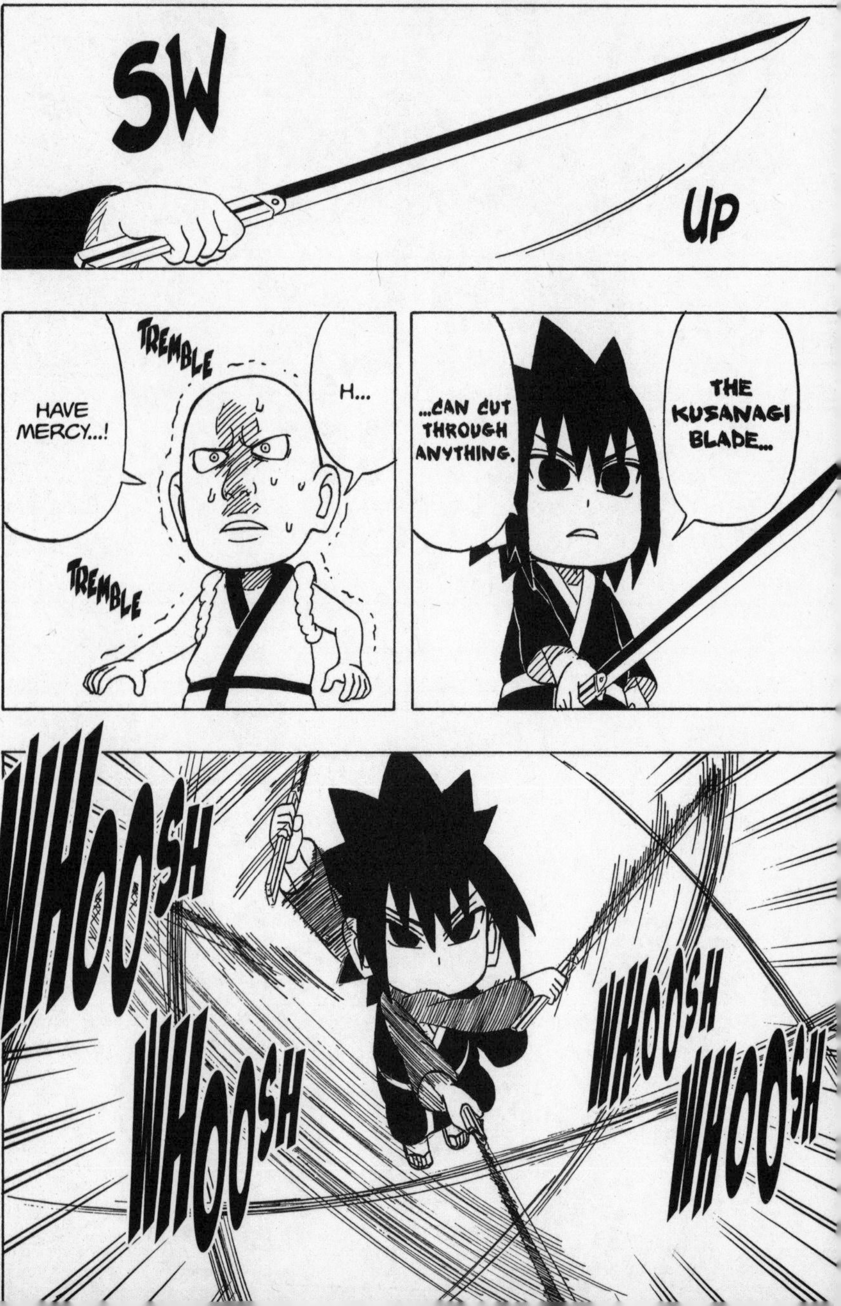
SW
UP
THE KUSANAGI BLADE...
...CAN CUT THROUGH ANYTHING.
H...
TREMBLE
HAVE MERCY...!
TREMBLE
WHOOSH
WHOOSH
WHOOSH
WHOOSH

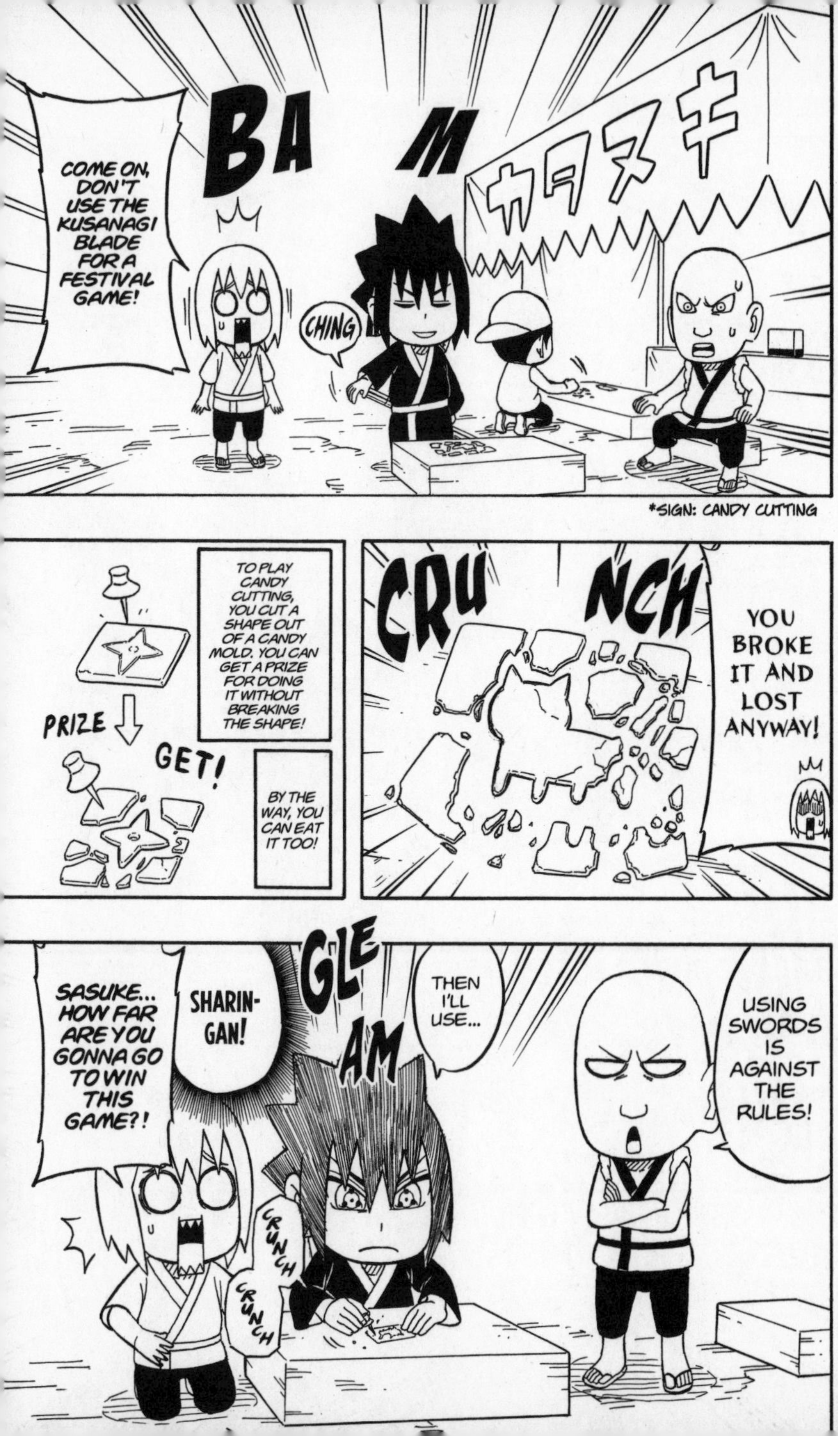
カタヌキ
BAM
CHING
COME ON, DON'T USE THE KUSANAGI BLADE FOR A FESTIVAL GAME!
*SIGN: CANDY CUTTING
CRUNCH
YOU BROKE IT AND LOST ANYWAY!
TO PLAY CANDY CUTTING, YOU CUT A SHAPE OUT OF A CANDY MOLD. YOU CAN GET A PRIZE FOR DOING IT WITHOUT BREAKING THE SHAPE!
PRIZE
GET!
BY THE WAY, YOU CAN EAT IT TOO!
USING SWORDS IS AGAINST THE RULES!
THEN I'LL USE...
GLEAM
SHARIN-GAN!
CRUNCH
CRUNCH
SASUKE... HOW FAR ARE YOU GONNA GO TO WIN THIS GAME?!

SASUKE VS. SUIGETSU?!

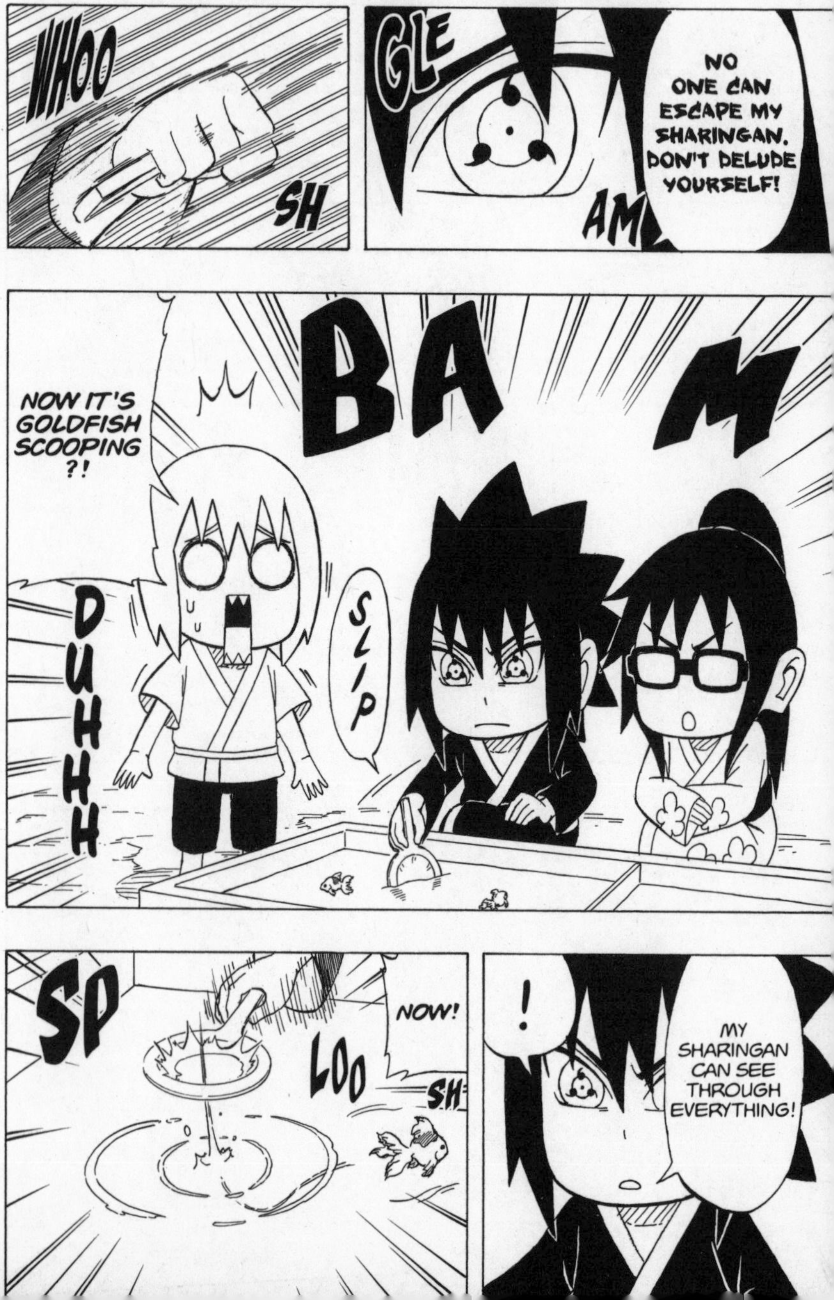
GLE
NO ONE CAN ESCAPE MY SHARINGAN. DON'T DELUDE YOURSELF!
AM
WHOO
SH
BAM
NOW IT'S GOLDFISH SCOOPING ?!
SLIP
DUHHH
!
MY SHARINGAN CAN SEE THROUGH EVERYTHING!
NOW!
SP
LOO
SH

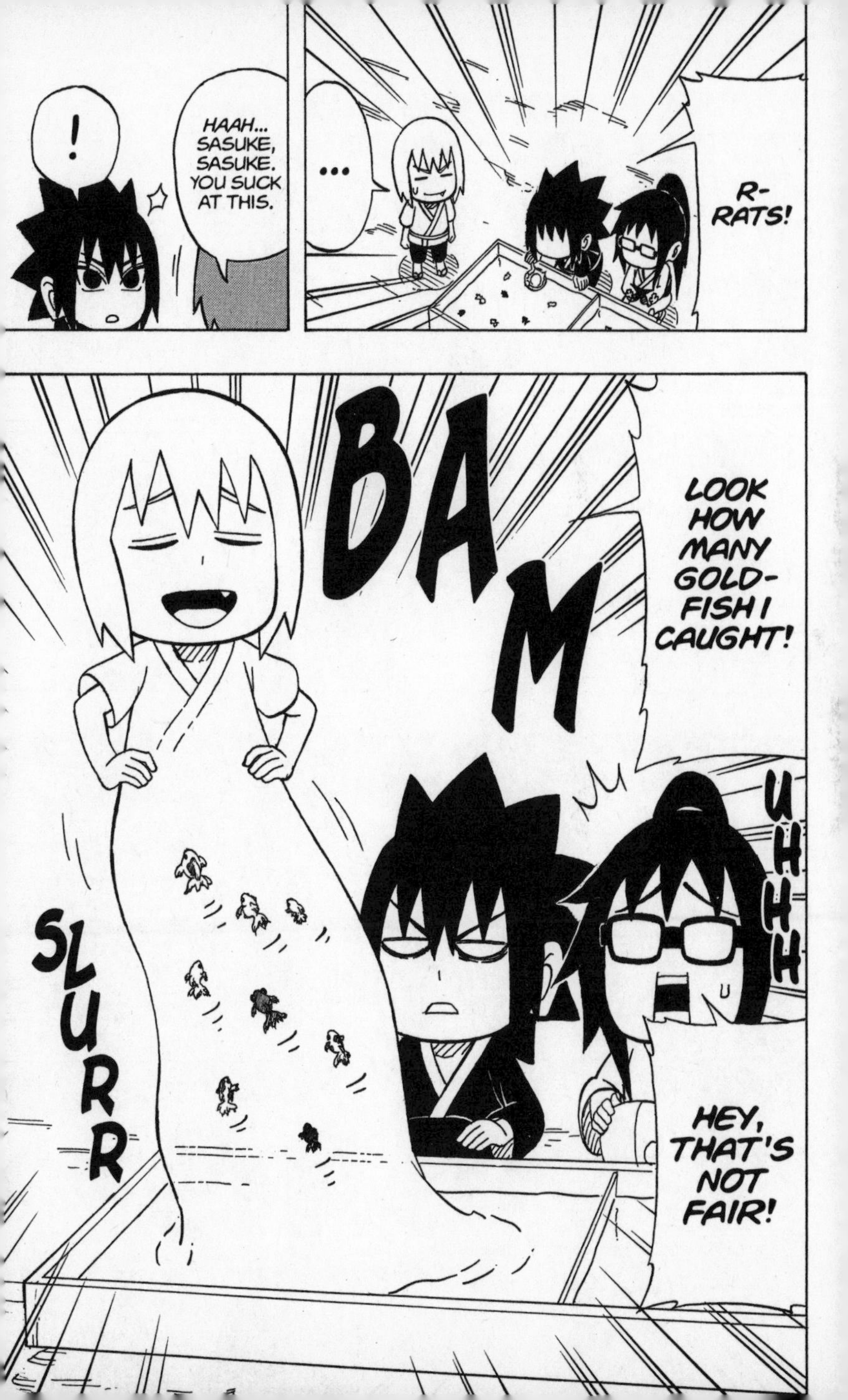
R-RATS!
...
HAAH... SASUKE, SASUKE. YOU SUCK AT THIS.
!
LOOK HOW MANY GOLD-FISH I CAUGHT!
BAM
UHHHH
HEY, THAT'S NOT FAIR!
SLURR

CONFESSION

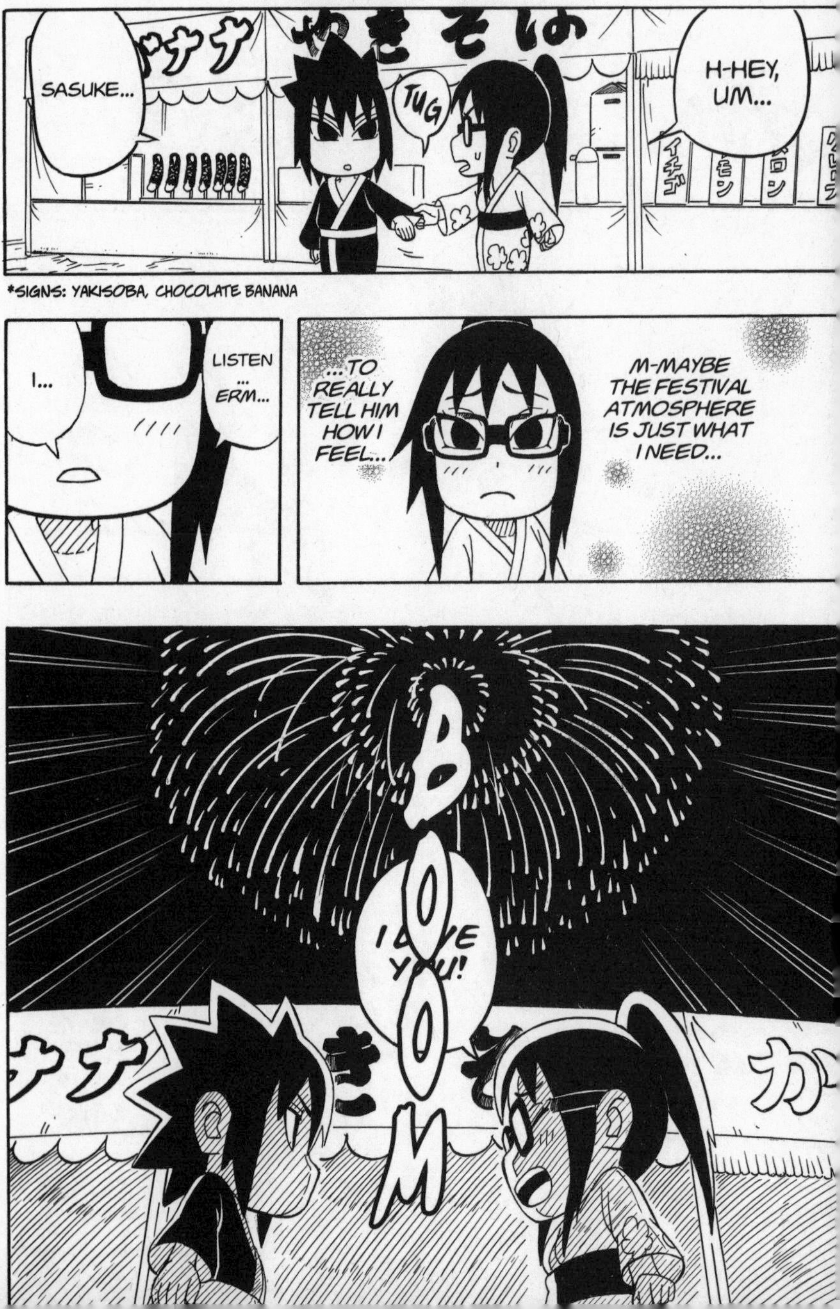
H-HEY, UM...
TUG
SASUKE...
*SIGNS: YAKISOBA, CHOCOLATE BANANA
M-MAYBE THE FESTIVAL ATMOSPHERE IS JUST WHAT I NEED...
...TO REALLY TELL HIM HOW I FEEL...
LISTEN ... ERM...
I...
BOOOOM
I LOVE YOU!

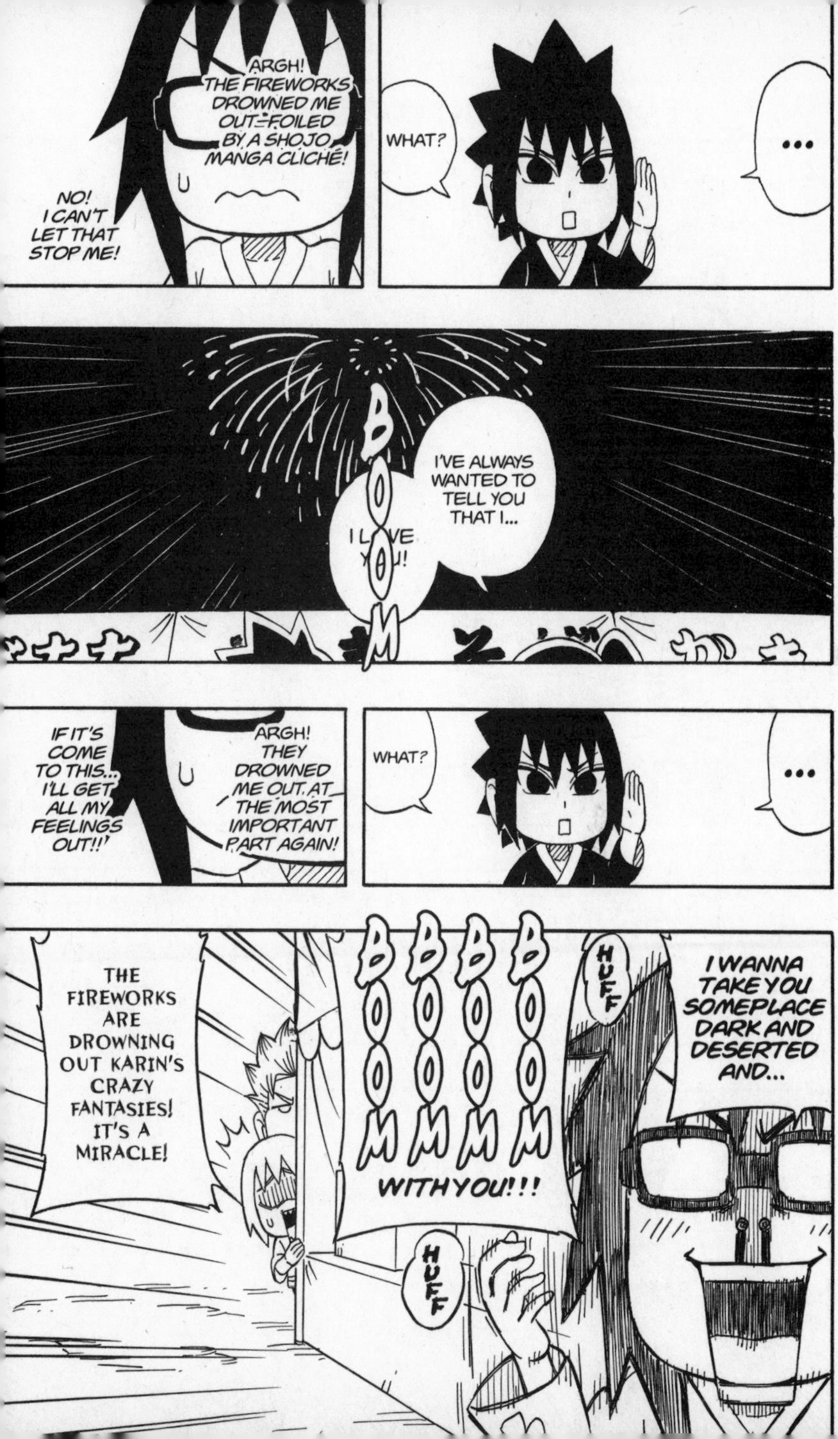
…
WHAT?
ARGH! THE FIREWORKS DROWNED ME OUT—FOILED BY A SHOJO MANGA CLICHÉ!
NO! I CAN'T LET THAT STOP ME!
I'VE ALWAYS WANTED TO TELL YOU THAT I...
BOOM
I L VE Y U!
…
WHAT?
ARGH! THEY DROWNED ME OUT AT THE MOST IMPORTANT PART AGAIN!
IF IT'S COME TO THIS... I'LL GET ALL MY FEELINGS OUT!!
I WANNA TAKE YOU SOMEPLACE DARK AND DESERTED AND...
HUFF
BOOOOM BOOOOM BOOOOM BOOOOM
WITH YOU!!!
HUFF
THE FIREWORKS ARE DROWNING OUT KARIN'S CRAZY FANTASIES! IT'S A MIRACLE!

SHOOTING GALLERY

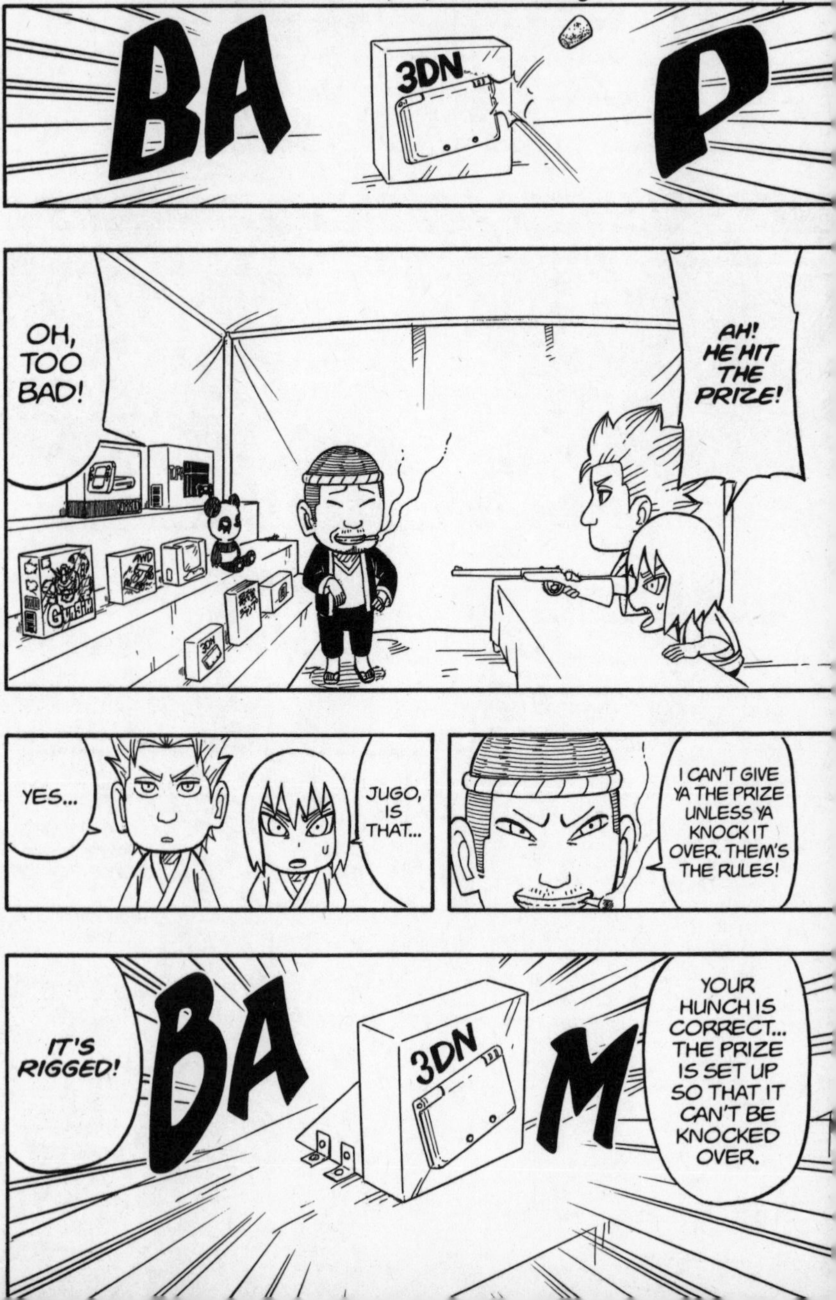
BA
3DN
P
AH! HE HIT THE PRIZE!
OH, TOO BAD!
I CAN'T GIVE YA THE PRIZE UNLESS YA KNOCK IT OVER. THEM'S THE RULES!
JUGO, IS THAT...
YES...
YOUR HUNCH IS CORRECT... THE PRIZE IS SET UP SO THAT IT CAN'T BE KNOCKED OVER.
BA
3DN
M
IT'S RIGGED!

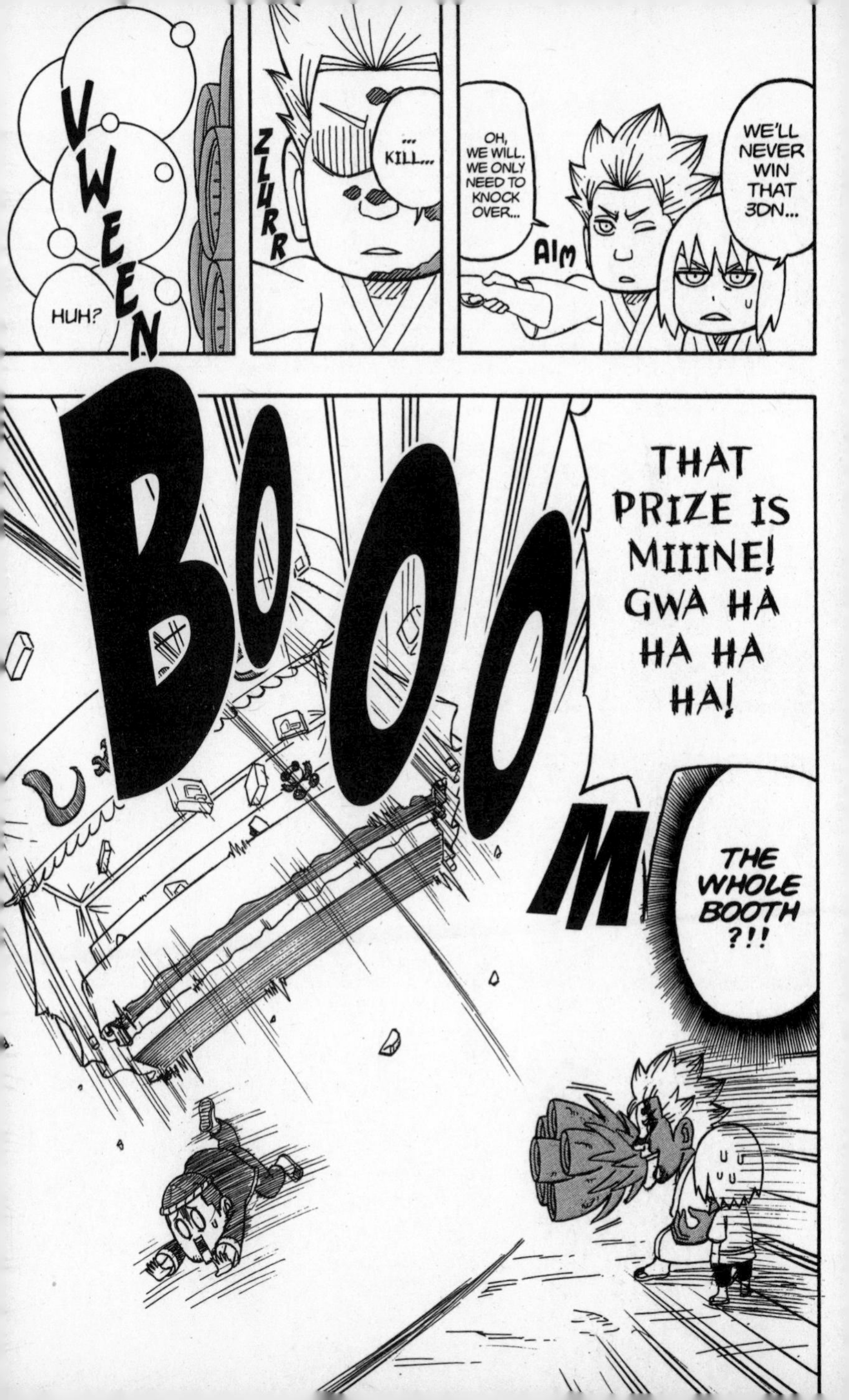
WE'LL NEVER WIN THAT 3DN...
OH, WE WILL. WE ONLY NEED TO KNOCK OVER...
AIM
ZLURR
... KILL...
VWEEN
HUH?
THAT PRIZE IS MIIINE! GWA HA HA HA HA!
BOOOM
THE WHOLE BOOTH ?!!

FIREWORKS SHOW

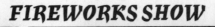

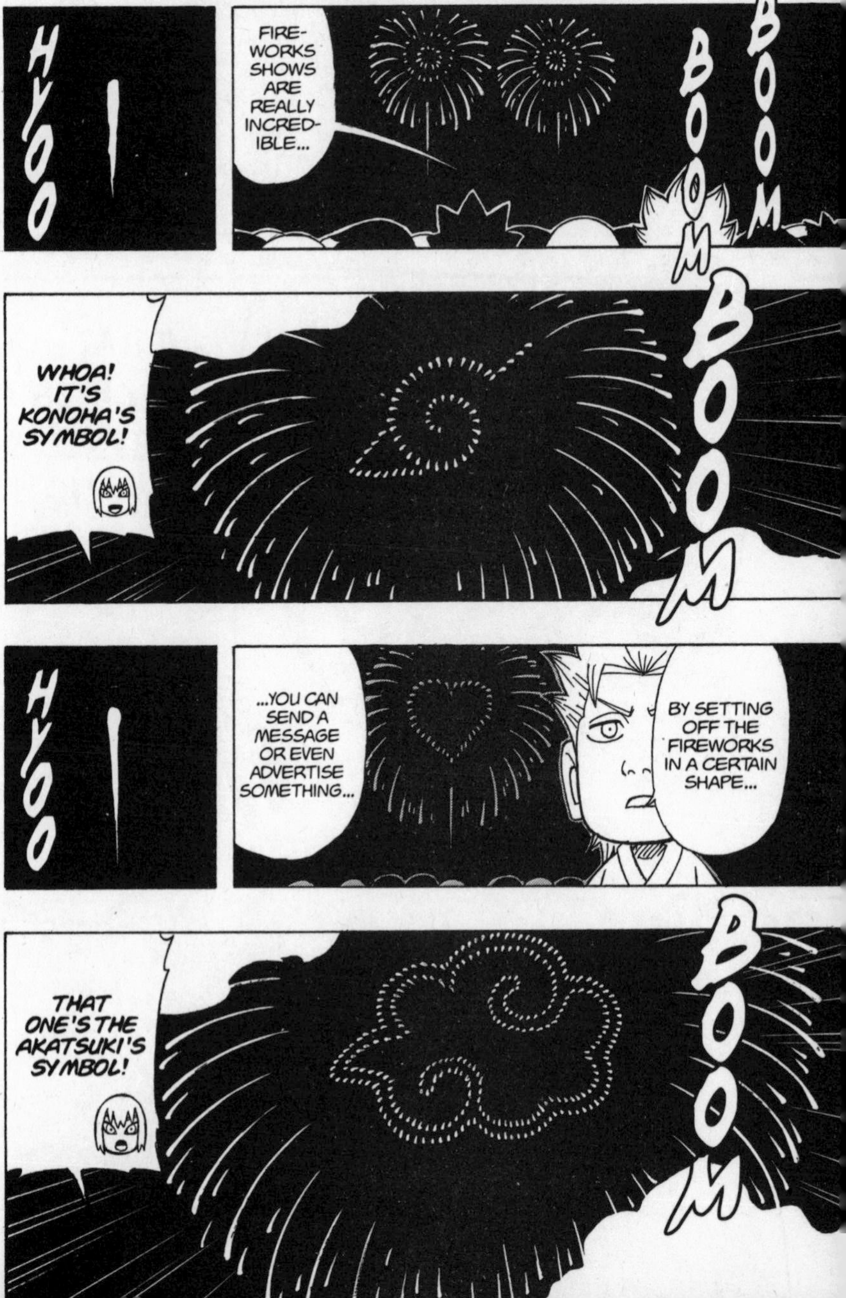
BOOM
BOOM
FIRE-WORKS SHOWS ARE REALLY INCREDIBLE...
HYOO
BOOM
WHOA! IT'S KONOHA'S SYMBOL!
BY SETTING OFF THE FIREWORKS IN A CERTAIN SHAPE...
...YOU CAN SEND A MESSAGE OR EVEN ADVERTISE SOMETHING...
HYOO
BOOM
THAT ONE'S THE AKATSUKI'S SYMBOL!

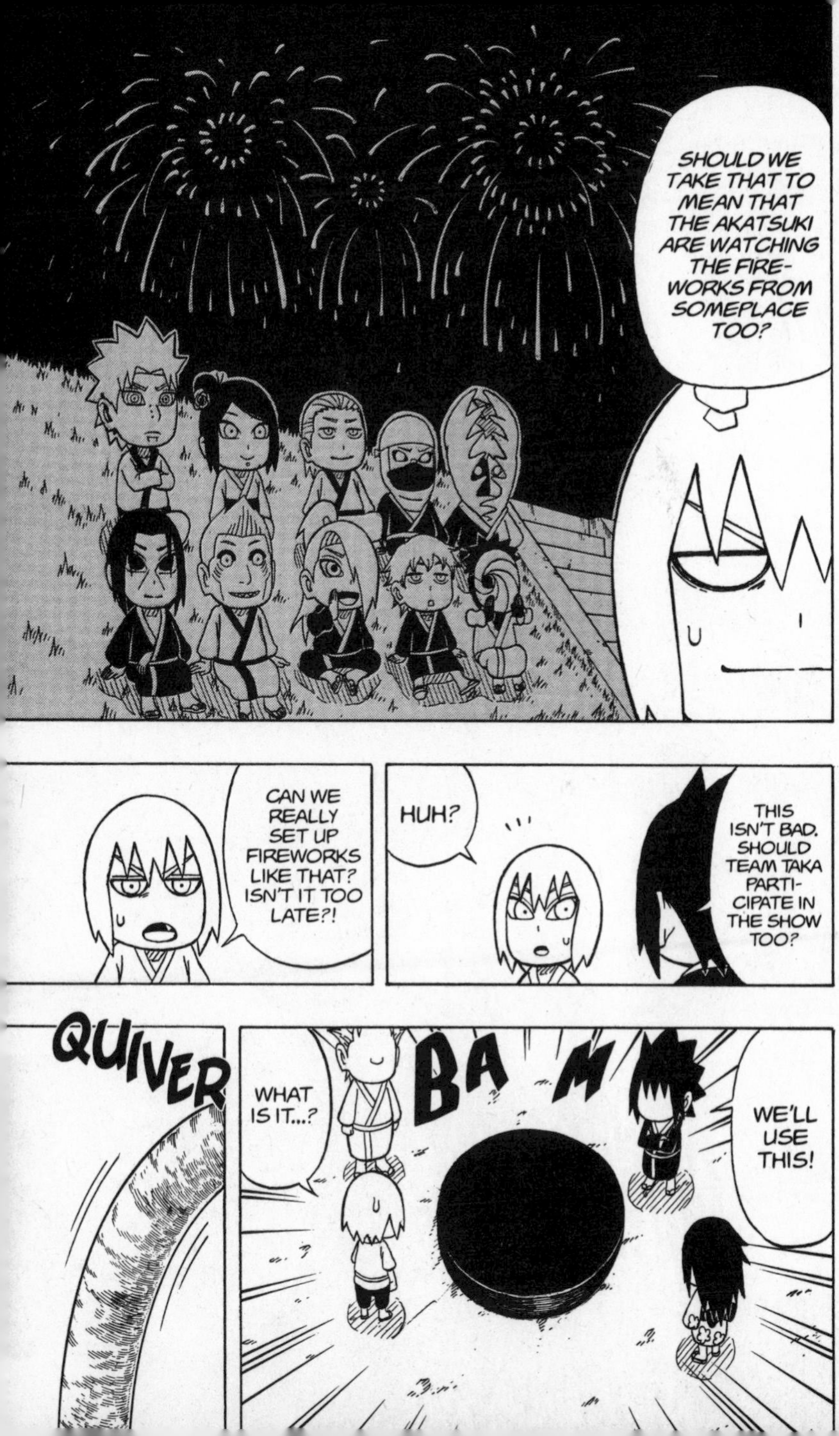
SHOULD WE TAKE THAT TO MEAN THAT THE AKATSUKI ARE WATCHING THE FIRE-WORKS FROM SOMEPLACE TOO?
THIS ISN'T BAD. SHOULD TEAM TAKA PARTI-CIPATE IN THE SHOW TOO?
HUH?
CAN WE REALLY SET UP FIREWORKS LIKE THAT? ISN'T IT TOO LATE?!
WE'LL USE THIS!
BAM
WHAT IS IT...?
QUIVER

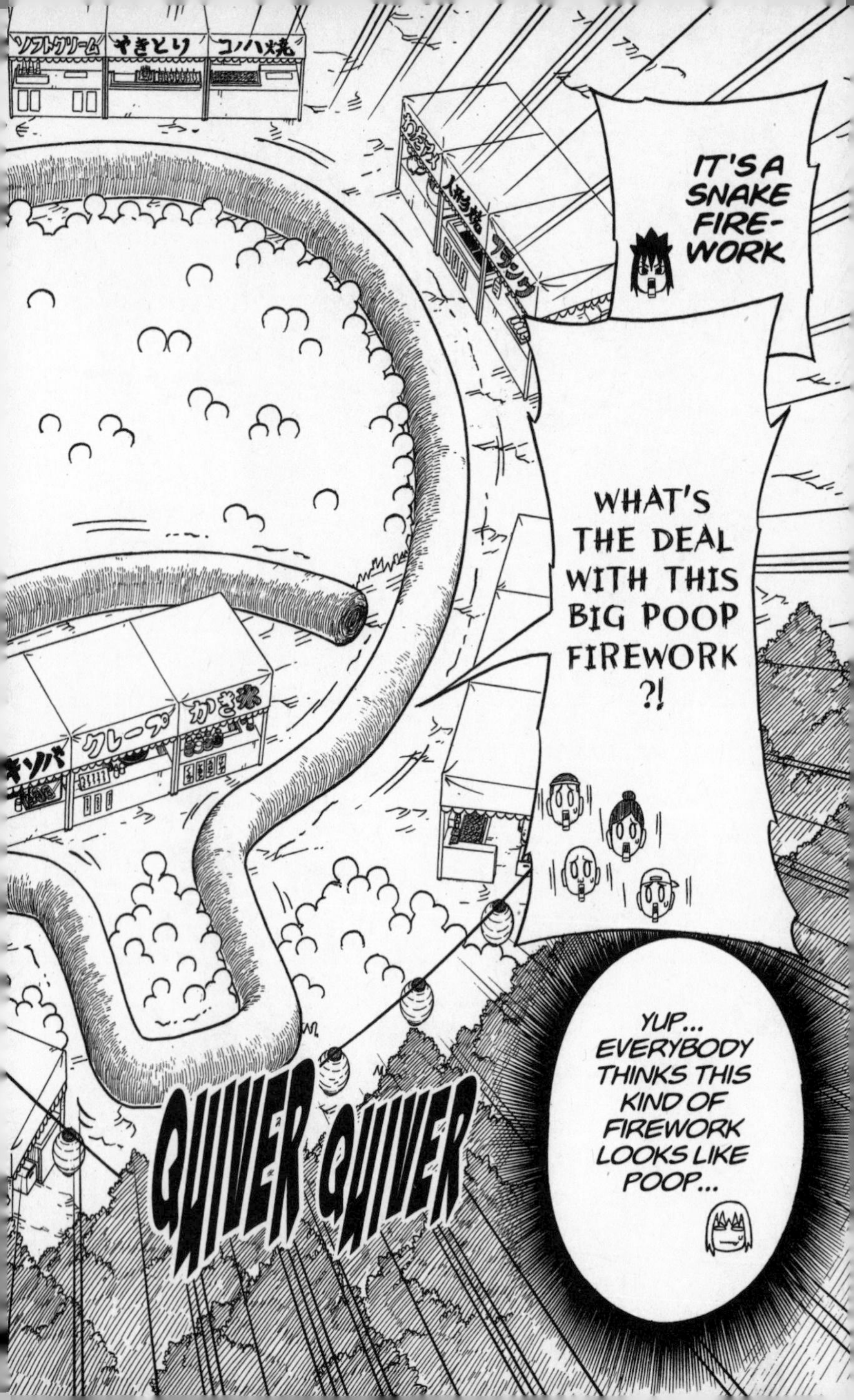

IT'S A SNAKE FIRE-WORK
WHAT'S THE DEAL WITH THIS BIG POOP FIREWORK ?!
YUP... EVERYBODY THINKS THIS KIND OF FIREWORK LOOKS LIKE POOP...
QUIVER QUIVER
ソフトクリーム
やきとり
クレープ
かき氷

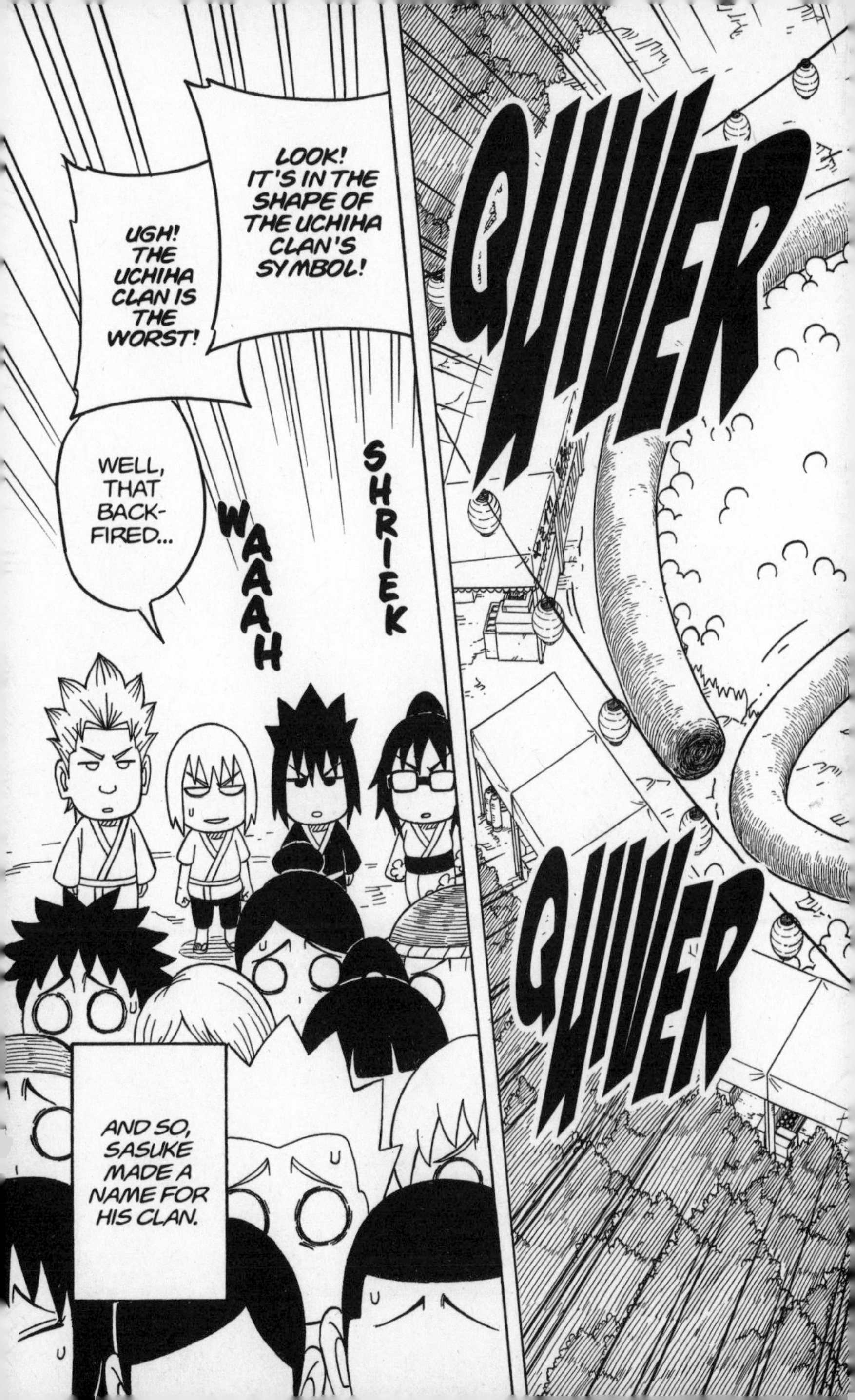
QUIVER
QUIVER
LOOK! IT'S IN THE SHAPE OF THE UCHIHA CLAN'S SYMBOL!
UGH! THE UCHIHA CLAN IS THE WORST!
SHRIEK
WAAAH
WELL, THAT BACK-FIRED...
AND SO, SASUKE MADE A NAME FOR HIS CLAN.

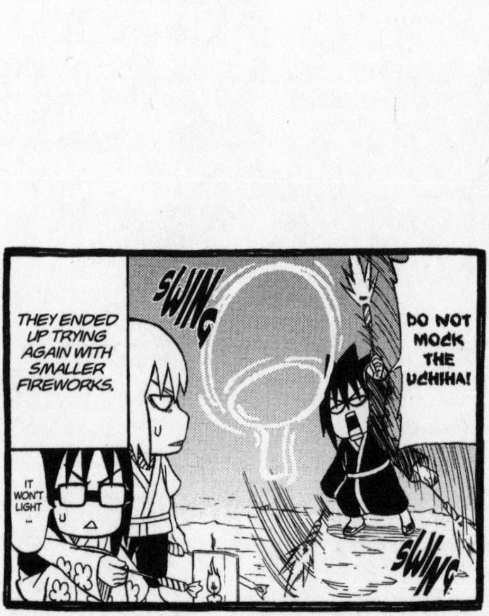
DO NOT MOCK THE UCHIHA!
SWING
THEY ENDED UP TRYING AGAIN WITH SMALLER FIREWORKS.
SWING
IT WON'T LIGHT ...

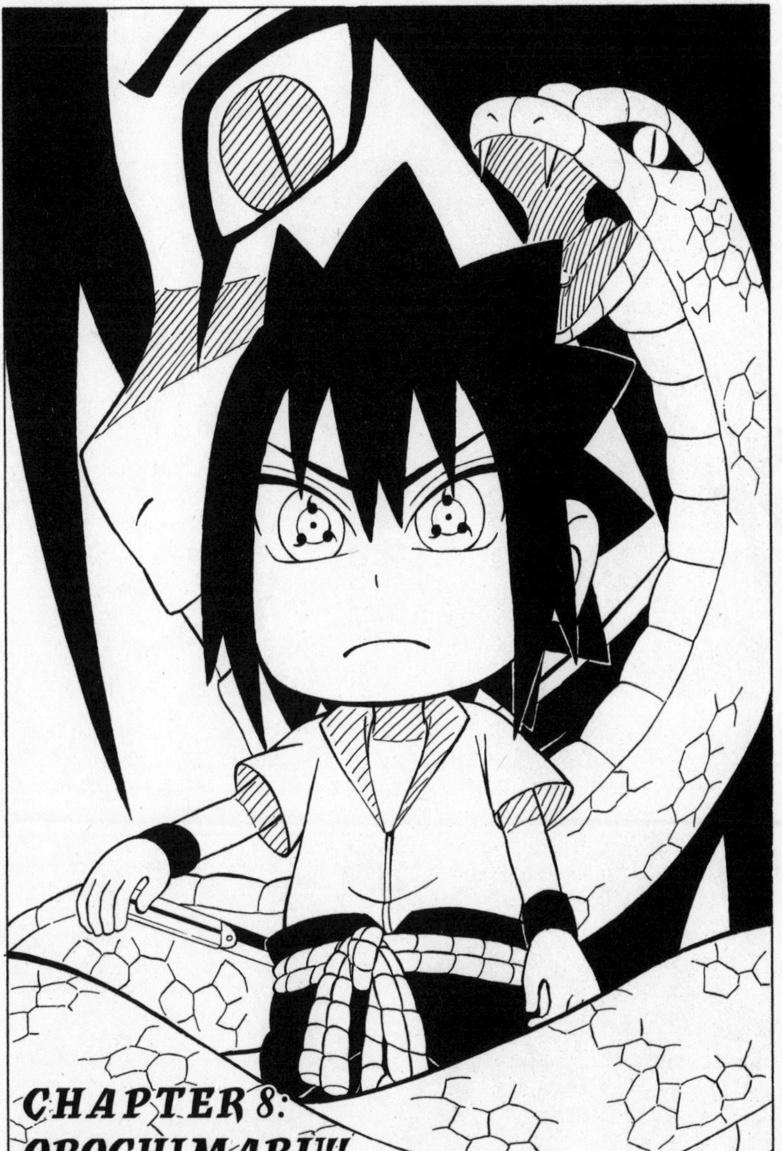
CHAPTER 8:
OROCHIMARU!!

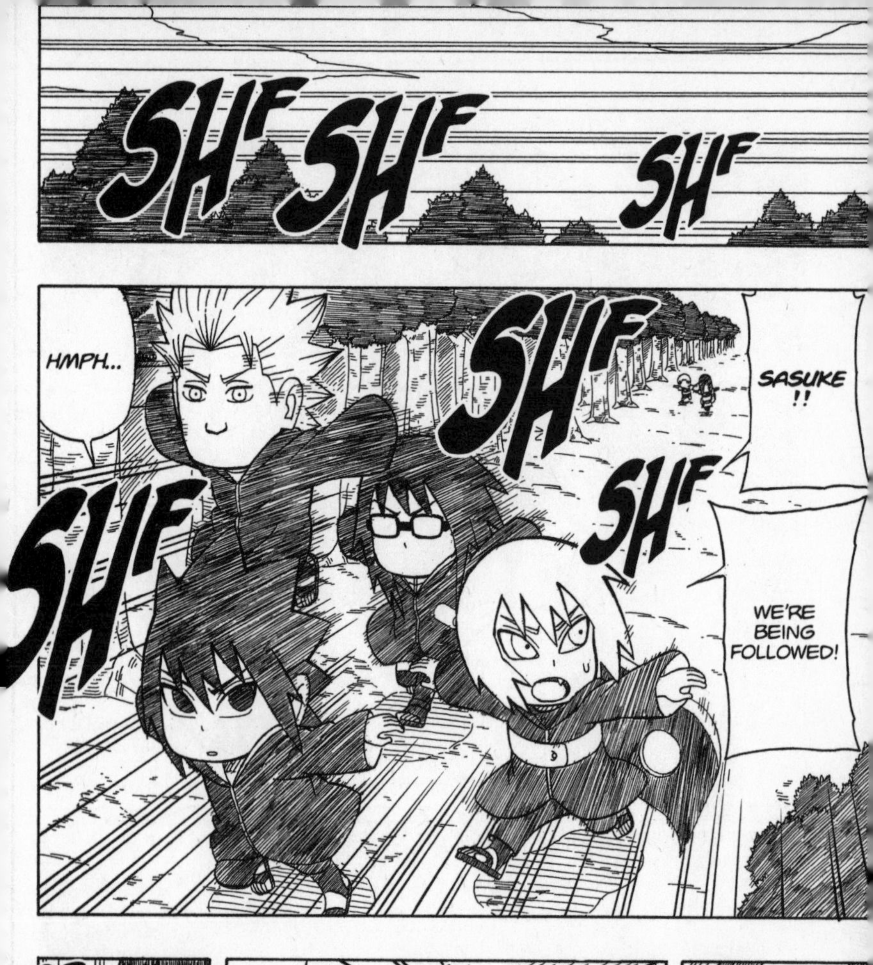
SHF
SHF
SHF
SASUKE!!
WE'RE BEING FOLLOWED!
SHF
SHF
HMPH...
SHF
!
HISSS!
GE
LUN
SNAKES!
GRP

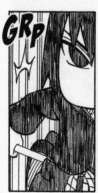

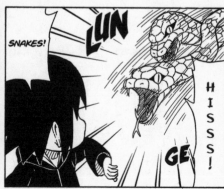

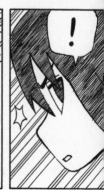

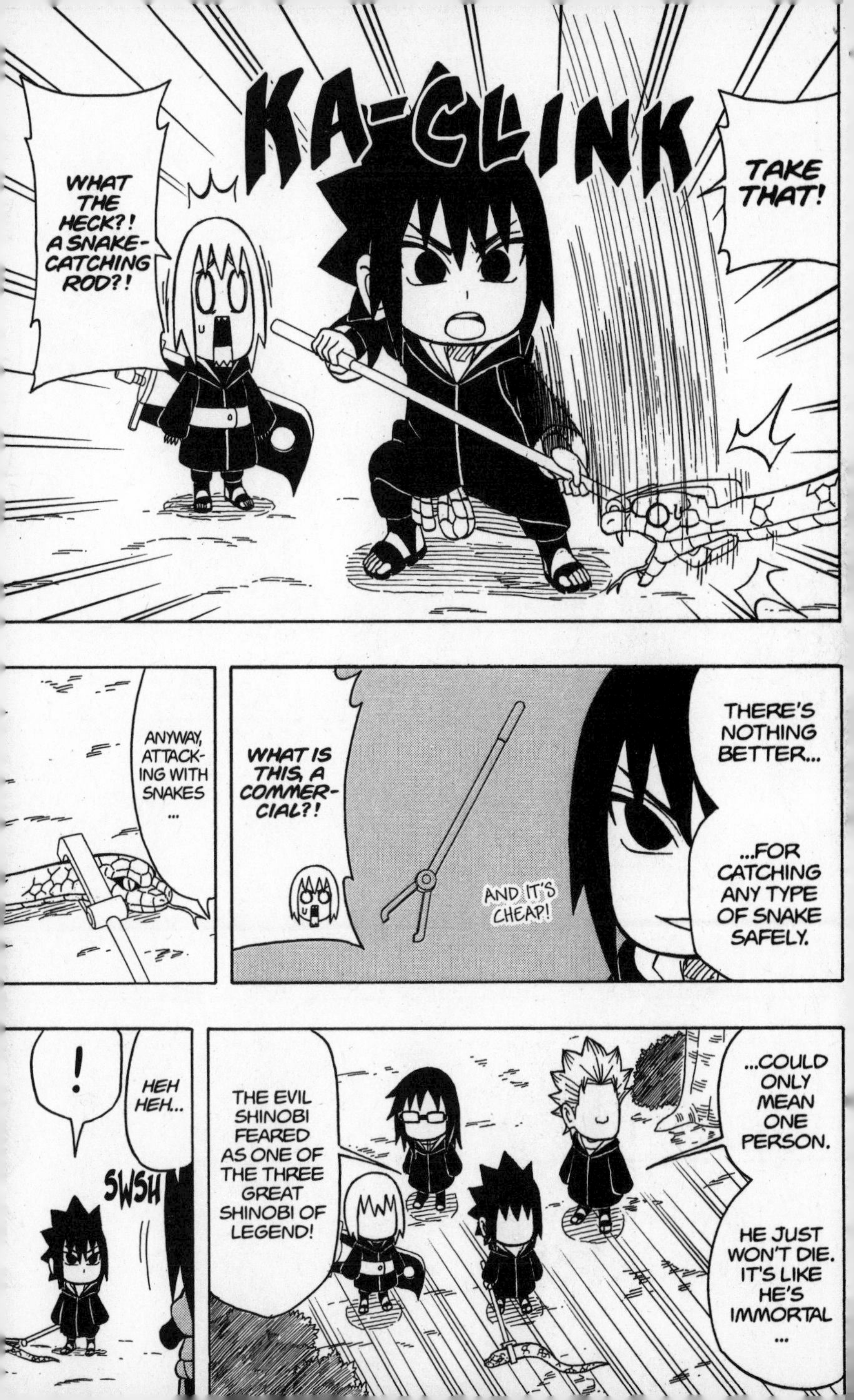
TAKE THAT!
KA-CLINK
WHAT THE HECK?! A SNAKE-CATCHING ROD?!
THERE'S NOTHING BETTER...
...FOR CATCHING ANY TYPE OF SNAKE SAFELY.
AND IT'S CHEAP!
WHAT IS THIS, A COMMERCIAL?!
ANYWAY, ATTACKING WITH SNAKES ...
...COULD ONLY MEAN ONE PERSON.
HE JUST WON'T DIE. IT'S LIKE HE'S IMMORTAL ...
THE EVIL SHINOBI FEARED AS ONE OF THE THREE GREAT SHINOBI OF LEGEND!
HEH HEH...
!
SWSH

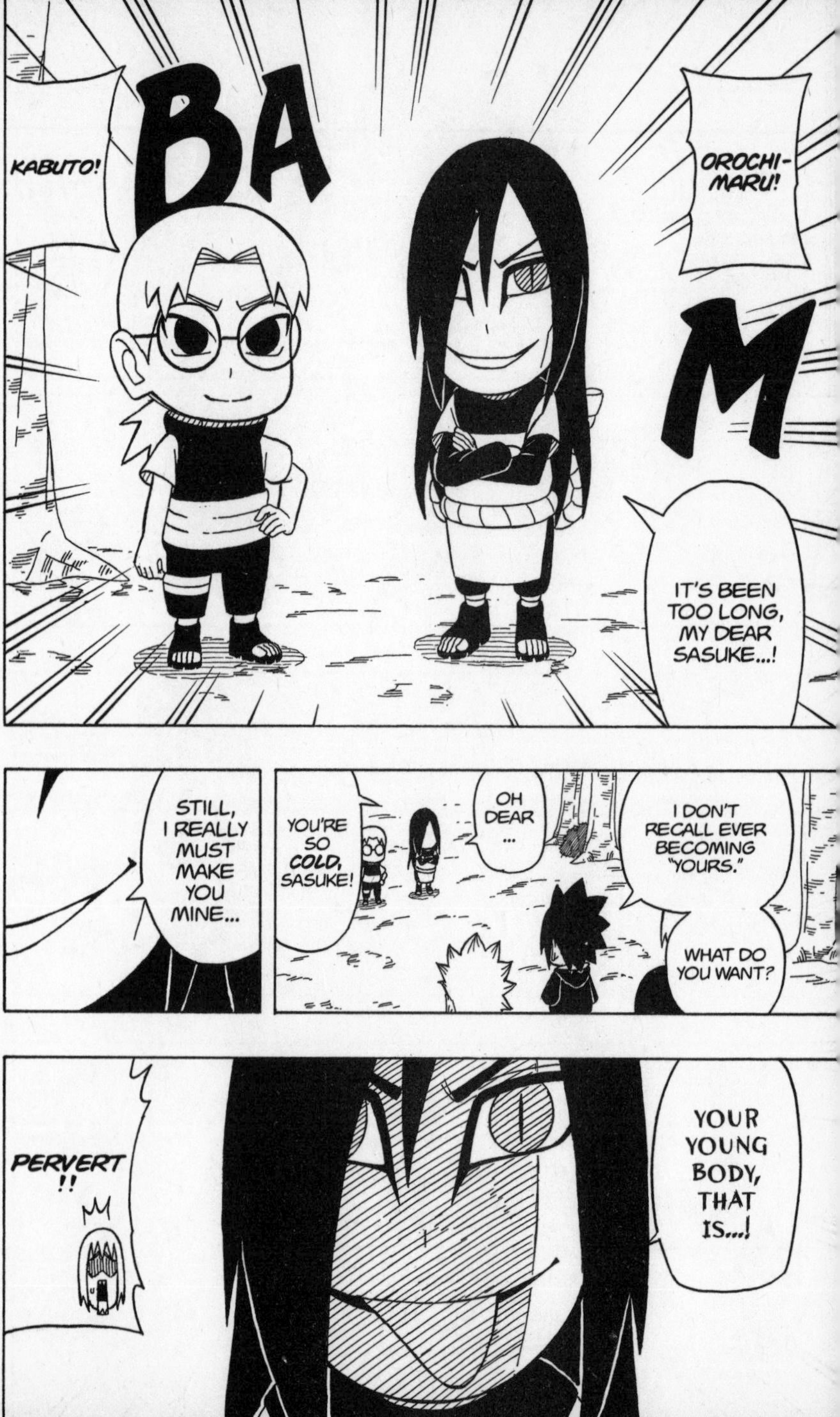
OROCHI-MARU!
KABUTO!
BAM
IT'S BEEN TOO LONG, MY DEAR SASUKE...!
I DON'T RECALL EVER BECOMING "YOURS."
WHAT DO YOU WANT?
OH DEAR ...
YOU'RE SO COLD, SASUKE!
STILL, I REALLY MUST MAKE YOU MINE...
YOUR YOUNG BODY, THAT IS...!
PERVERT !!

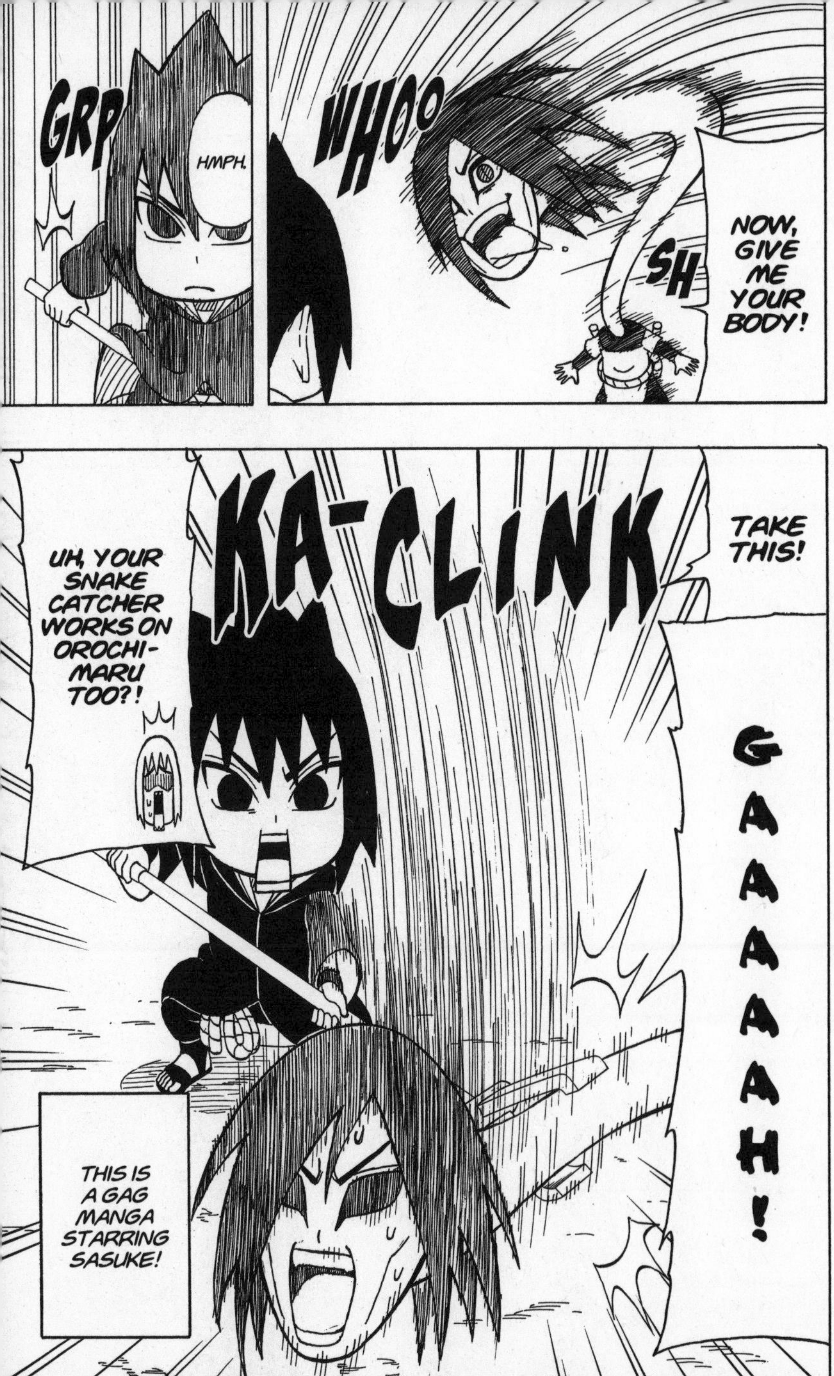
WHOO
NOW, GIVE ME YOUR BODY!
SH
GRP
HMPH.
TAKE THIS!
KA-CLINK
UH, YOUR SNAKE CATCHER WORKS ON OROCHI-MARU TOO?!
GAAAAAH!
THIS IS A GAG MANGA STARRING SASUKE!

SNAKE EXPERT

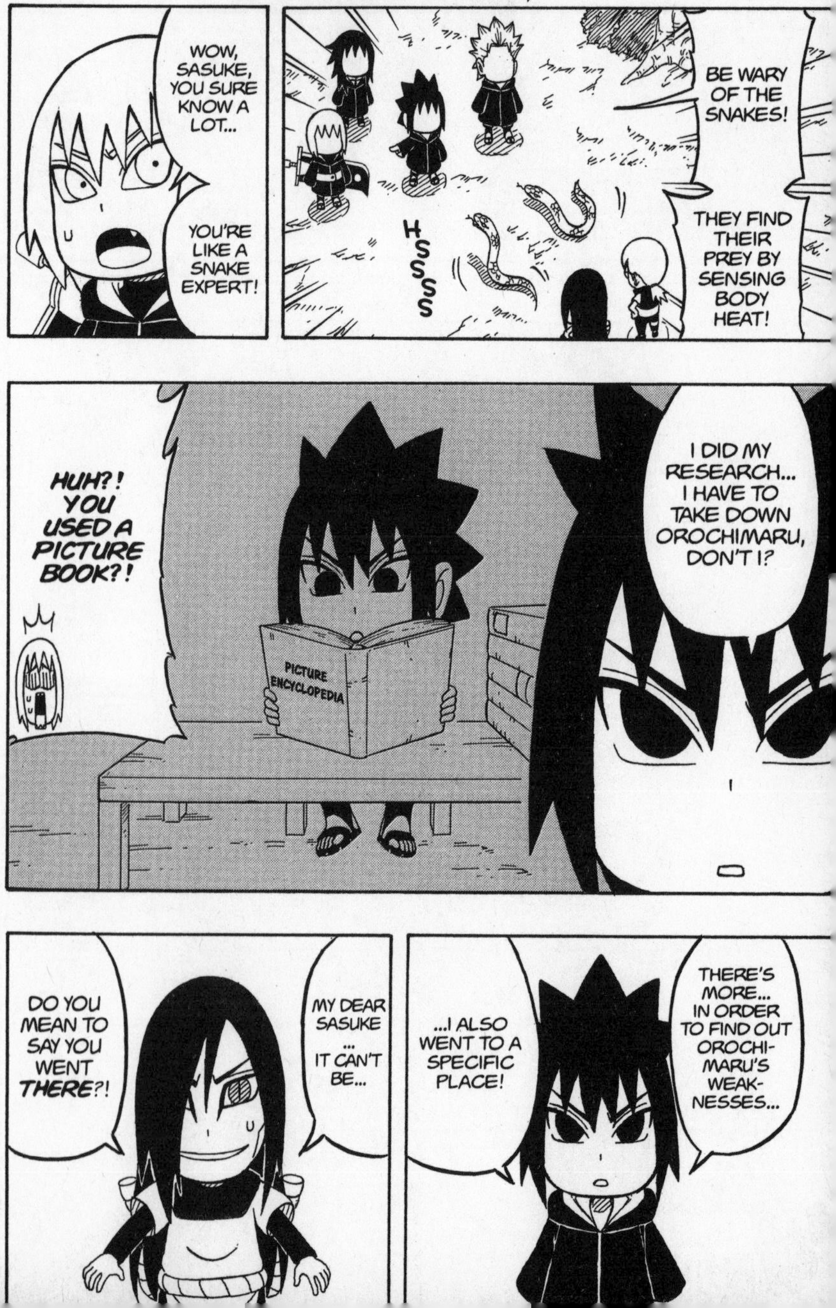
BE WARY OF THE SNAKES!
THEY FIND THEIR PREY BY SENSING BODY HEAT!
HSSSS
WOW, SASUKE, YOU SURE KNOW A LOT...
YOU'RE LIKE A SNAKE EXPERT!
I DID MY RESEARCH... I HAVE TO TAKE DOWN OROCHIMARU, DON'T I?
PICTURE ENCYCLOPEDIA
HUH?! YOU USED A PICTURE BOOK?!
THERE'S MORE... IN ORDER TO FIND OUT OROCHI-MARU'S WEAK-NESSES...
...I ALSO WENT TO A SPECIFIC PLACE!
MY DEAR SASUKE ... IT CAN'T BE...
DO YOU MEAN TO SAY YOU WENT THERE?!

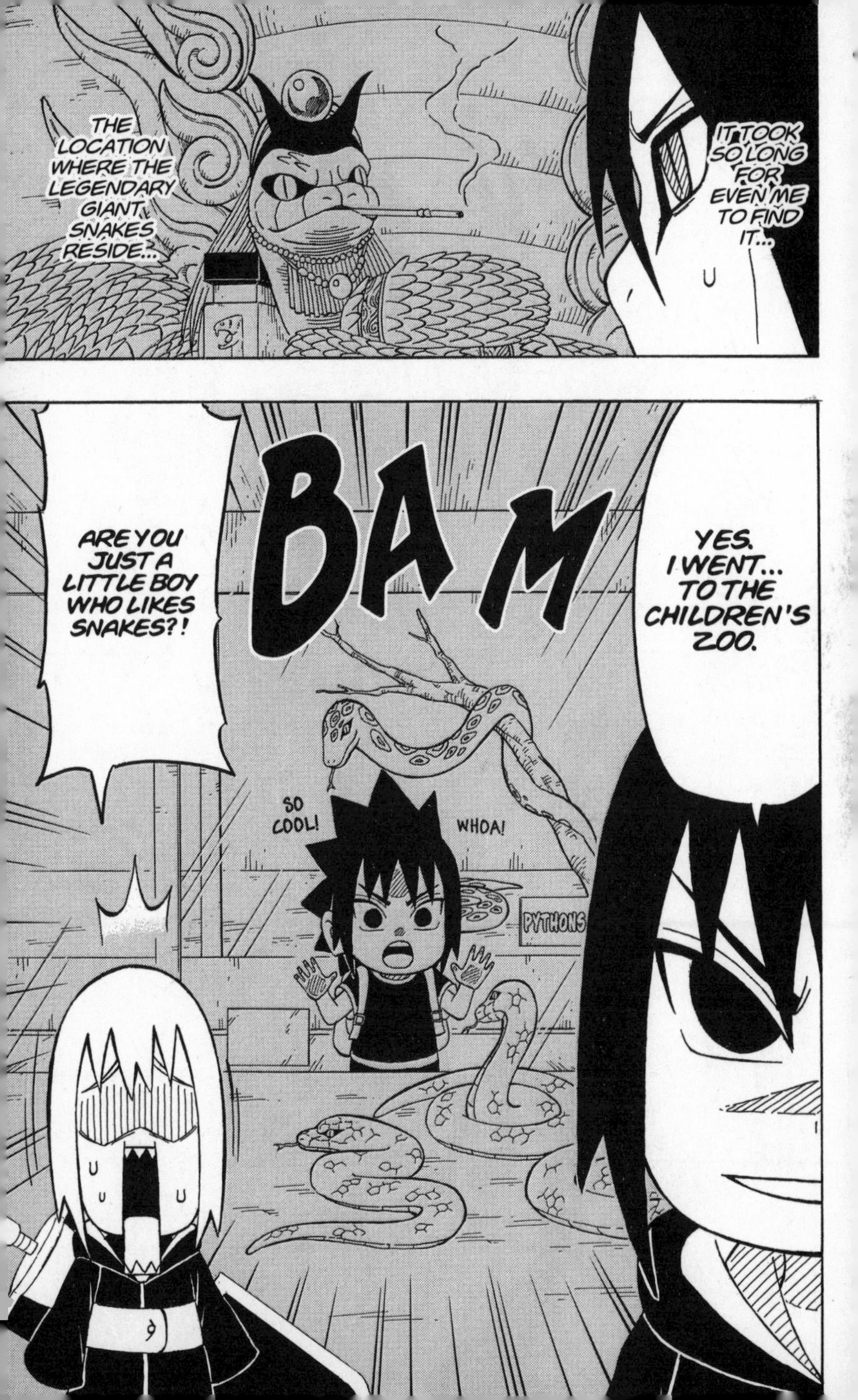
IT TOOK SO LONG FOR EVEN ME TO FIND IT...
THE LOCATION WHERE THE LEGENDARY GIANT SNAKES RESIDE...
YES. I WENT... TO THE CHILDREN'S ZOO.
BAM
ARE YOU JUST A LITTLE BOY WHO LIKES SNAKES?!
WHOA!
SO COOL!
PYTHONS

OROCHIMARU'S DISCIPLES

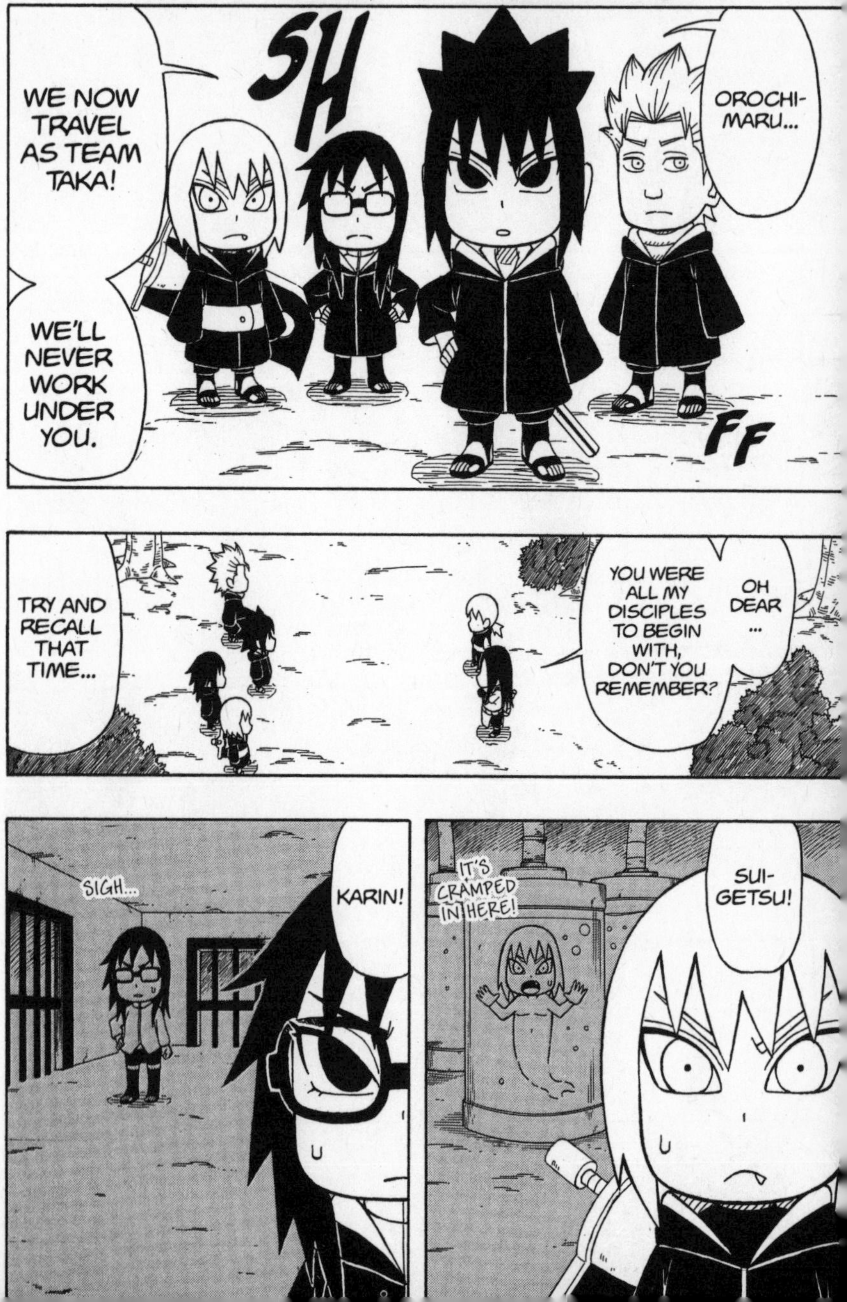
OROCHI-MARU...
SH
FF
WE NOW TRAVEL AS TEAM TAKA!
WE'LL NEVER WORK UNDER YOU.
OH DEAR ...
YOU WERE ALL MY DISCIPLES TO BEGIN WITH, DON'T YOU REMEMBER?
TRY AND RECALL THAT TIME...
SUI-GETSU!
IT'S CRAMPED IN HERE!
KARIN!
SIGH...

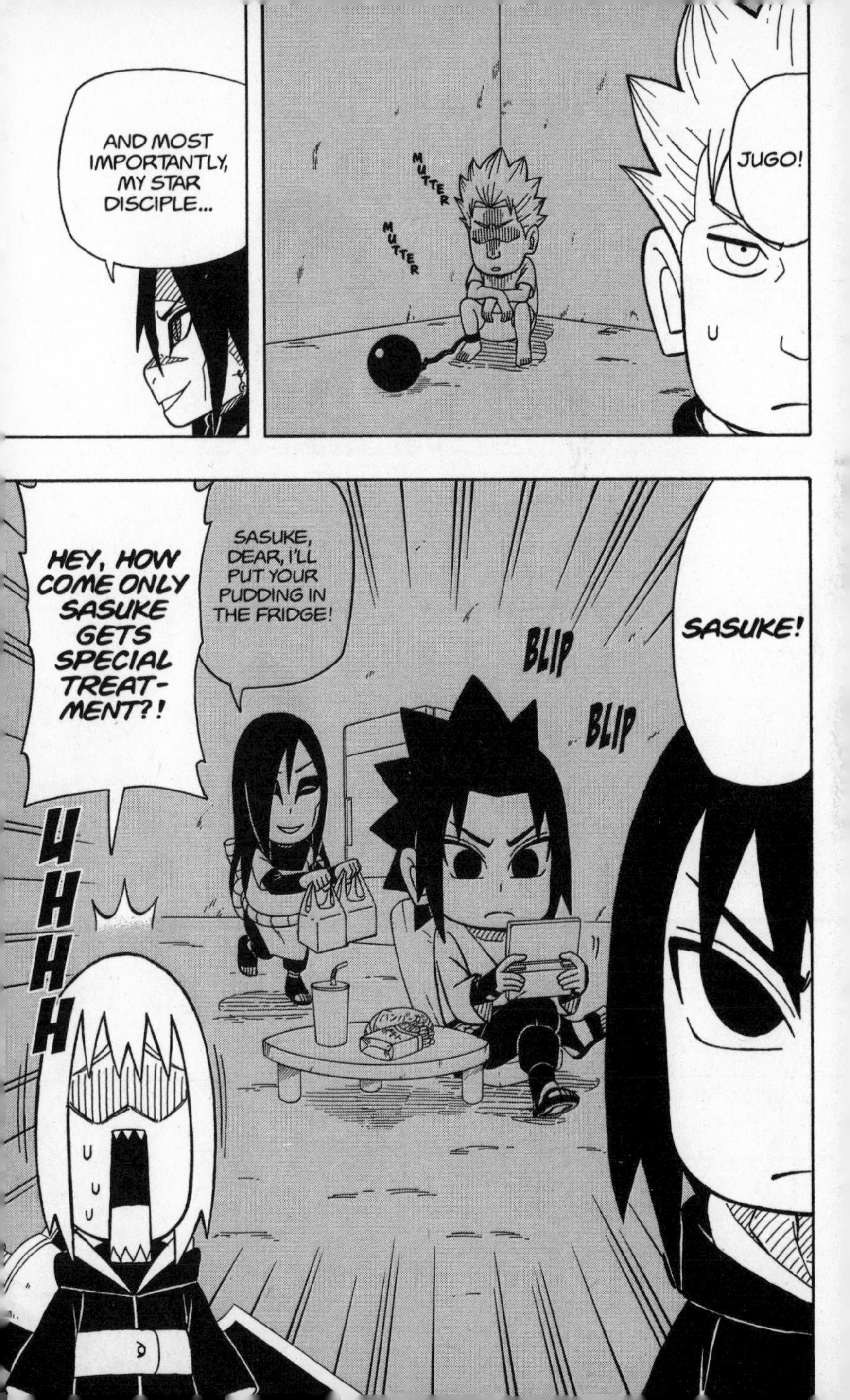
JUGO!
MUTTER
MUTTER
AND MOST IMPORTANTLY, MY STAR DISCIPLE...
SASUKE!
BLIP
BLIP
SASUKE, DEAR, I'LL PUT YOUR PUDDING IN THE FRIDGE!
HEY, HOW COME ONLY SASUKE GETS SPECIAL TREATMENT?!
UHHHH

SUIGETSU'S TERROR

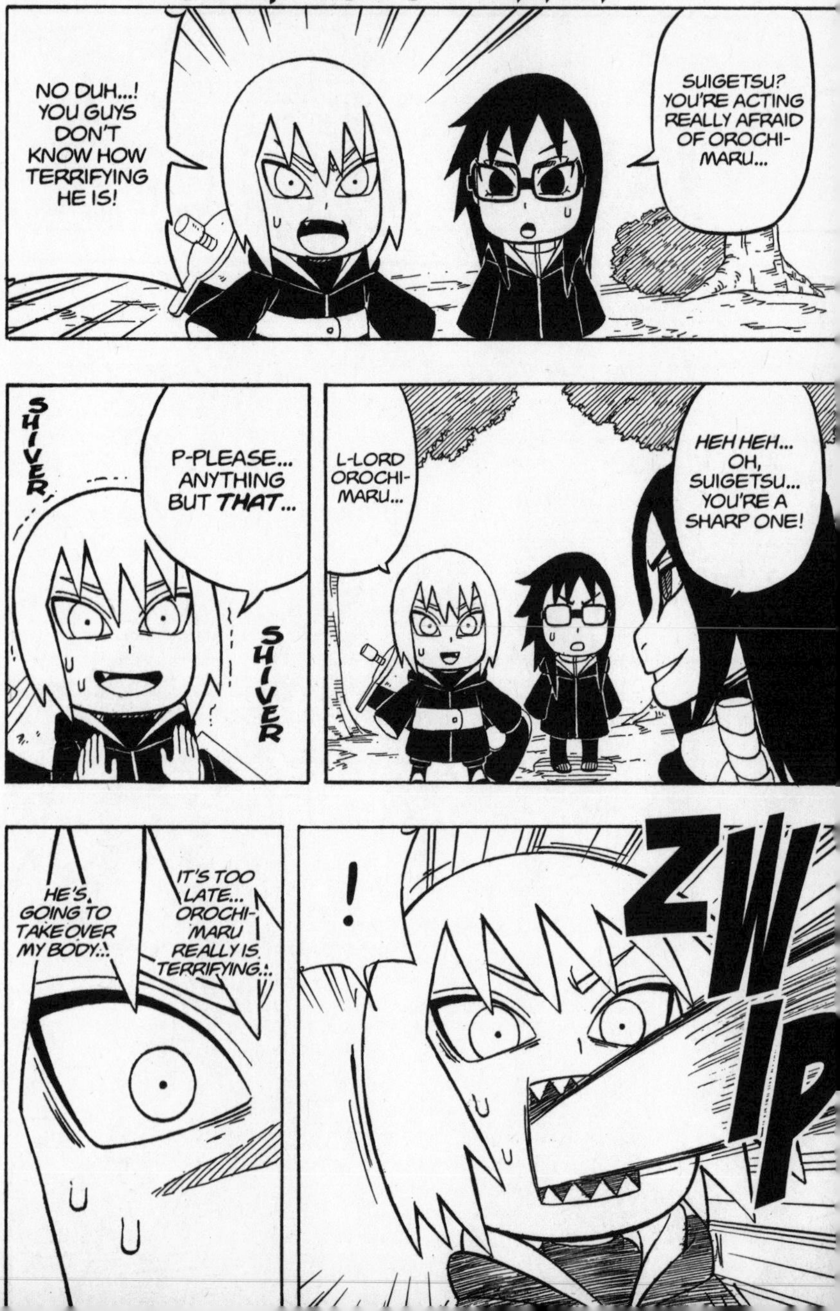

SUIGETSU? YOU'RE ACTING REALLY AFRAID OF OROCHI-MARU...
NO DUH...! YOU GUYS DON'T KNOW HOW TERRIFYING HE IS!
HEH HEH... OH, SUIGETSU... YOU'RE A SHARP ONE!
L-LORD OROCHI-MARU...
P-PLEASE... ANYTHING BUT *THAT*...
SHIVER
SHIVER
!
ZWIP
IT'S TOO LATE... OROCHI-MARU REALLY IS TERRIFYING...
HE'S GOING TO TAKE OVER MY BODY...

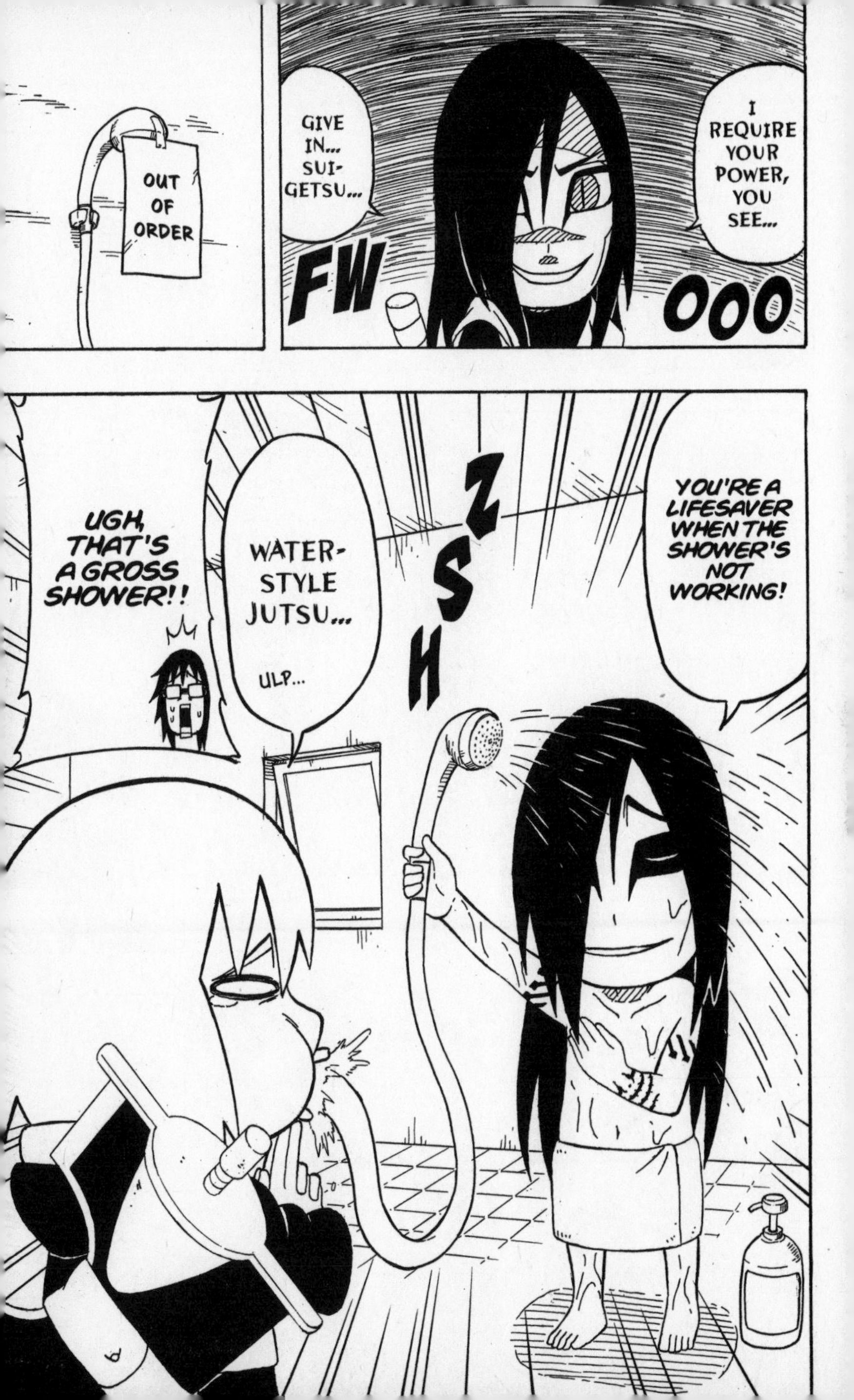
I REQUIRE YOUR POWER, YOU SEE...
GIVE IN... SUI-GETSU...
FW
OOO
OUT OF ORDER
YOU'RE A LIFESAVER WHEN THE SHOWER'S NOT WORKING!
ZSH
WATER-STYLE JUTSU...
ULP...
UGH, THAT'S A GROSS SHOWER!!

YOUNG BODY

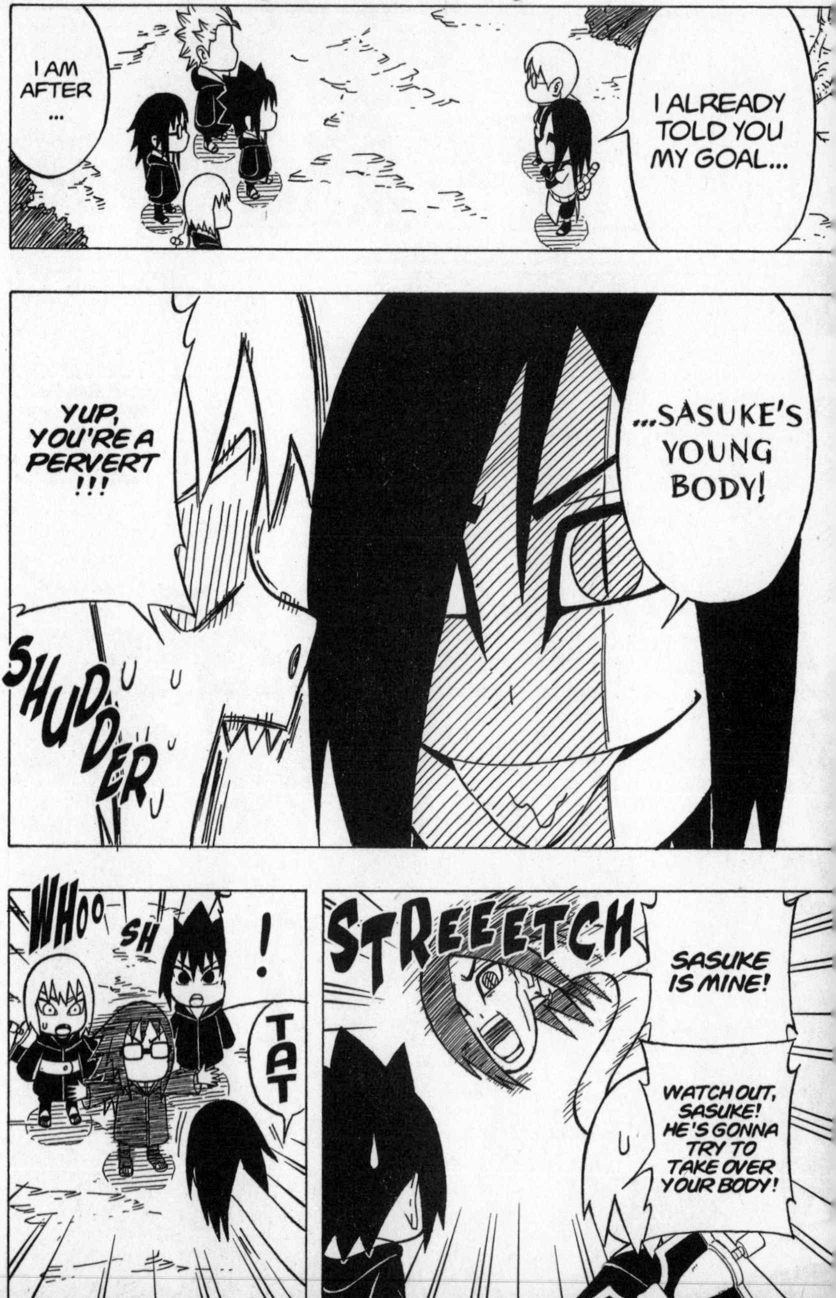
I ALREADY TOLD YOU MY GOAL...
I AM AFTER ...
...SASUKE'S YOUNG BODY!
YUP, YOU'RE A PERVERT!!!
SHUDDER
STREEETCH
SASUKE IS MINE!
WATCH OUT, SASUKE! HE'S GONNA TRY TO TAKE OVER YOUR BODY!
WHOOSH
!
TAT

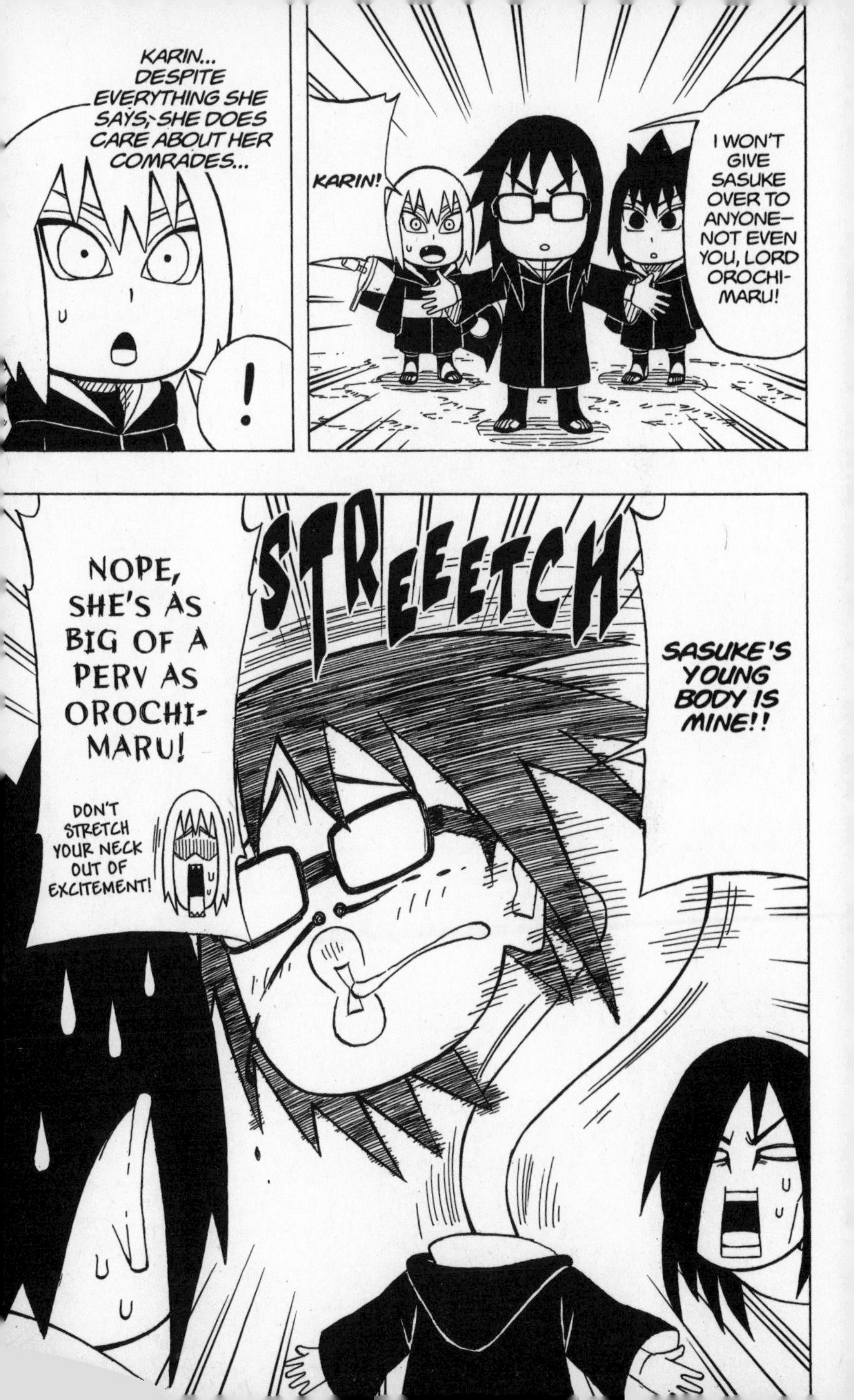
I WON'T GIVE SASUKE OVER TO ANYONE—NOT EVEN YOU, LORD OROCHIMARU!
KARIN!
KARIN... DESPITE EVERYTHING SHE SAYS, SHE DOES CARE ABOUT HER COMRADES...
!
STREEETCH
SASUKE'S YOUNG BODY IS MINE!!
NOPE, SHE'S AS BIG OF A PERV AS OROCHIMARU!
DON'T STRETCH YOUR NECK OUT OF EXCITEMENT!

KABUTO

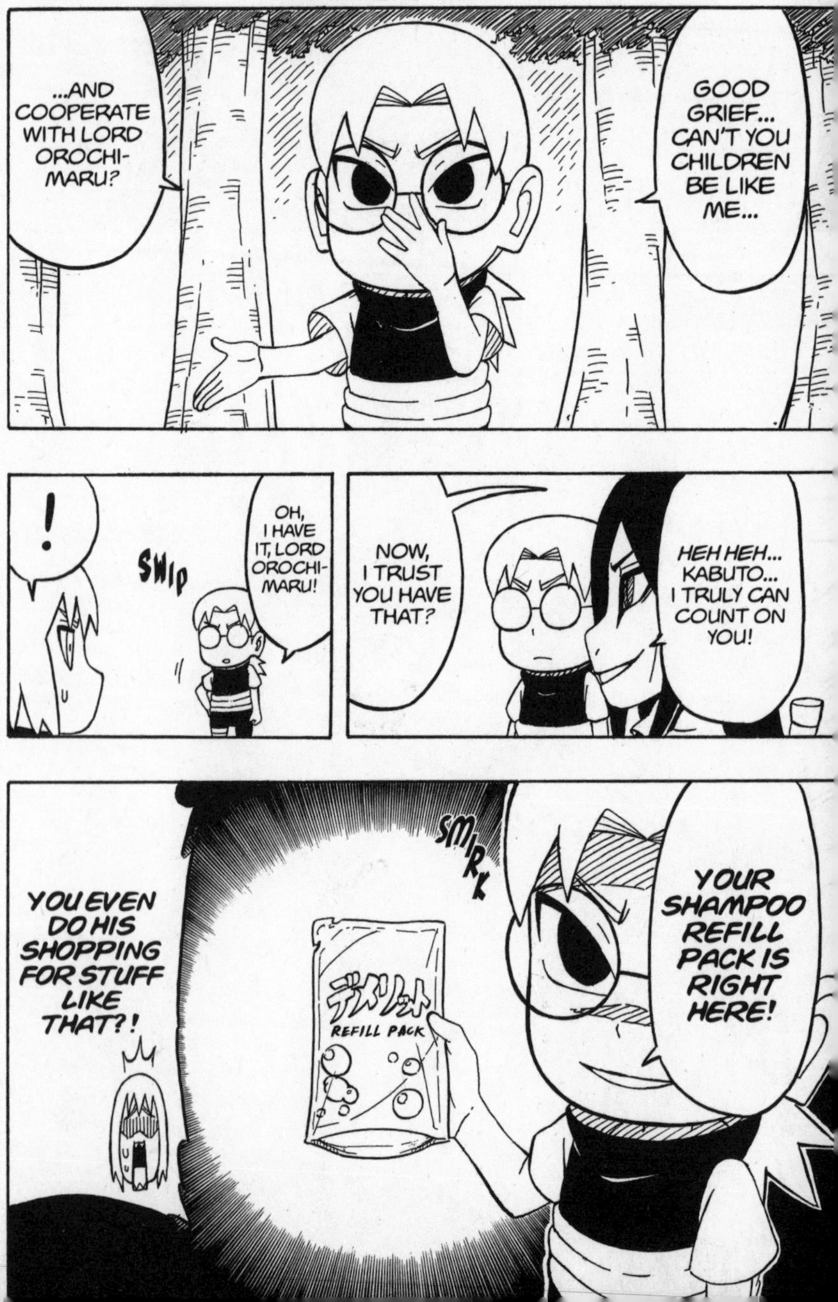
GOOD GRIEF... CAN'T YOU CHILDREN BE LIKE ME...
...AND COOPERATE WITH LORD OROCHI-MARU?
HEH HEH... KABUTO... I TRULY CAN COUNT ON YOU!
NOW, I TRUST YOU HAVE THAT?
OH, I HAVE IT, LORD OROCHI-MARU!
SWIP
!
SMIRK
YOUR SHAMPOO REFILL PACK IS RIGHT HERE!
REFILL PACK
YOU EVEN DO HIS SHOPPING FOR STUFF LIKE THAT?!

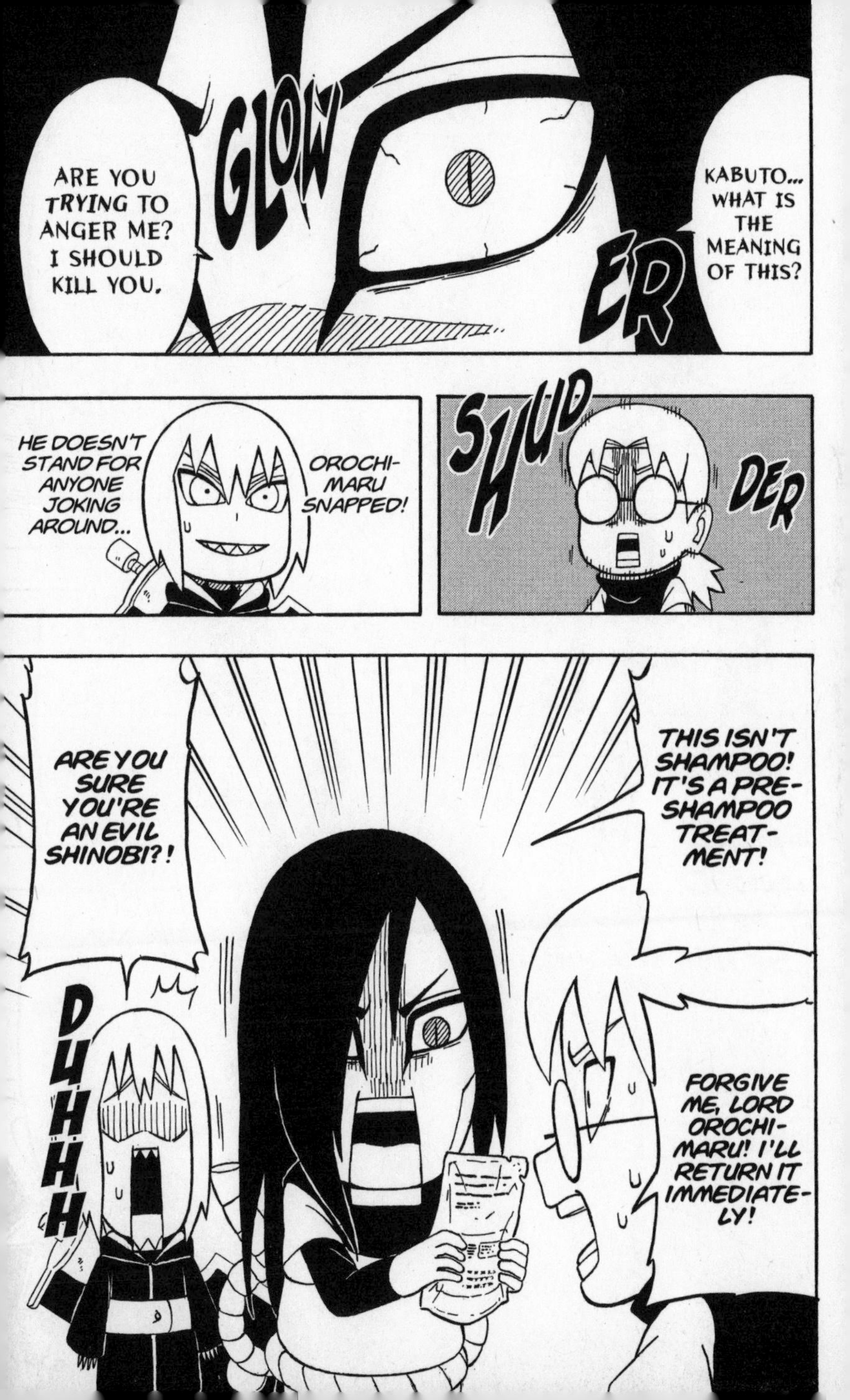
KABUTO... WHAT IS THE MEANING OF THIS?
ARE YOU TRYING TO ANGER ME? I SHOULD KILL YOU.
GLOW
ER
SHUD
DER
OROCHI-MARU SNAPPED!
HE DOESN'T STAND FOR ANYONE JOKING AROUND...
THIS ISN'T SHAMPOO! IT'S A PRE-SHAMPOO TREAT-MENT!
FORGIVE ME, LORD OROCHI-MARU! I'LL RETURN IT IMMEDIATE-LY!
ARE YOU SURE YOU'RE AN EVIL SHINOBI?!
DUHHHH

SHEDDING SKIN

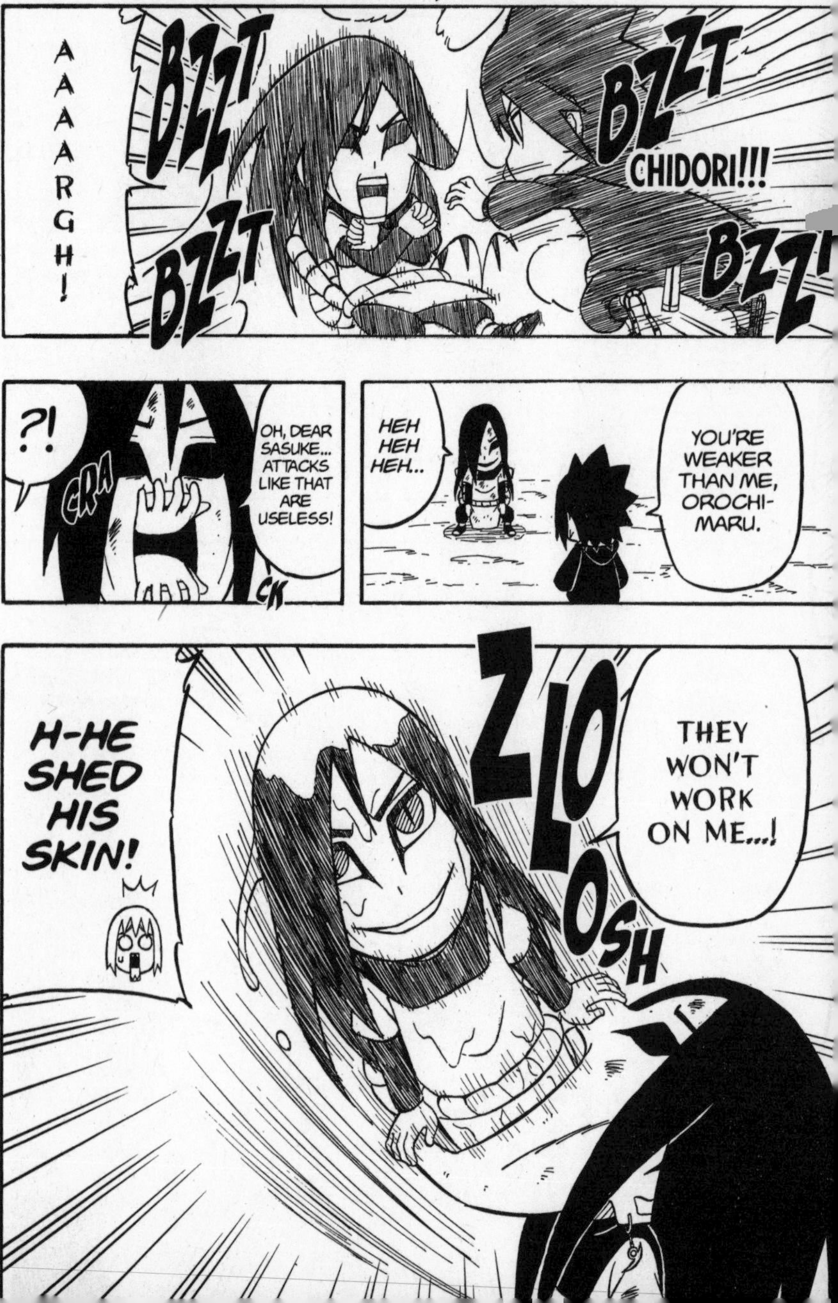
BZZT
CHIDORI!!!
BZZ
BZZT
AAAAARGH!
BZZT
YOU'RE WEAKER THAN ME, OROCHI-MARU.
HEH HEH HEH...
OH, DEAR SASUKE... ATTACKS LIKE THAT ARE USELESS!
?!
CRA
CK
THEY WON'T WORK ON ME...!
ZLOOSH
H-HE SHED HIS SKIN!

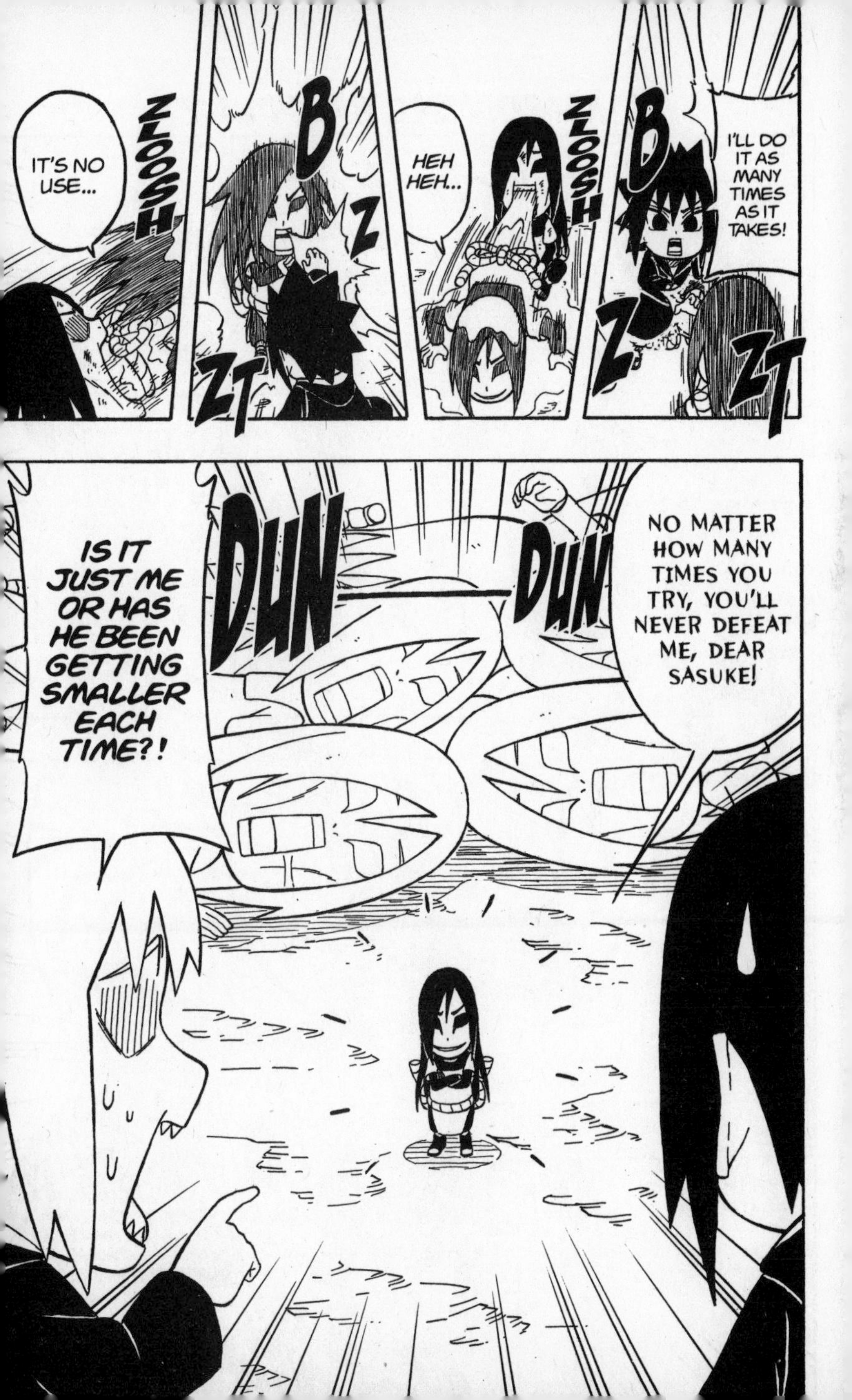
I'LL DO IT AS MANY TIMES AS IT TAKES!
B
Z
ZT
ZLOOSH
HEH HEH...
B
Z
ZT
ZLOOSH
IT'S NO USE...
NO MATTER HOW MANY TIMES YOU TRY, YOU'LL NEVER DEFEAT ME, DEAR SASUKE!
DUN—DUN
IS IT JUST ME OR HAS HE BEEN GETTING SMALLER EACH TIME?!

SUMMONING BATTLE!!

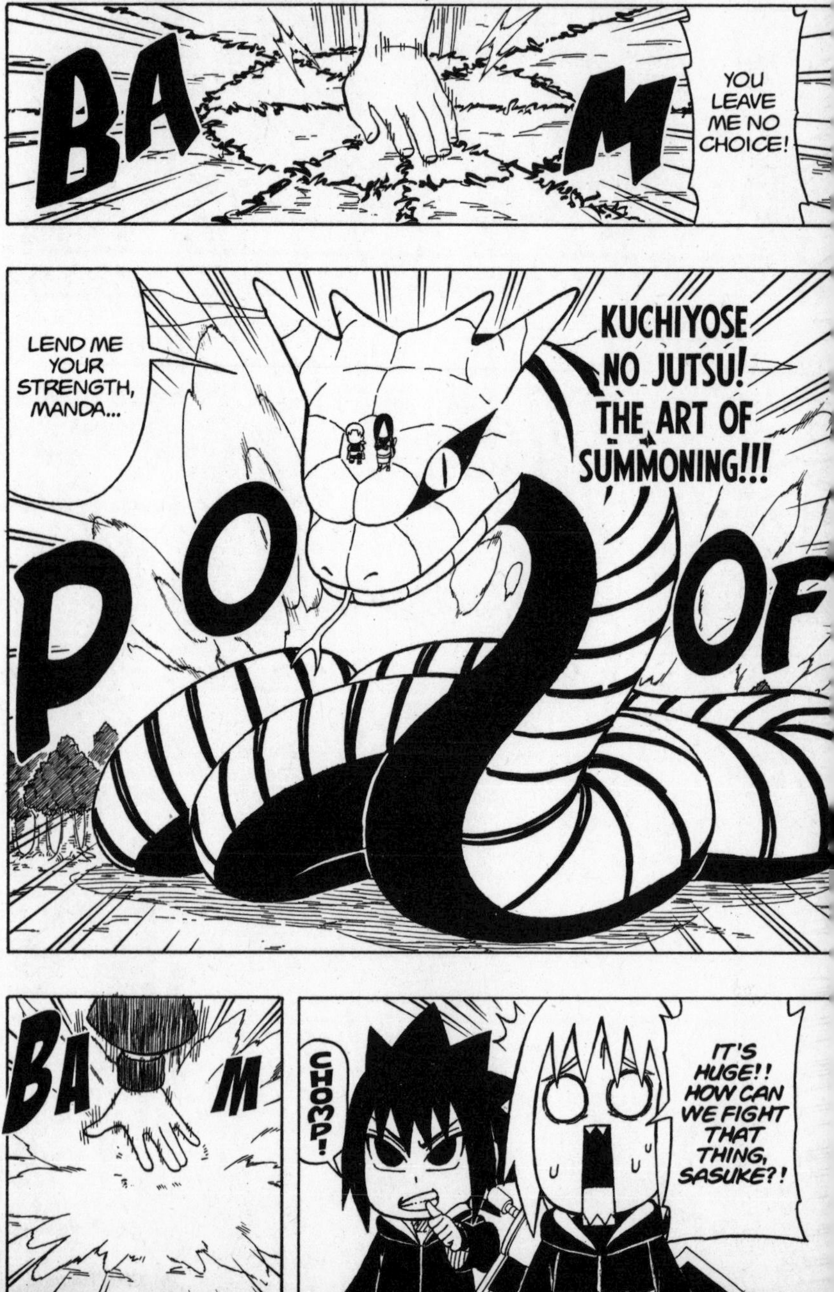
YOU LEAVE ME NO CHOICE!
BAM
KUCHIYOSE NO JUTSU! THE ART OF SUMMONING!!!
LEND ME YOUR STRENGTH, MANDA...
POOF
IT'S HUGE!! HOW CAN WE FIGHT THAT THING, SASUKE?!
CHOMP!
BAM

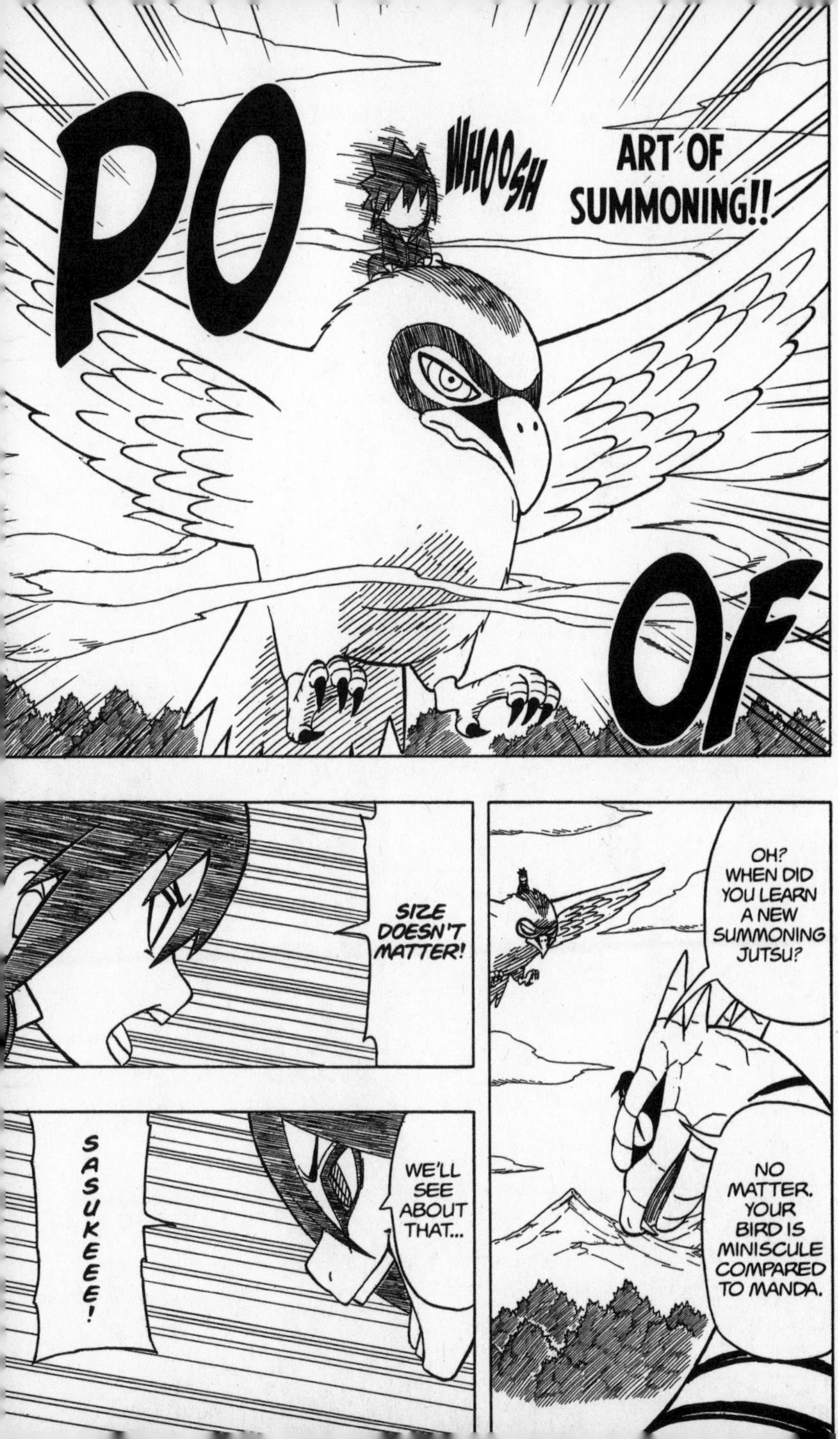
ART OF SUMMONING!!
WHOOSH
PO
OF
OH? WHEN DID YOU LEARN A NEW SUMMONING JUTSU?
NO MATTER. YOUR BIRD IS MINISCULE COMPARED TO MANDA.
SIZE DOESN'T MATTER!
WE'LL SEE ABOUT THAT...
SASUKEEE!

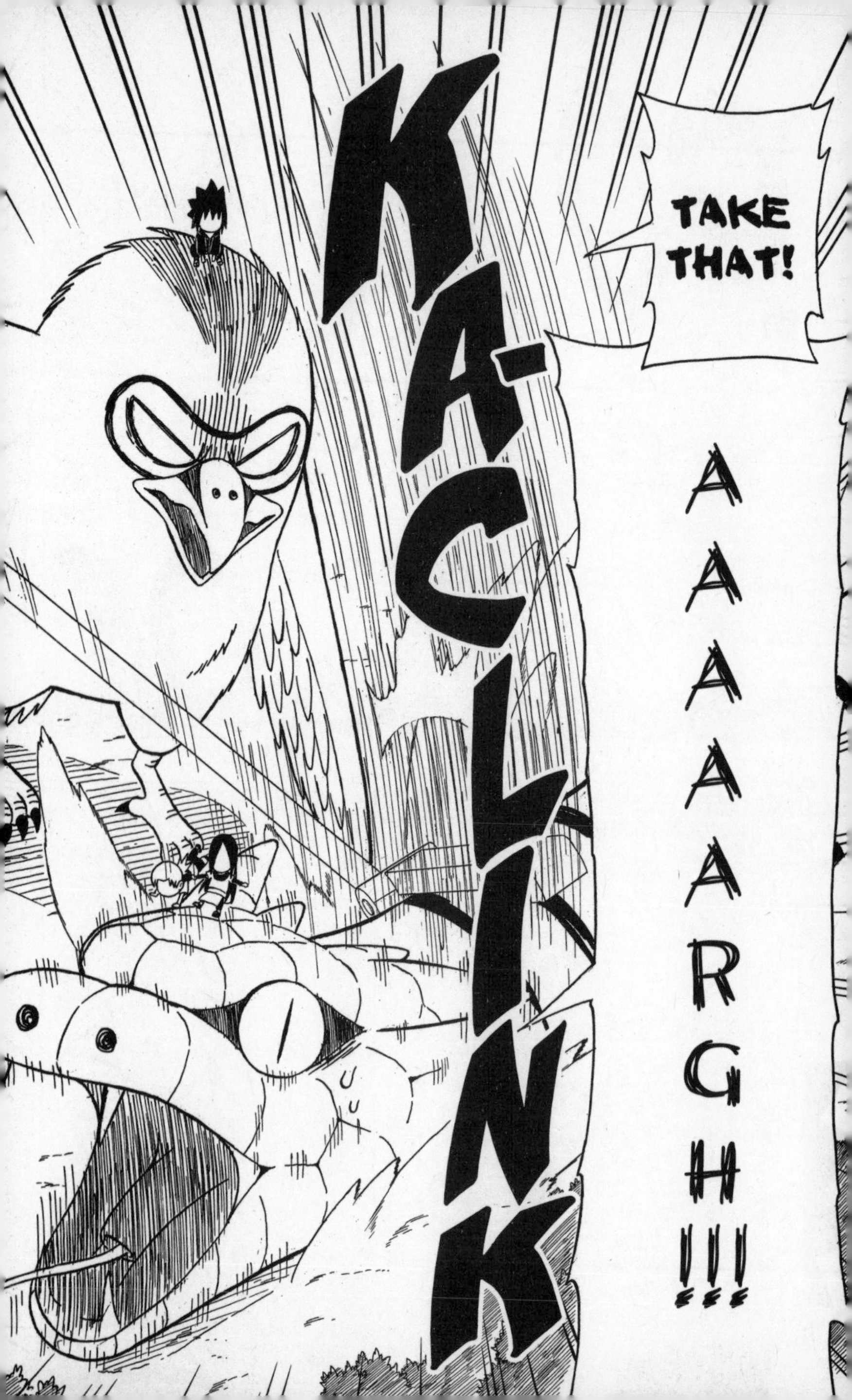
TAKE THAT!
AAAAAARGH!!!
KA-CLINK

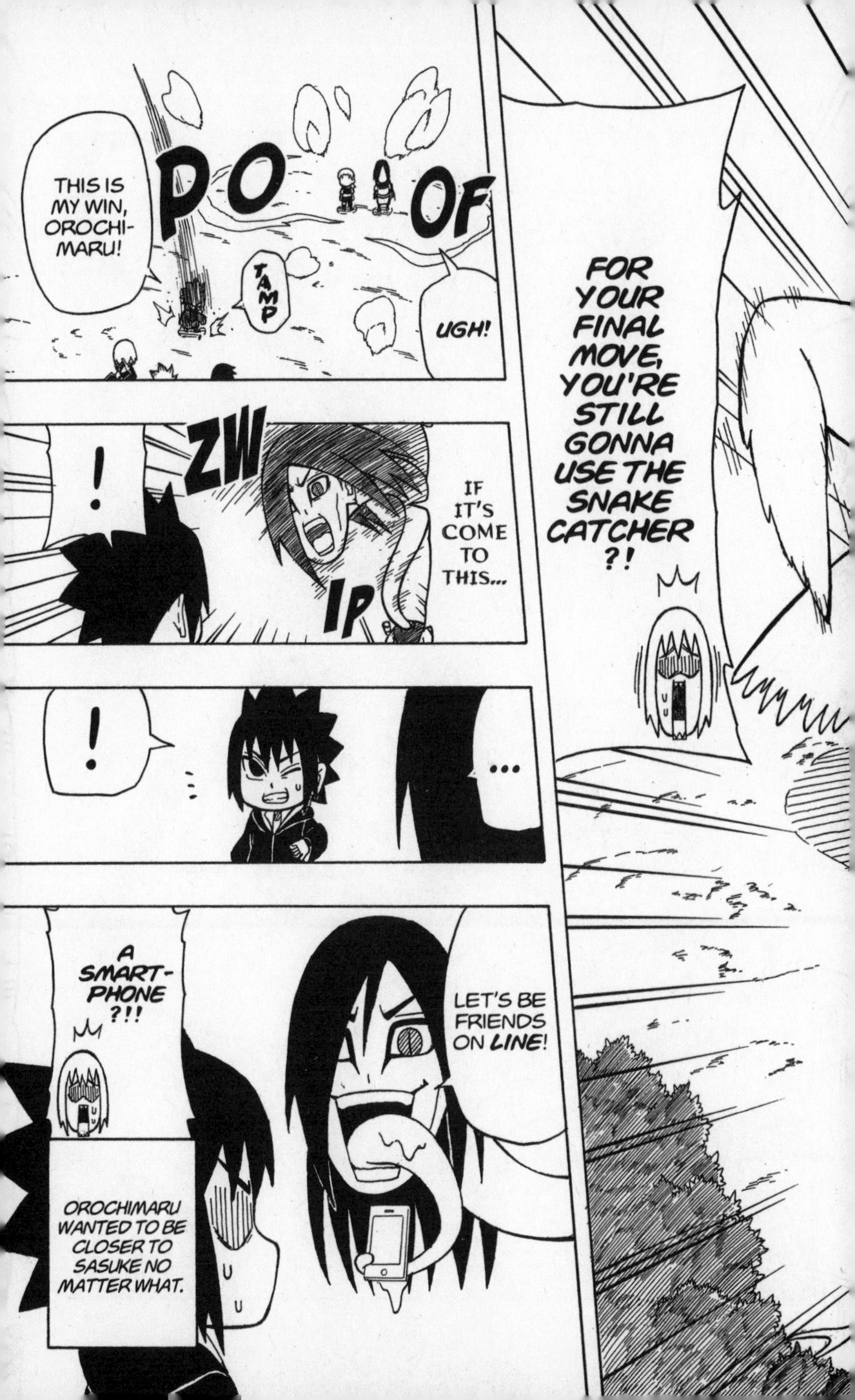
FOR YOUR FINAL MOVE, YOU'RE STILL GONNA USE THE SNAKE CATCHER?!
POOF
UGH!
TAMP
THIS IS MY WIN, OROCHIMARU!
IF IT'S COME TO THIS...
ZWIP
!
...
!
LET'S BE FRIENDS ON **LINE**!
A SMARTPHONE?!!
OROCHIMARU WANTED TO BE CLOSER TO SASUKE NO MATTER WHAT.

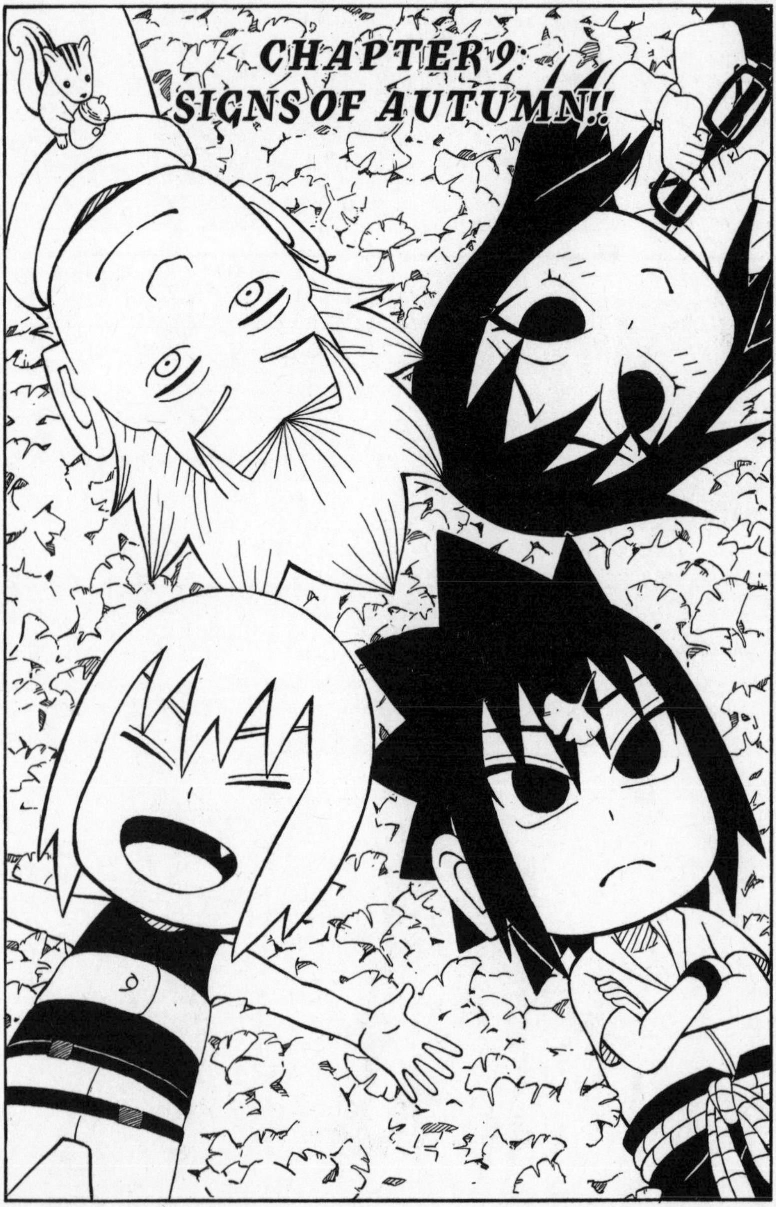
CHAPTER 9:
SIGNS OF AUTUMN!!

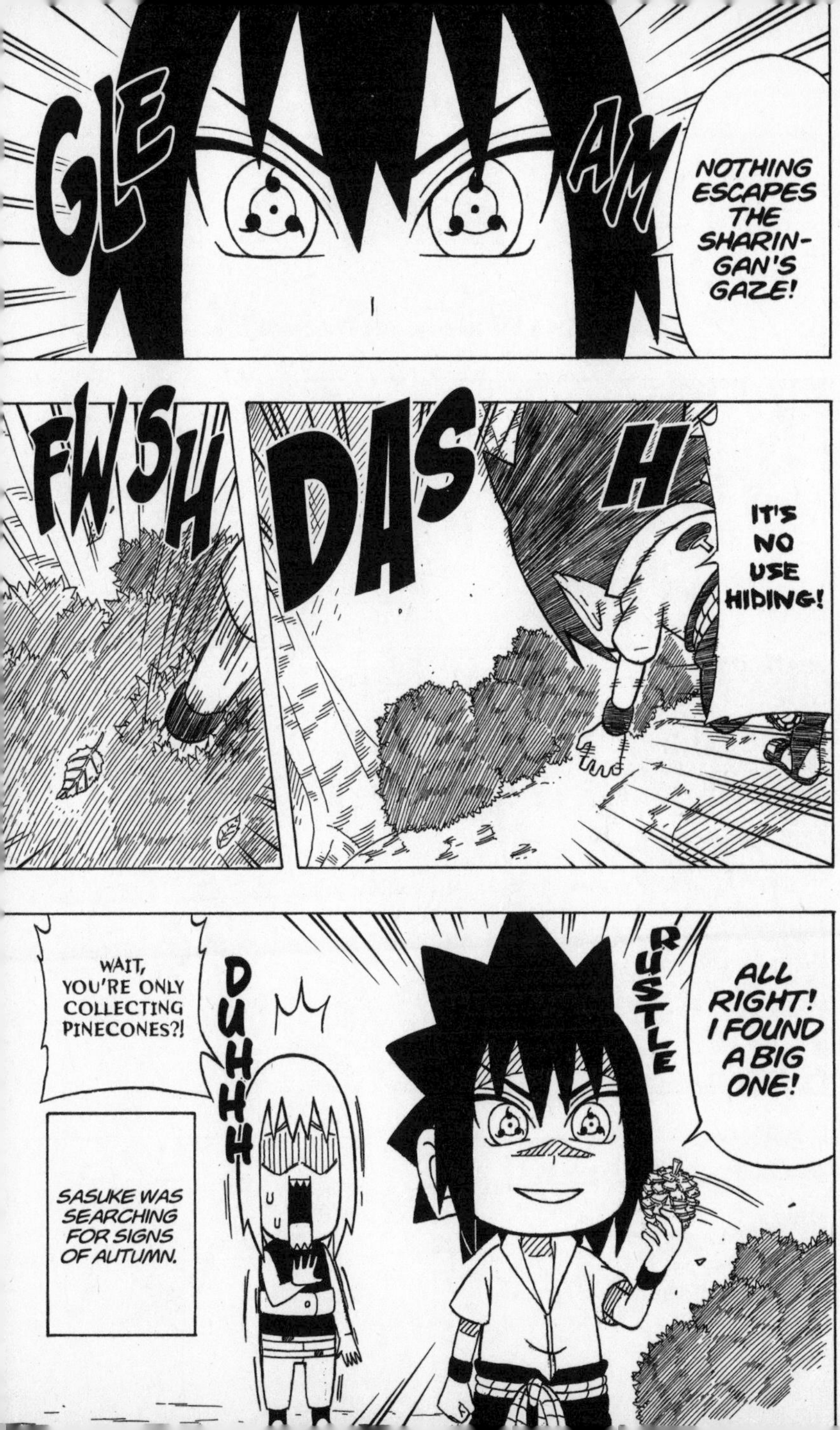
GLEAM
NOTHING ESCAPES THE SHARIN-GAN'S GAZE!
DASH
IT'S NO USE HIDING!
FWSH
ALL RIGHT! I FOUND A BIG ONE!
RUSTLE
DUHHH
WAIT, YOU'RE ONLY COLLECTING PINECONES?!
SASUKE WAS SEARCHING FOR SIGNS OF AUTUMN.

GAS

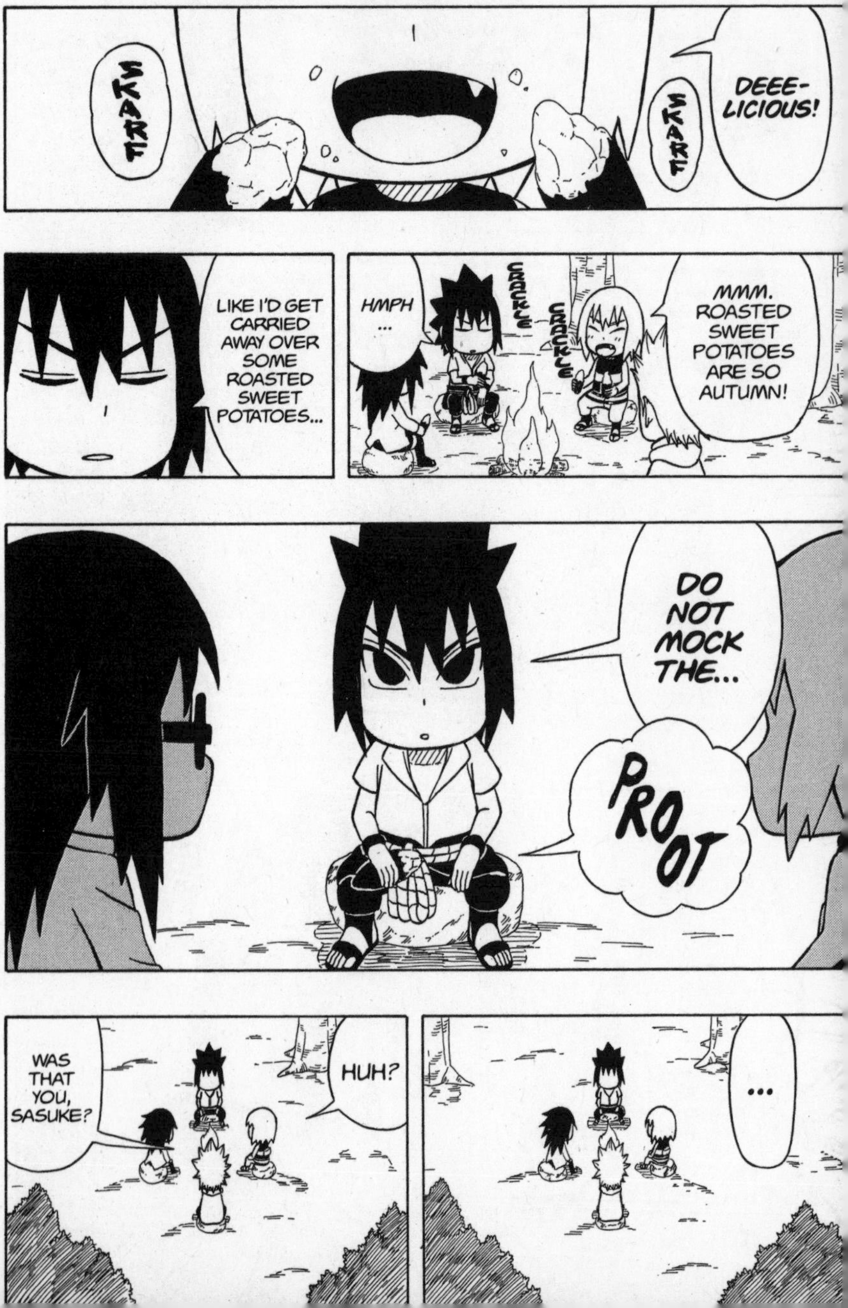
DEEE-LICIOUS!
SKARF
SKARF
MMM. ROASTED SWEET POTATOES ARE SO AUTUMN!
CRACKLE
CRACKLE
HMPH ...
LIKE I'D GET CARRIED AWAY OVER SOME ROASTED SWEET POTATOES...
DO NOT MOCK THE...
PROOT
...
HUH?
WAS THAT YOU, SASUKE?

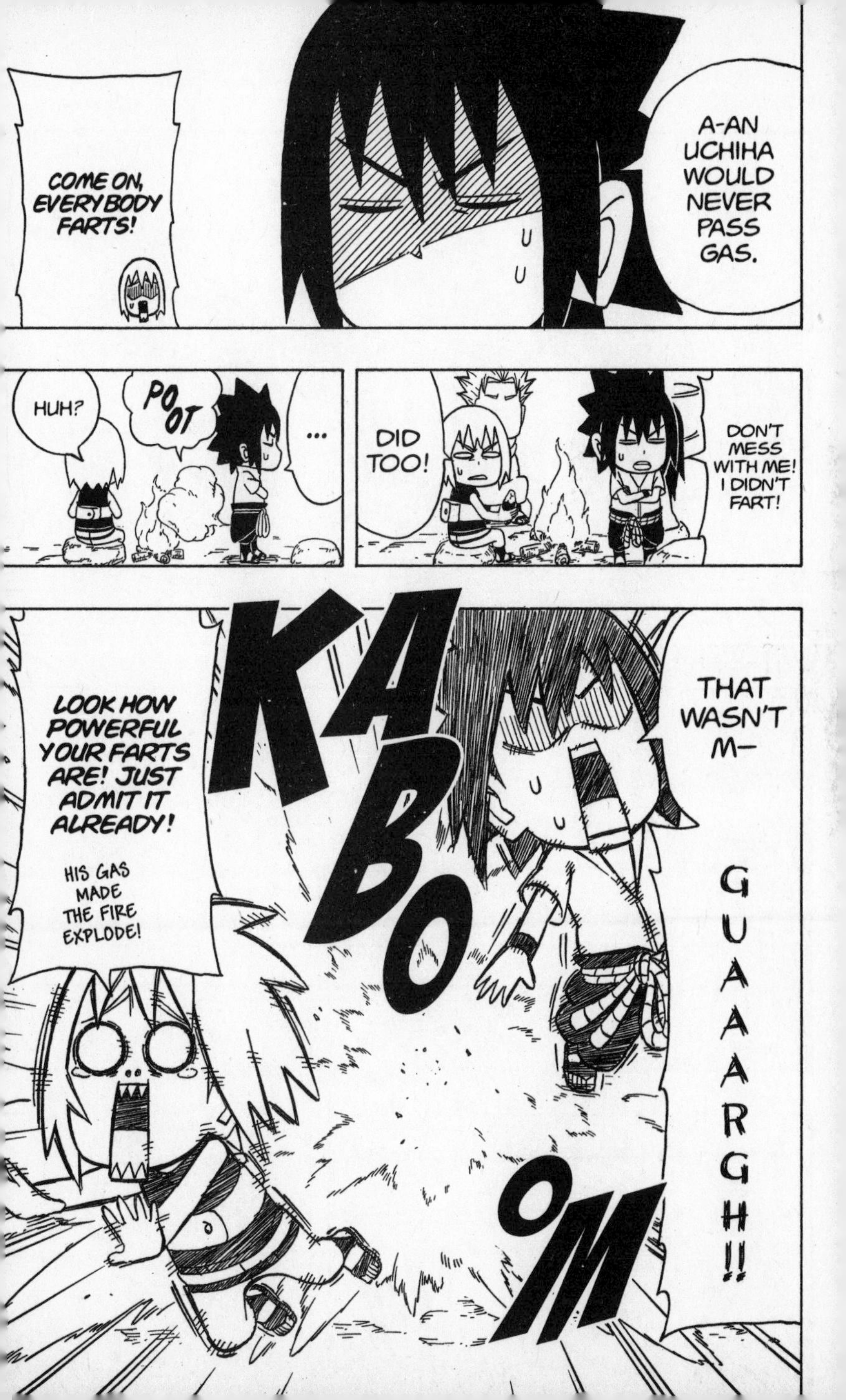
A-AN UCHIHA WOULD NEVER PASS GAS.
COME ON, EVERYBODY FARTS!
DON'T MESS WITH ME! I DIDN'T FART!
DID TOO!
...
POOT
HUH?
THAT WASN'T M—
GUAAAARGH!!
KABOOM
LOOK HOW POWERFUL YOUR FARTS ARE! JUST ADMIT IT ALREADY!
HIS GAS MADE THE FIRE EXPLODE!

HUNTING

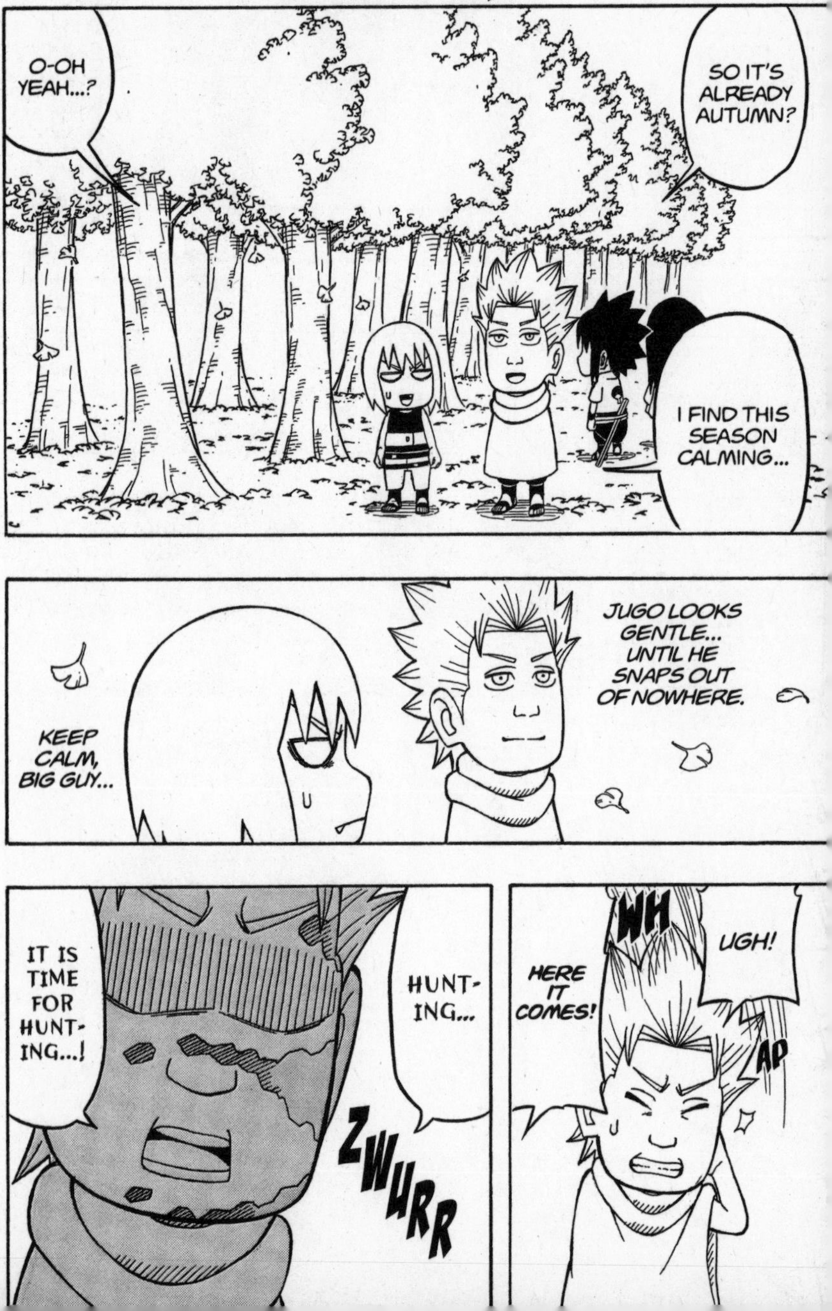
SO IT'S ALREADY AUTUMN?
I FIND THIS SEASON CALMING...
O-OH YEAH...?
JUGO LOOKS GENTLE... UNTIL HE SNAPS OUT OF NOWHERE.
KEEP CALM, BIG GUY...
WH
UGH!
HERE IT COMES!
AP
HUNT-ING...
IT IS TIME FOR HUNT-ING...!
ZWURR

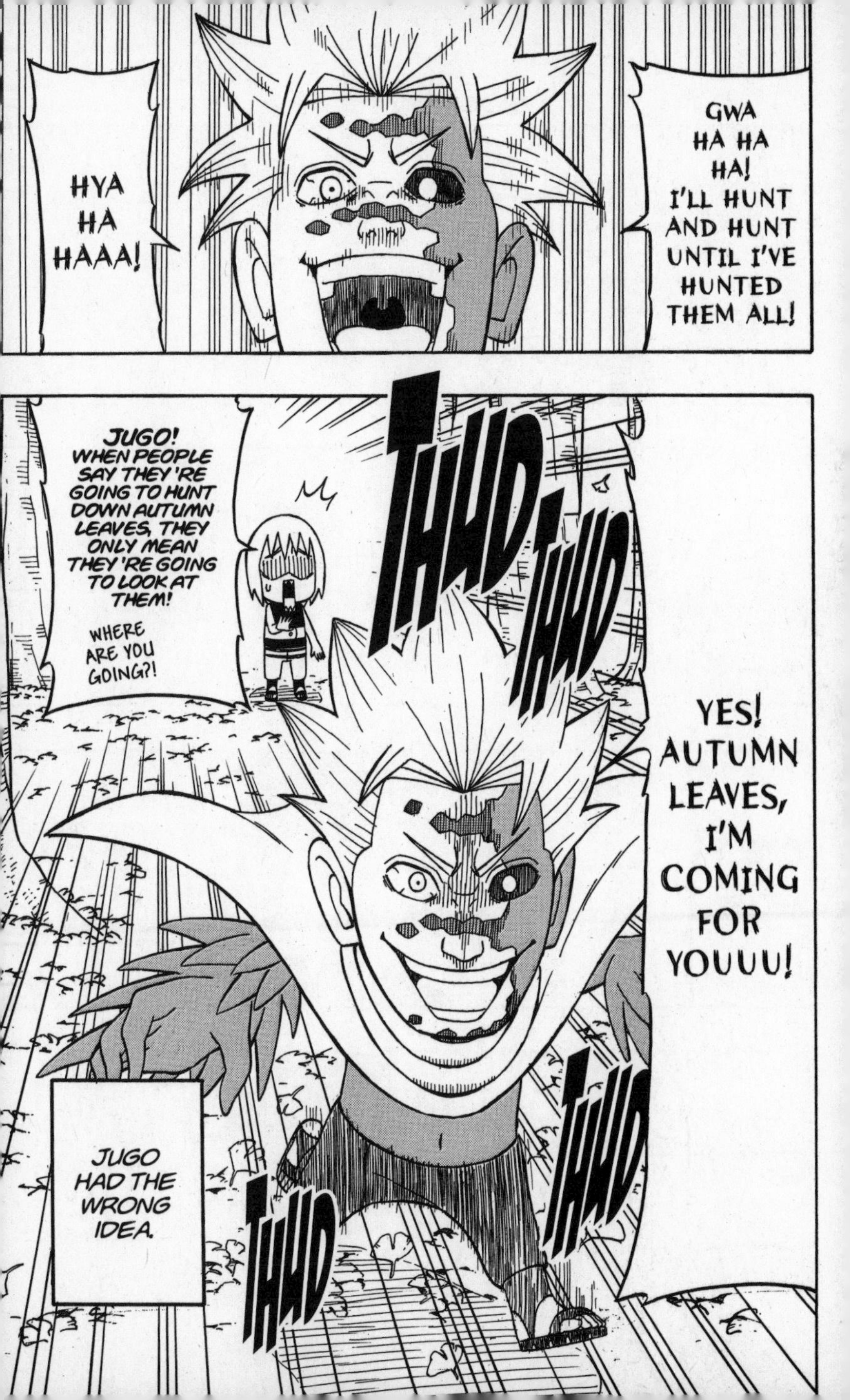
GWA HA HA HA! I'LL HUNT AND HUNT UNTIL I'VE HUNTED THEM ALL!
HYA HA HAAA!
THUD THUD
YES! AUTUMN LEAVES, I'M COMING FOR YOUUU!
JUGO! WHEN PEOPLE SAY THEY'RE GOING TO HUNT DOWN AUTUMN LEAVES, THEY ONLY MEAN THEY'RE GOING TO LOOK AT THEM!
WHERE ARE YOU GOING?!
THUD THUD
JUGO HAD THE WRONG IDEA.

HALLOWEEN

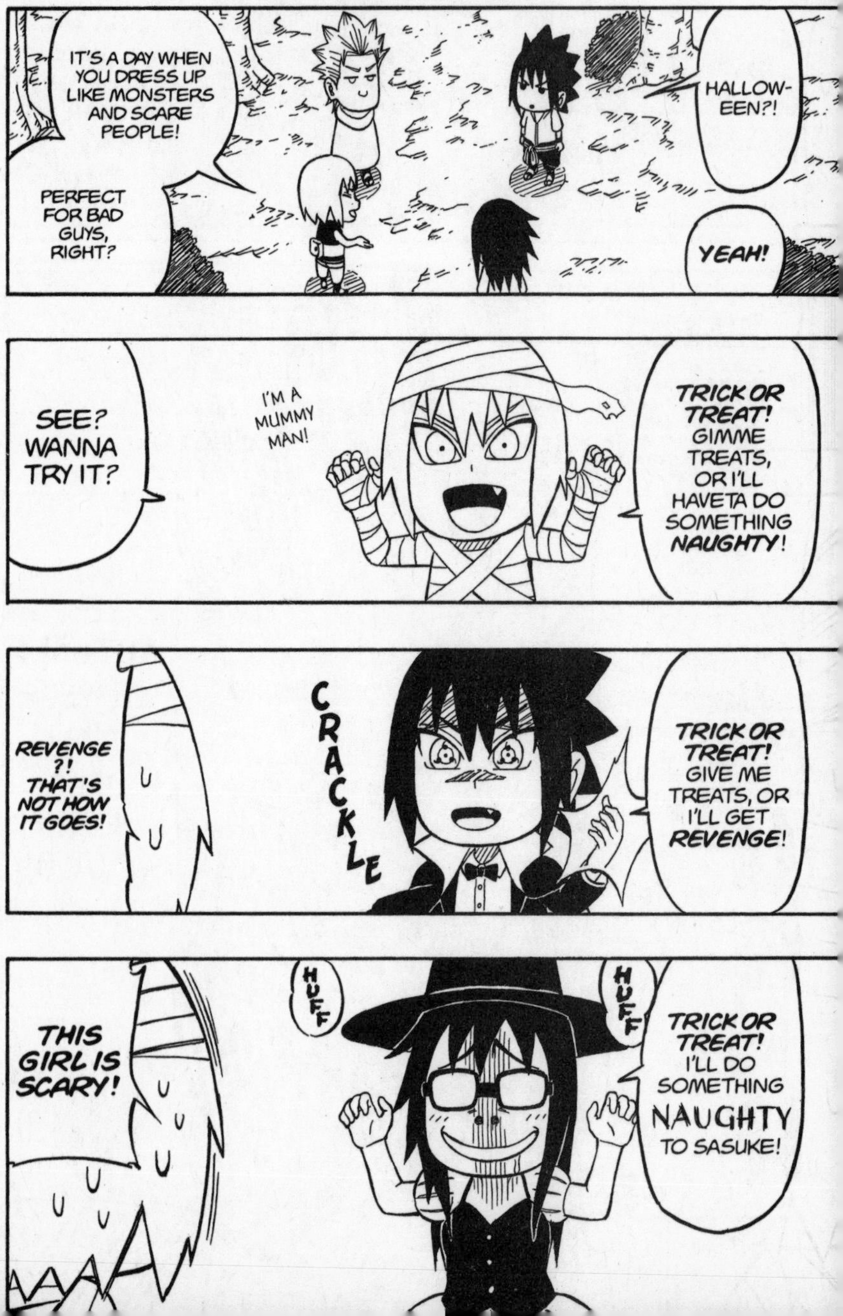
HALLOWEEN?!
YEAH!
IT'S A DAY WHEN YOU DRESS UP LIKE MONSTERS AND SCARE PEOPLE!
PERFECT FOR BAD GUYS, RIGHT?
TRICK OR TREAT! GIMME TREATS, OR I'LL HAVETA DO SOMETHING NAUGHTY!
I'M A MUMMY MAN!
SEE? WANNA TRY IT?
TRICK OR TREAT! GIVE ME TREATS, OR I'LL GET REVENGE!
CRACKLE
REVENGE?! THAT'S NOT HOW IT GOES!
HUFF
TRICK OR TREAT! I'LL DO SOMETHING NAUGHTY TO SASUKE!
HUFF
THIS GIRL IS SCARY!

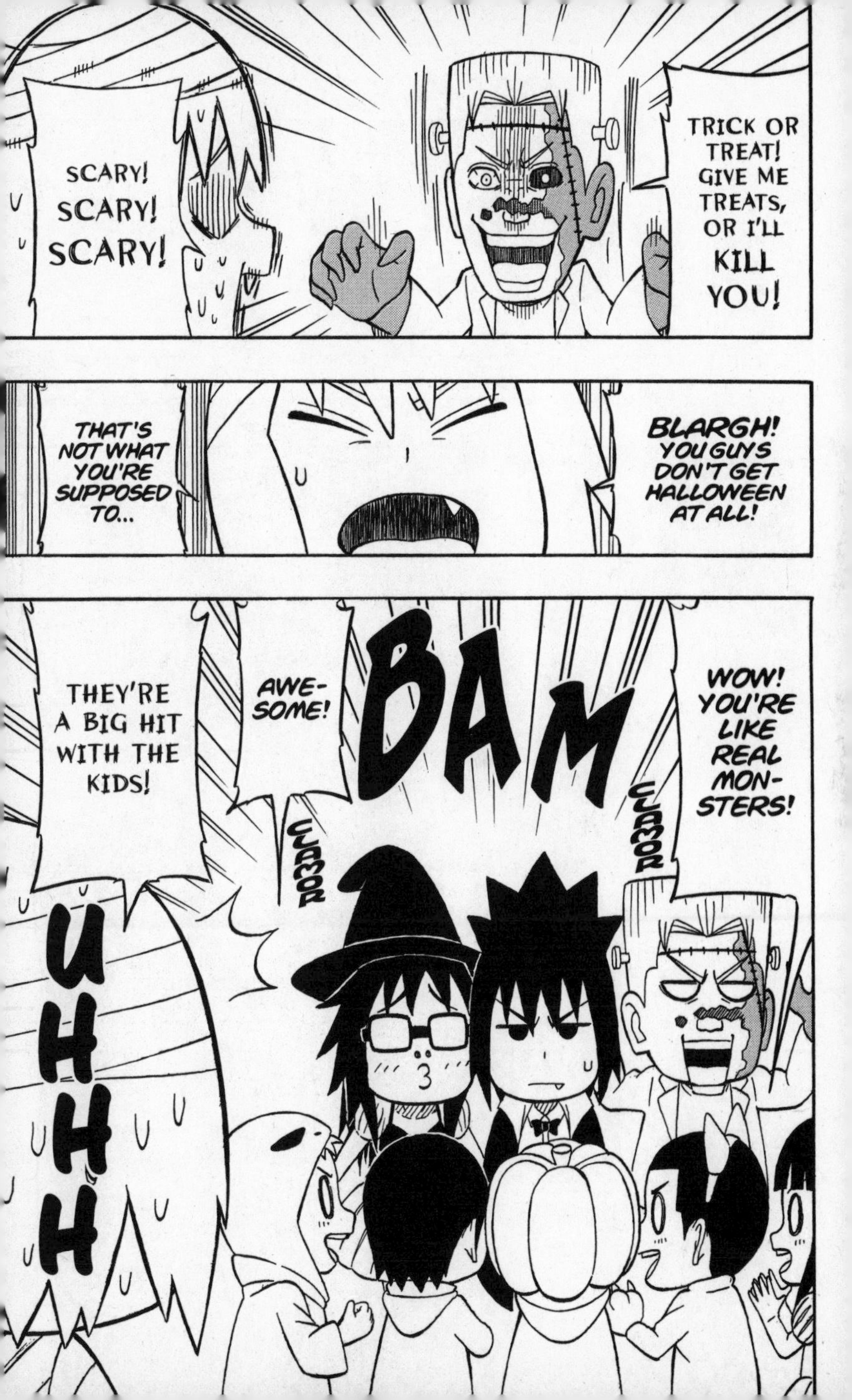
TRICK OR TREAT! GIVE ME TREATS, OR I'LL KILL YOU!
SCARY! SCARY! SCARY!
BLARGH! YOU GUYS DON'T GET HALLOWEEN AT ALL!
THAT'S NOT WHAT YOU'RE SUPPOSED TO...
WOW! YOU'RE LIKE REAL MON-STERS!
CLAMOR
BAM
AWE-SOME!
CLAMOR
THEY'RE A BIG HIT WITH THE KIDS!
UHHHH

HALLOWEEN 2

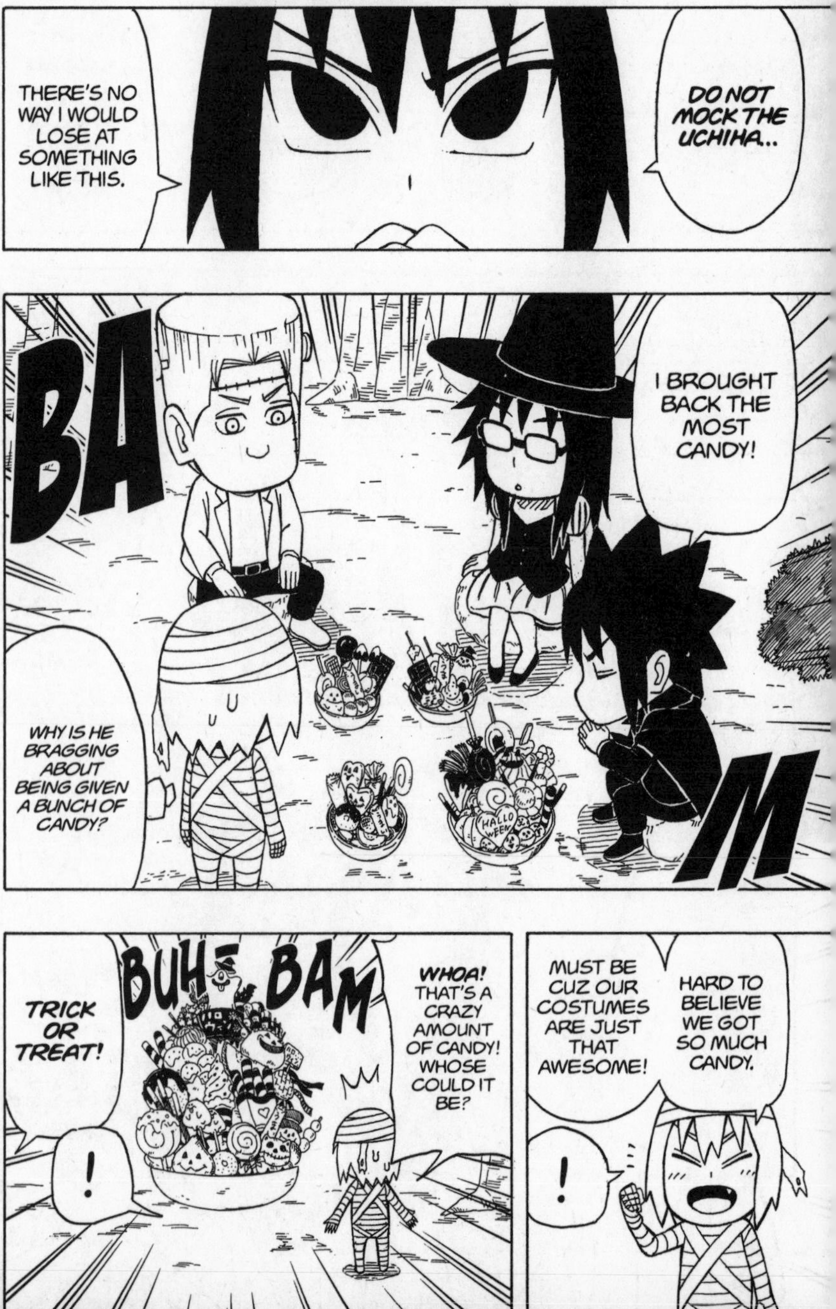
DO NOT MOCK THE UCHIHA...
THERE'S NO WAY I WOULD LOSE AT SOMETHING LIKE THIS.
I BROUGHT BACK THE MOST CANDY!
BAM
WHY IS HE BRAGGING ABOUT BEING GIVEN A BUNCH OF CANDY?
HARD TO BELIEVE WE GOT SO MUCH CANDY.
MUST BE CUZ OUR COSTUMES ARE JUST THAT AWESOME!
!
WHOA! THAT'S A CRAZY AMOUNT OF CANDY! WHOSE COULD IT BE?
BUH-BAM
TRICK OR TREAT!
!

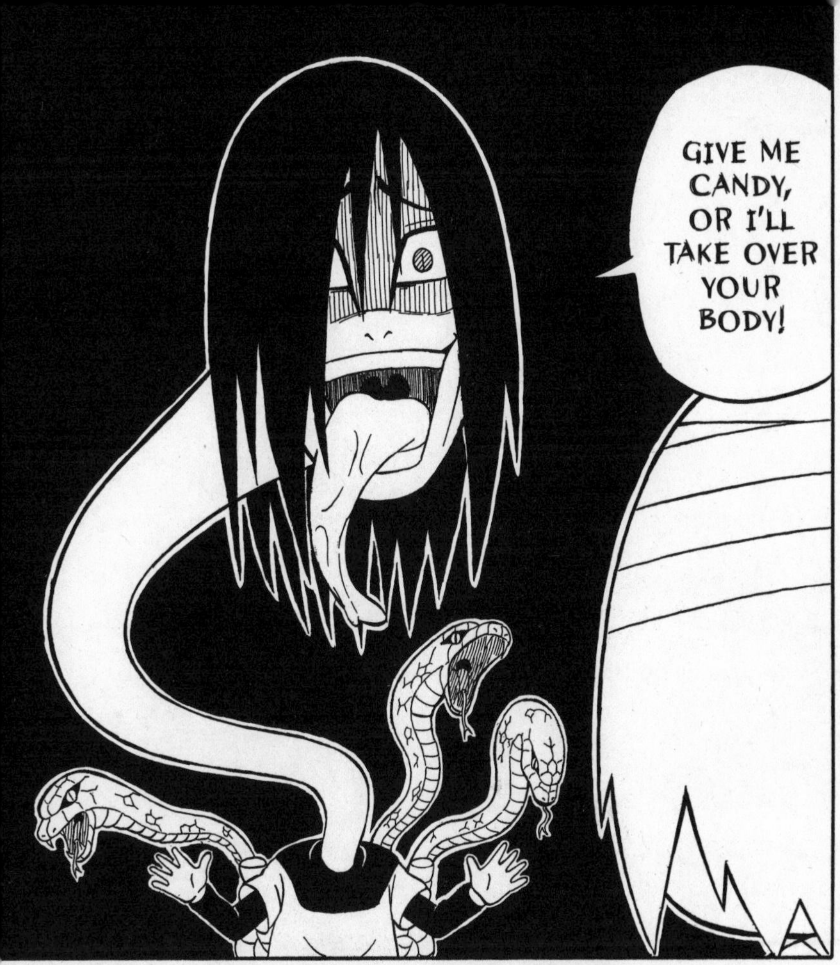
GIVE ME CANDY, OR I'LL TAKE OVER YOUR BODY!

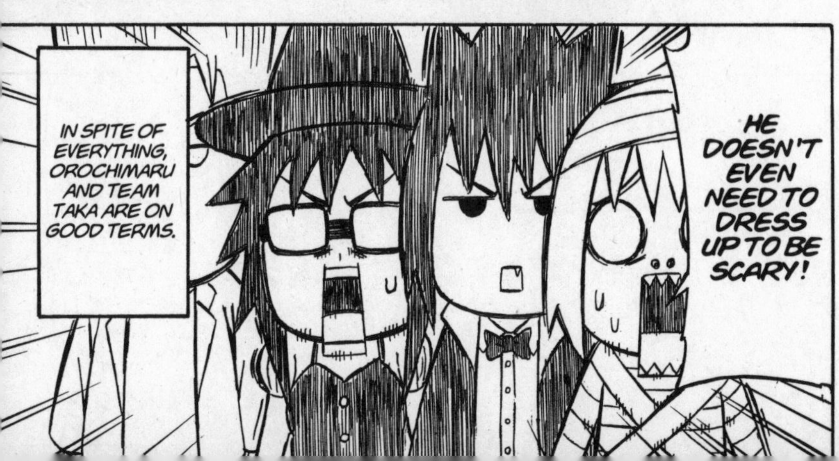
HE DOESN'T EVEN NEED TO DRESS UP TO BE SCARY!
IN SPITE OF EVERYTHING, OROCHIMARU AND TEAM TAKA ARE ON GOOD TERMS.

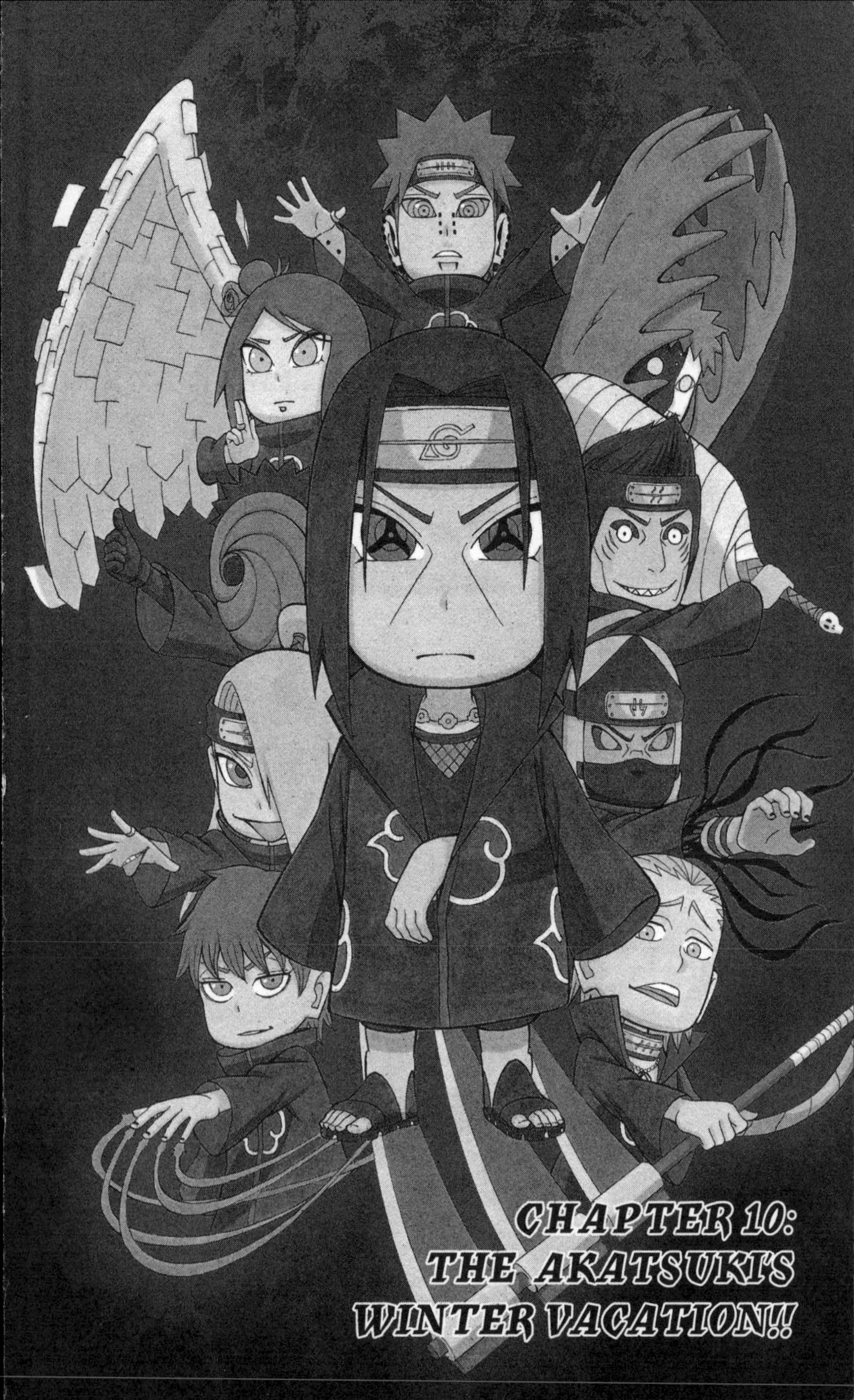
CHAPTER 10:
THE AKATSUKI'S
WINTER VACATION!!

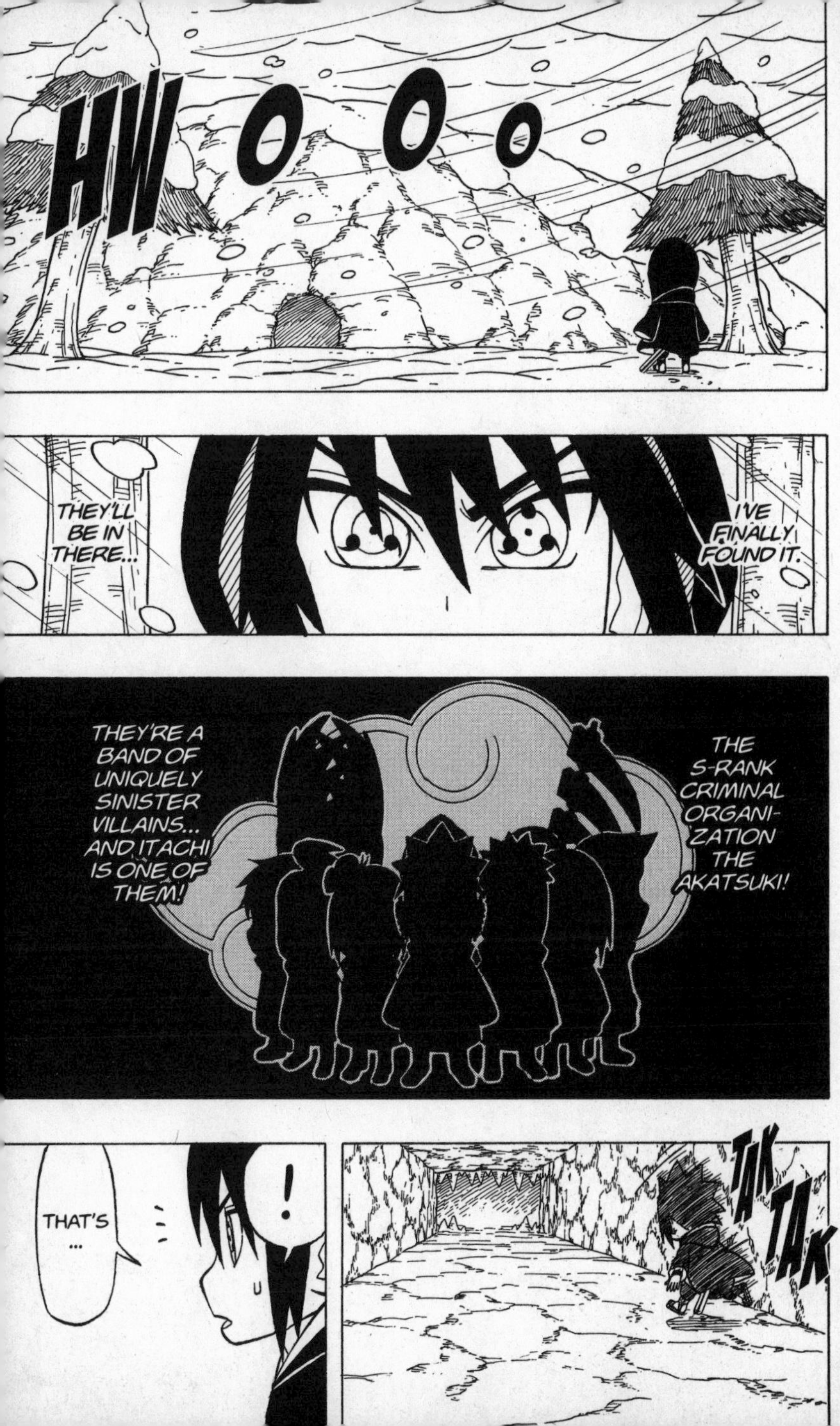
HWOOOO
I'VE FINALLY FOUND IT.
THEY'LL BE IN THERE...
THE S-RANK CRIMINAL ORGANI-ZATION THE AKATSUKI!
THEY'RE A BAND OF UNIQUELY SINISTER VILLAINS... AND ITACHI IS ONE OF THEM!
TAK TAK
!
THAT'S ...

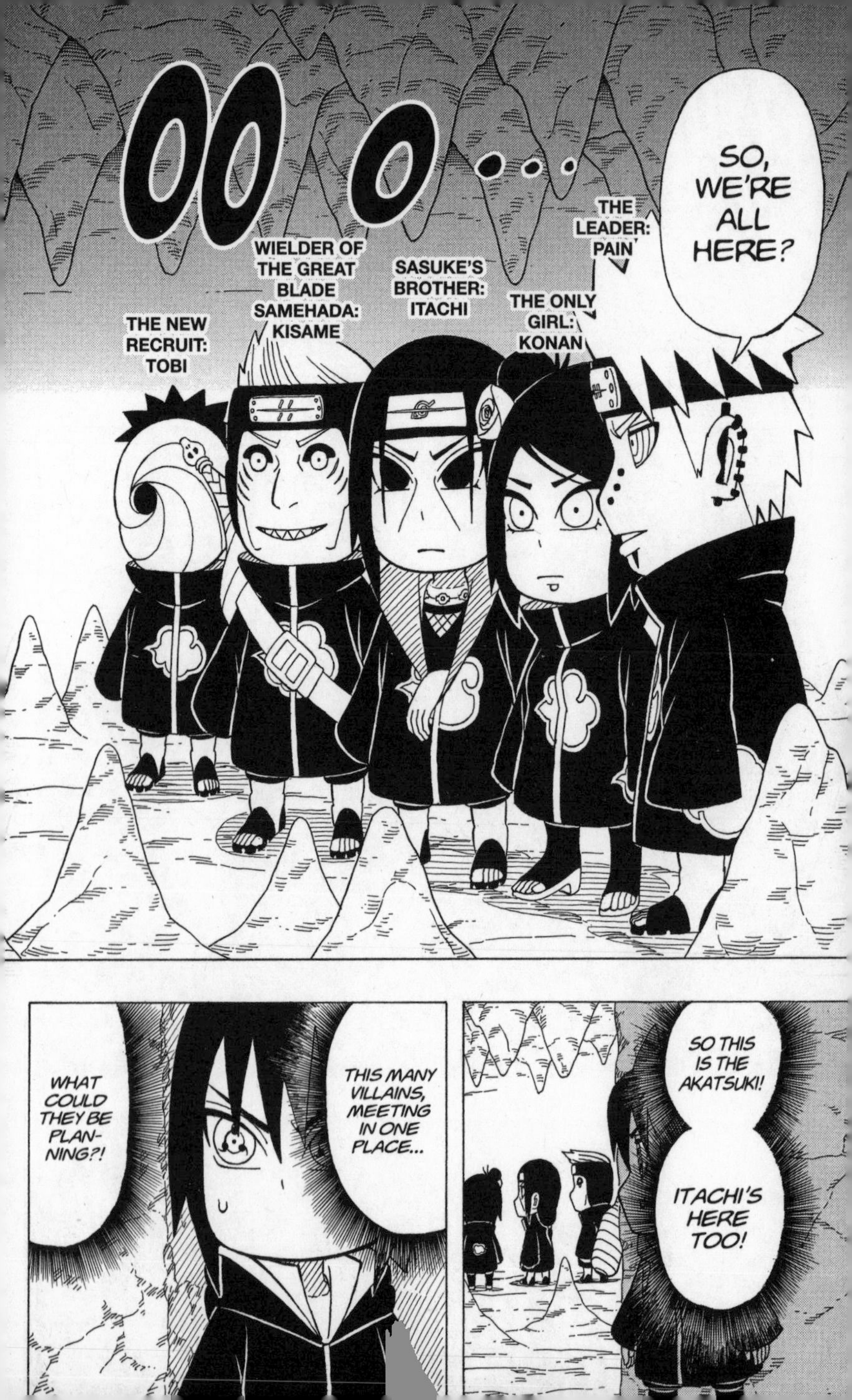
OOO...
SO, WE'RE ALL HERE?
THE LEADER: PAIN
THE ONLY GIRL: KONAN
SASUKE'S BROTHER: ITACHI
WIELDER OF THE GREAT BLADE SAMEHADA: KISAME
THE NEW RECRUIT: TOBI
SO THIS IS THE AKATSUKI!
ITACHI'S HERE TOO!
THIS MANY VILLAINS, MEETING IN ONE PLACE...
WHAT COULD THEY BE PLAN-NING?!

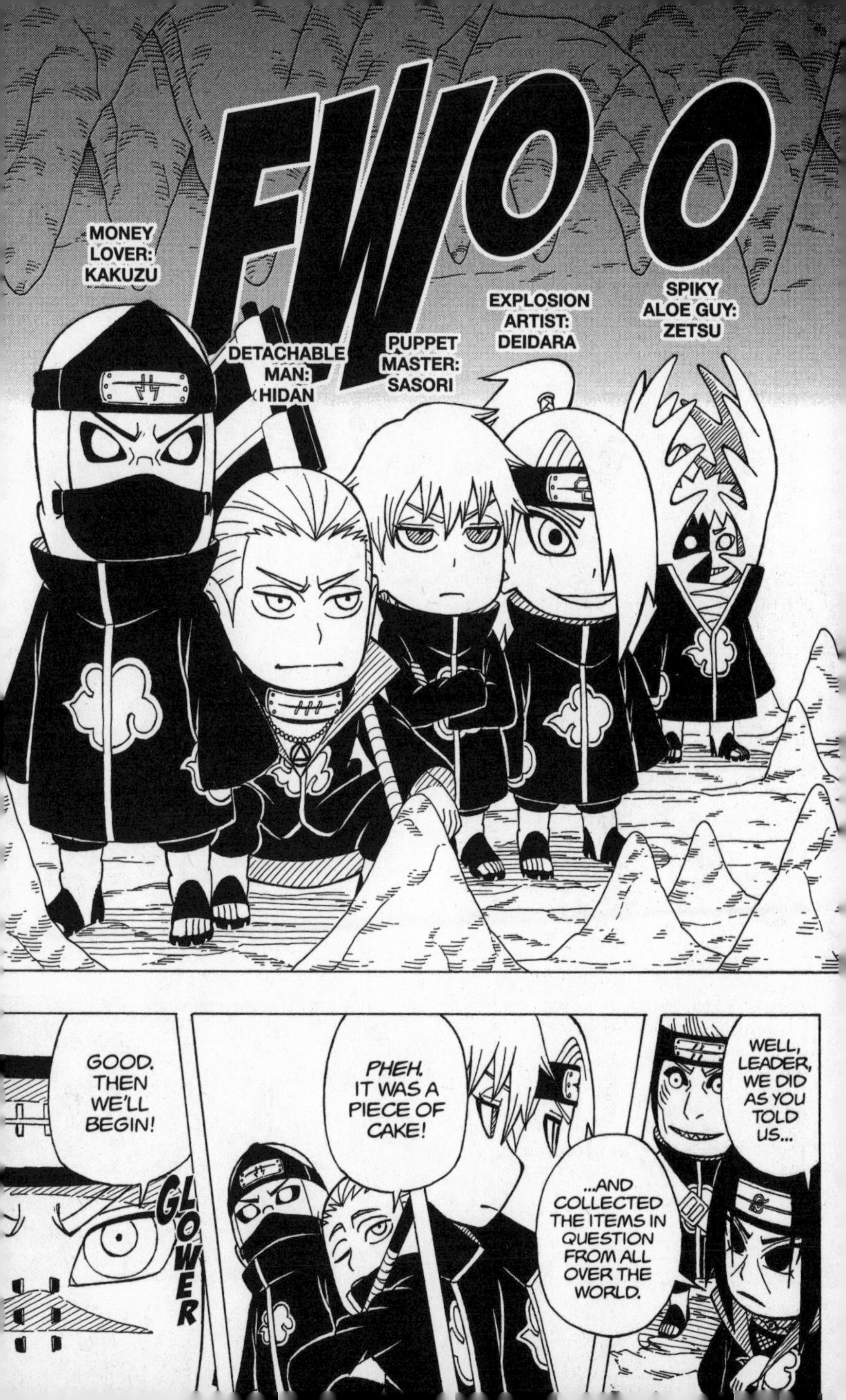
FWOO O
SPIKY ALOE GUY: ZETSU
EXPLOSION ARTIST: DEIDARA
PUPPET MASTER: SASORI
DETACHABLE MAN: HIDAN
MONEY LOVER: KAKUZU
WELL, LEADER, WE DID AS YOU TOLD US...
...AND COLLECTED THE ITEMS IN QUESTION FROM ALL OVER THE WORLD.
PHEH. IT WAS A PIECE OF CAKE!
GOOD. THEN WE'LL BEGIN!
GLOWER

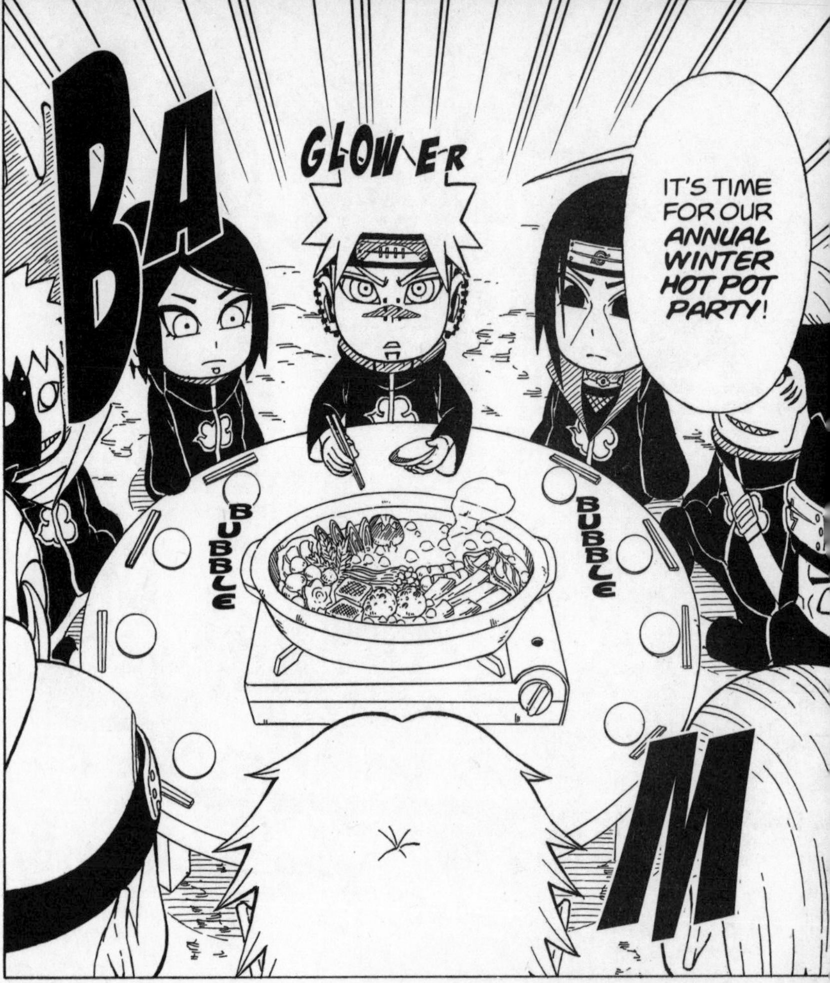
IT'S TIME FOR OUR ANNUAL WINTER HOT POT PARTY!
GLOW ER
BA
BUBBLE
BUBBLE
M

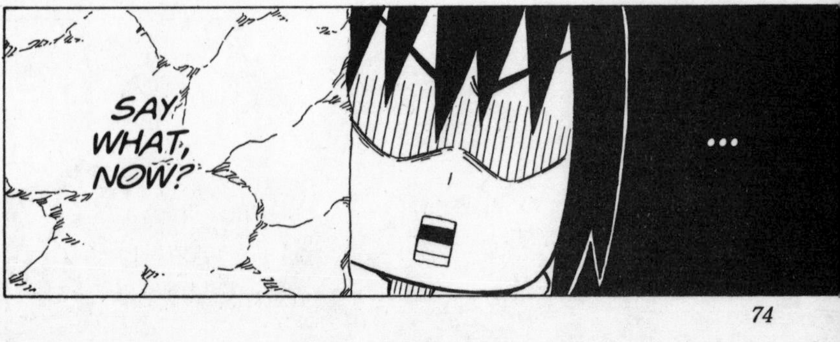
...
SAY WHAT, NOW?

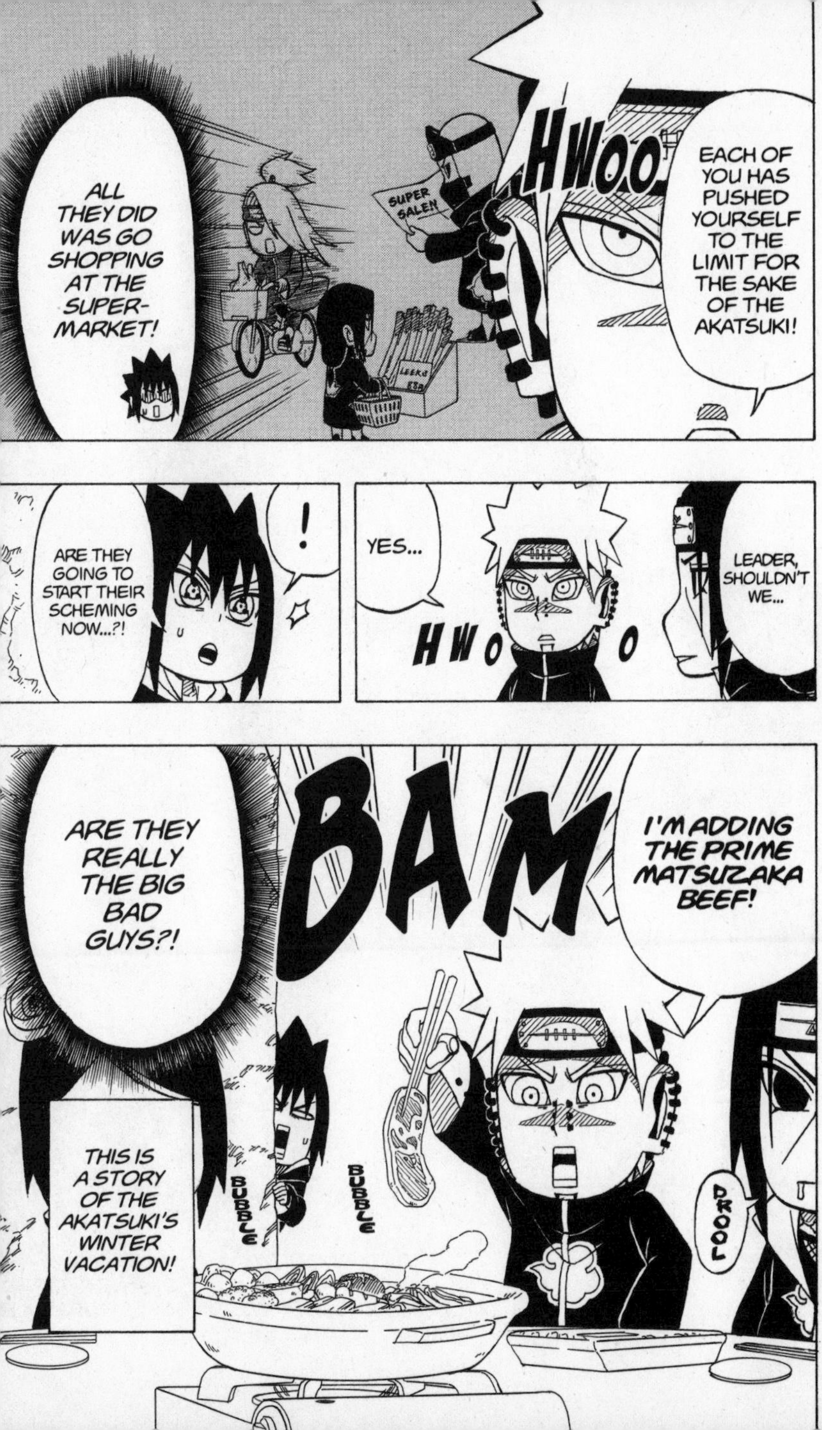
EACH OF YOU HAS PUSHED YOURSELF TO THE LIMIT FOR THE SAKE OF THE AKATSUKI!
HWOO
ALL THEY DID WAS GO SHOPPING AT THE SUPER-MARKET!
LEADER, SHOULDN'T WE...
YES...
HWO O
!
ARE THEY GOING TO START THEIR SCHEMING NOW...?!
I'M ADDING THE PRIME MATSUZAKA BEEF!
BAM
DROOL
BUBBLE
BUBBLE
ARE THEY REALLY THE BIG BAD GUYS?!
THIS IS A STORY OF THE AKATSUKI'S WINTER VACATION!

CHRISTMAS MEMORIES

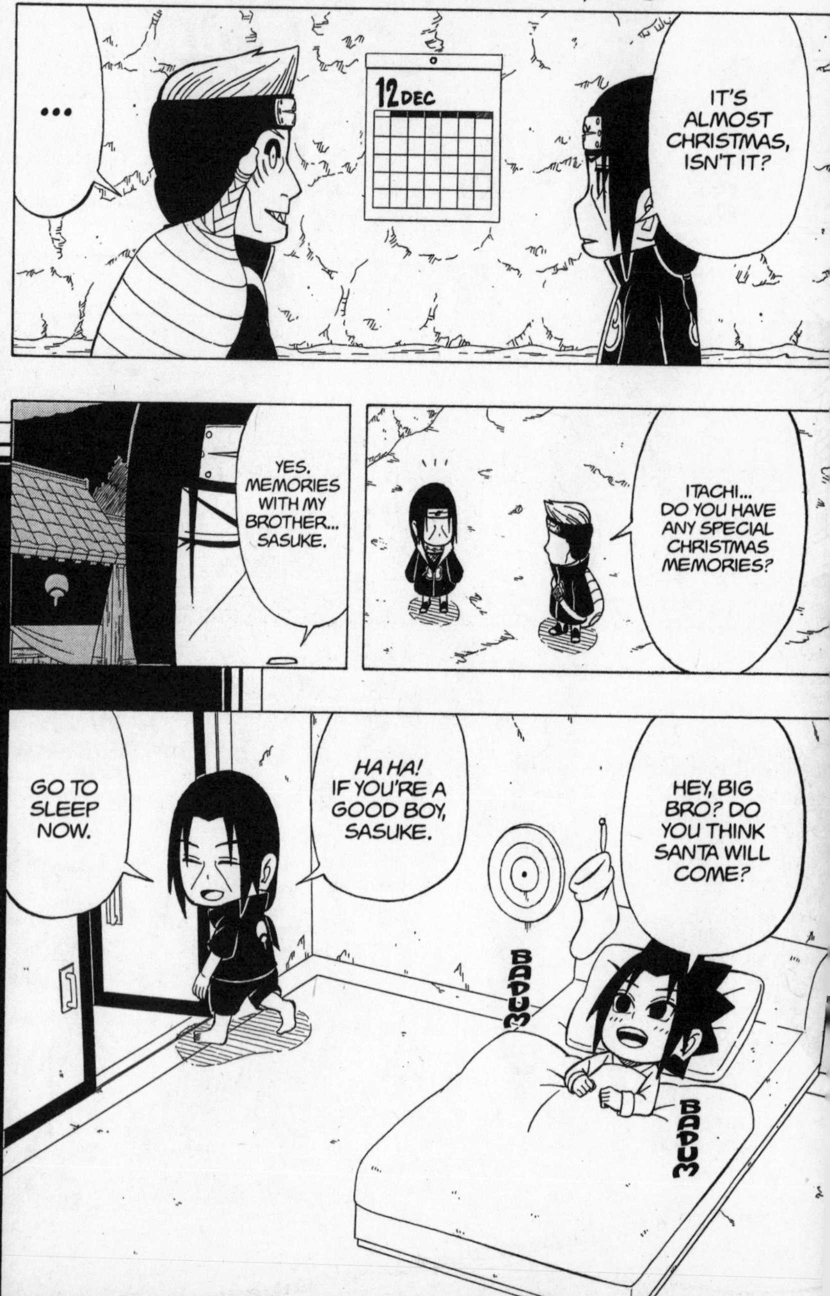
IT'S ALMOST CHRISTMAS, ISN'T IT?
...
12 DEC
ITACHI... DO YOU HAVE ANY SPECIAL CHRISTMAS MEMORIES?
YES. MEMORIES WITH MY BROTHER... SASUKE.
HEY, BIG BRO? DO YOU THINK SANTA WILL COME?
BADUM
BADUM
HA HA! IF YOU'RE A GOOD BOY, SASUKE.
GO TO SLEEP NOW.

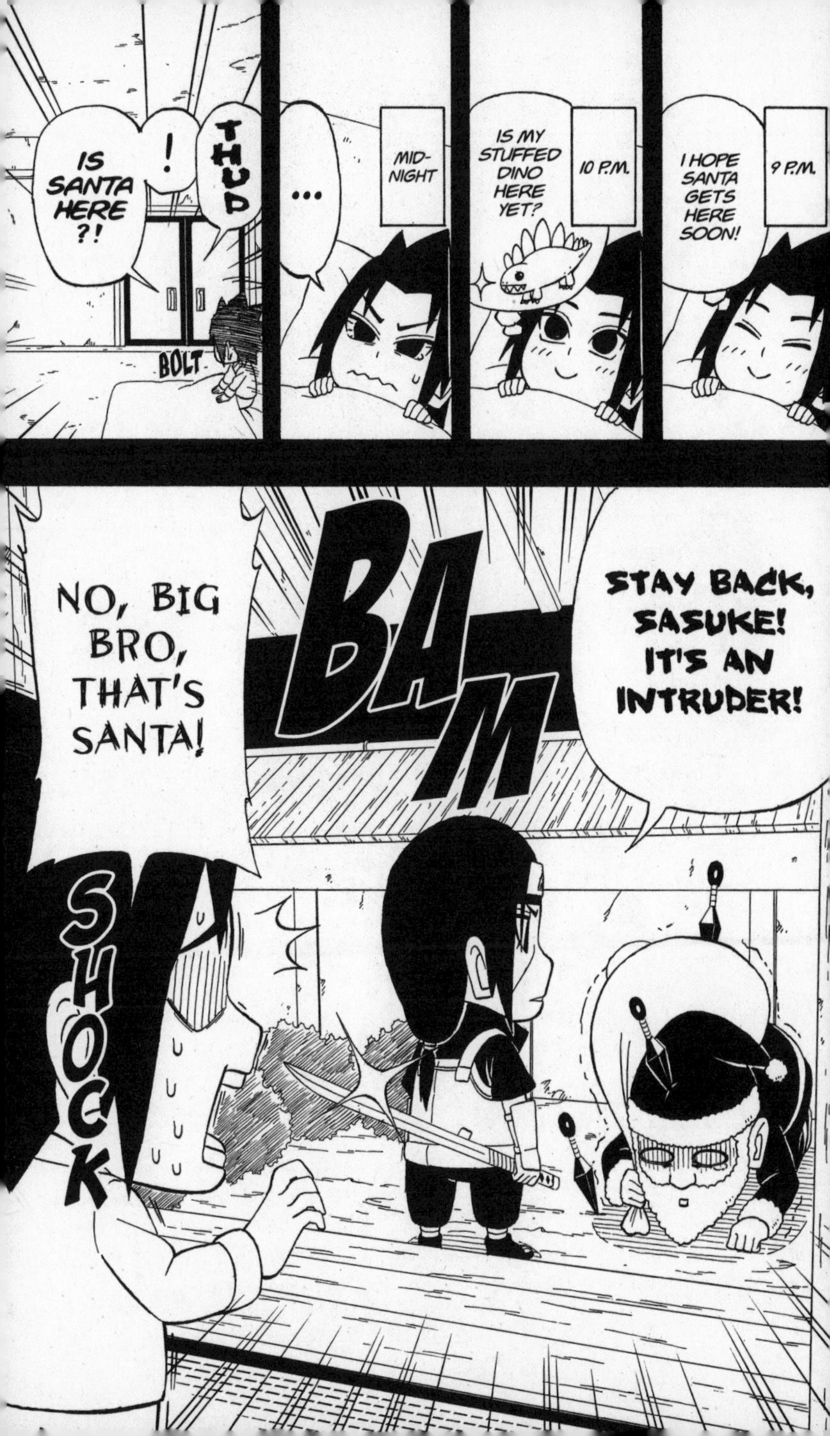
9 P.M.
I HOPE SANTA GETS HERE SOON!
10 P.M.
IS MY STUFFED DINO HERE YET?
MID-NIGHT
...
THUD
!
IS SANTA HERE ?!
BOLT
STAY BACK, SASUKE! IT'S AN INTRUDER!
BAM
NO, BIG BRO, THAT'S SANTA!
SHOCK

SLEDDING

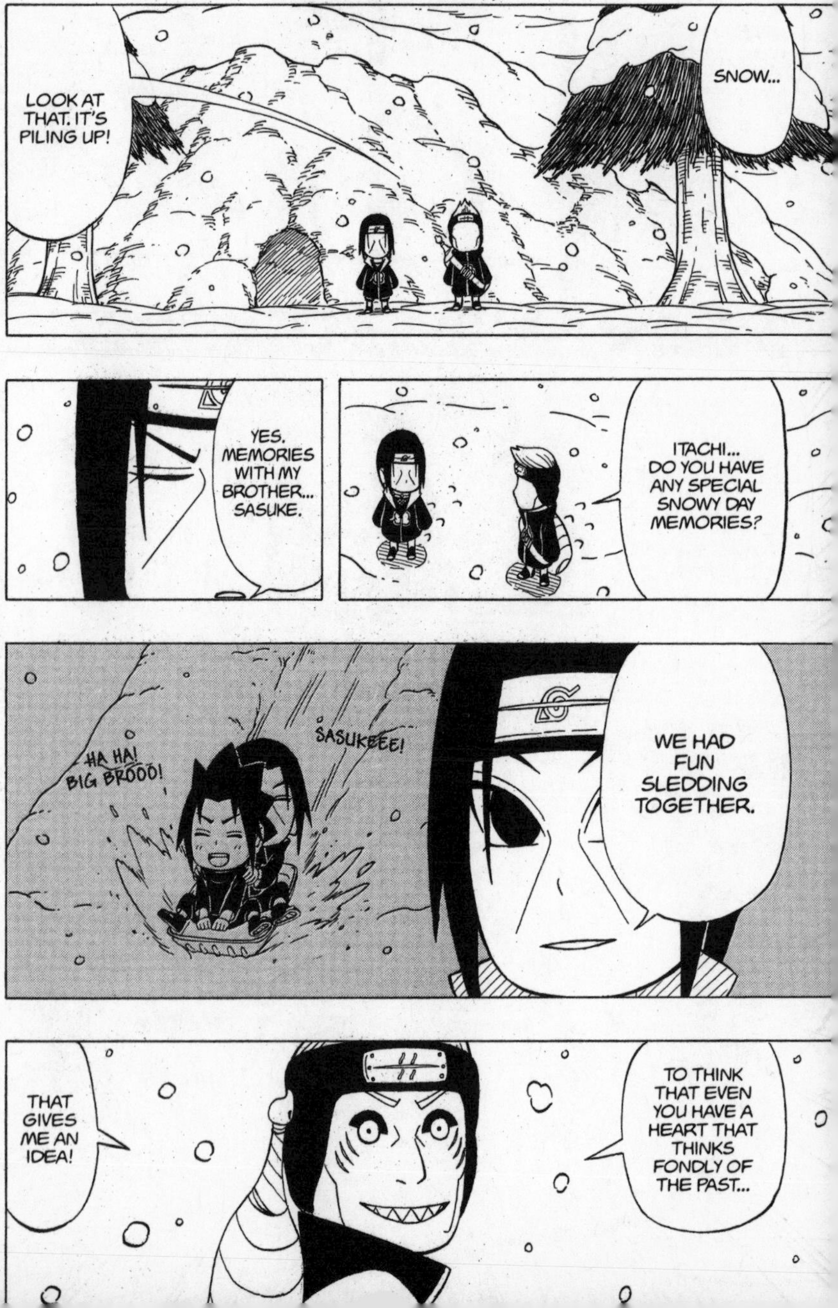
SNOW...
LOOK AT THAT. IT'S PILING UP!
ITACHI... DO YOU HAVE ANY SPECIAL SNOWY DAY MEMORIES?
YES. MEMORIES WITH MY BROTHER... SASUKE.
WE HAD FUN SLEDDING TOGETHER.
SASUKEEE!
HA HA! BIG BROOO!
TO THINK THAT EVEN YOU HAVE A HEART THAT THINKS FONDLY OF THE PAST...
THAT GIVES ME AN IDEA!

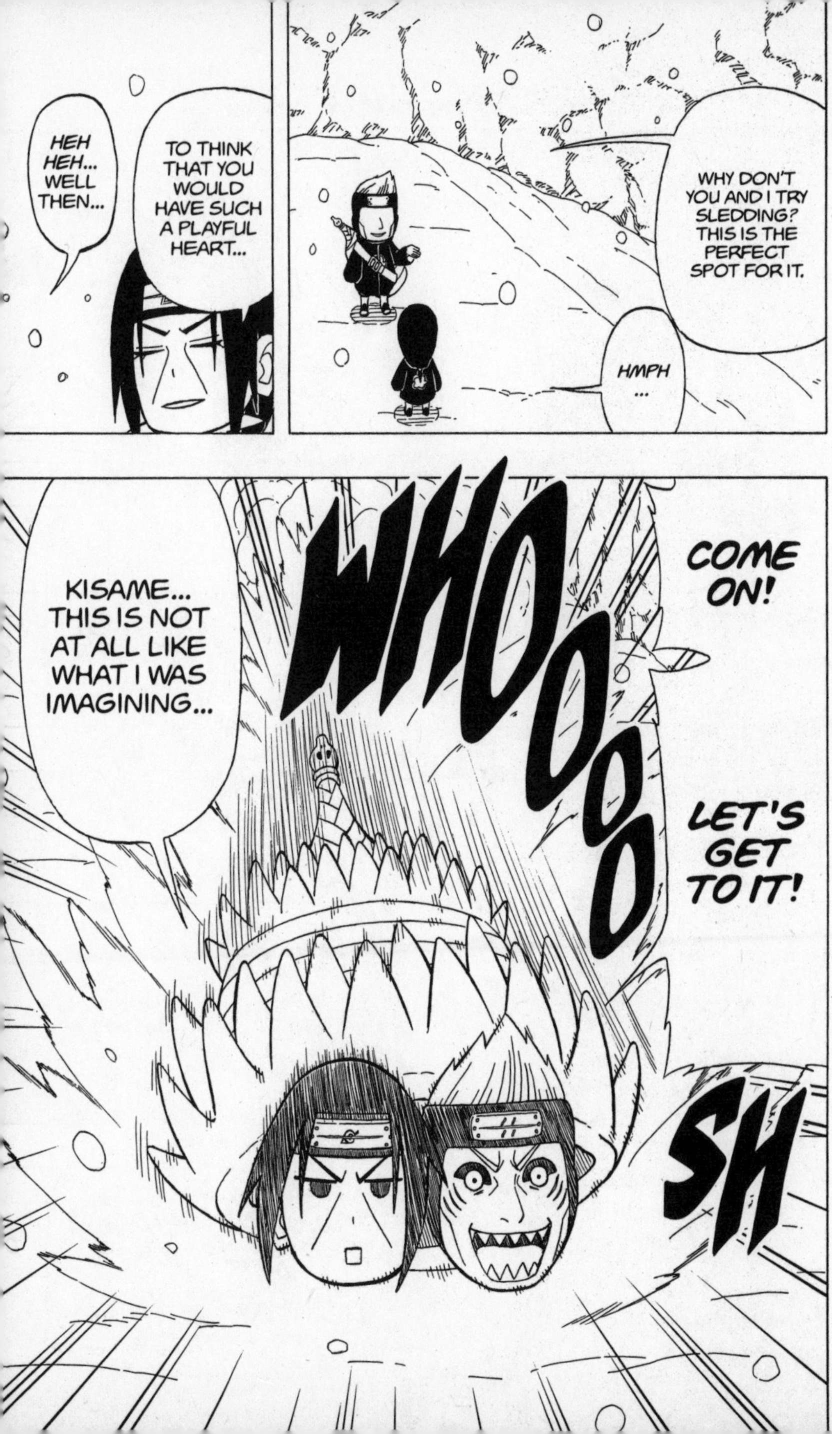
WHY DON'T YOU AND I TRY SLEDDING? THIS IS THE PERFECT SPOT FOR IT.
HMPH ...
TO THINK THAT YOU WOULD HAVE SUCH A PLAYFUL HEART...
HEH HEH... WELL THEN...
COME ON!
LET'S GET TO IT!
WHOOOOO
KISAME... THIS IS NOT AT ALL LIKE WHAT I WAS IMAGINING...
SH

SNOWMAN SHOWDOWN

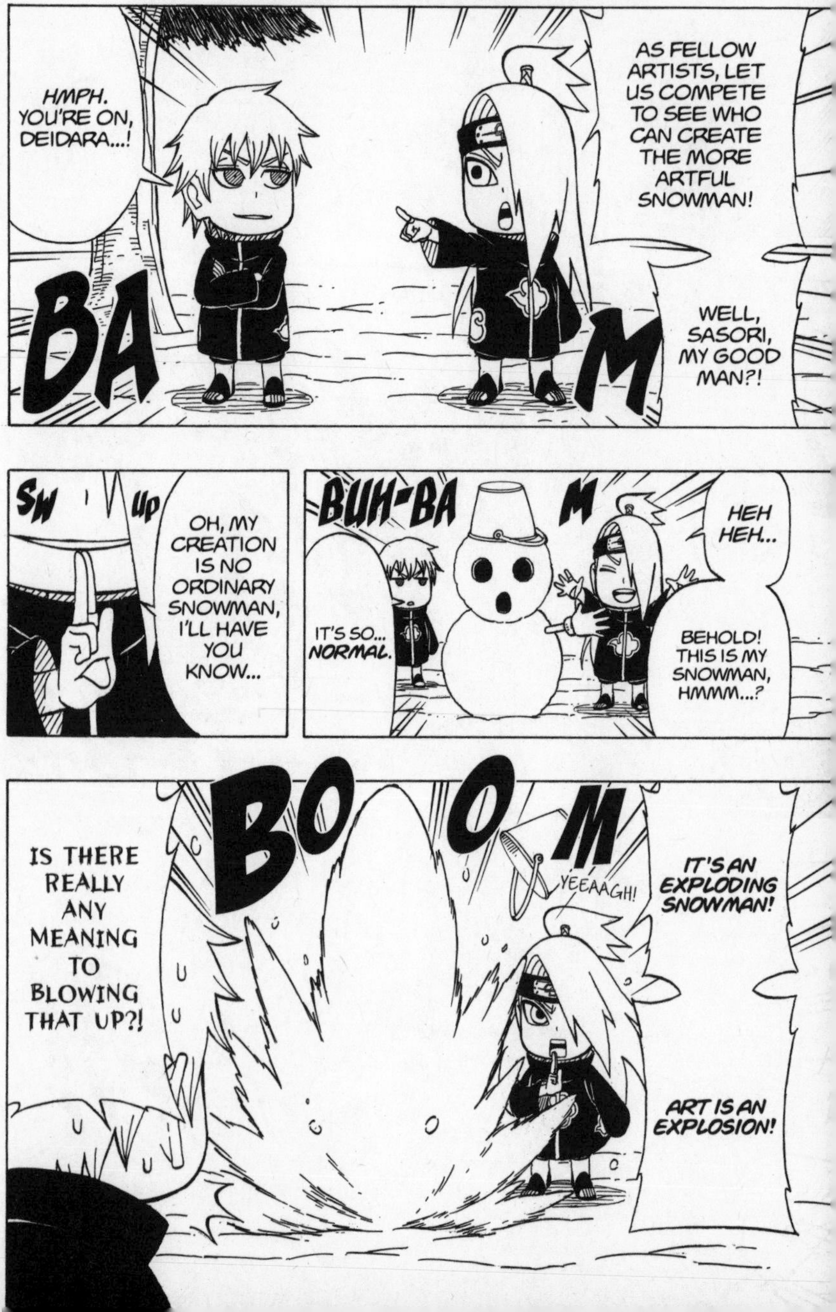
AS FELLOW ARTISTS, LET US COMPETE TO SEE WHO CAN CREATE THE MORE ARTFUL SNOWMAN!
WELL, SASORI, MY GOOD MAN?!
BAM
HMPH. YOU'RE ON, DEIDARA...!
BUH-BAM
HEH HEH...
BEHOLD! THIS IS MY SNOWMAN, HMMM...?
IT'S SO... NORMAL.
SWUP
OH, MY CREATION IS NO ORDINARY SNOWMAN, I'LL HAVE YOU KNOW...
IT'S AN EXPLODING SNOWMAN!
BOOM
YEEAAGH!
ART IS AN EXPLOSION!
IS THERE REALLY ANY MEANING TO BLOWING THAT UP?!

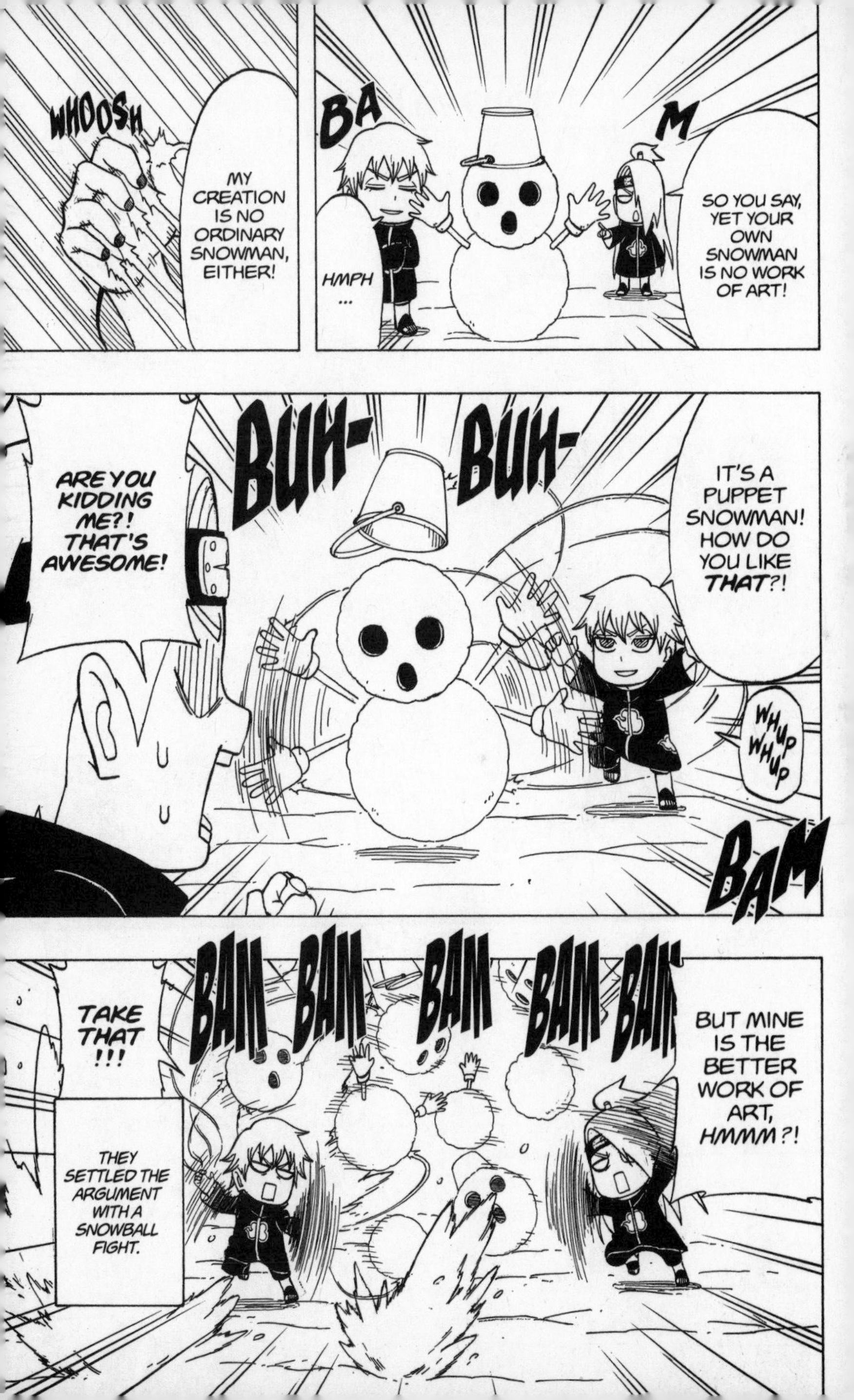
BAM
SO YOU SAY, YET YOUR OWN SNOWMAN IS NO WORK OF ART!
HMPH ...
WHOOSH
MY CREATION IS NO ORDINARY SNOWMAN, EITHER!
IT'S A PUPPET SNOWMAN! HOW DO YOU LIKE THAT?!
BUH- BUH-
WHUP WHUP
BAM
ARE YOU KIDDING ME?! THAT'S AWESOME!
BUT MINE IS THE BETTER WORK OF ART, HMMM?!
BAM BAM BAM BAM BAM
TAKE THAT!!!
THEY SETTLED THE ARGUMENT WITH A SNOWBALL FIGHT.

LAND MINES

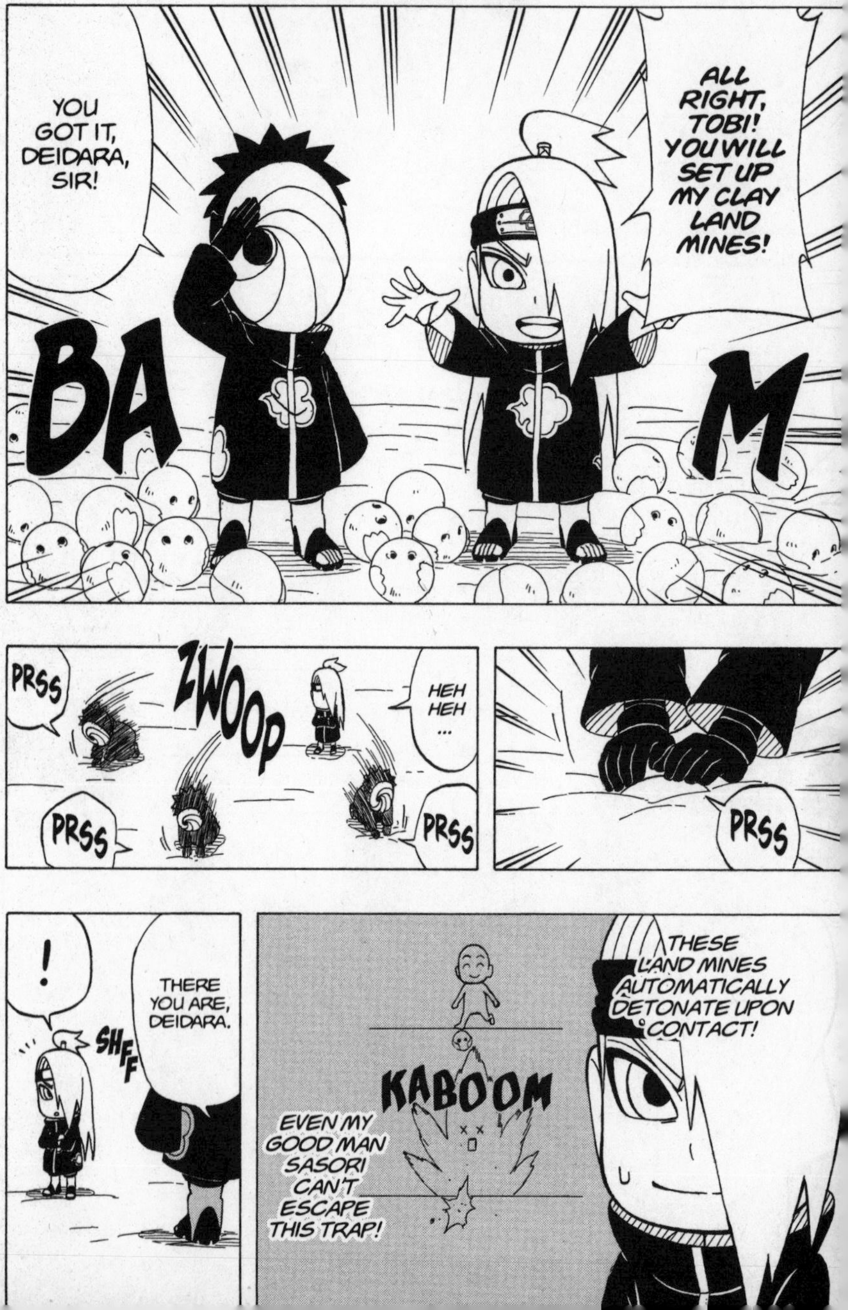
ALL RIGHT, TOBI! YOU WILL SET UP MY CLAY LAND MINES!
YOU GOT IT, DEIDARA, SIR!
BAM
PRSS
HEH HEH ...
ZWOOP
PRSS
PRSS
PRSS
THESE LAND MINES AUTOMATICALLY DETONATE UPON CONTACT!
KABOOM
EVEN MY GOOD MAN SASORI CAN'T ESCAPE THIS TRAP!
THERE YOU ARE, DEIDARA.
SHFF
!

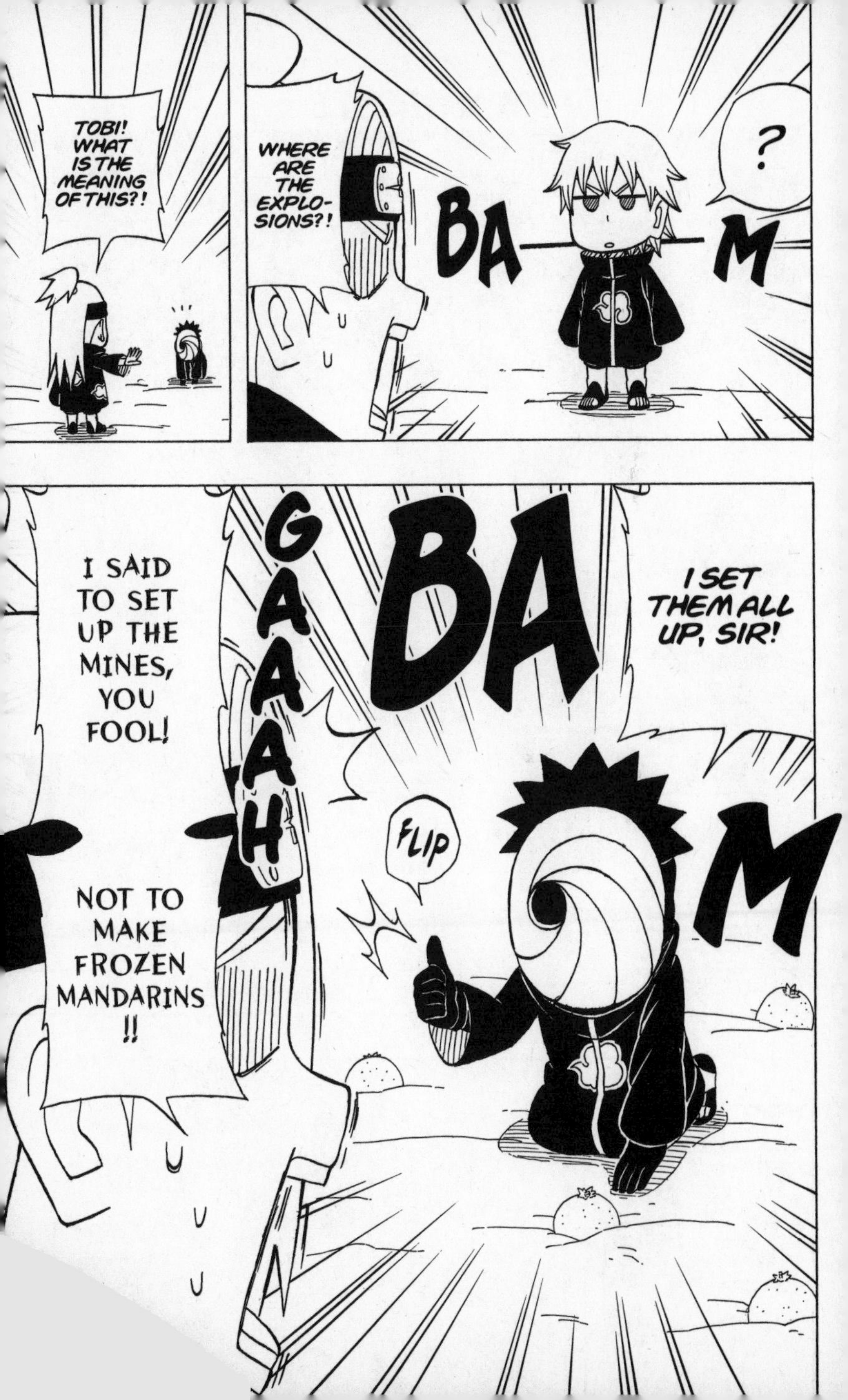
?
BA—M
WHERE ARE THE EXPLOSIONS?!
TOBI! WHAT IS THE MEANING OF THIS?!
I SET THEM ALL UP, SIR!
BABAM
GAAAAH
FLIP
I SAID TO SET UP THE MINES, YOU FOOL!
NOT TO MAKE FROZEN MANDARINS!!

IMMORTAL

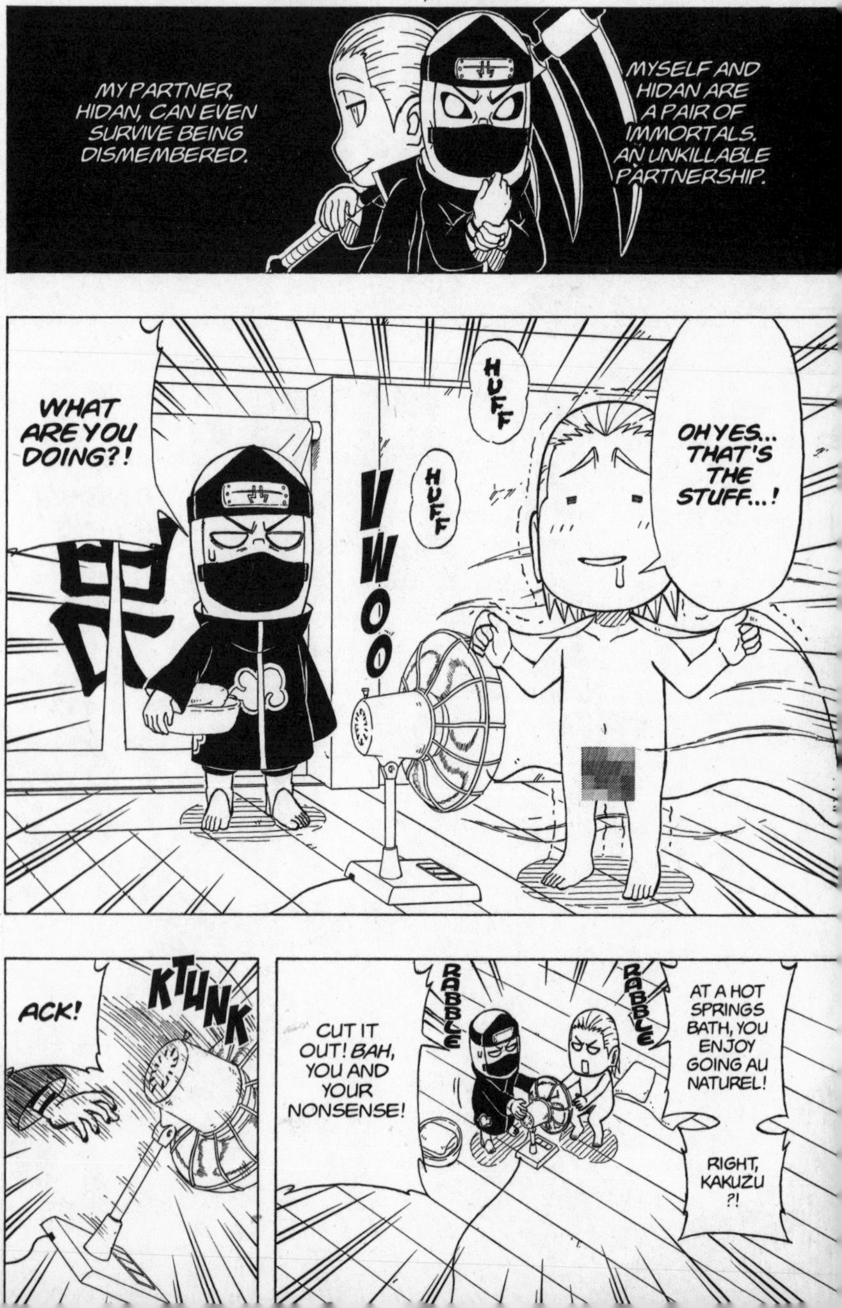
MYSELF AND HIDAN ARE A PAIR OF IMMORTALS. AN UNKILLABLE PARTNERSHIP.
MY PARTNER, HIDAN, CAN EVEN SURVIVE BEING DISMEMBERED.
OH YES... THAT'S THE STUFF...!
HUFF
HUFF
VWOO
WHAT ARE YOU DOING?!
AT A HOT SPRINGS BATH, YOU ENJOY GOING AU NATUREL!
RIGHT, KAKUZU ?!
RABBLE
RABBLE
CUT IT OUT! BAH, YOU AND YOUR NONSENSE!
KTUNK
ACK!

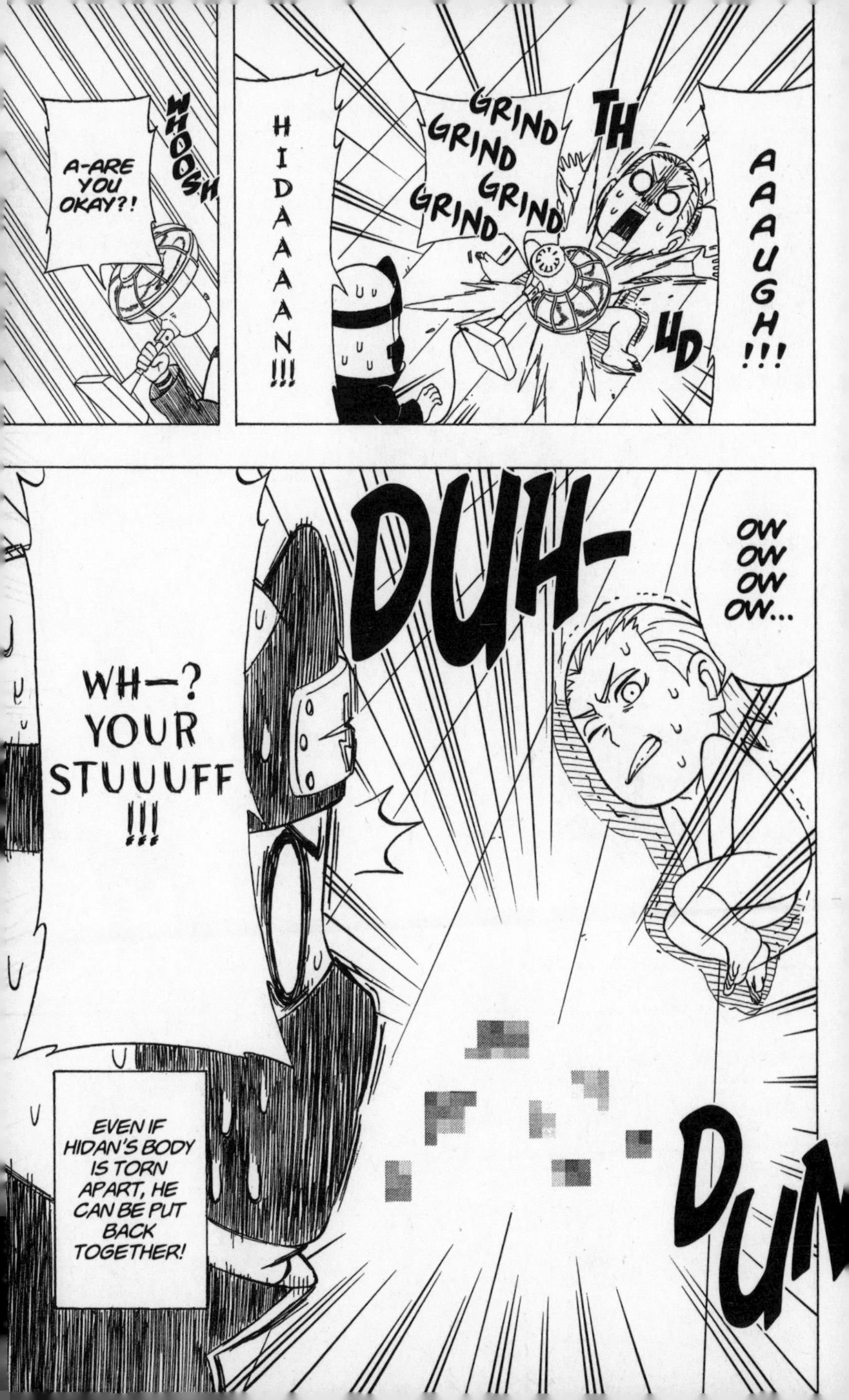
AAAAUGH!!!
TH
UD
GRIND GRIND GRIND GRIND
HIDAAAAN!!!
WHOOSH
A-ARE YOU OKAY?!
OW OW OW OW...
DUH-
DUN
WH—? YOUR STUUUFF!!!
EVEN IF HIDAN'S BODY IS TORN APART, HE CAN BE PUT BACK TOGETHER!

HOT SPRINGS

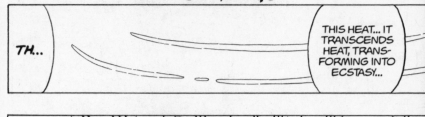

THIS HEAT... IT TRANSCENDS HEAT, TRANSFORMING INTO ECSTASY...
TH...
THAT'S THE STUFF...
HUFF
BAM
HUFF
THAT'S CREEPY!
HIDAN... CAN'T YOU EVEN SOAK IN A HOT SPRING LIKE A NORMAL PERSON?
SHUT UP ALREADY, KAKUZU...
NOW, TO WARM UP PROPERLY, SOAK WITH THE WATER UP TO YOUR SHOULDERS AND COUNT TO 100!
DO YOU EVER GIVE IT A REST, OLD MAN?

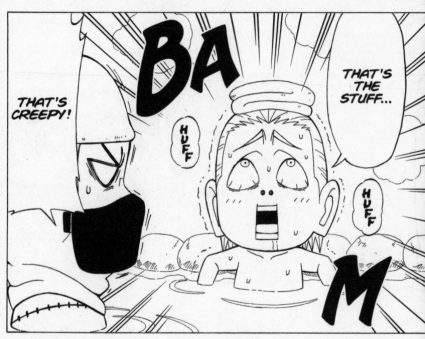

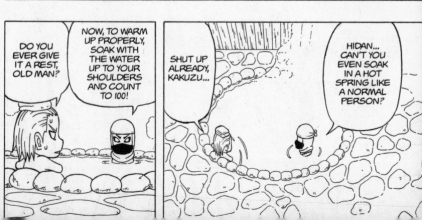

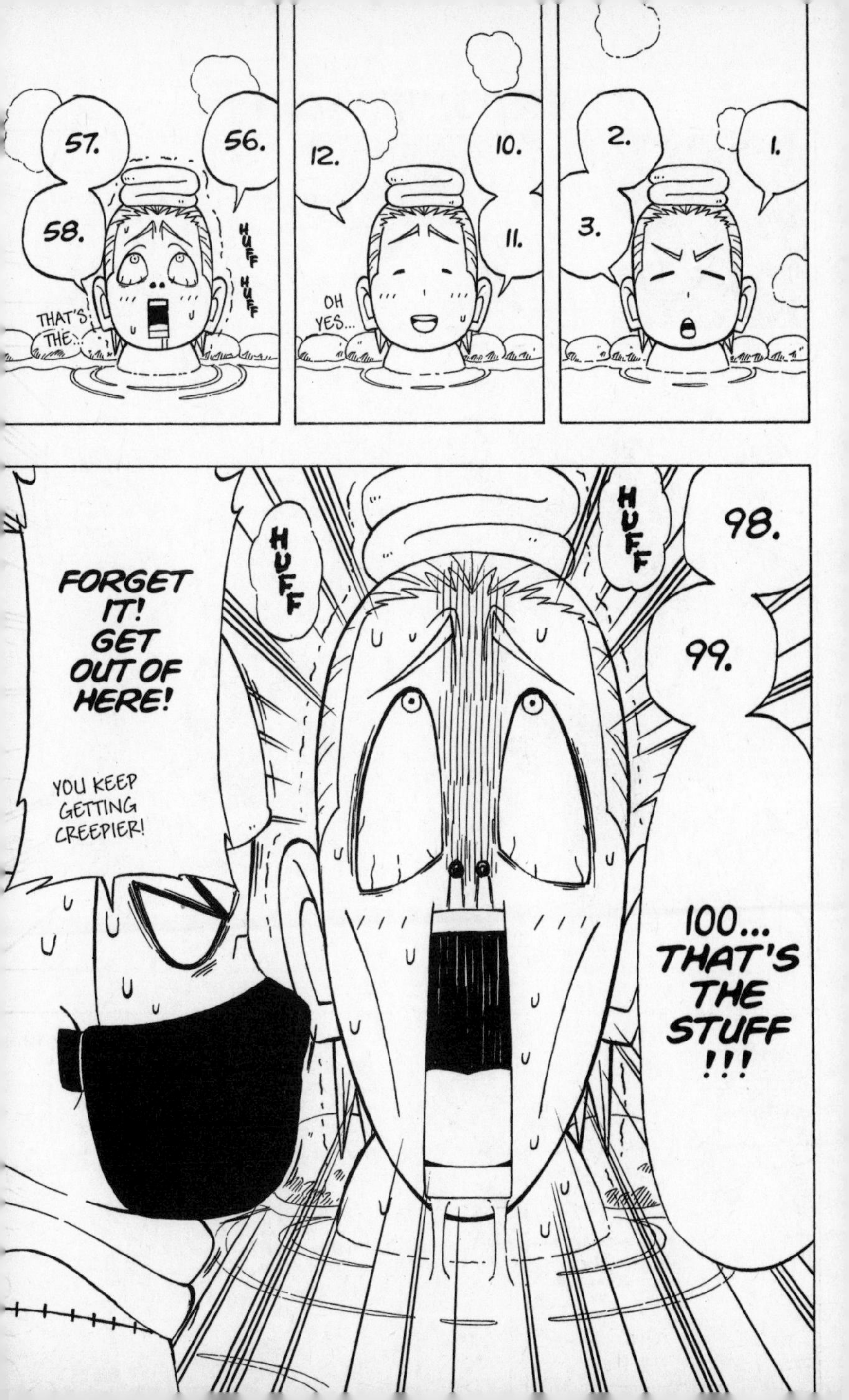
1.
2.
3.
10.
11.
12.
OH YES...
56.
57.
58.
HUFF HUFF
THAT'S THE...
98.
99.
100... THAT'S THE STUFF!!!
HUFF HUFF
FORGET IT! GET OUT OF HERE!
YOU KEEP GETTING CREEPIER!

A HAND-KNIT SCARF

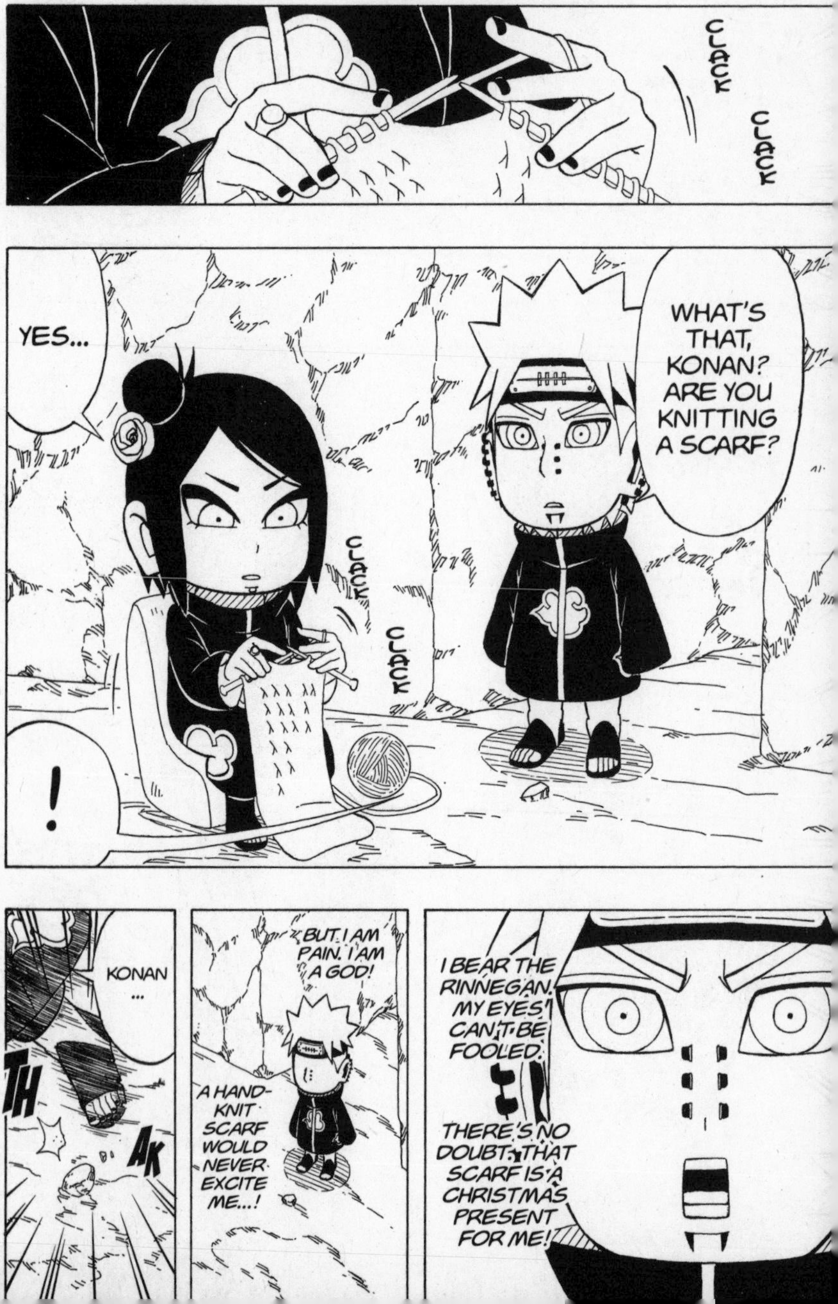
CLACK
CLACK
WHAT'S THAT, KONAN? ARE YOU KNITTING A SCARF?
CLACK
CLACK
YES...
!
I BEAR THE RINNEGAN. MY EYES CAN'T BE FOOLED.
THERE'S NO DOUBT THAT SCARF IS A CHRISTMAS PRESENT FOR ME!
BUT I AM PAIN. I AM A GOD!
A HAND-KNIT SCARF WOULD NEVER EXCITE ME...!
KONAN ...

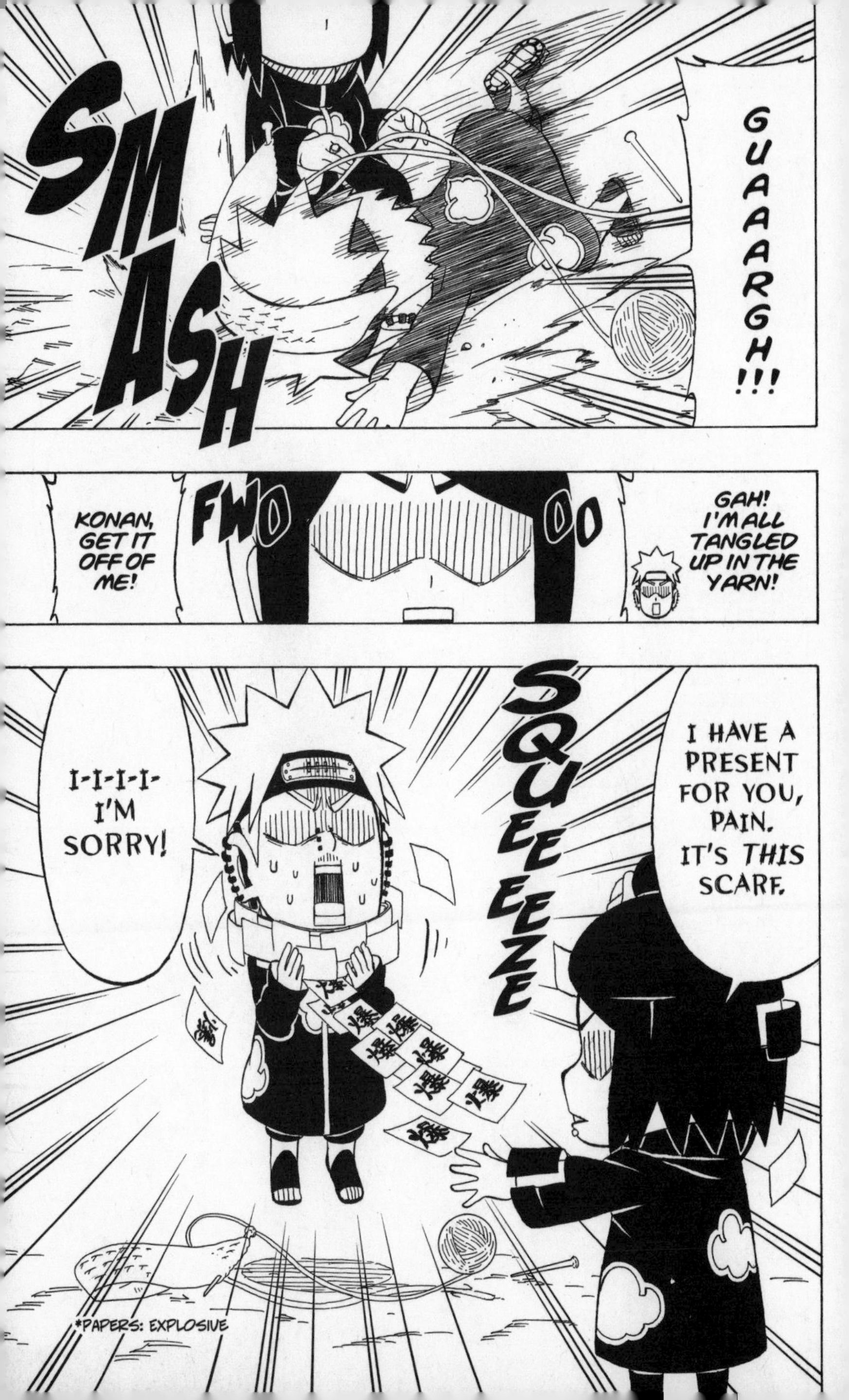
GUAAAARGH!!!
SMASH
GAH! I'M ALL TANGLED UP IN THE YARN!
FWOOO
KONAN, GET IT OFF OF ME!
I HAVE A PRESENT FOR YOU, PAIN. IT'S THIS SCARF.
SQUEEEEEZE
I-I-I-I-I'M SORRY!
*PAPERS: EXPLOSIVE

STATIC ELECTRICITY

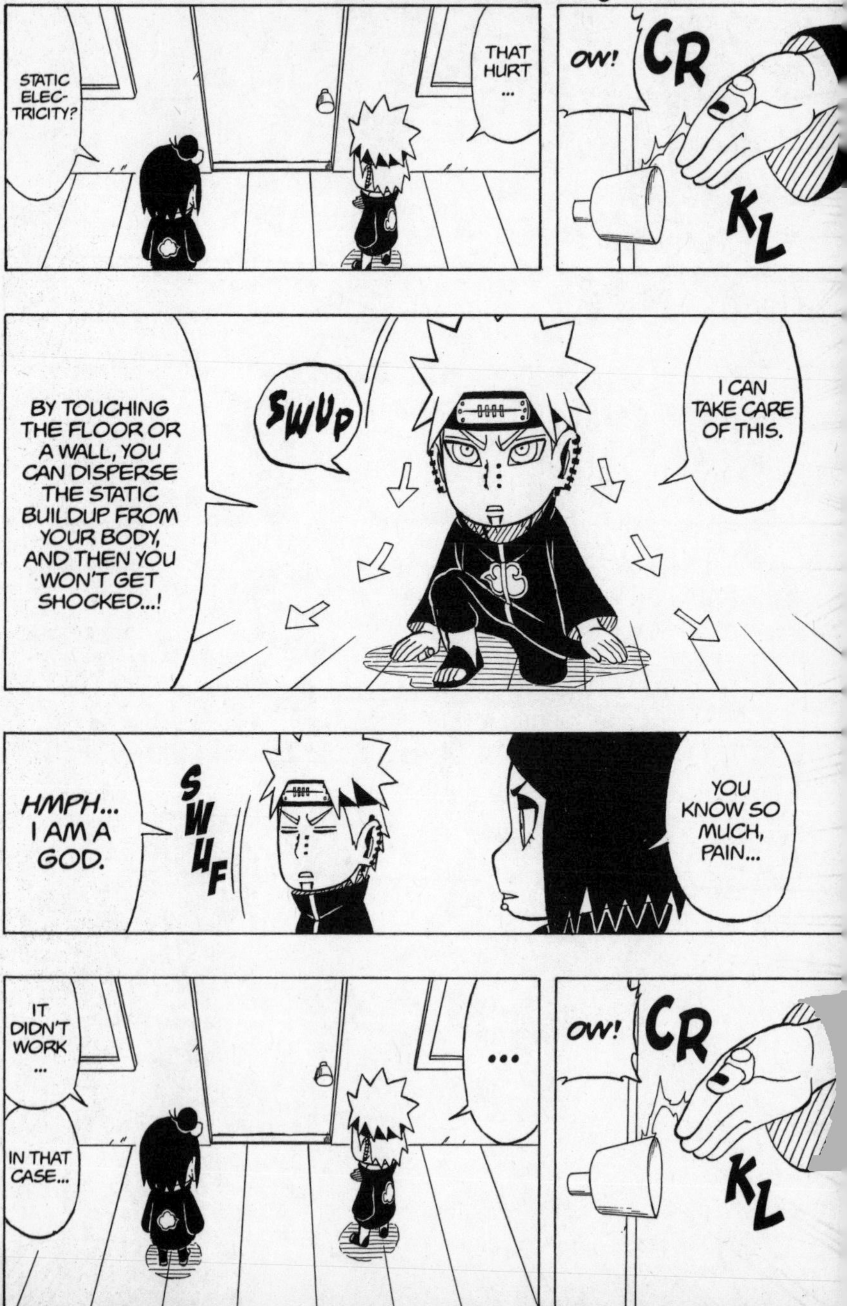

OW!
CRKL
THAT HURT...
STATIC ELEC-TRICITY?
I CAN TAKE CARE OF THIS.
SWUP
BY TOUCHING THE FLOOR OR A WALL, YOU CAN DISPERSE THE STATIC BUILDUP FROM YOUR BODY, AND THEN YOU WON'T GET SHOCKED...!
YOU KNOW SO MUCH, PAIN...
SWUF
HMPH... I AM A GOD.
OW!
CRKL
...
IT DIDN'T WORK...
IN THAT CASE...

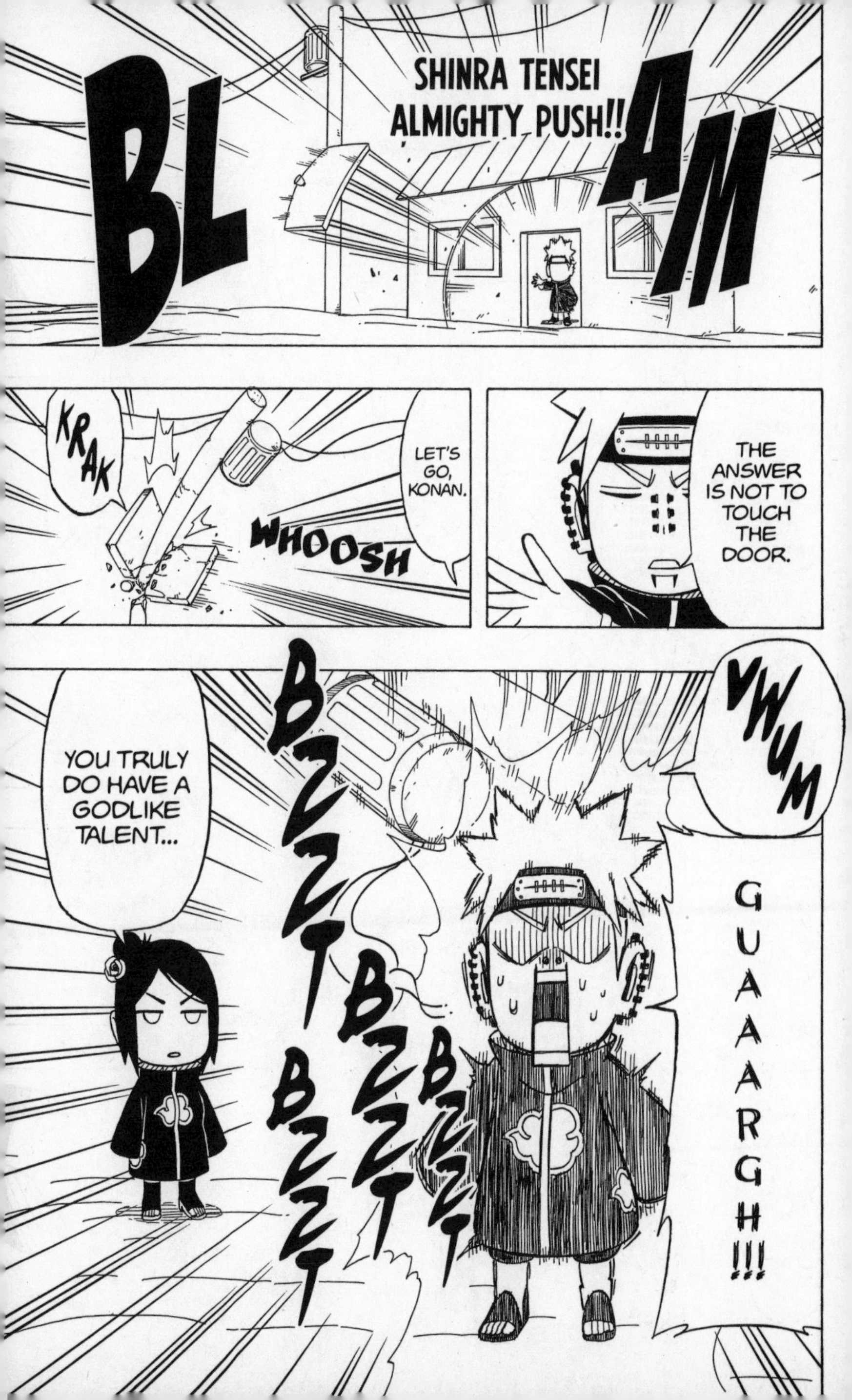
SHINRA TENSEI ALMIGHTY PUSH!!
BL AM
THE ANSWER IS NOT TO TOUCH THE DOOR.
LET'S GO, KONAN.
WHOOSH
KRAK
VWUM
GUAAARGH!!!
BZZZT BZZT BZZZT BZZZT
YOU TRULY DO HAVE A GODLIKE TALENT...

CHRISTMAS

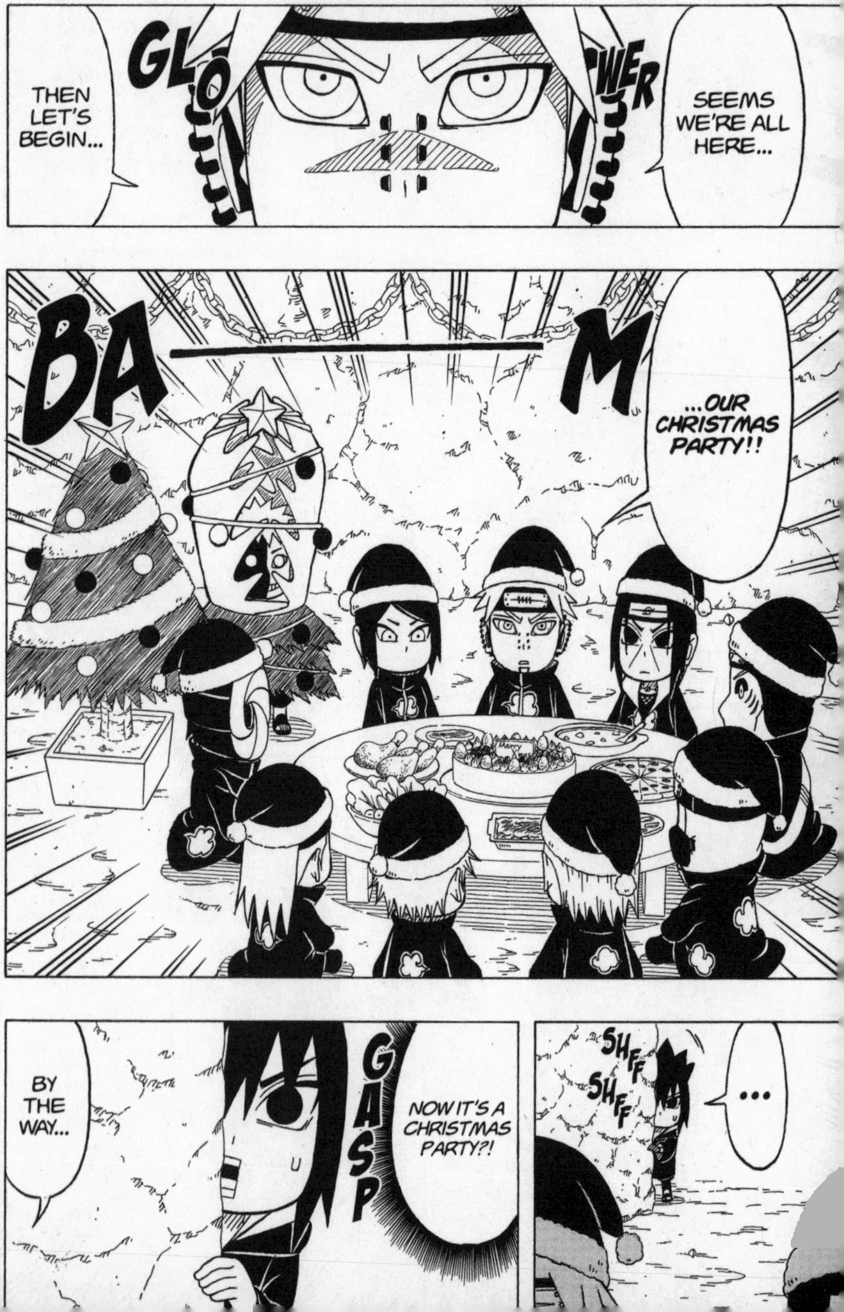
SEEMS WE'RE ALL HERE...
GLOWER
THEN LET'S BEGIN...
...OUR CHRISTMAS PARTY!!
BAM
SHFF SHFF
...
NOW IT'S A CHRISTMAS PARTY?!
GASP
BY THE WAY...

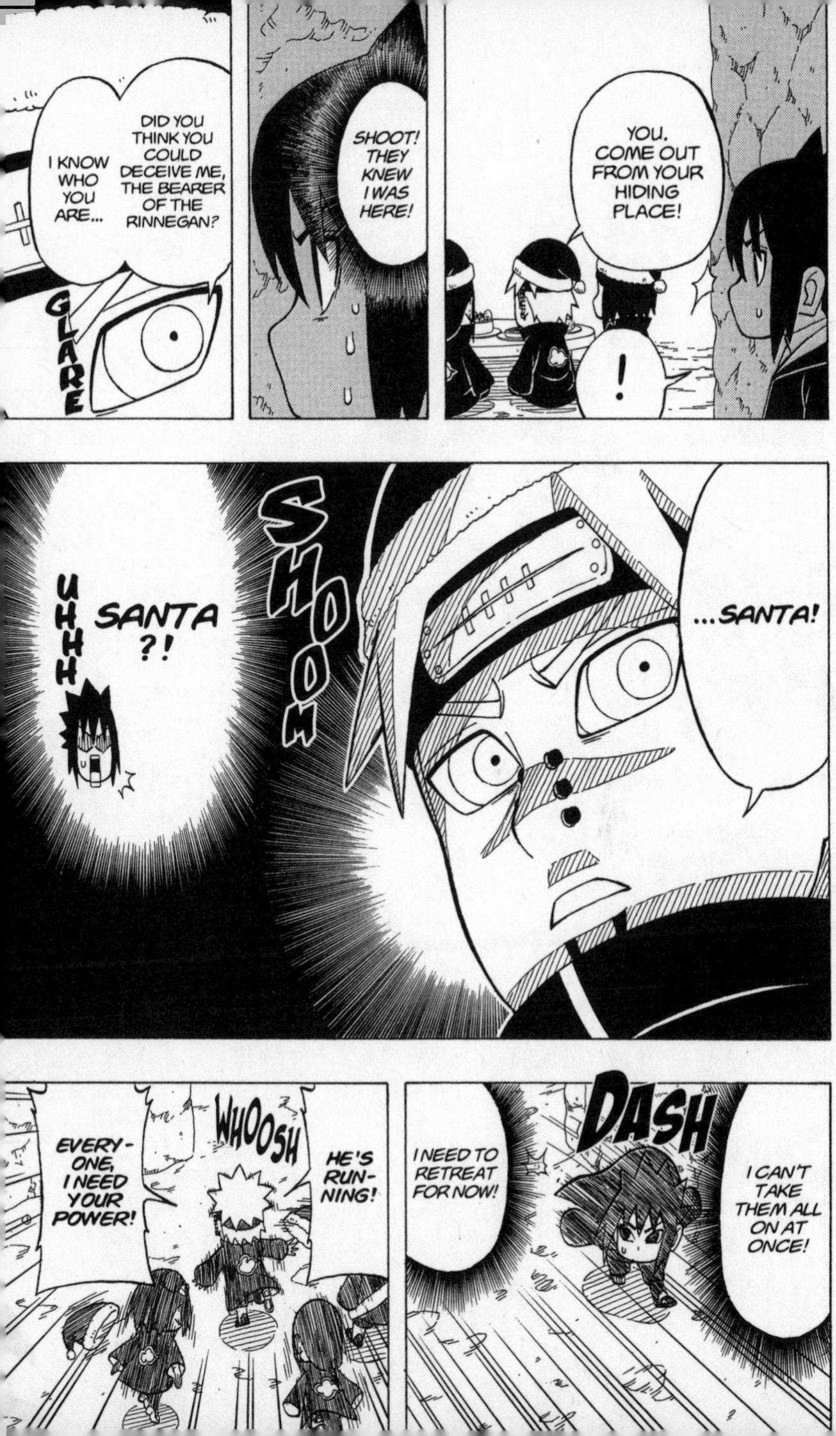
YOU. COME OUT FROM YOUR HIDING PLACE!
!
SHOOT! THEY KNEW I WAS HERE!
DID YOU THINK YOU COULD DECEIVE ME, THE BEARER OF THE RINNEGAN?
I KNOW WHO YOU ARE...
GLARE
...SANTA!
SHOOM
SANTA?!
UHHH
I CAN'T TAKE THEM ALL ON AT ONCE!
DASH
I NEED TO RETREAT FOR NOW!
HE'S RUNNING!
WHOOSH
EVERYONE, I NEED YOUR POWER!

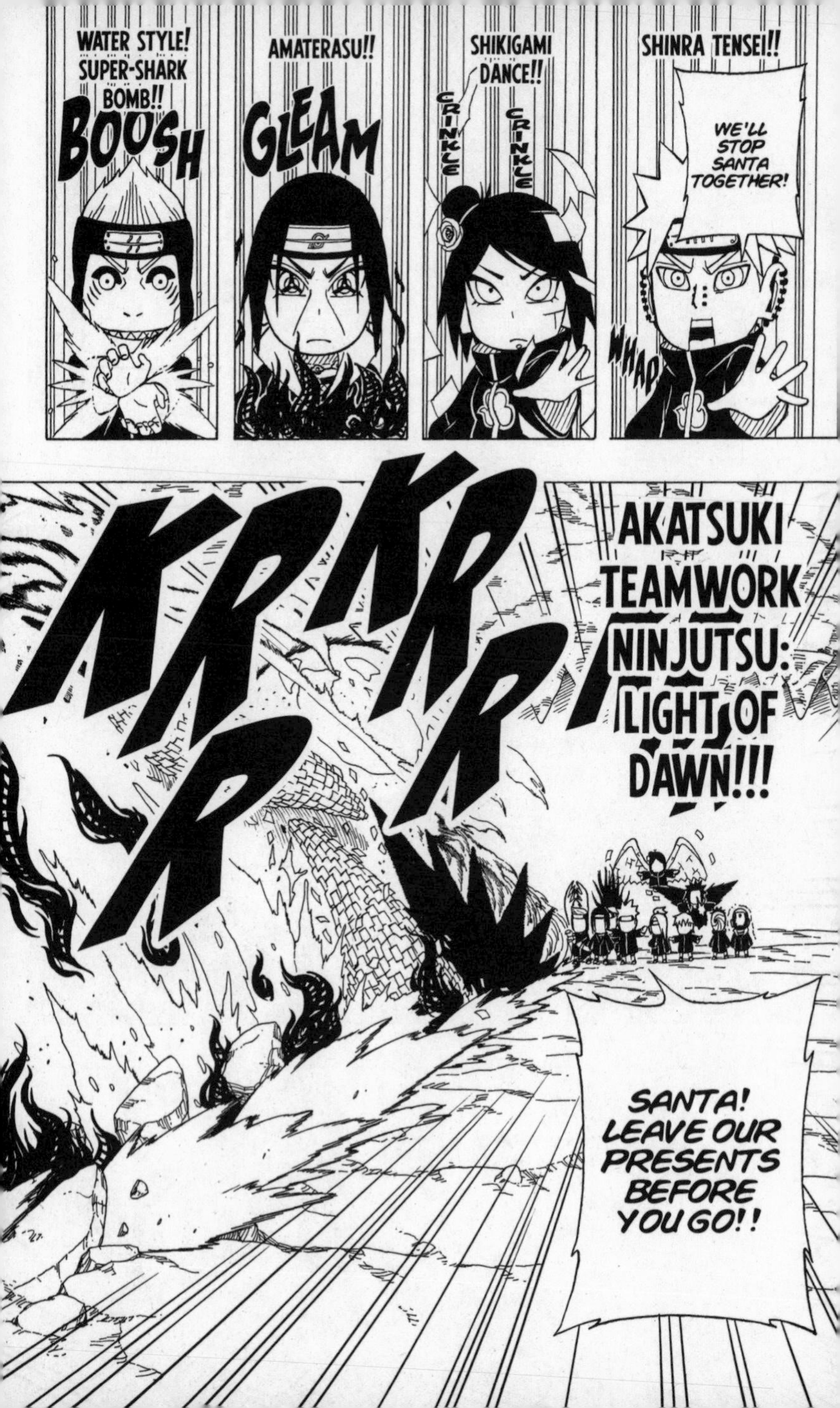
SHINRA TENSEI!!
WE'LL STOP SANTA TOGETHER!
WHAP
SHIKIGAMI DANCE!!
CRINKLE
CRINKLE
AMATERASU!!
GLEAM
WATER STYLE! SUPER-SHARK BOMB!!
BOOSH
AKATSUKI TEAMWORK NINJUTSU: LIGHT OF DAWN!!!
KRKRKRKR
SANTA! LEAVE OUR PRESENTS BEFORE YOU GO!!

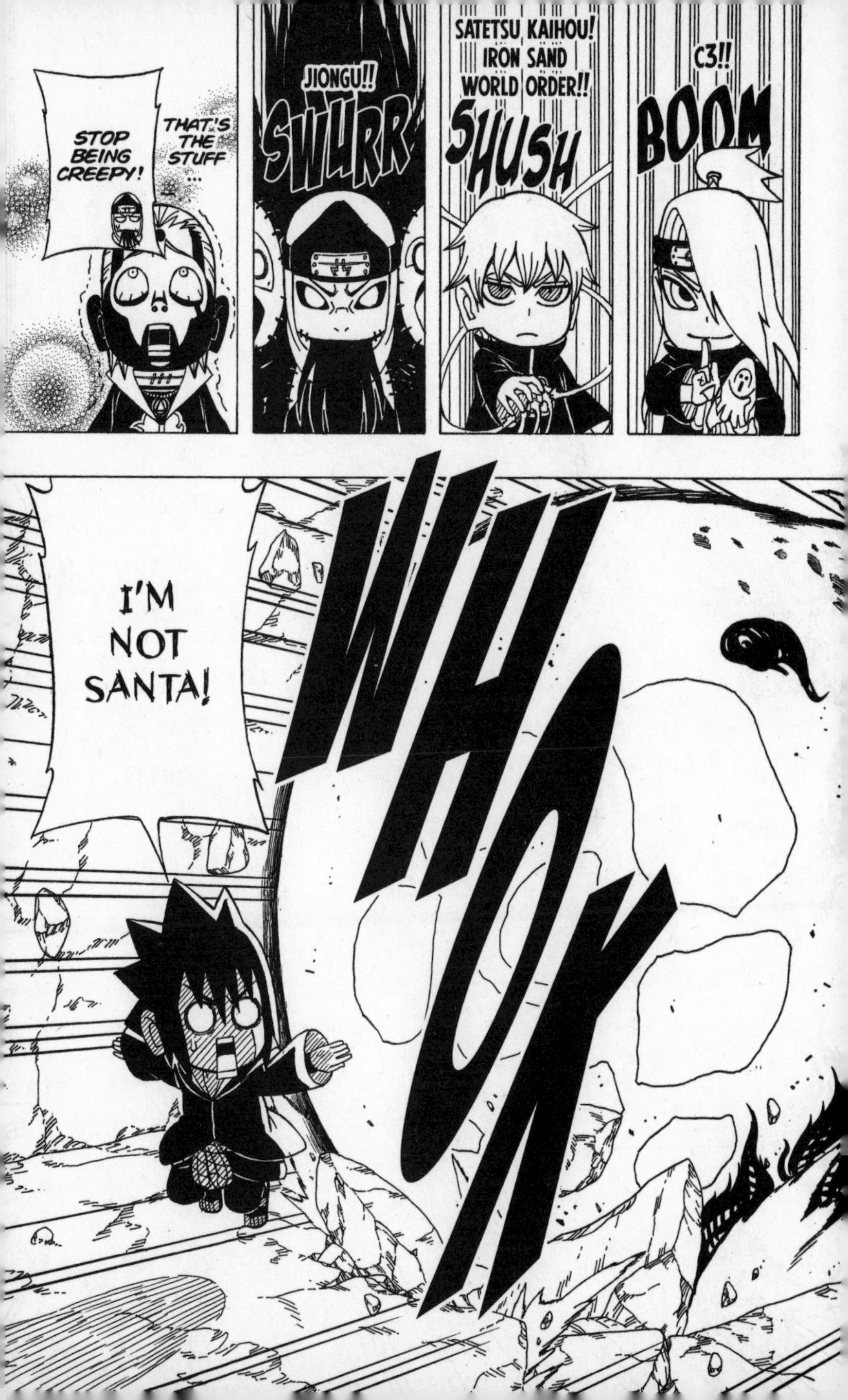
C3!!
BOOM
SATETSU KAIHOU! IRON SAND WORLD ORDER!!
SHUSH
JIONGU!!
SWURR
THAT'S THE STUFF...
STOP BEING CREEPY!
I'M NOT SANTA!

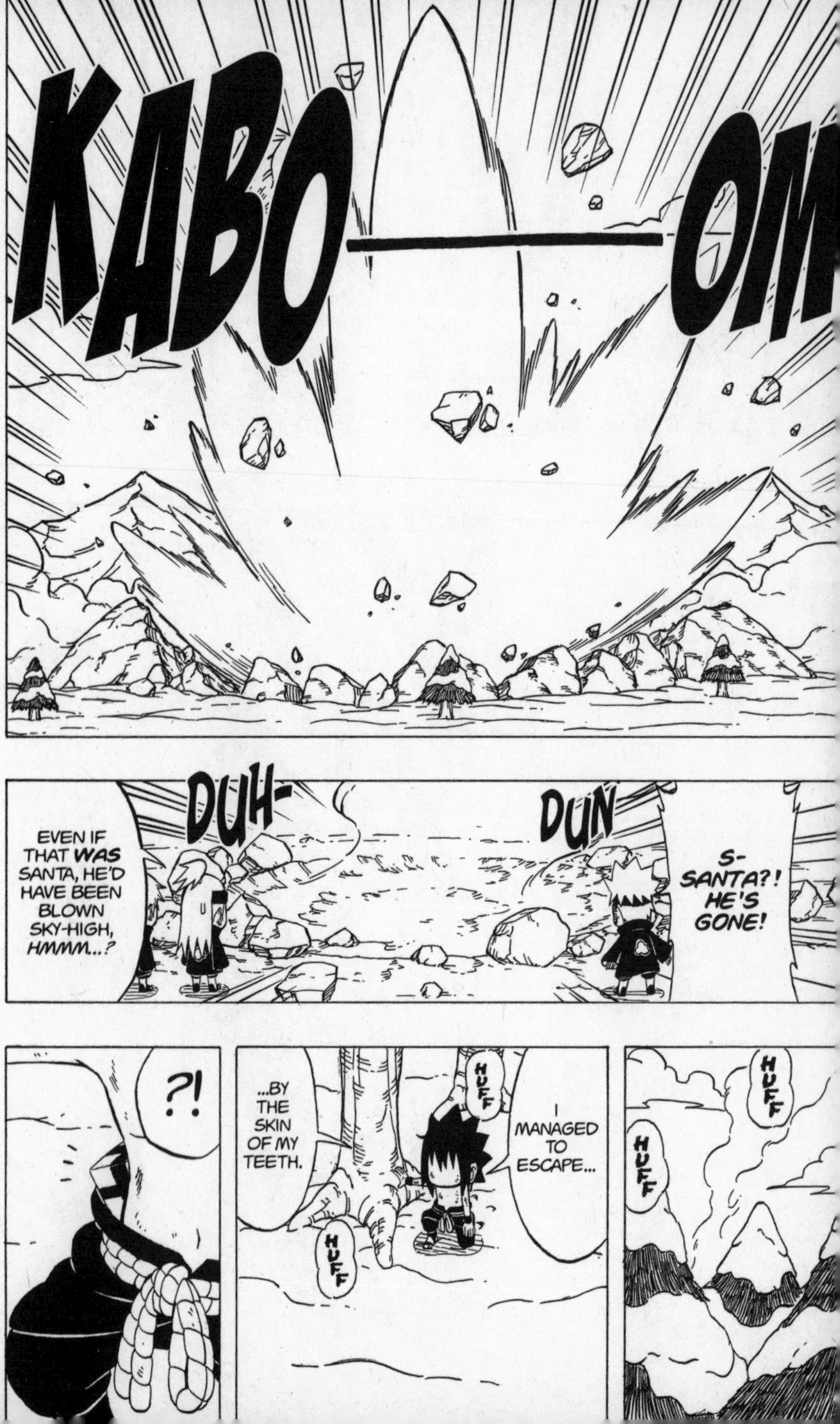
KABO—OOM
S-SANTA?! HE'S GONE!
DUH-DUN
EVEN IF THAT WAS SANTA, HE'D HAVE BEEN BLOWN SKY-HIGH, HMMM...?
HUFF
HUFF
HUFF
I MANAGED TO ESCAPE...
...BY THE SKIN OF MY TEETH.
HUFF
?!

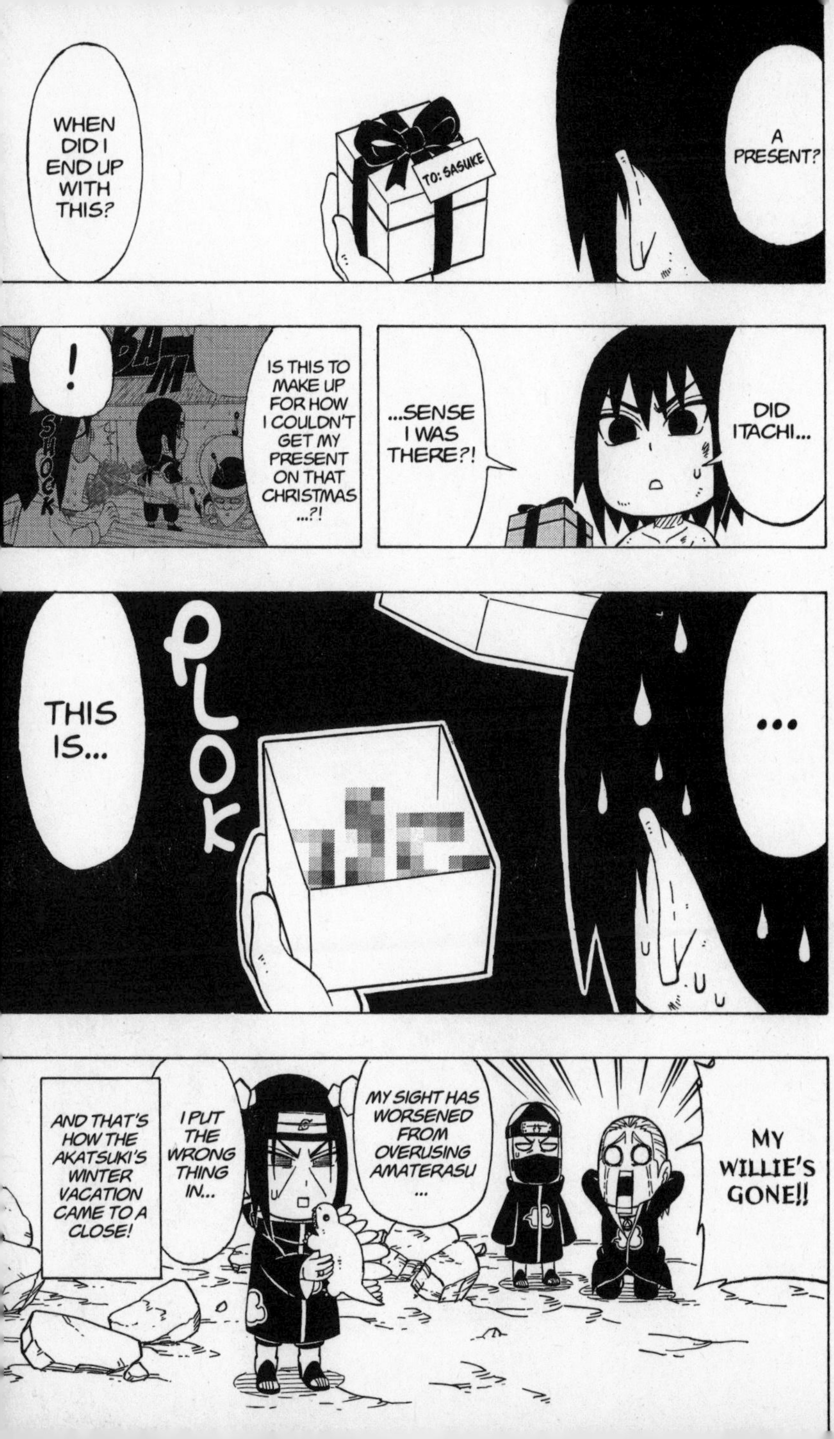
A PRESENT?
TO: SASUKE
WHEN DID I END UP WITH THIS?
DID ITACHI...
...SENSE I WAS THERE?!
IS THIS TO MAKE UP FOR HOW I COULDN'T GET MY PRESENT ON THAT CHRISTMAS ...?!
BAM
!
SHOCK
...
PLOK
THIS IS...
MY WILLIE'S GONE!!
MY SIGHT HAS WORSENED FROM OVERUSING AMATERASU ...
I PUT THE WRONG THING IN...
AND THAT'S HOW THE AKATSUKI'S WINTER VACATION CAME TO A CLOSE!

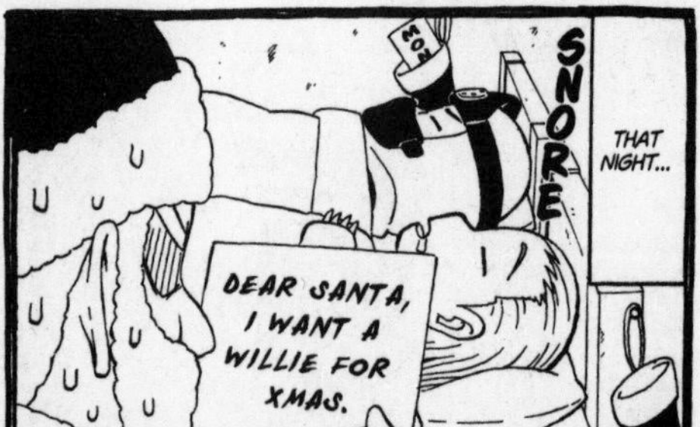
THAT NIGHT...
SNORE
DEAR SANTA, I WANT A WILLIE FOR XMAS.

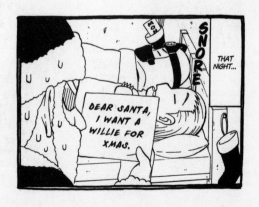

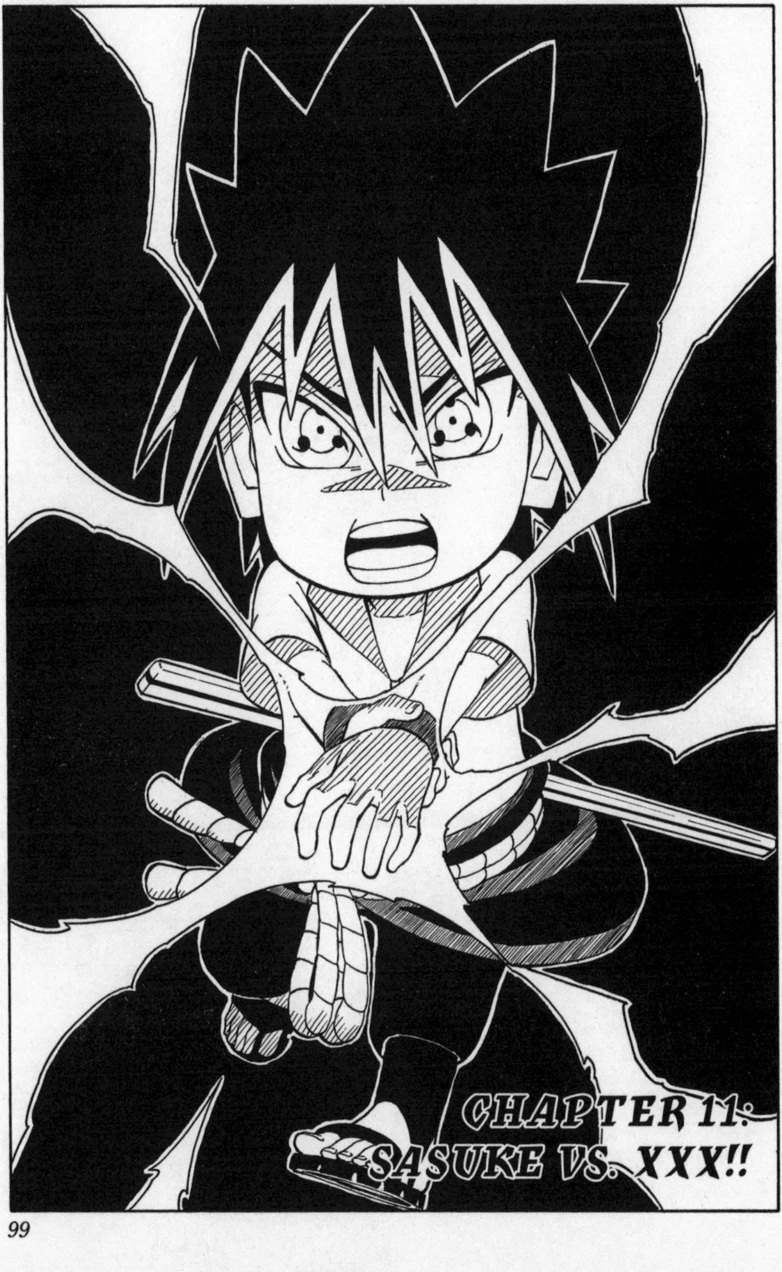
CHAPTER 11:
SASUKE VS. XXX!!

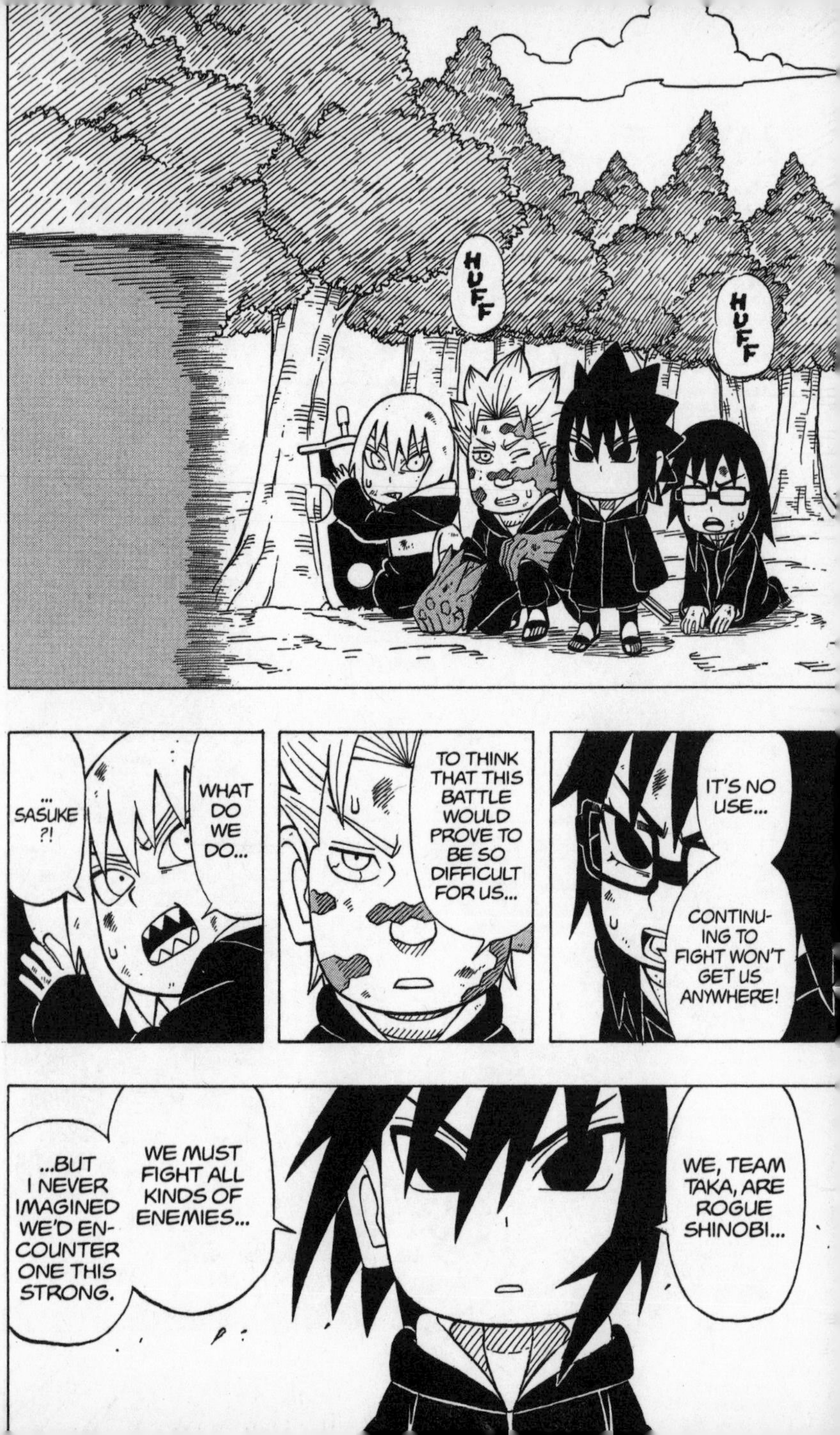
HUFF
HUFF
IT'S NO USE...
CONTINUING TO FIGHT WON'T GET US ANYWHERE!
TO THINK THAT THIS BATTLE WOULD PROVE TO BE SO DIFFICULT FOR US...
WHAT DO WE DO...
...SASUKE?!
WE, TEAM TAKA, ARE ROGUE SHINOBI...
WE MUST FIGHT ALL KINDS OF ENEMIES...
...BUT I NEVER IMAGINED WE'D ENCOUNTER ONE THIS STRONG.

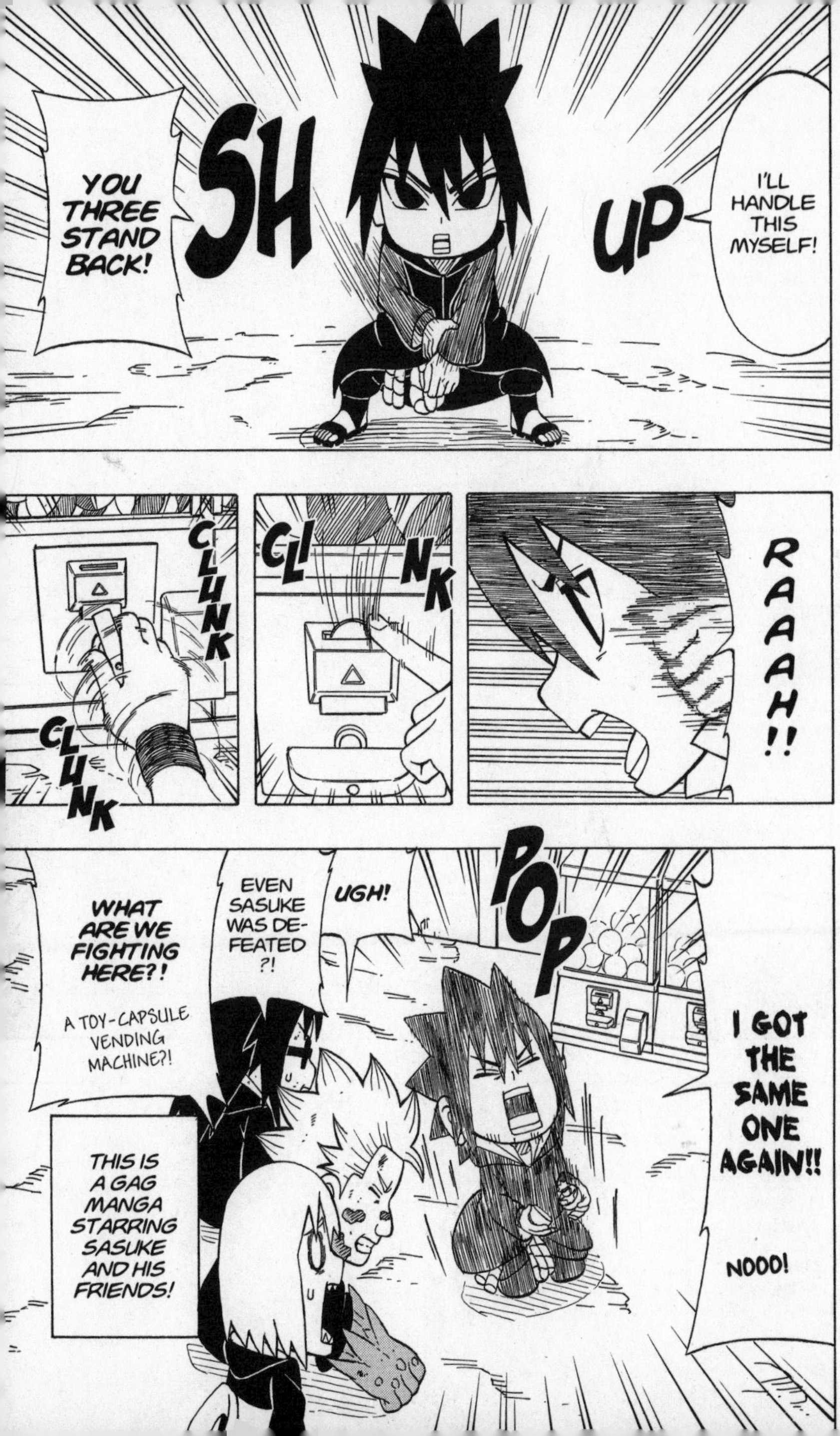
SHUP
I'LL HANDLE THIS MYSELF!
YOU THREE STAND BACK!
RAAAAH!!
CLINK
CLUNK
CLUNK
I GOT THE SAME ONE AGAIN!!
NOOO!
POP
UGH!
EVEN SASUKE WAS DE-FEATED?!
WHAT ARE WE FIGHTING HERE?!
A TOY-CAPSULE VENDING MACHINE?!
THIS IS A GAG MANGA STARRING SASUKE AND HIS FRIENDS!

SASUKE VS. THE TABLE!!

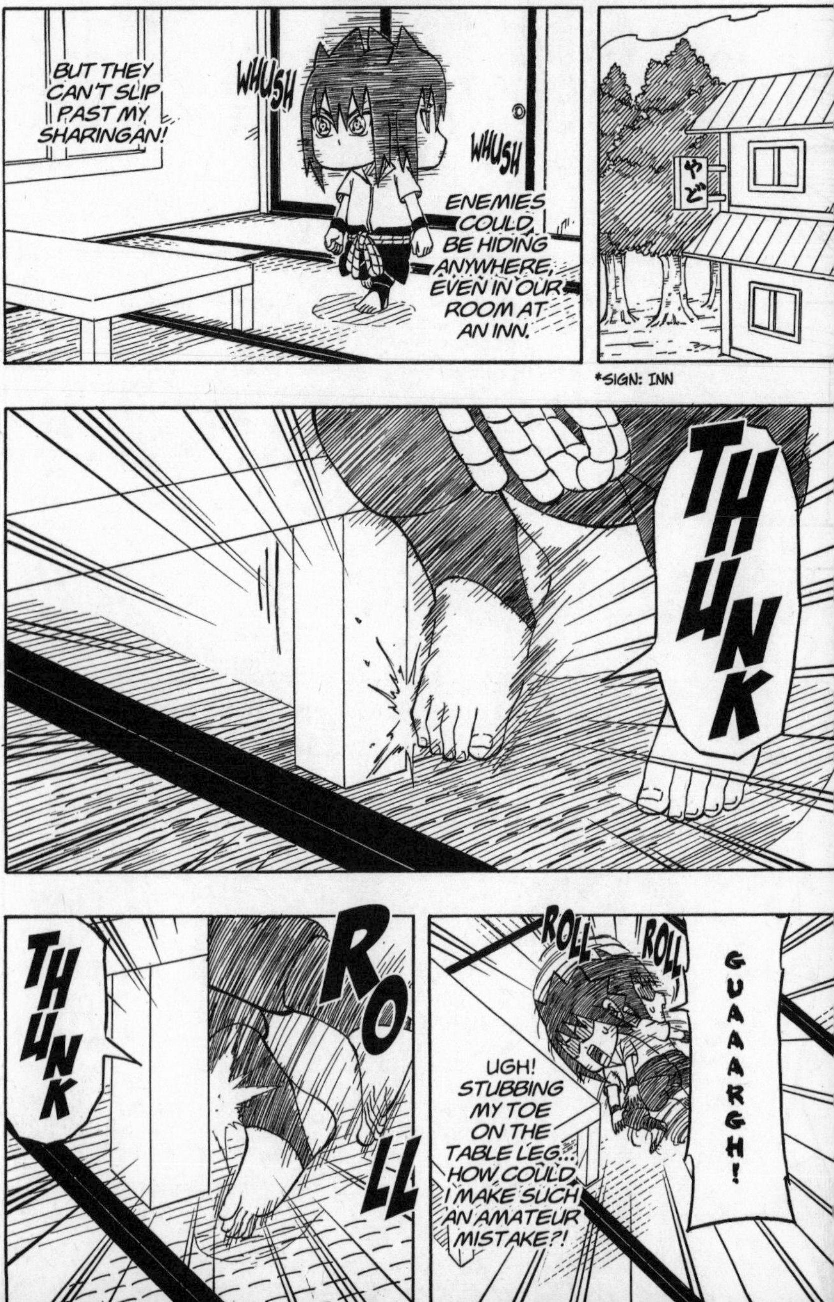
やど
*SIGN: INN
WHUSH
WHUSH
ENEMIES COULD BE HIDING ANYWHERE, EVEN IN OUR ROOM AT AN INN.
BUT THEY CAN'T SLIP PAST MY SHARINGAN!
THUNK
GUAAARGH!
ROLL ROLL
UGH! STUBBING MY TOE ON THE TABLE LEG... HOW COULD I MAKE SUCH AN AMATEUR MISTAKE?!
ROLL
THUNK

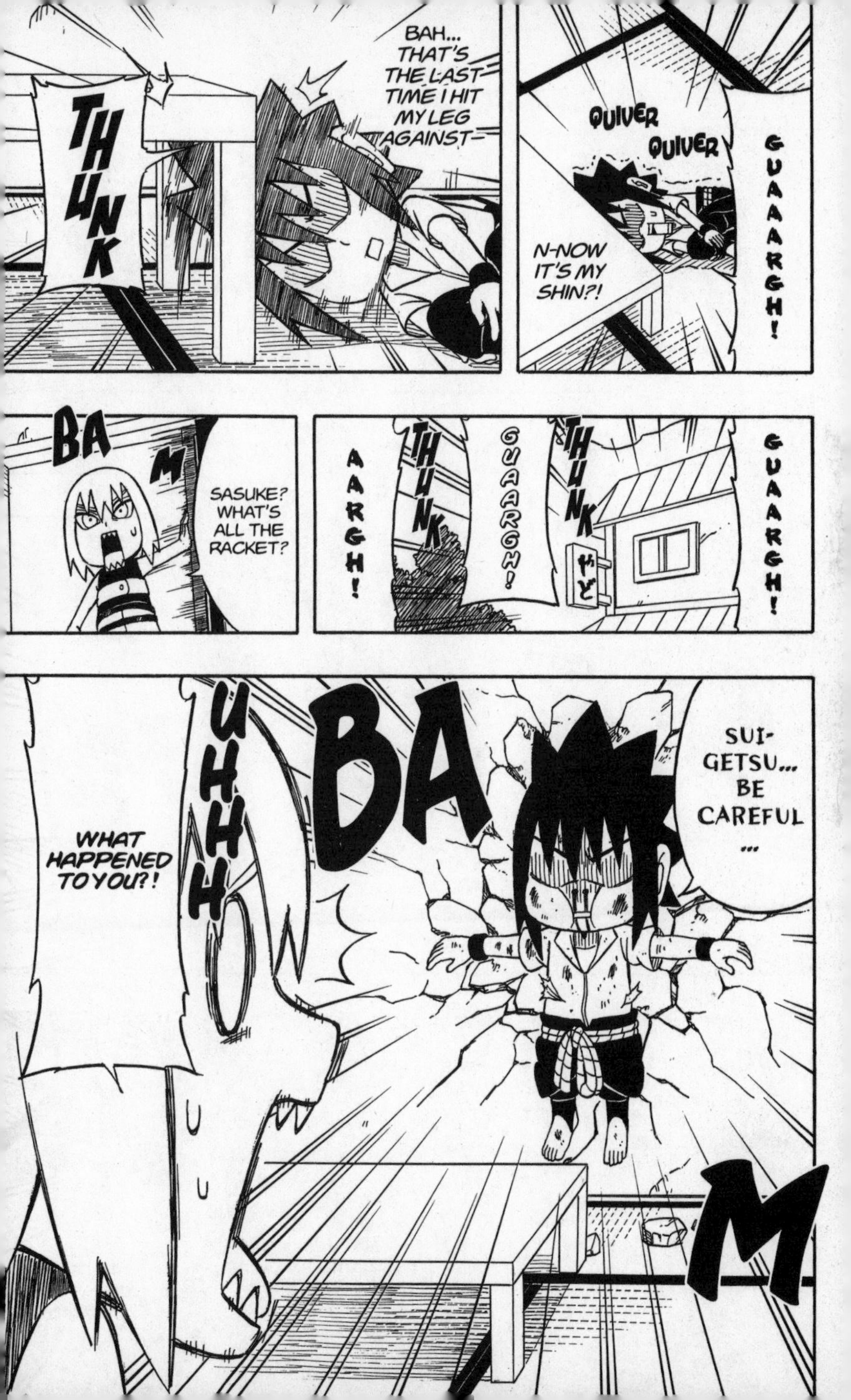
QUIVER
QUIVER
GUAAARGH!
N-NOW IT'S MY SHIN?!
BAH... THAT'S THE LAST TIME I HIT MY LEG AGAINST—
THUNK
GUAARGH!
THUNK
GUAARGH!
THUNK
AARGH!
BAM
SASUKE? WHAT'S ALL THE RACKET?
SUI-GETSU... BE CAREFUL...
BAM
UHHHH
WHAT HAPPENED TO YOU?!

SASUKE VS. NATTO!!

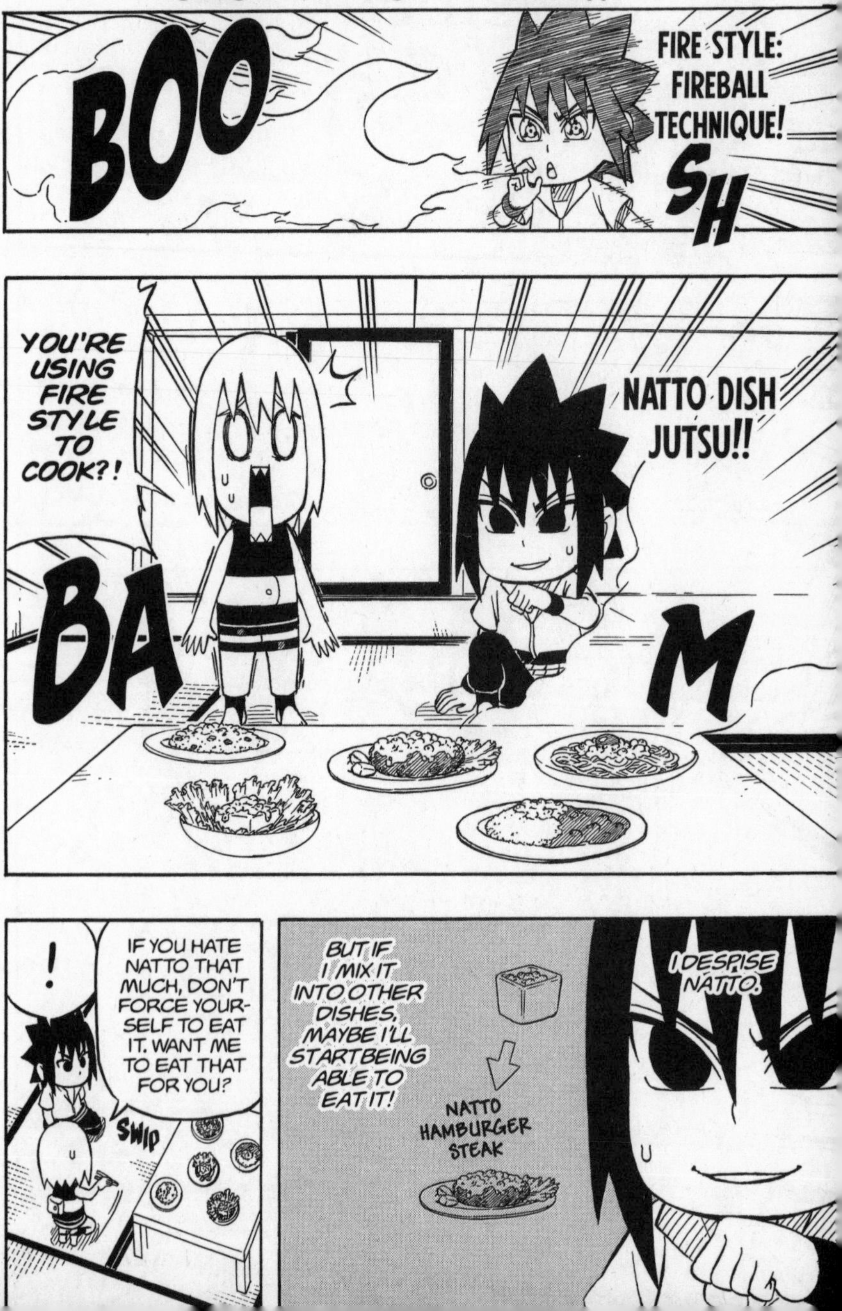
FIRE STYLE: FIREBALL TECHNIQUE!
SH
BOO
NATTO DISH JUTSU!!
YOU'RE USING FIRE STYLE TO COOK?!
BAM
I DESPISE NATTO.
BUT IF I MIX IT INTO OTHER DISHES, MAYBE I'LL START BEING ABLE TO EAT IT!
NATTO HAMBURGER STEAK
IF YOU HATE NATTO THAT MUCH, DON'T FORCE YOURSELF TO EAT IT. WANT ME TO EAT THAT FOR YOU?
!
SWIP

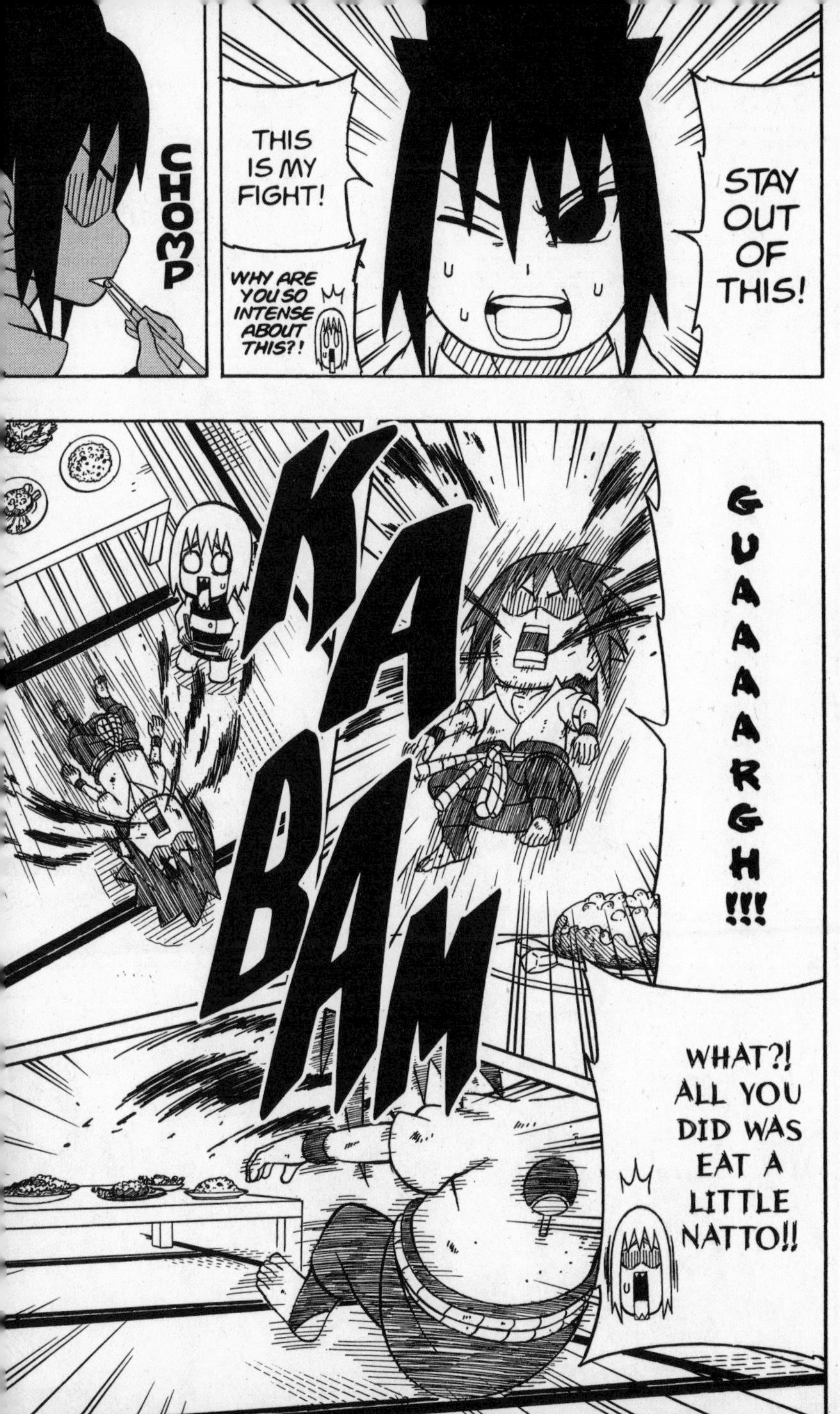
STAY OUT OF THIS!
THIS IS MY FIGHT!
WHY ARE YOU SO INTENSE ABOUT THIS?!
CHOMP
GUAAAAARGH!!!
KA-BAM
WHAT?! ALL YOU DID WAS EAT A LITTLE NATTO!!

SASUKE VS. THE LIGHT PULL STRING!!

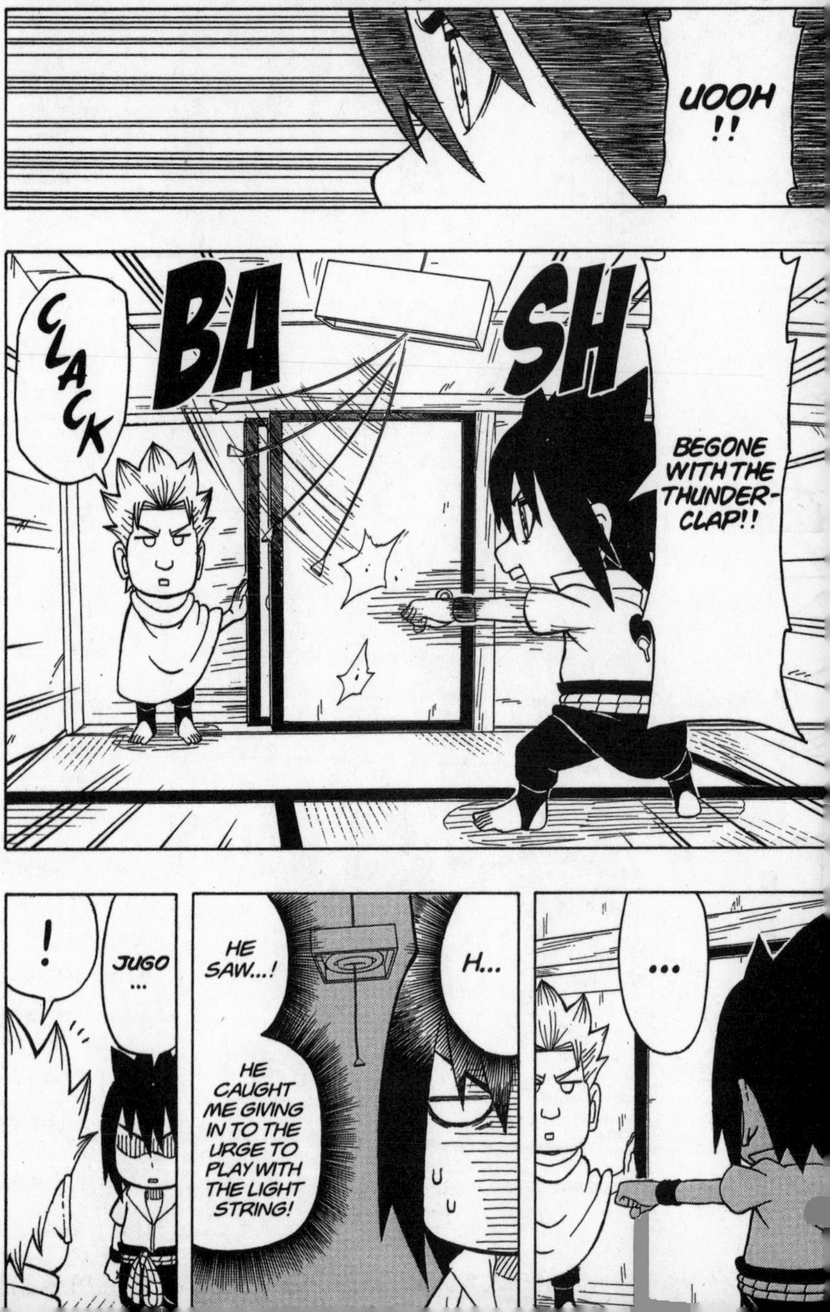
UOOH!!
BEGONE WITH THE THUNDER-CLAP!!
BASH
CLACK
...
H...
HE SAW...!
HE CAUGHT ME GIVING IN TO THE URGE TO PLAY WITH THE LIGHT STRING!
JUGO ...
!

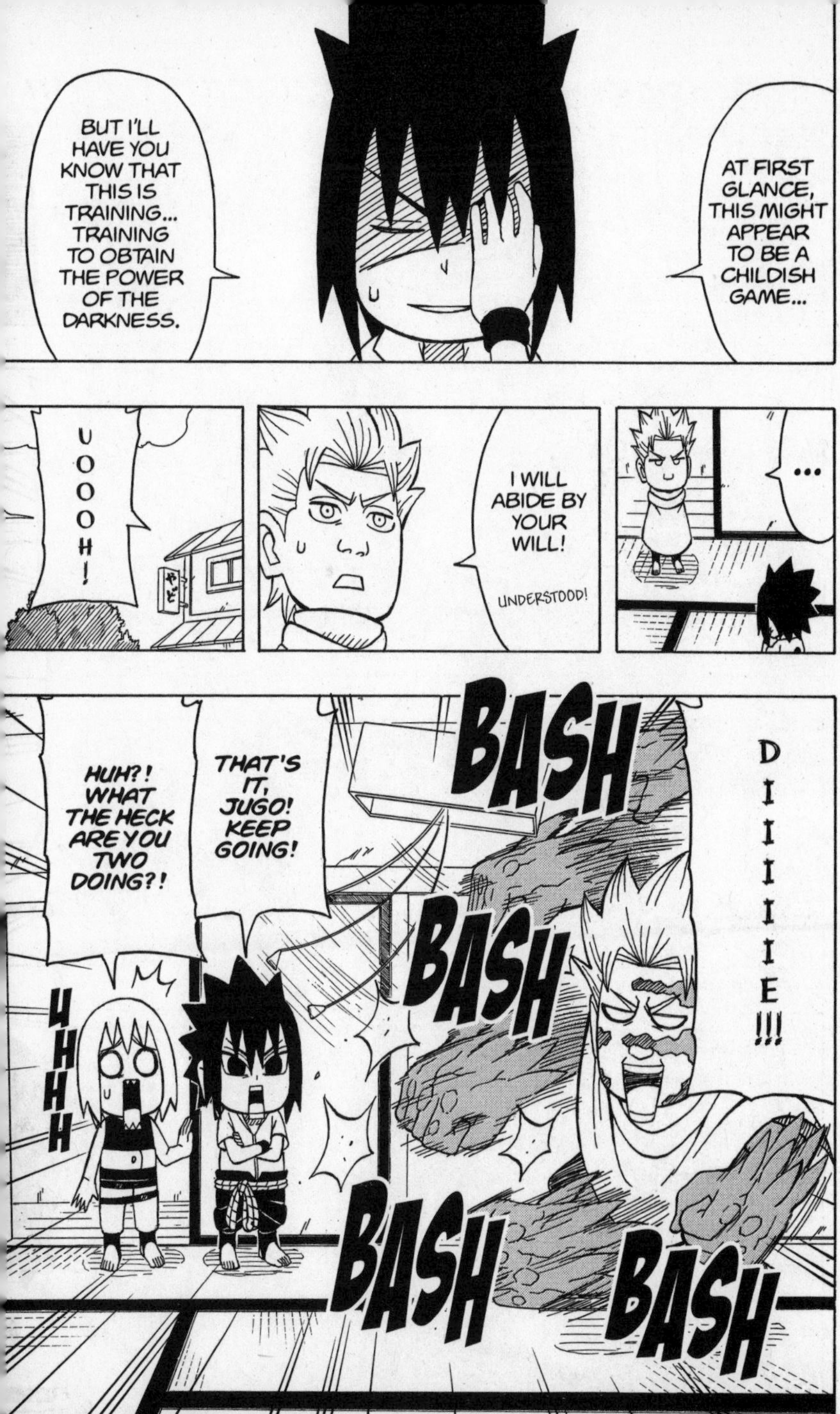
AT FIRST GLANCE, THIS MIGHT APPEAR TO BE A CHILDISH GAME...
BUT I'LL HAVE YOU KNOW THAT THIS IS TRAINING... TRAINING TO OBTAIN THE POWER OF THE DARKNESS.
...
I WILL ABIDE BY YOUR WILL!
UNDERSTOOD!
UOOOH!
DIIIIIE!!!
BASH
BASH
BASH
BASH
THAT'S IT, JUGO! KEEP GOING!
HUH?! WHAT THE HECK ARE YOU TWO DOING?!
UHHHH

SASUKE VS. BOWLING!!

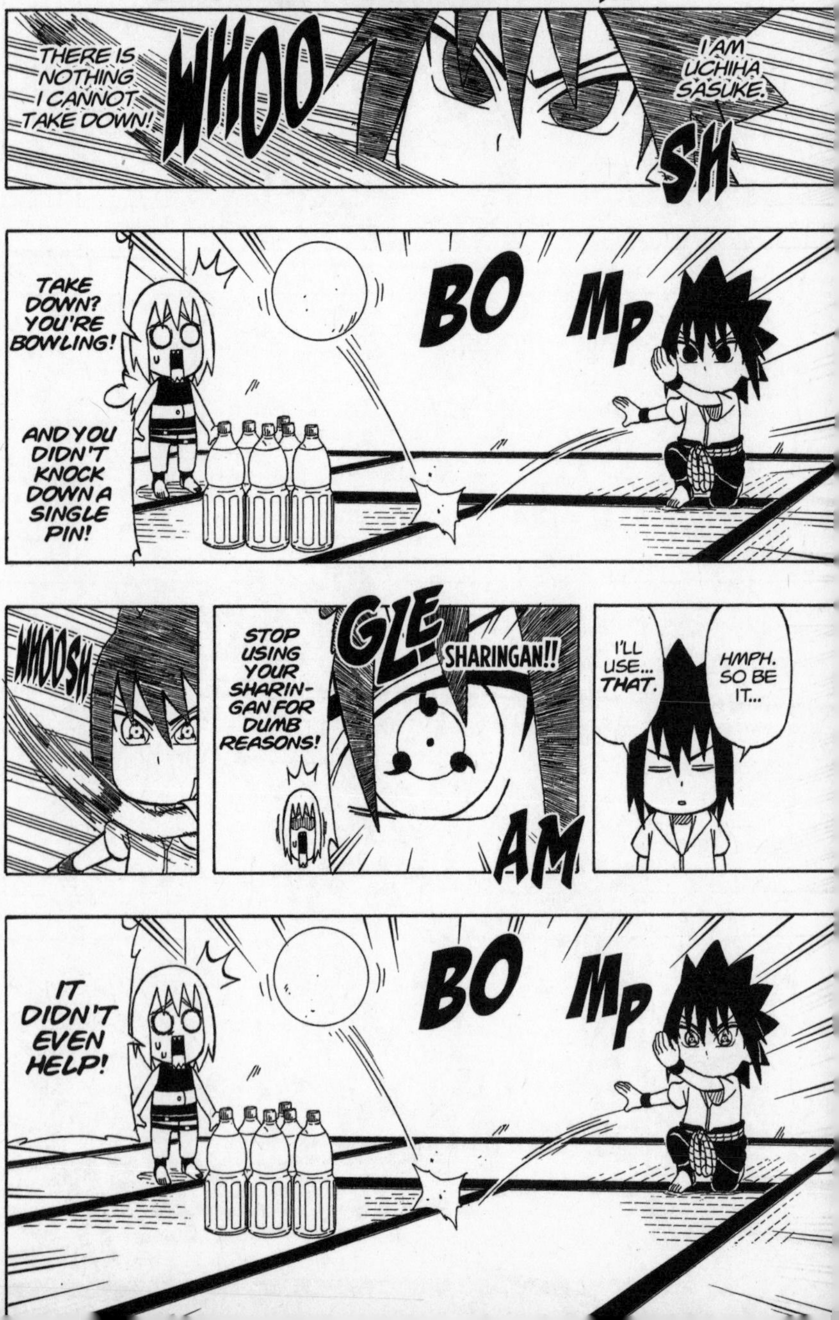
I AM UCHIHA SASUKE.
SH
WHOO
THERE IS NOTHING I CANNOT TAKE DOWN!
MP
BO
TAKE DOWN? YOU'RE BOWLING!
AND YOU DIDN'T KNOCK DOWN A SINGLE PIN!
HMPH. SO BE IT...
I'LL USE... THAT.
GLE
SHARINGAN!!
STOP USING YOUR SHARIN-GAN FOR DUMB REASONS!
AM
WHOOSH
MP
BO
IT DIDN'T EVEN HELP!

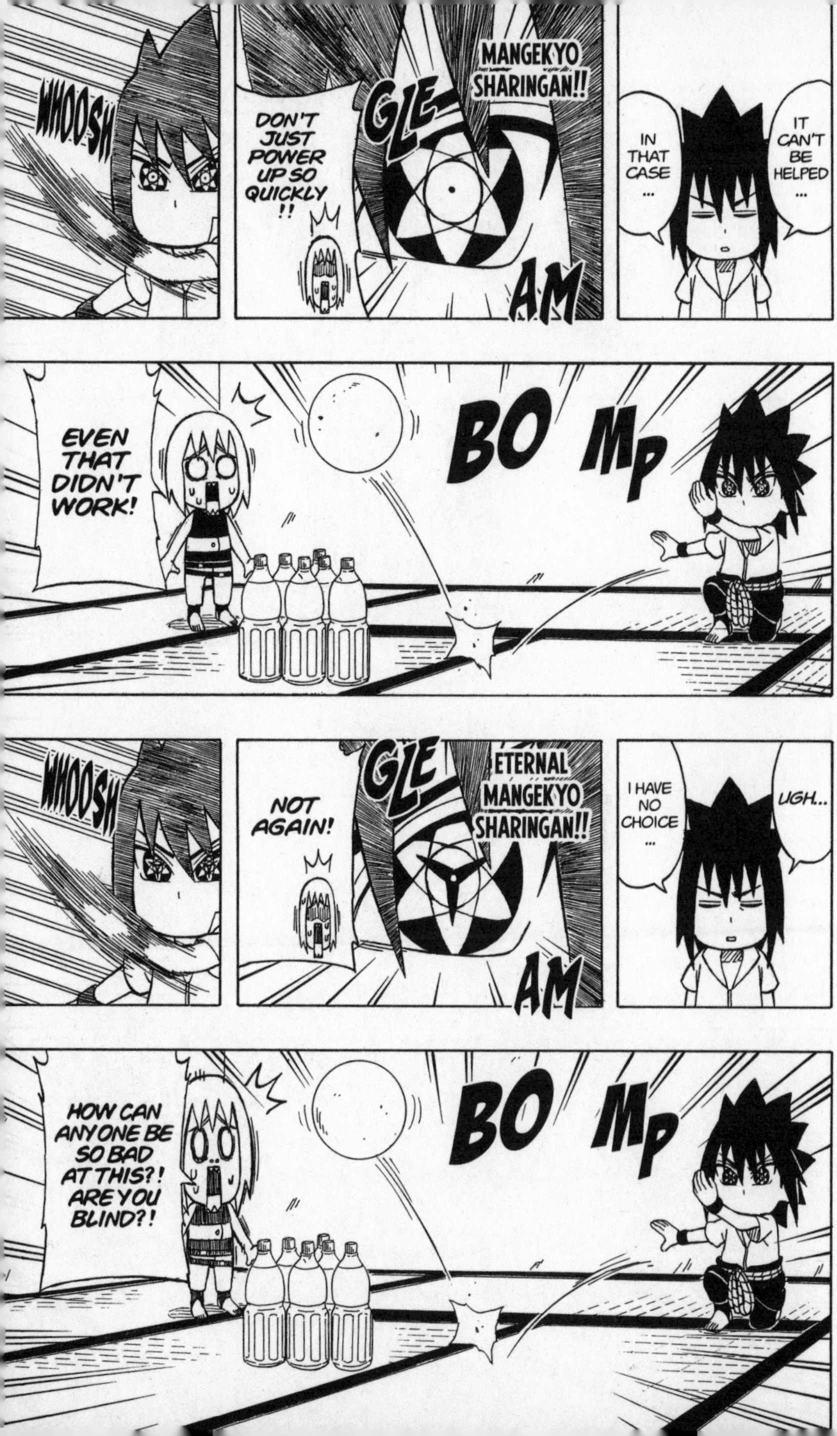
IT CAN'T BE HELPED...
IN THAT CASE...
MANGEKYO SHARINGAN!!
GLE
AM
DON'T JUST POWER UP SO QUICKLY!!
WHOOSH
BO MP
EVEN THAT DIDN'T WORK!
UGH...
I HAVE NO CHOICE...
ETERNAL MANGEKYO SHARINGAN!!
GLE
AM
NOT AGAIN!
WHOOSH
BO MP
HOW CAN ANYONE BE SO BAD AT THIS?! ARE YOU BLIND?!

SASUKE VS. THE TOILET!!

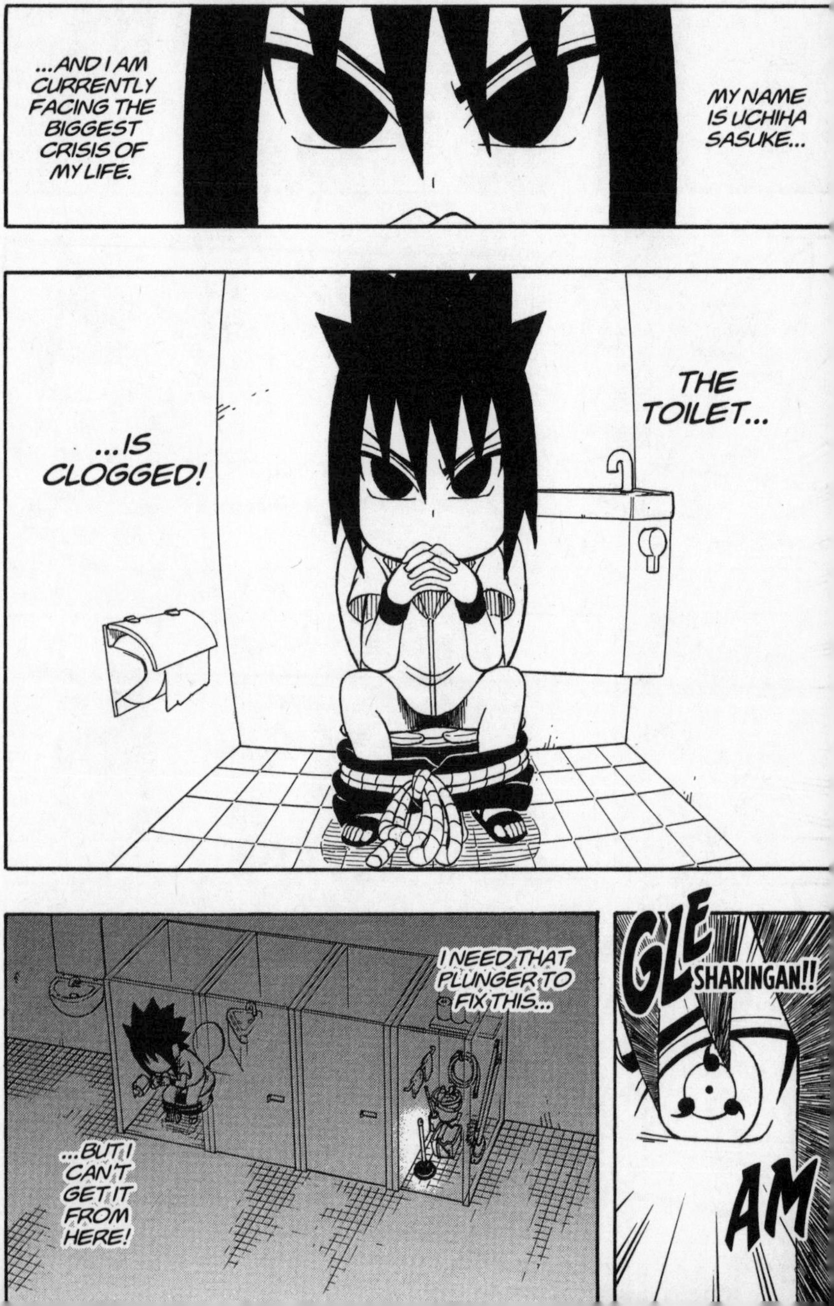
MY NAME IS UCHIHA SASUKE...
...AND I AM CURRENTLY FACING THE BIGGEST CRISIS OF MY LIFE.
THE TOILET...
...IS CLOGGED!
GLE
SHARINGAN!!
AM
I NEED THAT PLUNGER TO FIX THIS...
...BUT I CAN'T GET IT FROM HERE!

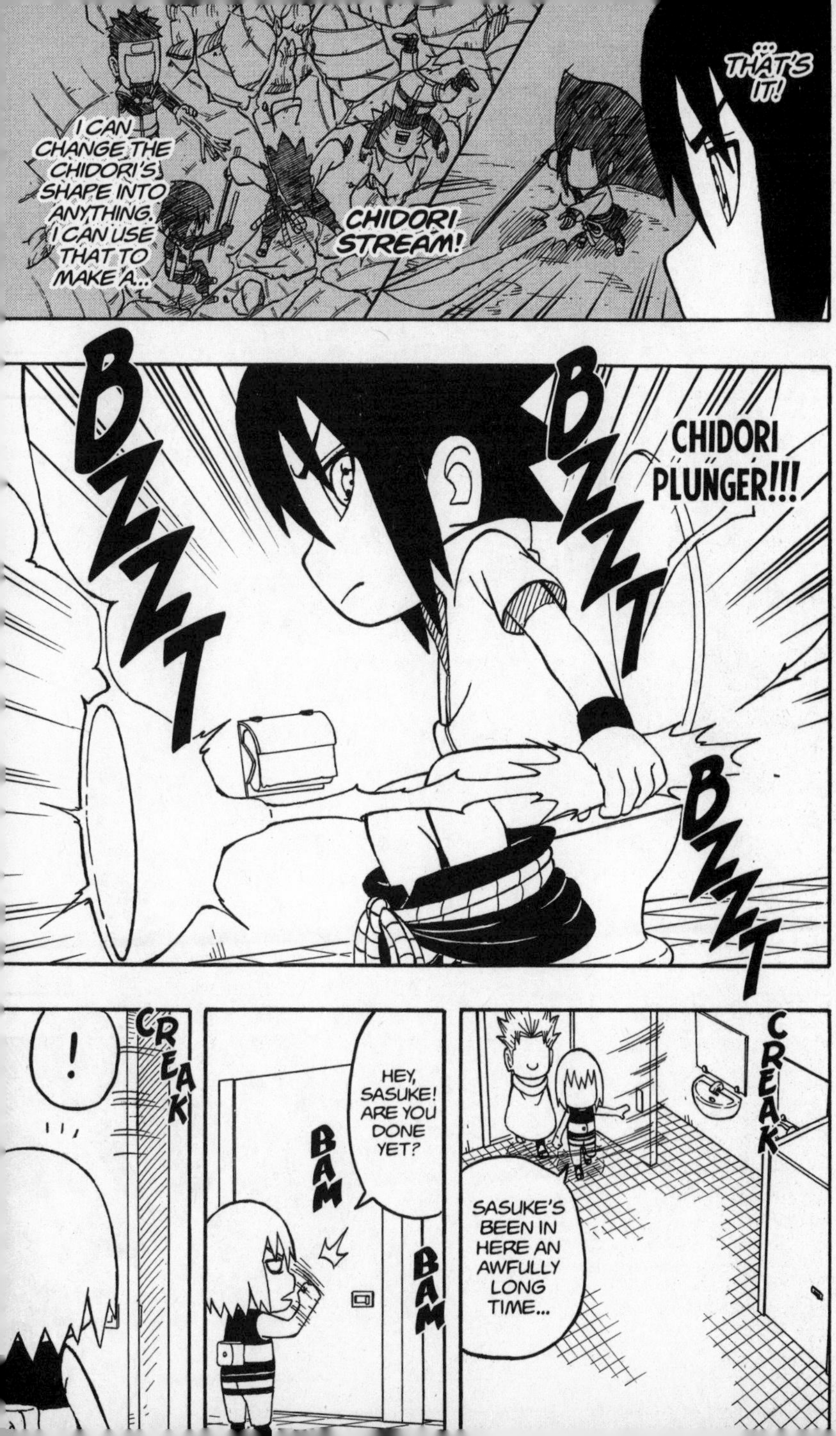

...THAT'S IT!
CHIDORI STREAM!
I CAN CHANGE THE CHIDORI'S SHAPE INTO ANYTHING. I CAN USE THAT TO MAKE A...
BZZZT
CHIDORI PLUNGER!!!
BZZZT
BZZZT
CREAK
SASUKE'S BEEN IN HERE AN AWFULLY LONG TIME...
HEY, SASUKE! ARE YOU DONE YET?
BAM
BAM
!
CREAK

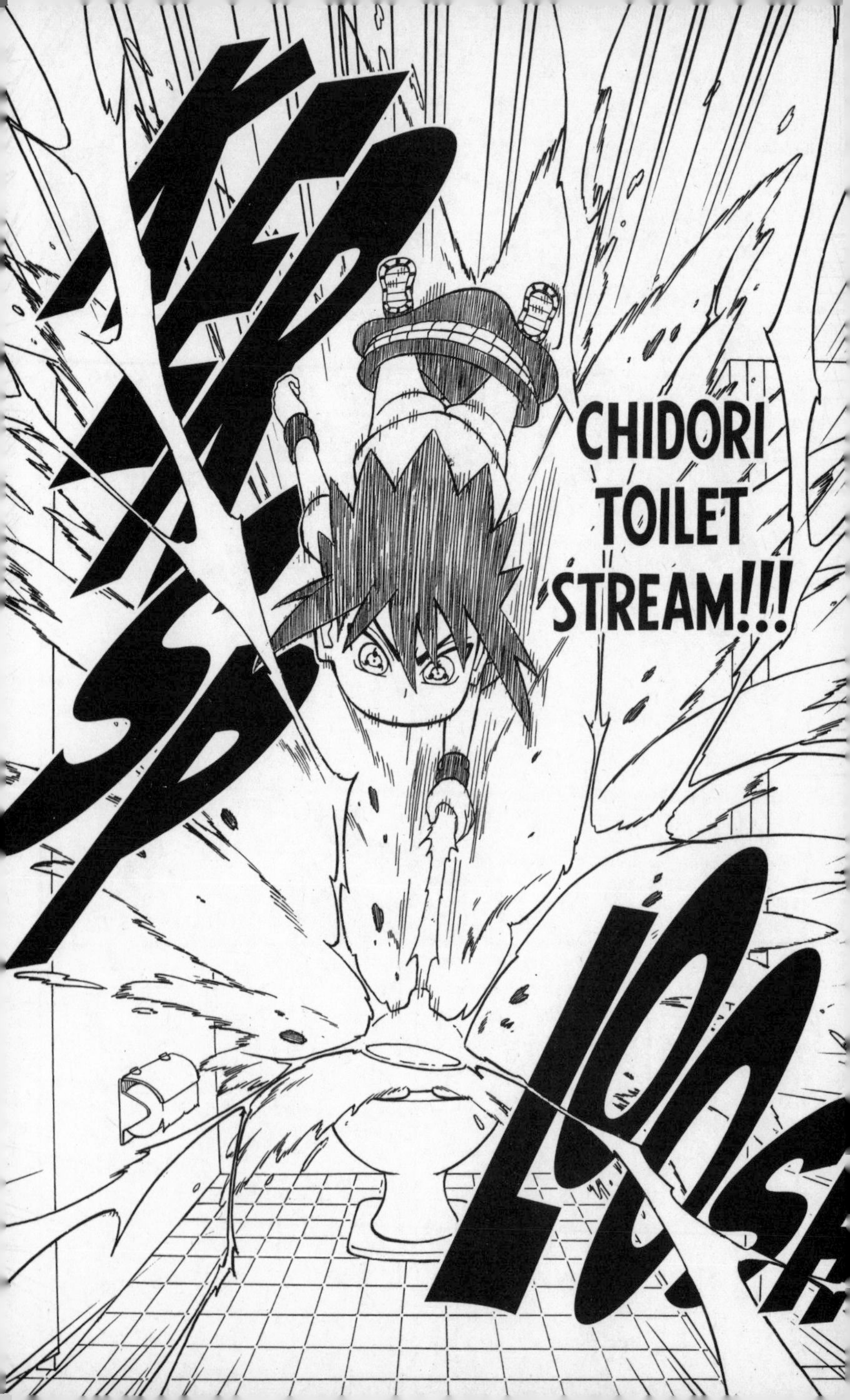
CHIDORI TOILET STREAM!!!

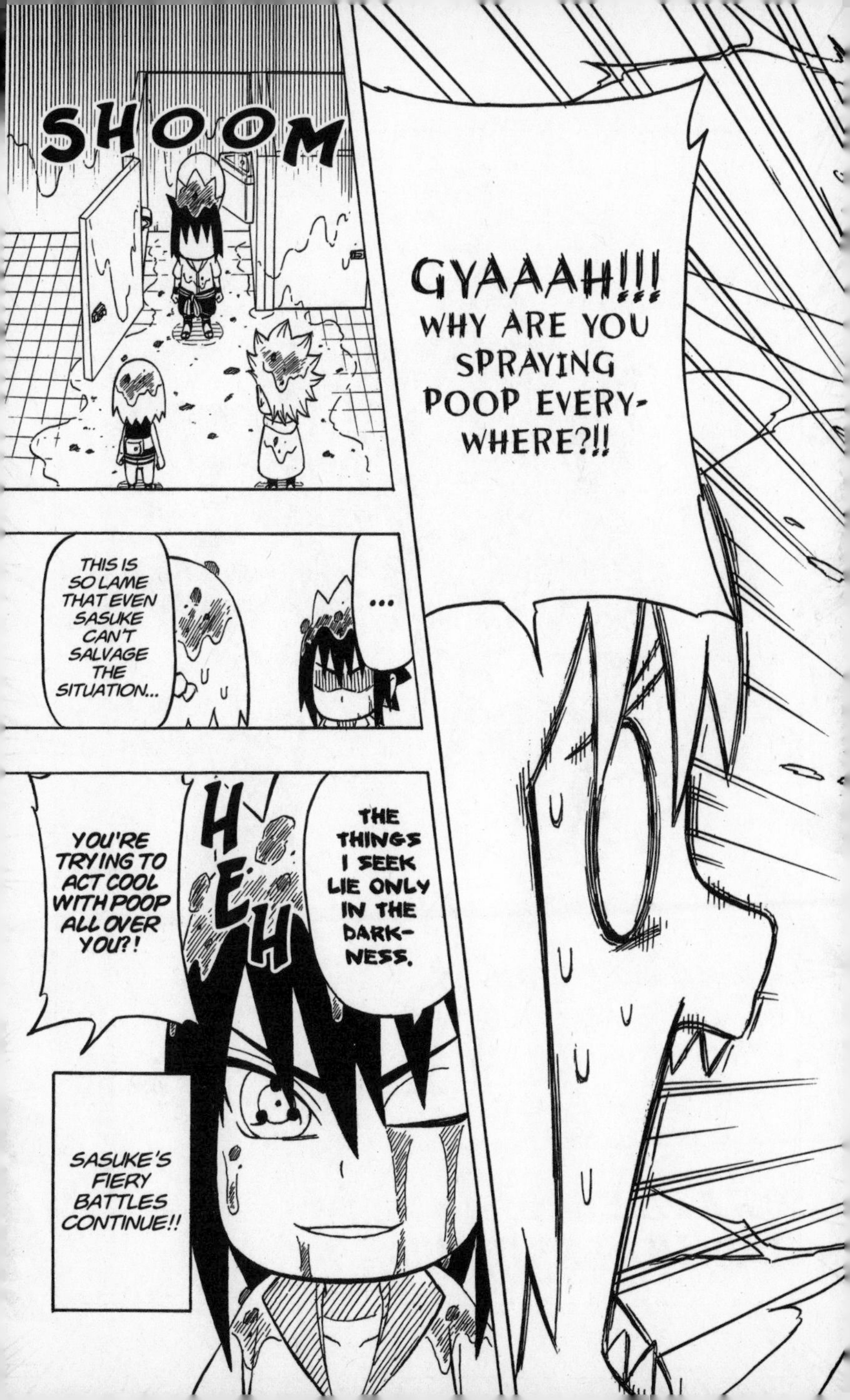
GYAAAH!!! WHY ARE YOU SPRAYING POOP EVERY-WHERE?!!
SHOOM
...
THIS IS SO LAME THAT EVEN SASUKE CAN'T SALVAGE THE SITUATION...
THE THINGS I SEEK LIE ONLY IN THE DARK-NESS.
HEH
YOU'RE TRYING TO ACT COOL WITH POOP ALL OVER YOU?!
SASUKE'S FIERY BATTLES CONTINUE!!

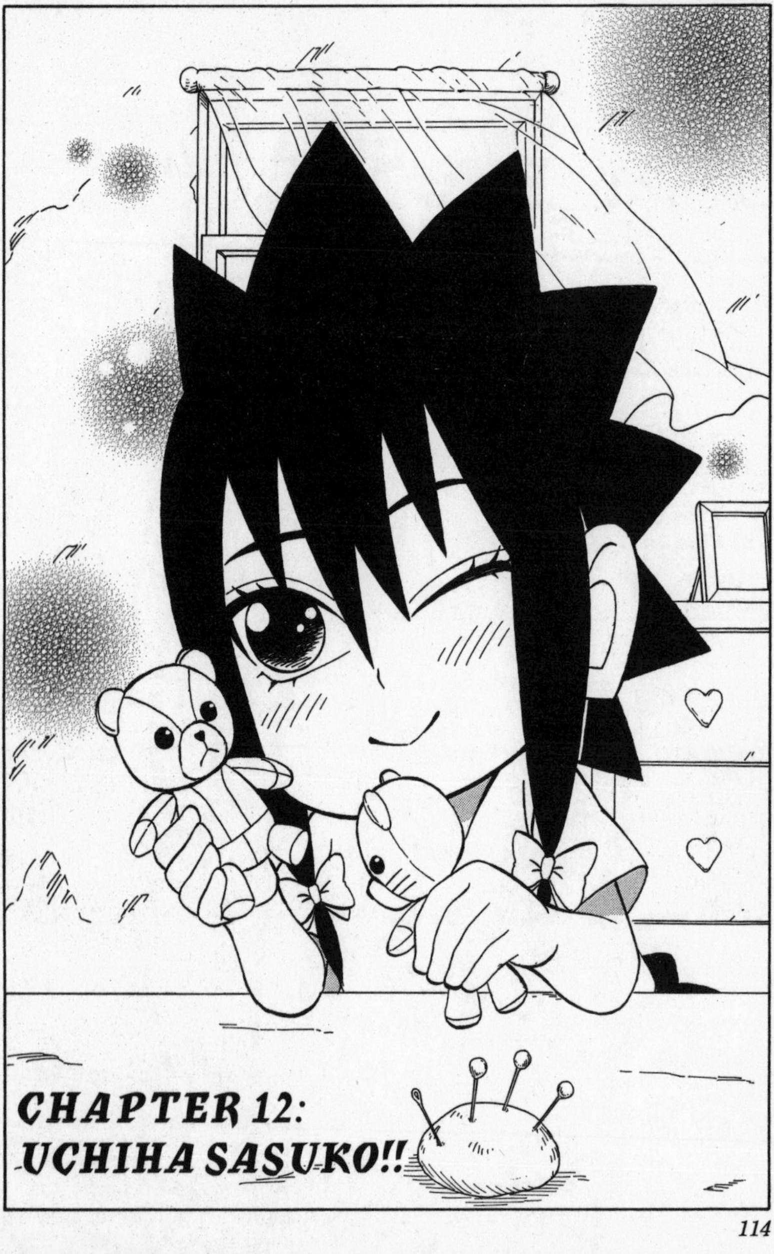
CHAPTER 12:
UCHIHA SASUKO!!

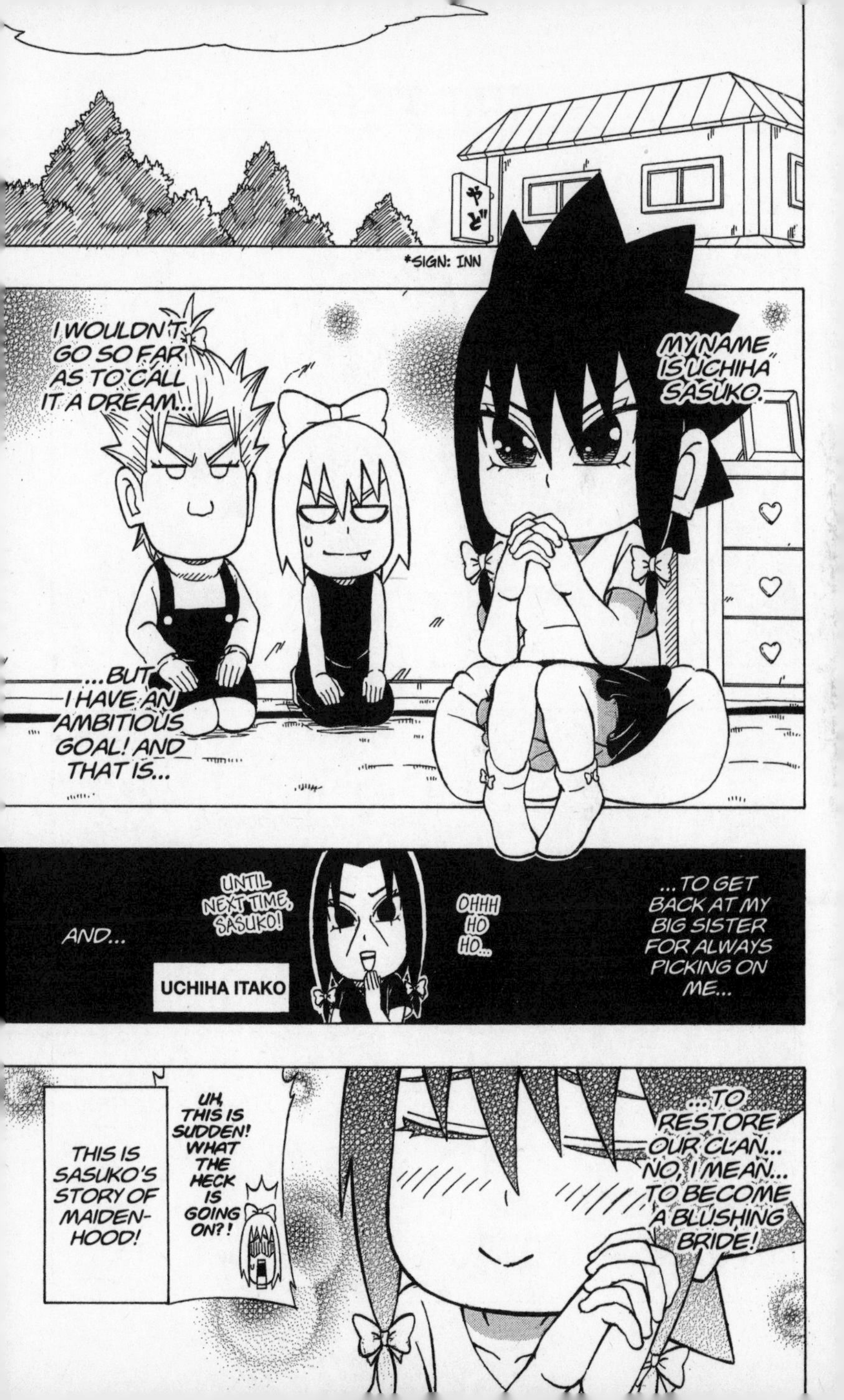
やど
*SIGN: INN
MY NAME IS UCHIHA SASUKO.
I WOULDN'T GO SO FAR AS TO CALL IT A DREAM...
...BUT I HAVE AN AMBITIOUS GOAL! AND THAT IS...
...TO GET BACK AT MY BIG SISTER FOR ALWAYS PICKING ON ME...
OHHH HO HO...
UNTIL NEXT TIME, SASUKO!
UCHIHA ITAKO
AND...
...TO RESTORE OUR CLAN... NO, I MEAN... TO BECOME A BLUSHING BRIDE!
UH, THIS IS SUDDEN! WHAT THE HECK IS GOING ON?!
THIS IS SASUKO'S STORY OF MAIDENHOOD!

GIRL TALK

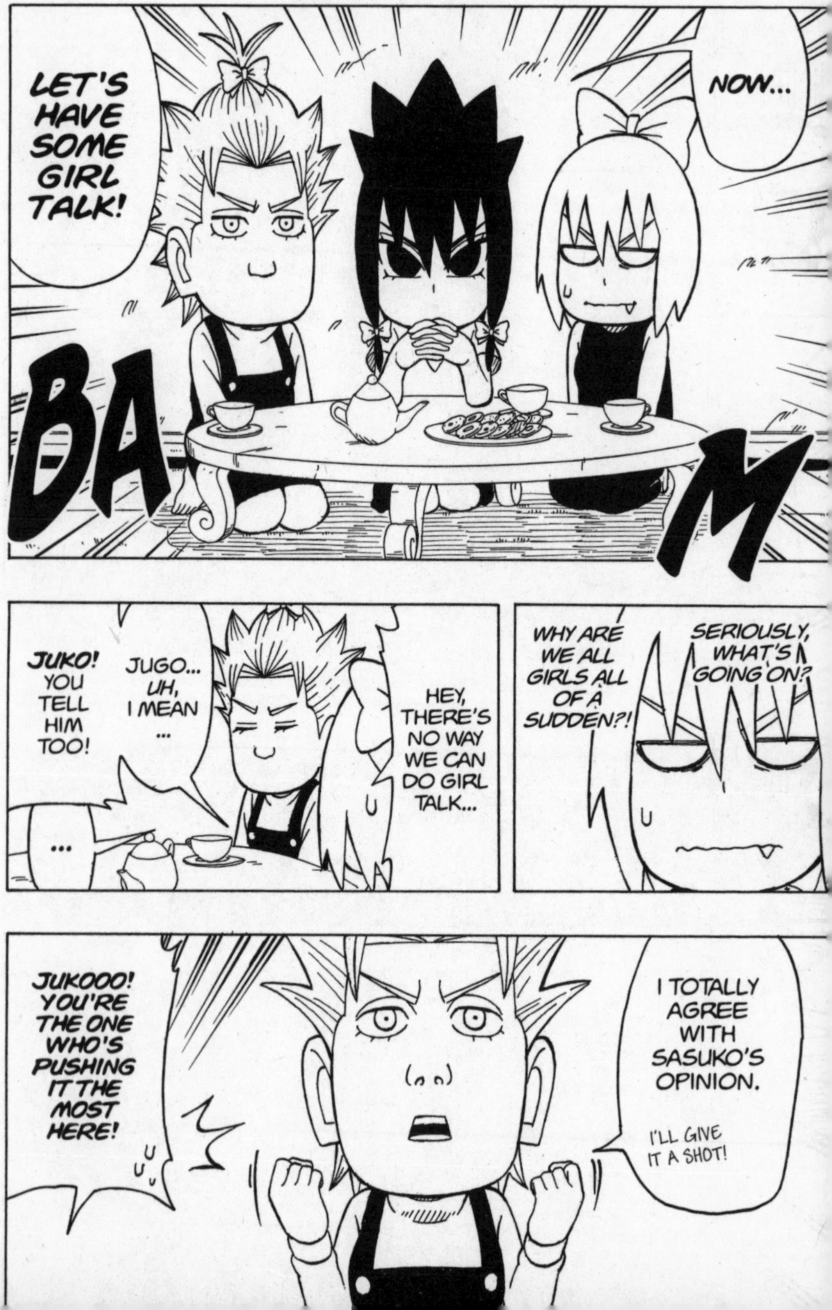
NOW...
LET'S HAVE SOME GIRL TALK!
BAM
SERIOUSLY, WHAT'S GOING ON?
WHY ARE WE ALL GIRLS ALL OF A SUDDEN?!
HEY, THERE'S NO WAY WE CAN DO GIRL TALK...
JUGO... UH, I MEAN ...
JUKO! YOU TELL HIM TOO!
...
I TOTALLY AGREE WITH SASUKO'S OPINION.
I'LL GIVE IT A SHOT!
JUKOOO! YOU'RE THE ONE WHO'S PUSHING IT THE MOST HERE!

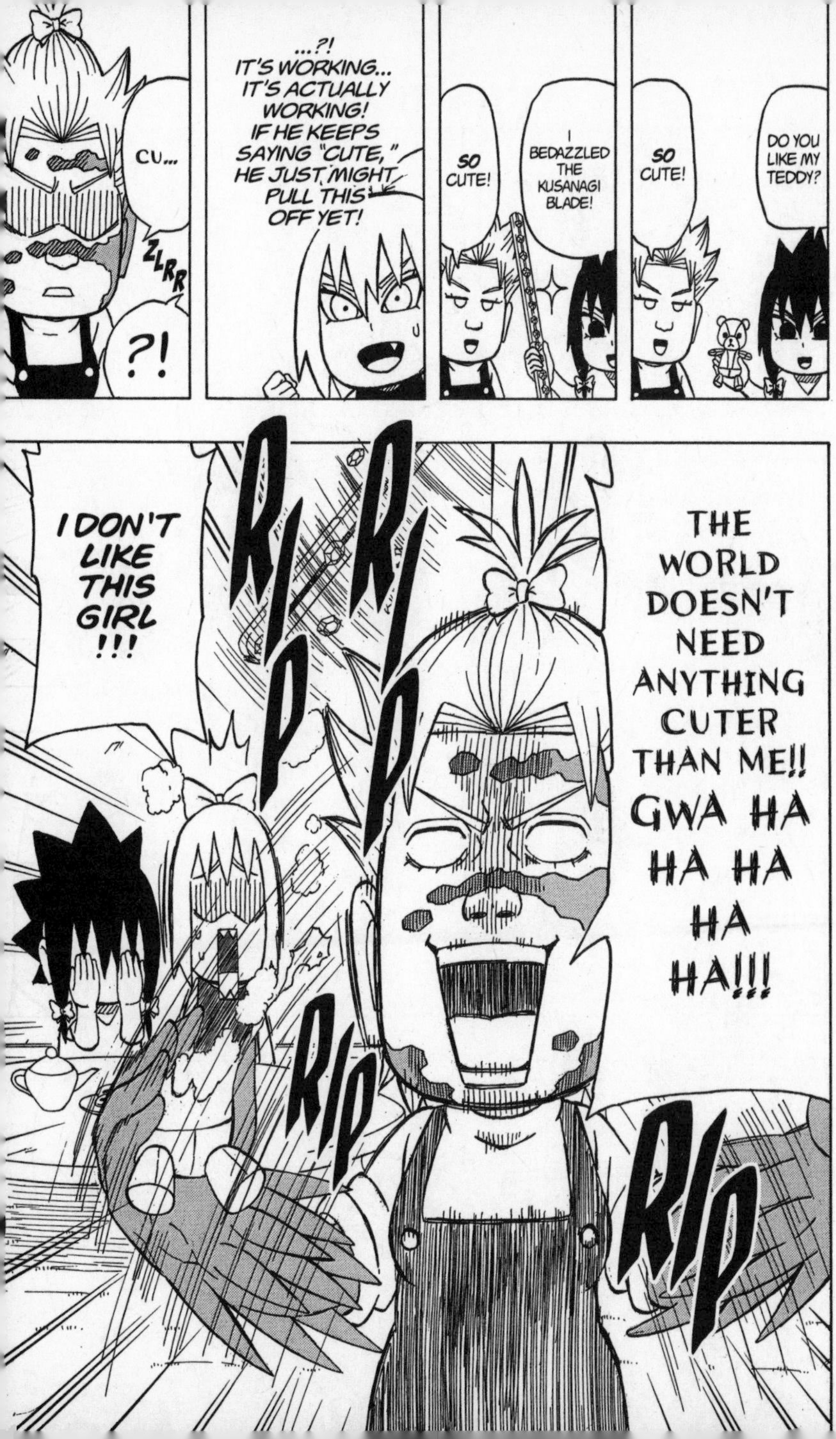
DO YOU LIKE MY TEDDY?
SO CUTE!
I BEDAZZLED THE KUSANAGI BLADE!
SO CUTE!
...?! IT'S WORKING... IT'S ACTUALLY WORKING! IF HE KEEPS SAYING "CUTE," HE JUST MIGHT PULL THIS OFF YET!
CU...
ZLRR
?!
THE WORLD DOESN'T NEED ANYTHING CUTER THAN ME!! GWA HA HA HA HA HA!!!
RIP
RIP
I DON'T LIKE THIS GIRL!!!
RIP
RIP

KARIO

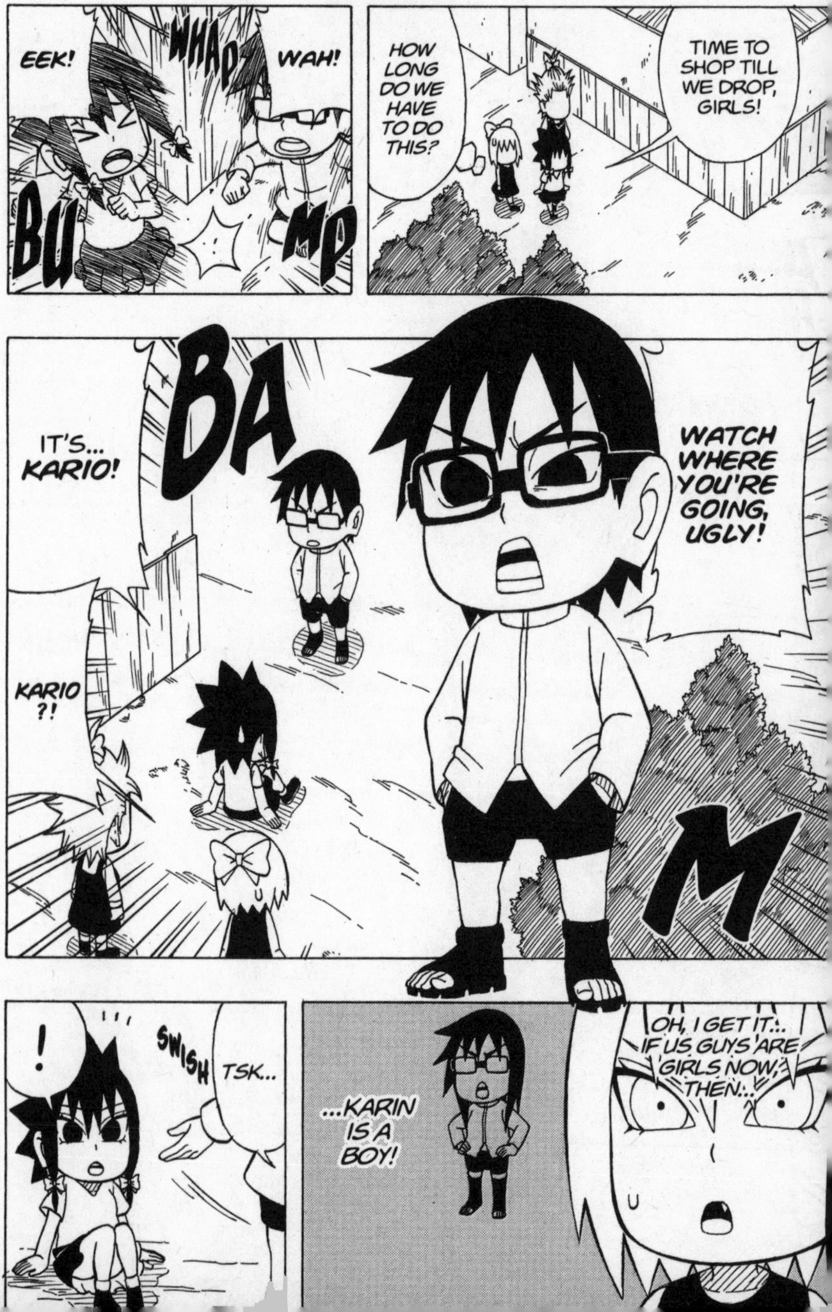
TIME TO SHOP TILL WE DROP, GIRLS!
HOW LONG DO WE HAVE TO DO THIS?
WHAP
WAH!
EEK!
BUMP
WATCH WHERE YOU'RE GOING, UGLY!
BAM
IT'S... KARIO!
KARIO ?!
OH, I GET IT... IF US GUYS ARE GIRLS NOW, THEN...
...KARIN IS A BOY!
TSK...
SWISH
!

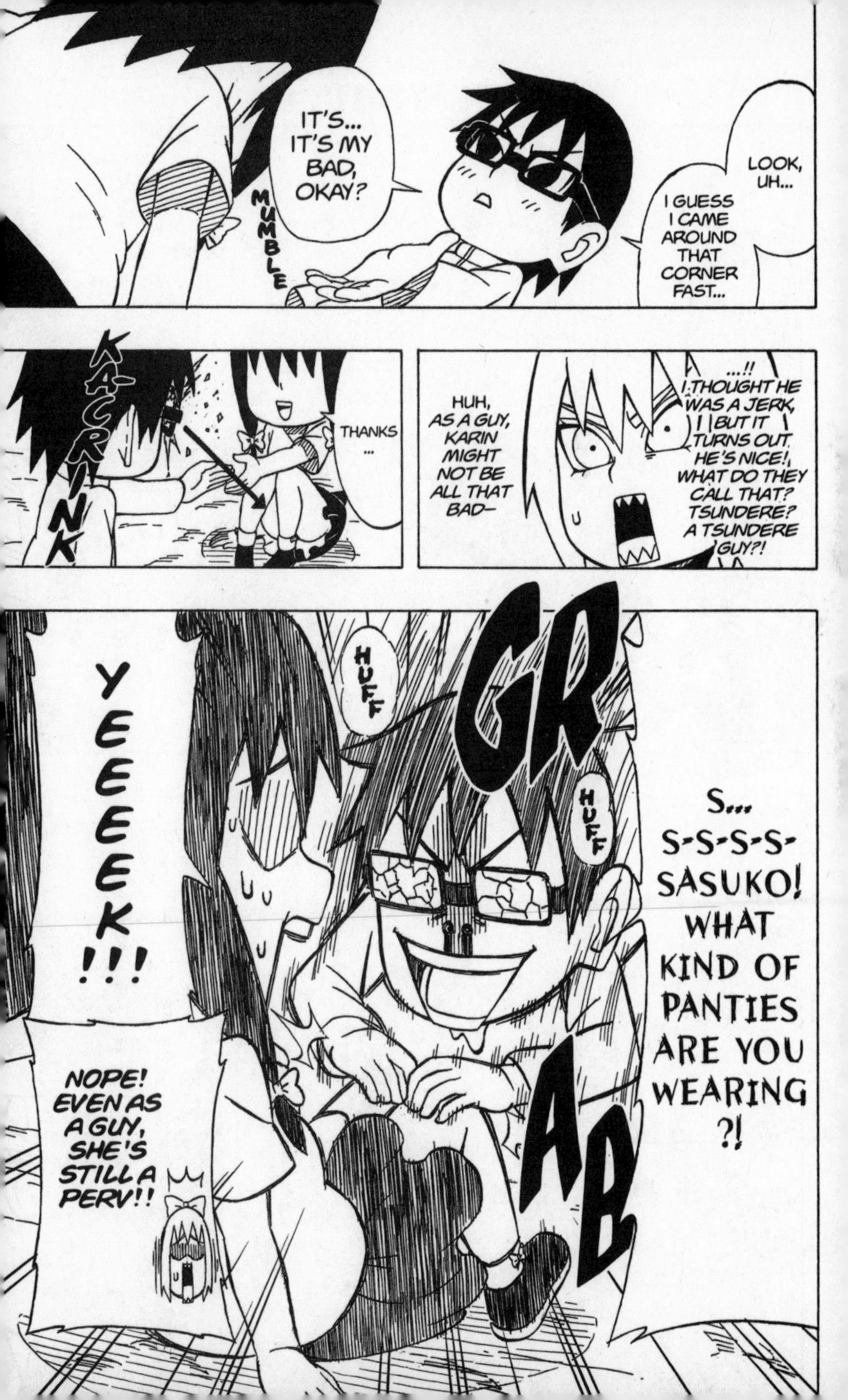
LOOK, UH...
I GUESS I CAME AROUND THAT CORNER FAST...
IT'S... IT'S MY BAD, OKAY?
MUMBLE
...!! I THOUGHT HE WAS A JERK, BUT IT TURNS OUT HE'S NICE! WHAT DO THEY CALL THAT? TSUNDERE? A TSUNDERE GUY?!
HUH, AS A GUY, KARIN MIGHT NOT BE ALL THAT BAD—
THANKS...
KA-CRINK
S... S-S-S-S-SASUKO! WHAT KIND OF PANTIES ARE YOU WEARING?!
GRAB
HUFF
HUFF
YEEEEEK!!!
NOPE! EVEN AS A GUY, SHE'S STILL A PERV!!

GIRL→BOY

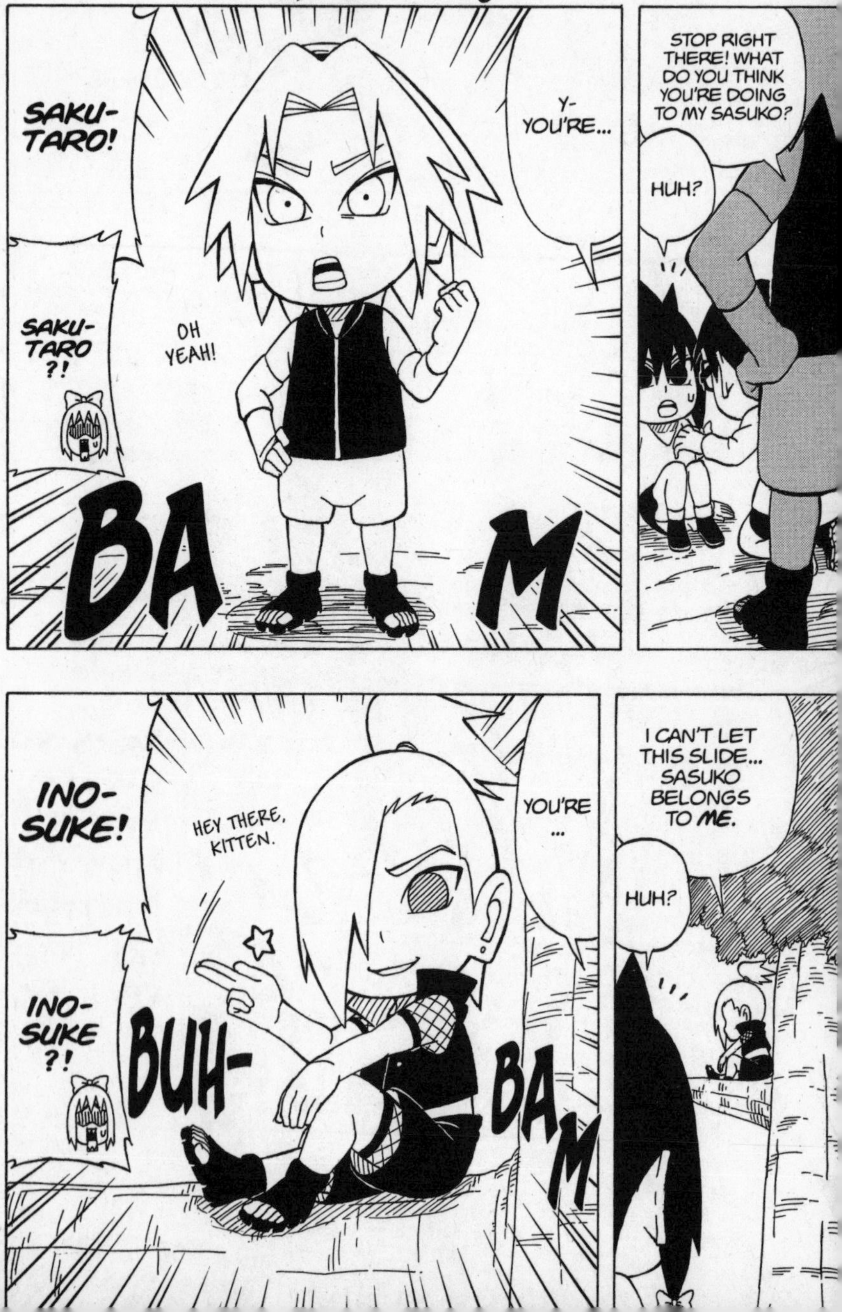
STOP RIGHT THERE! WHAT DO YOU THINK YOU'RE DOING TO MY SASUKO?
HUH?
Y- YOU'RE...
SAKU-TARO!
OH YEAH!
SAKU-TARO ?!
BAM
I CAN'T LET THIS SLIDE... SASUKO BELONGS TO *ME*.
HUH?
YOU'RE ...
INO-SUKE!
HEY THERE, KITTEN.
INO-SUKE ?!
BUH-BAM

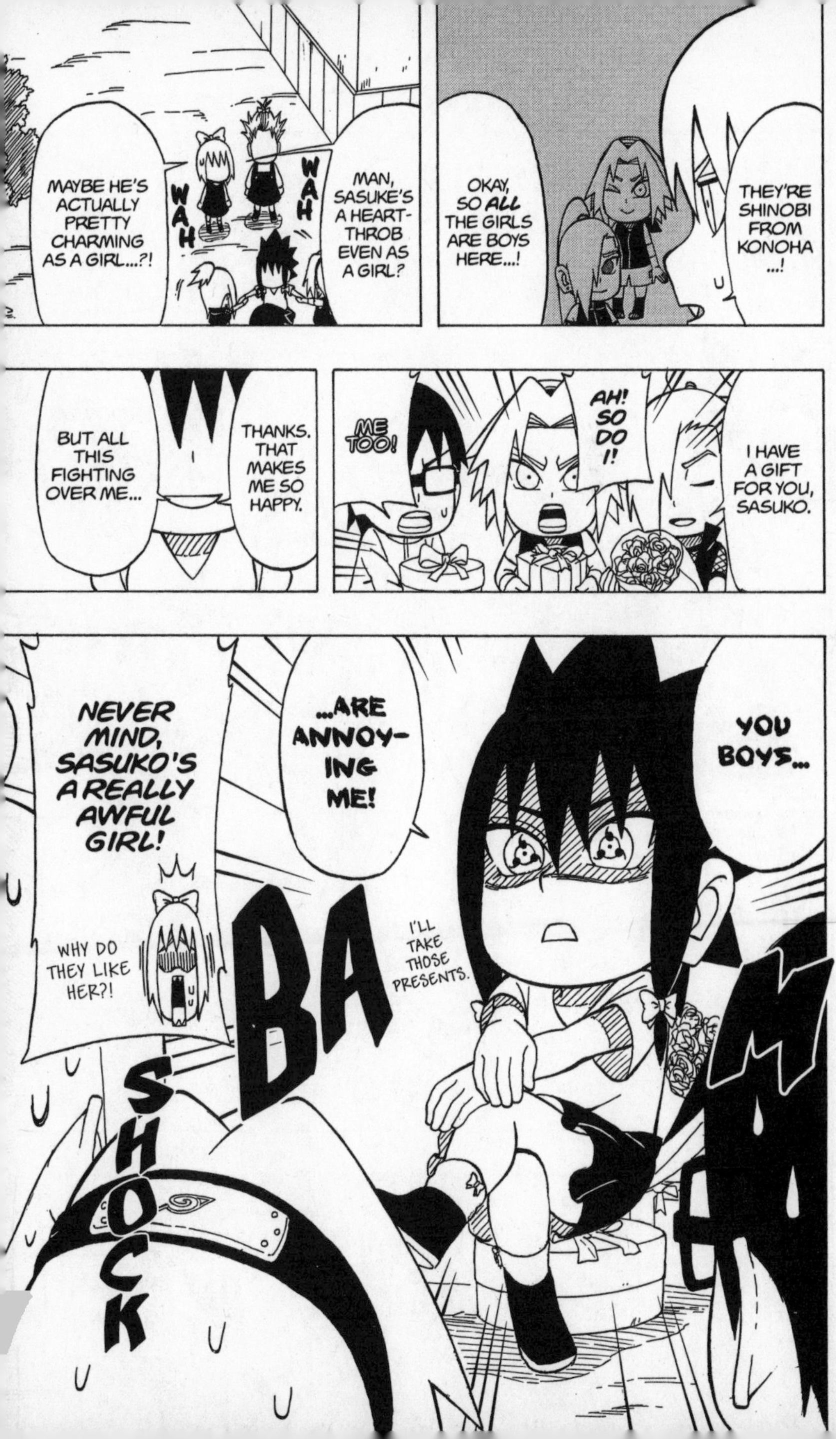
THEY'RE SHINOBI FROM KONOHA ...!
OKAY, SO ALL THE GIRLS ARE BOYS HERE...!
MAN, SASUKE'S A HEART-THROB EVEN AS A GIRL?
WAH WAH
MAYBE HE'S ACTUALLY PRETTY CHARMING AS A GIRL...?!
I HAVE A GIFT FOR YOU, SASUKO.
AH! SO DO I!
ME TOO!
THANKS. THAT MAKES ME SO HAPPY.
BUT ALL THIS FIGHTING OVER ME...
YOU BOYS...
...ARE ANNOY-ING ME!
I'LL TAKE THOSE PRESENTS.
BAM
NEVER MIND, SASUKO'S A REALLY AWFUL GIRL!
WHY DO THEY LIKE HER?!
SHOCK

BOY→GIRL

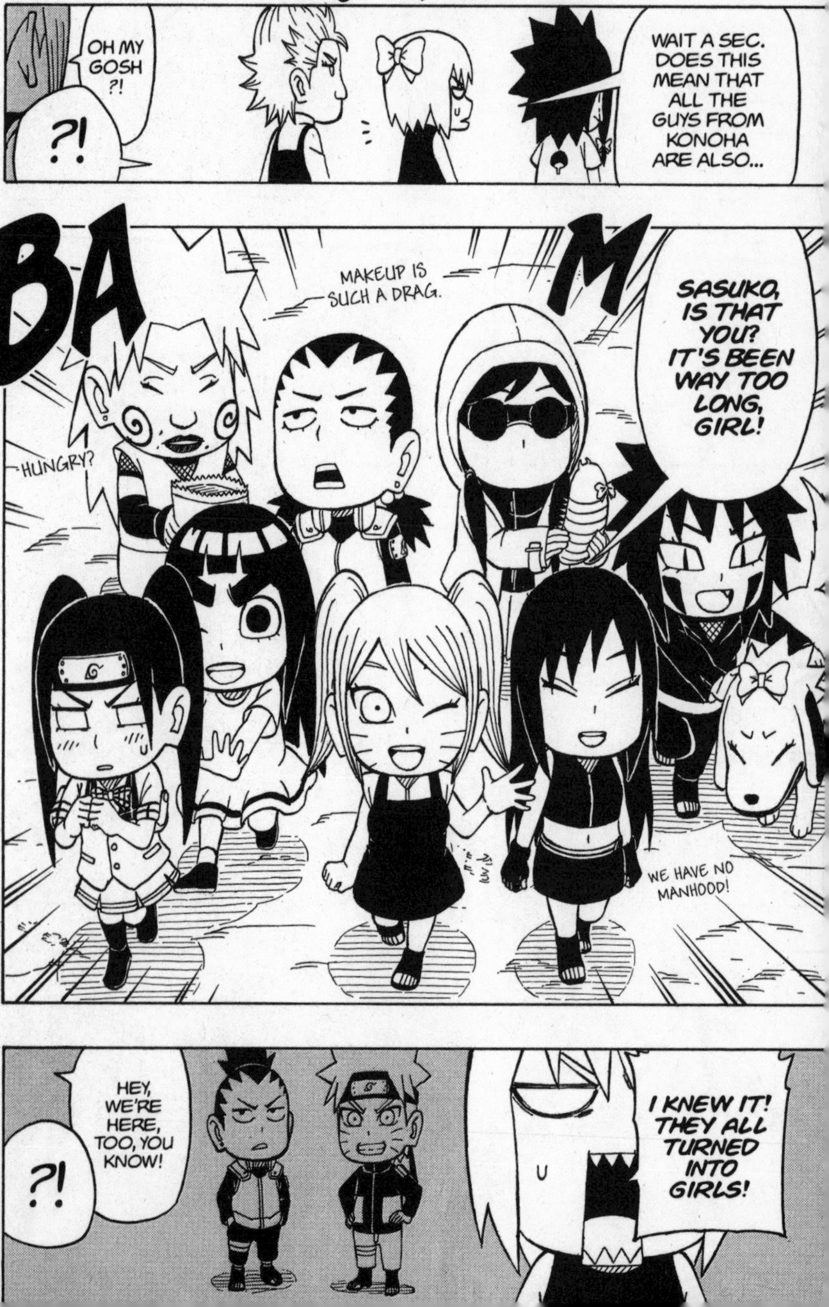
WAIT A SEC. DOES THIS MEAN THAT ALL THE GUYS FROM KONOHA ARE ALSO...
OH MY GOSH ?!
?!
BAM
SASUKO, IS THAT YOU? IT'S BEEN WAY TOO LONG, GIRL!
MAKEUP IS SUCH A DRAG.
HUNGRY?
WE HAVE NO MANHOOD!
I KNEW IT! THEY ALL TURNED INTO GIRLS!
HEY, WE'RE HERE, TOO, YOU KNOW!
?!

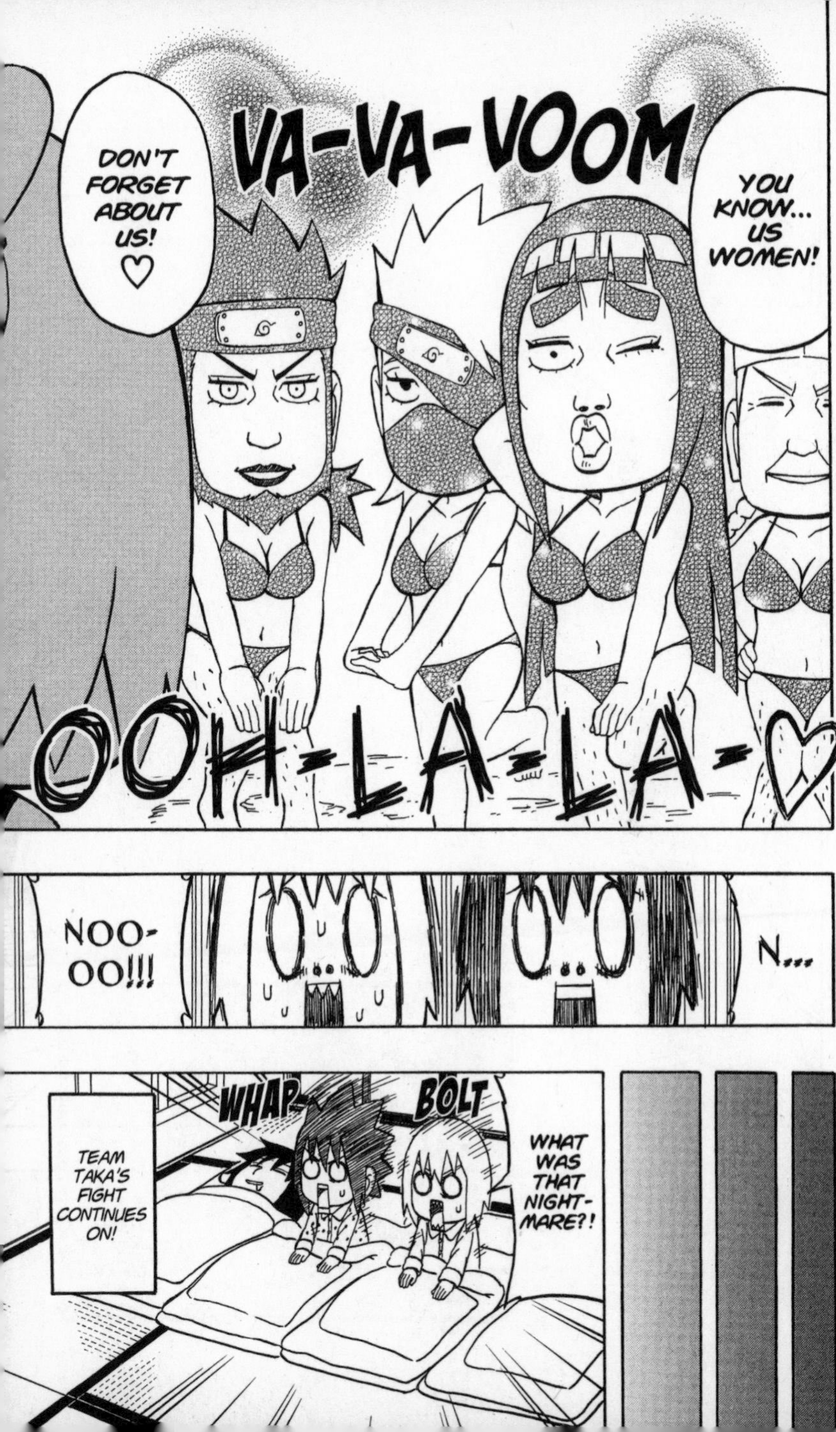
VA-VA-VOOM
YOU KNOW... US WOMEN!
DON'T FORGET ABOUT US! ♡
OOH-LA-LA-♡
N...
NOO-OO!!!
BOLT
WHAT WAS THAT NIGHT-MARE?!
WHAP
TEAM TAKA'S FIGHT CONTINUES ON!

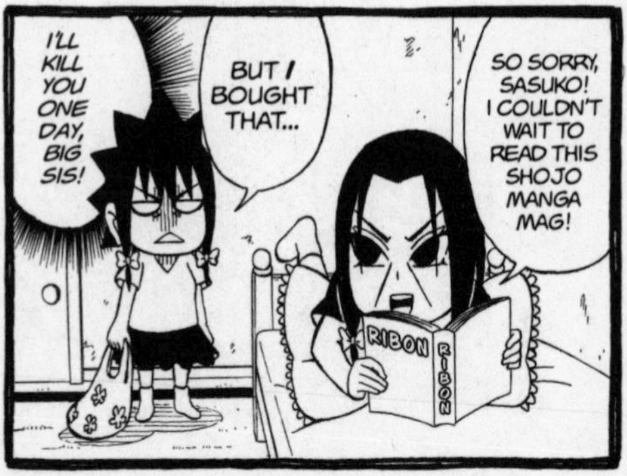
SO SORRY, SASUKO! I COULDN'T WAIT TO READ THIS SHOJO MANGA MAG!
RIBON
RIBON
BUT I BOUGHT THAT...
I'LL KILL YOU ONE DAY, BIG SIS!

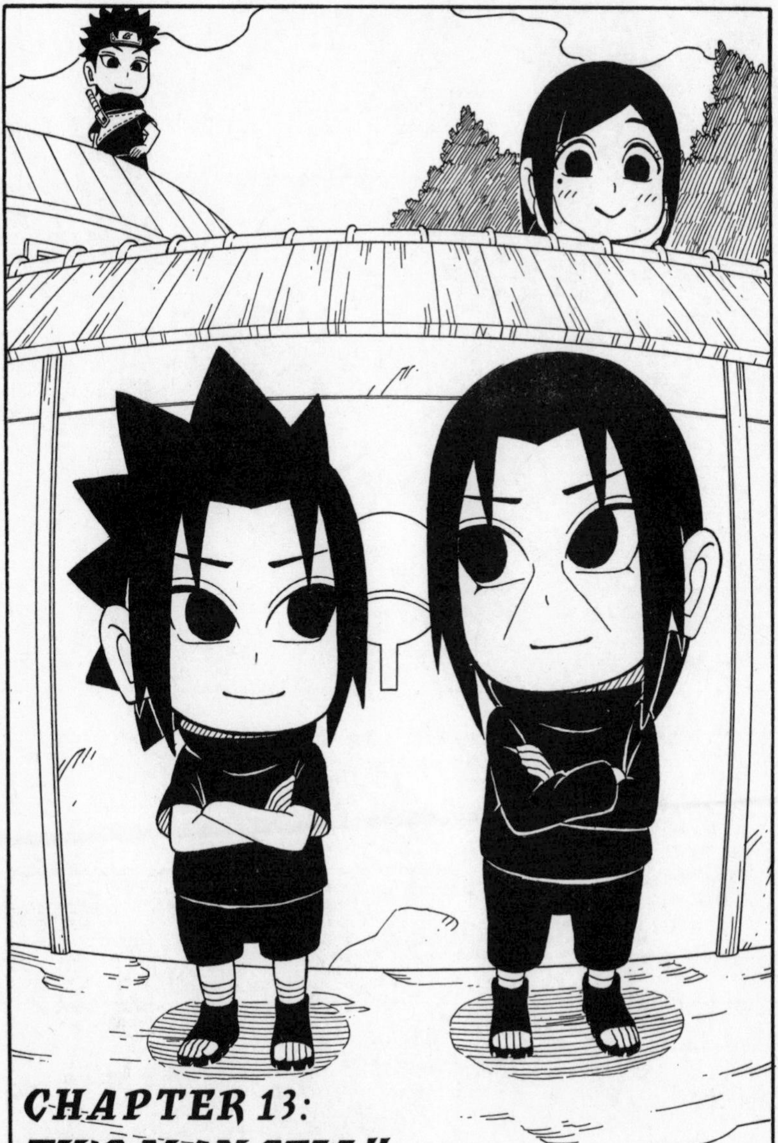
CHAPTER 13:
TWO-MAN CELL!!

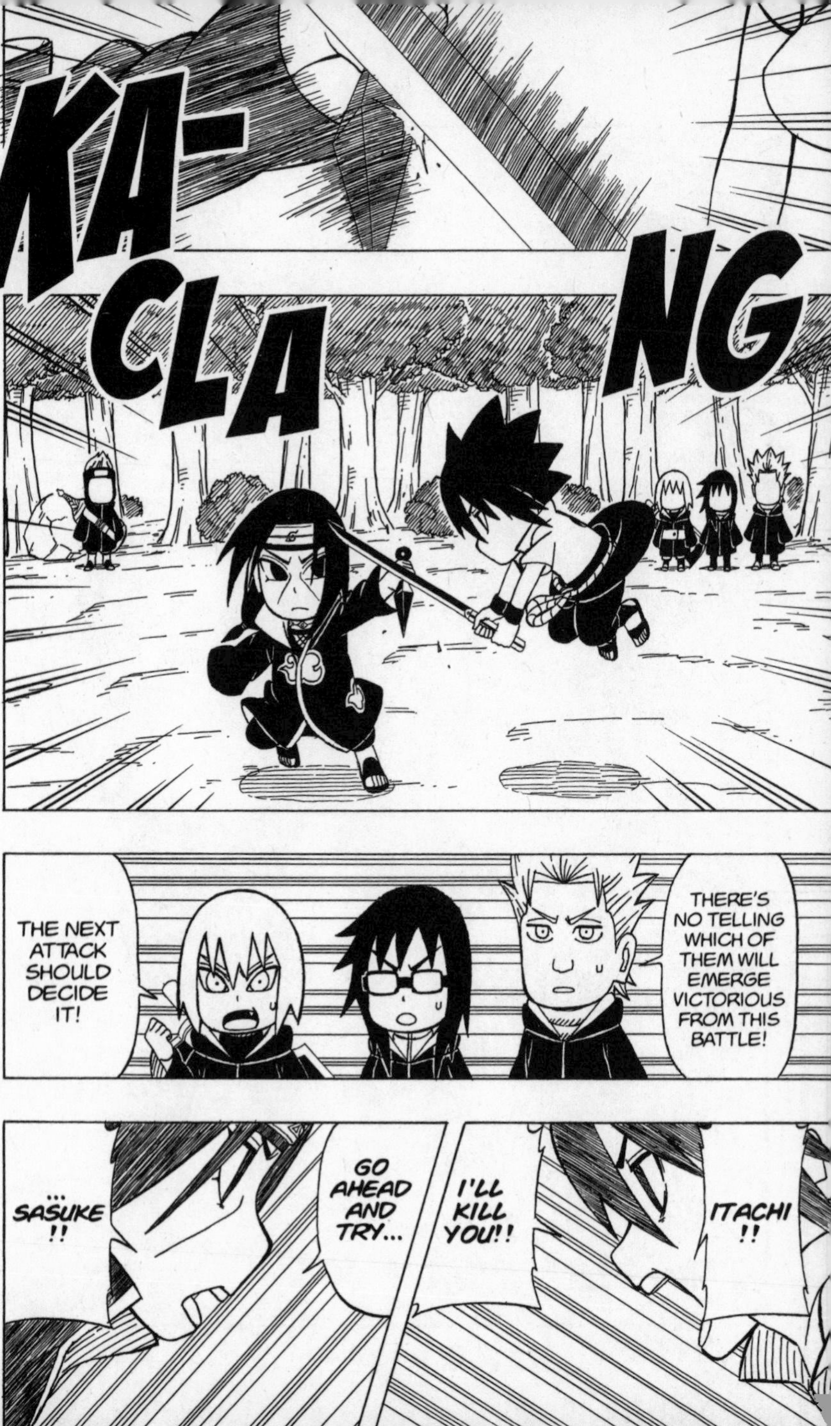
KA-CLA-NG
THERE'S NO TELLING WHICH OF THEM WILL EMERGE VICTORIOUS FROM THIS BATTLE!
THE NEXT ATTACK SHOULD DECIDE IT!
ITACHI !!
I'LL KILL YOU!!
GO AHEAD AND TRY...
... SASUKE !!

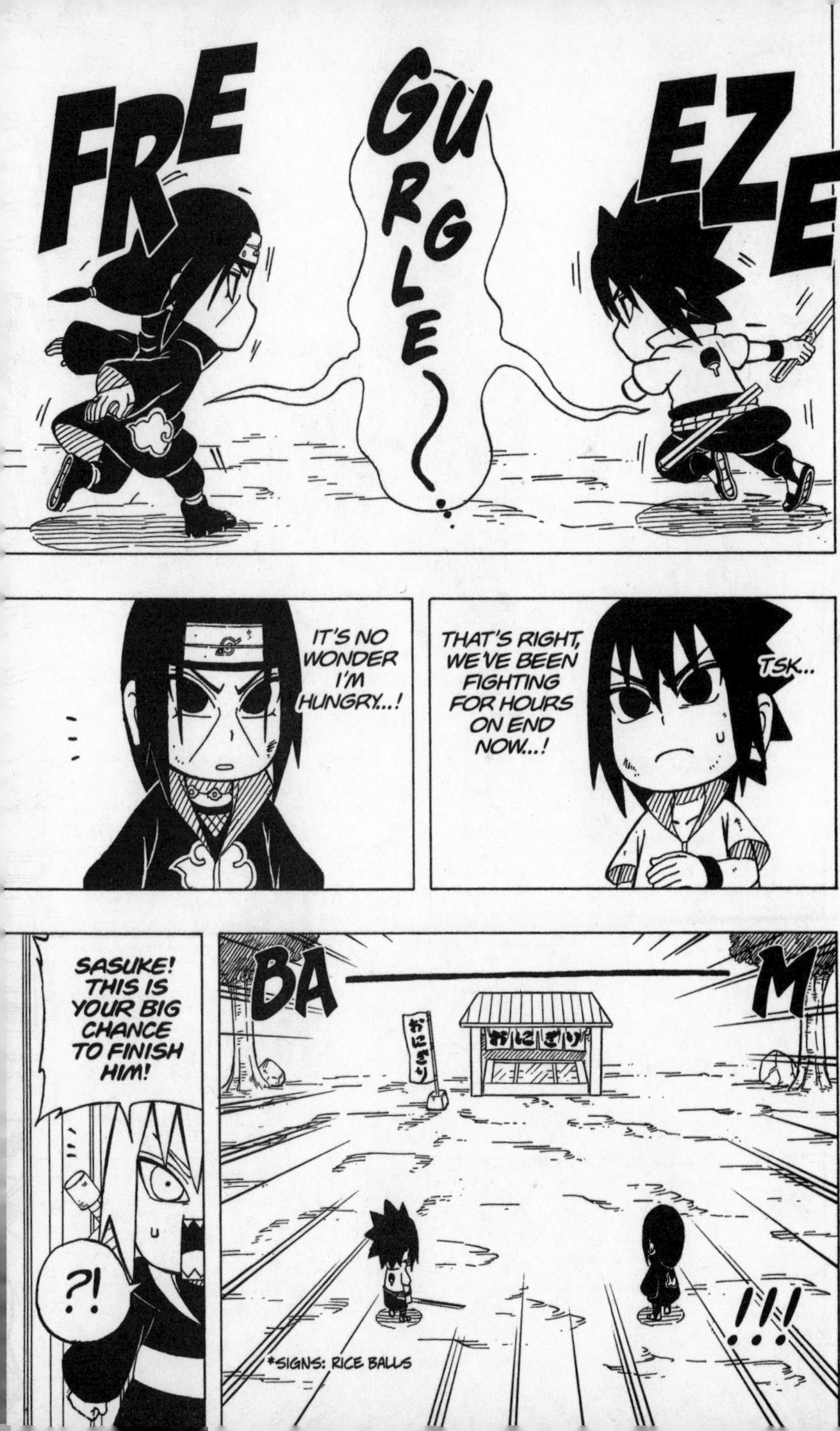

FRE
GURGLE
EZE
IT'S NO WONDER I'M HUNGRY...!
THAT'S RIGHT, WE'VE BEEN FIGHTING FOR HOURS ON END NOW...!
TSK...
SASUKE! THIS IS YOUR BIG CHANCE TO FINISH HIM!
?!
BA———M
おにぎり
おにぎり
!!!
*SIGNS: RICE BALLS

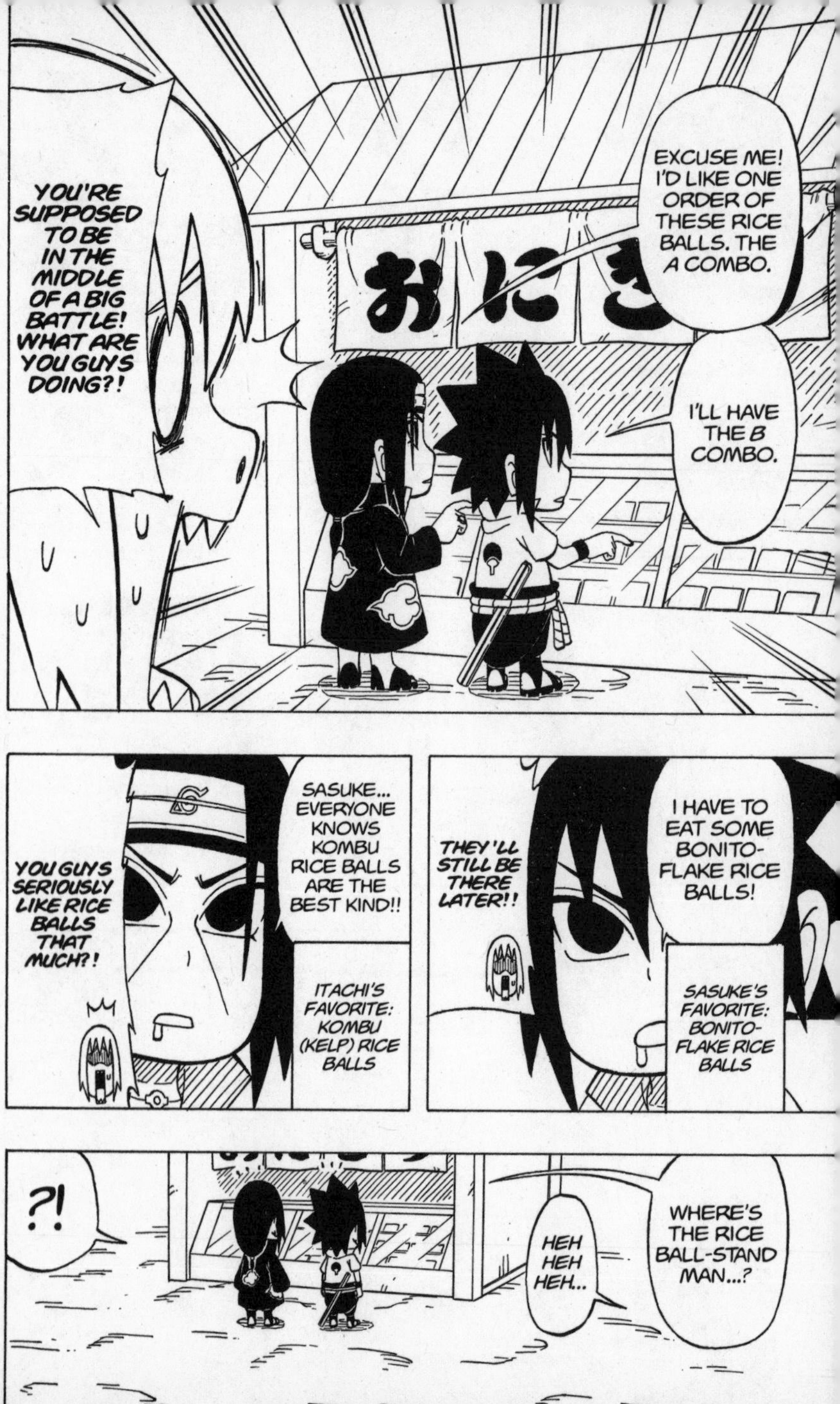
EXCUSE ME! I'D LIKE ONE ORDER OF THESE RICE BALLS. THE A COMBO.
おにぎ
I'LL HAVE THE B COMBO.
YOU'RE SUPPOSED TO BE IN THE MIDDLE OF A BIG BATTLE! WHAT ARE YOU GUYS DOING?!
I HAVE TO EAT SOME BONITO-FLAKE RICE BALLS!
SASUKE'S FAVORITE: BONITO-FLAKE RICE BALLS
THEY'LL STILL BE THERE LATER!!
SASUKE... EVERYONE KNOWS KOMBU RICE BALLS ARE THE BEST KIND!!
ITACHI'S FAVORITE: KOMBU (KELP) RICE BALLS
YOU GUYS SERIOUSLY LIKE RICE BALLS THAT MUCH?!
WHERE'S THE RICE BALL-STAND MAN...?
HEH HEH HEH...
?!

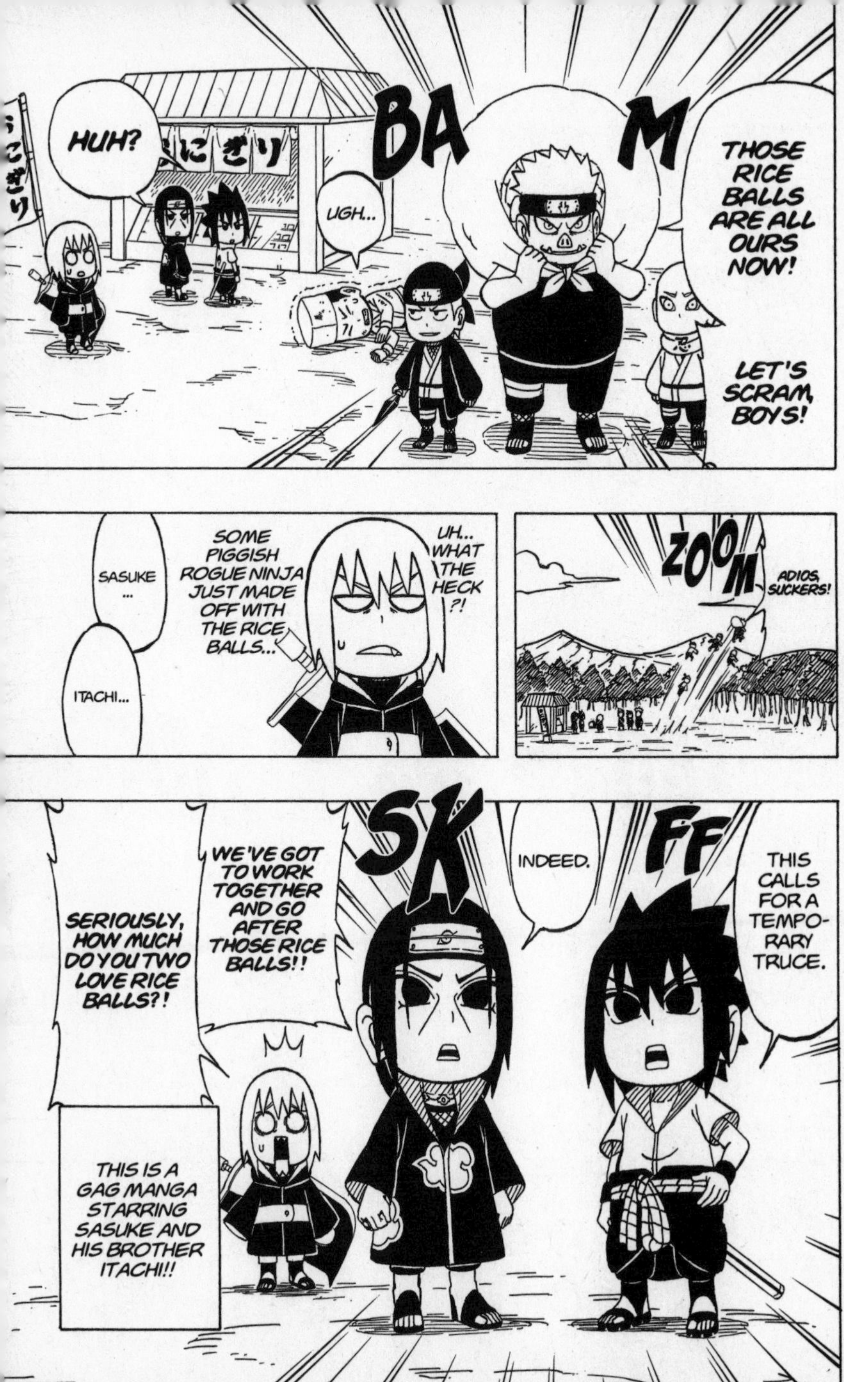
THOSE RICE BALLS ARE ALL OURS NOW!
LET'S SCRAM, BOYS!
BAM
UGH...
HUH?
ZOOM
ADIOS, SUCKERS!
UH... WHAT THE HECK?!
SOME PIGGISH ROGUE NINJA JUST MADE OFF WITH THE RICE BALLS...
SASUKE...
ITACHI...
SKFF
THIS CALLS FOR A TEMPORARY TRUCE.
INDEED.
WE'VE GOT TO WORK TOGETHER AND GO AFTER THOSE RICE BALLS!!
SERIOUSLY, HOW MUCH DO YOU TWO LOVE RICE BALLS?!
THIS IS A GAG MANGA STARRING SASUKE AND HIS BROTHER ITACHI!!

COMBINATION!

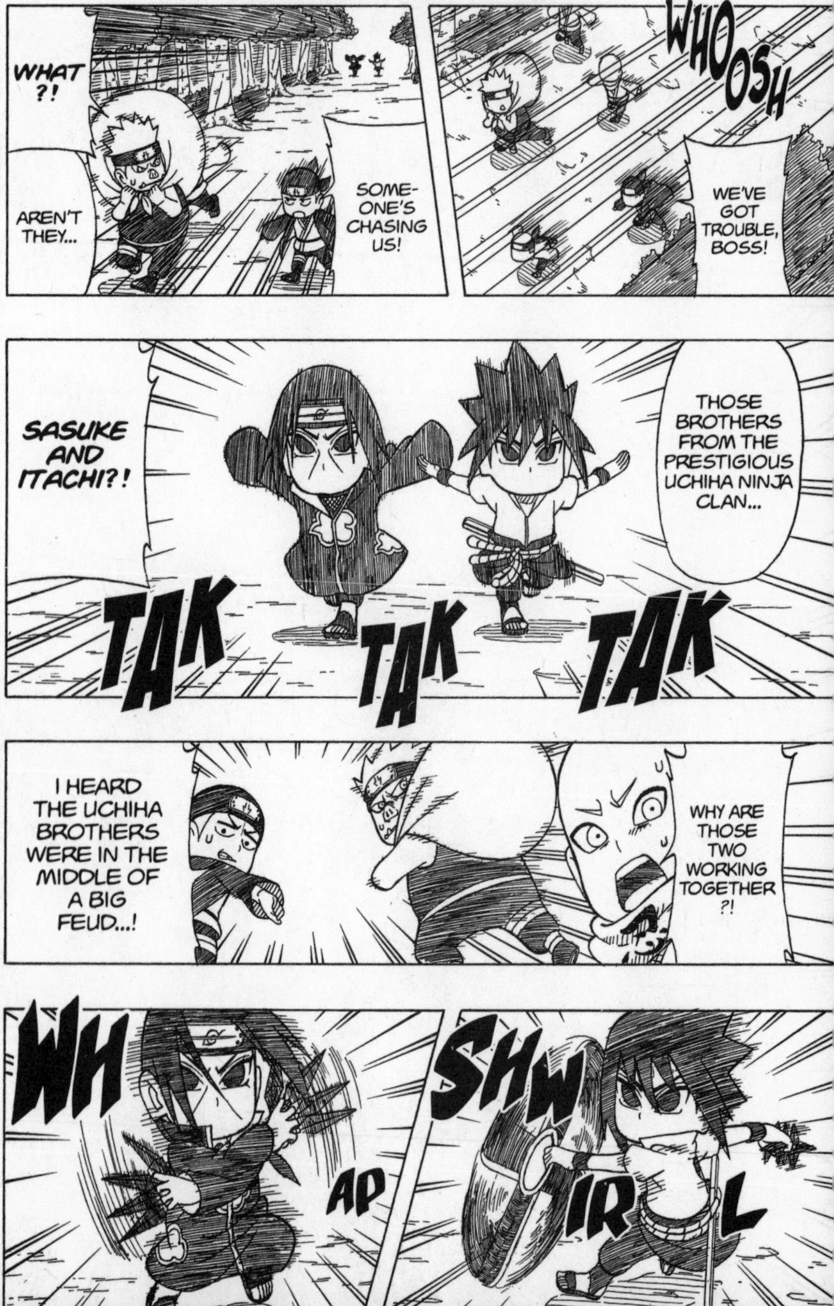
WHOOSH
WE'VE GOT TROUBLE, BOSS!
SOME-ONE'S CHASING US!
WHAT ?!
AREN'T THEY...
THOSE BROTHERS FROM THE PRESTIGIOUS UCHIHA NINJA CLAN...
SASUKE AND ITACHI?!
TAK TAK TAK
WHY ARE THOSE TWO WORKING TOGETHER ?!
I HEARD THE UCHIHA BROTHERS WERE IN THE MIDDLE OF A BIG FEUD...!
SHWIRL
WHAP

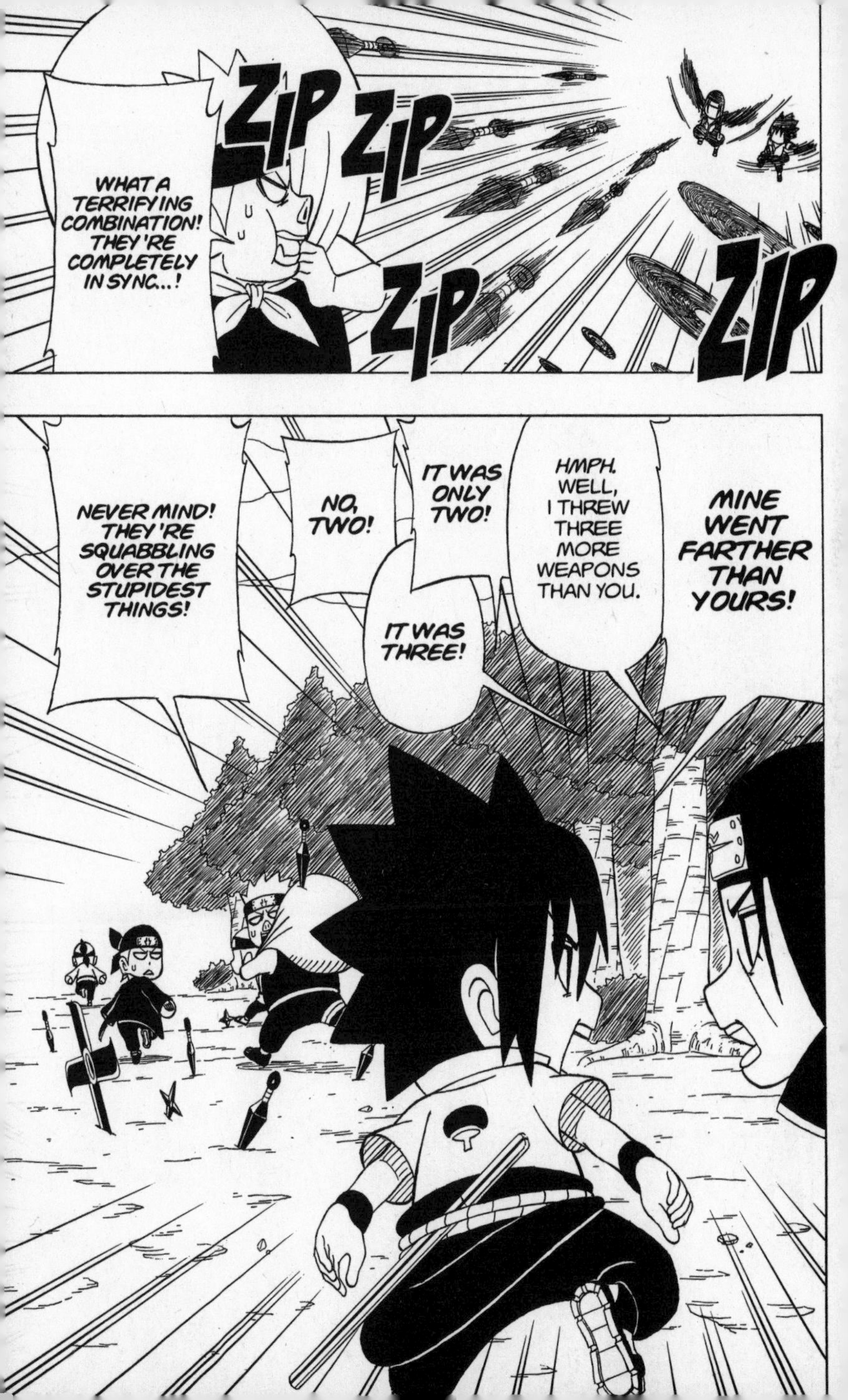
ZIP
ZIP ZIP
ZIP
WHAT A TERRIFYING COMBINATION! THEY'RE COMPLETELY IN SYNC...!
MINE WENT FARTHER THAN YOURS!
HMPH. WELL, I THREW THREE MORE WEAPONS THAN YOU.
IT WAS ONLY TWO!
IT WAS THREE!
NO, TWO!
NEVER MIND! THEY'RE SQUABBLING OVER THE STUPIDEST THINGS!

FIRE STYLE

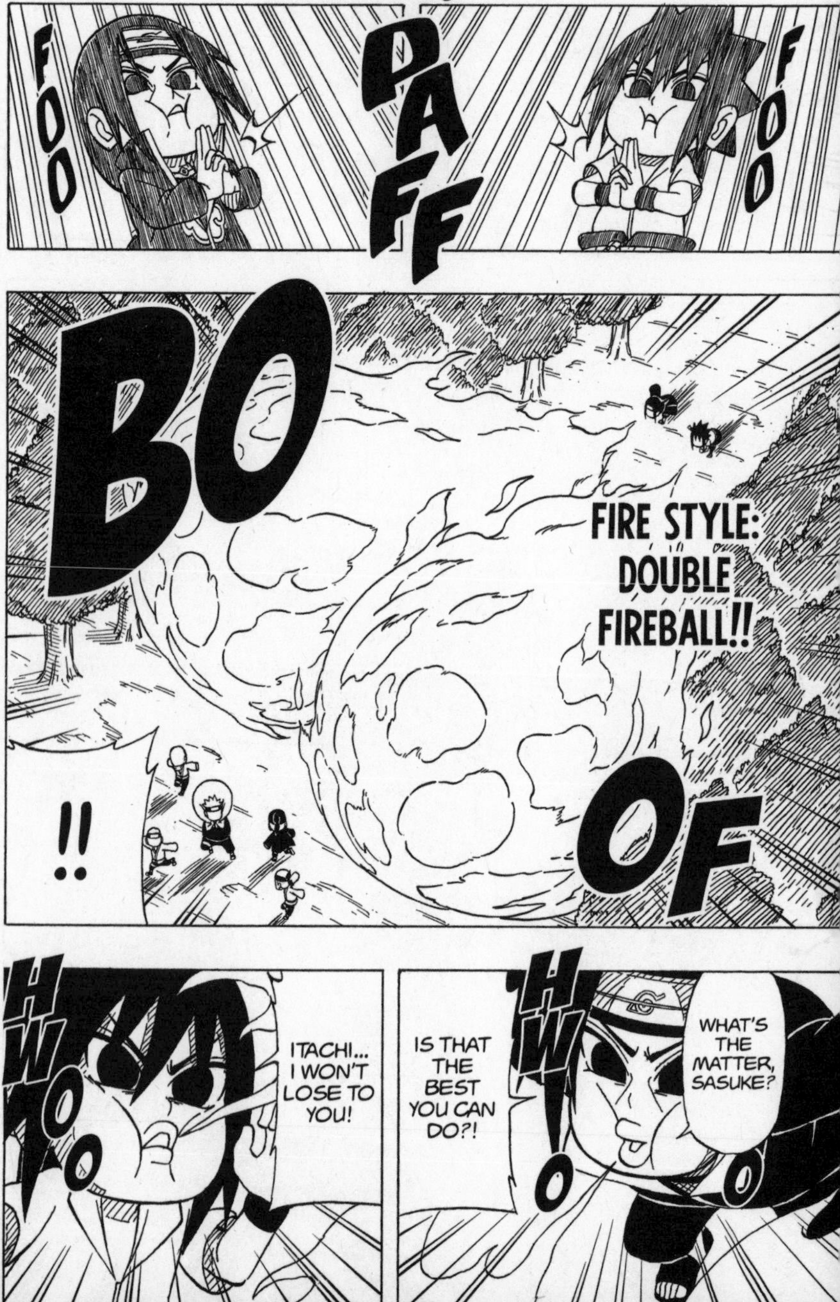
FOO
DAFF
FOO
FIRE STYLE: DOUBLE FIREBALL!!
BO
OF
!!
WHAT'S THE MATTER, SASUKE?
IS THAT THE BEST YOU CAN DO?!
HWO
ITACHI... I WON'T LOSE TO YOU!
HWOOO

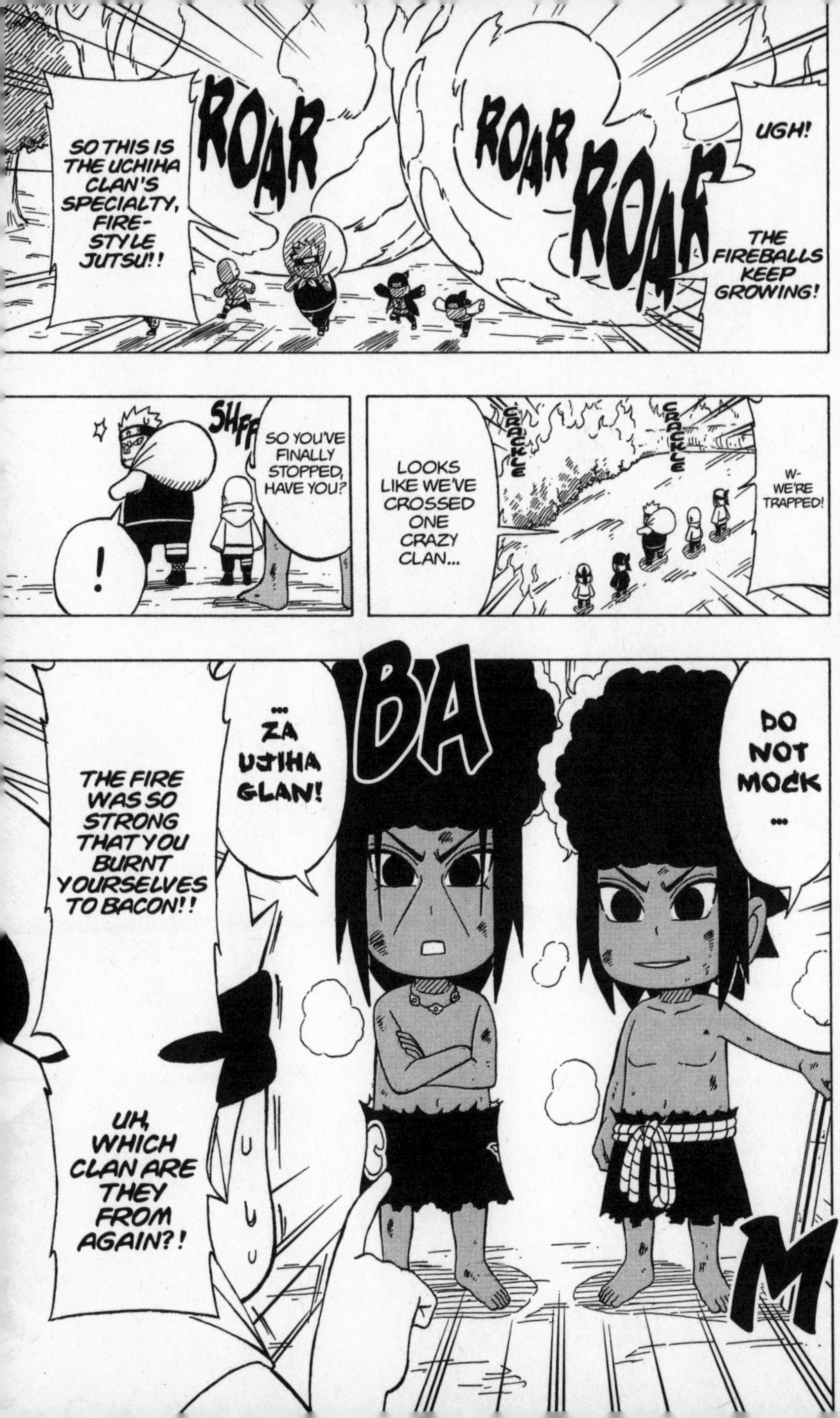
UGH!
THE FIREBALLS KEEP GROWING!
ROAR ROAR
ROAR
SO THIS IS THE UCHIHA CLAN'S SPECIALTY, FIRE-STYLE JUTSU!!
CRACKLE
CRACKLE
W-WE'RE TRAPPED!
LOOKS LIKE WE'VE CROSSED ONE CRAZY CLAN...
SO YOU'VE FINALLY STOPPED, HAVE YOU?
SHFF
!
DO NOT MOCK ...
M
BA
... ZA UJIHA GLAN!
THE FIRE WAS SO STRONG THAT YOU BURNT YOURSELVES TO BACON!!
UH, WHICH CLAN ARE THEY FROM AGAIN?!

TEAMWORK

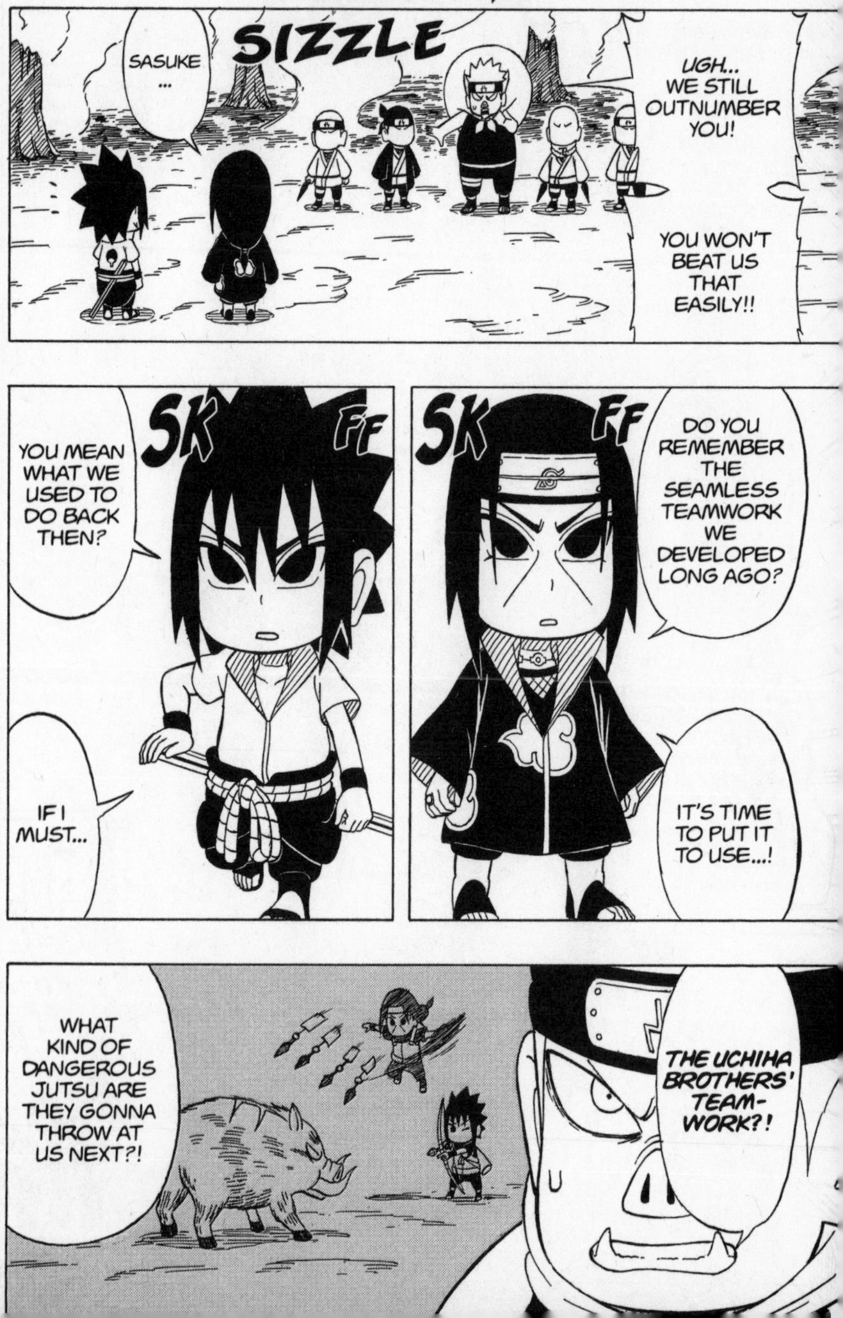
SIZZLE
UGH... WE STILL OUTNUMBER YOU!
YOU WON'T BEAT US THAT EASILY!!
SASUKE ...
SKFF
DO YOU REMEMBER THE SEAMLESS TEAMWORK WE DEVELOPED LONG AGO?
IT'S TIME TO PUT IT TO USE...!
SKFF
YOU MEAN WHAT WE USED TO DO BACK THEN?
IF I MUST...
THE UCHIHA BROTHERS' TEAM-WORK?!
WHAT KIND OF DANGEROUS JUTSU ARE THEY GONNA THROW AT US NEXT?!

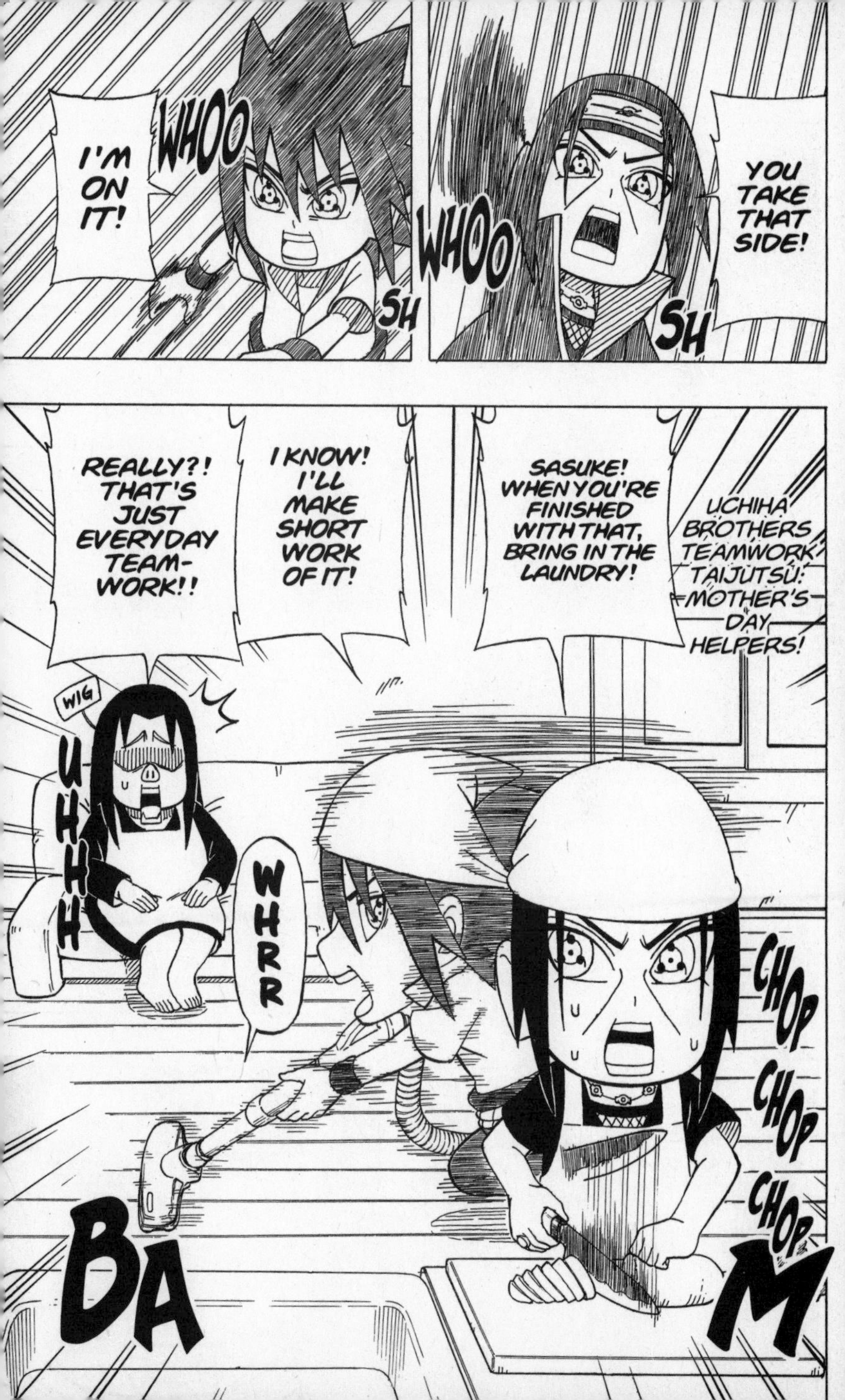
YOU TAKE THAT SIDE!
WHOO
SH
I'M ON IT!
WHOO
SH
UCHIHA BROTHERS TEAMWORK TAIJUTSU: MOTHER'S DAY HELPERS!
SASUKE! WHEN YOU'RE FINISHED WITH THAT, BRING IN THE LAUNDRY!
I KNOW! I'LL MAKE SHORT WORK OF IT!
REALLY?! THAT'S JUST EVERYDAY TEAM-WORK!!
CHOP
CHOP
CHOP
M
WHRR
WIG
UHHH
BA

COMBINED SKILLS!

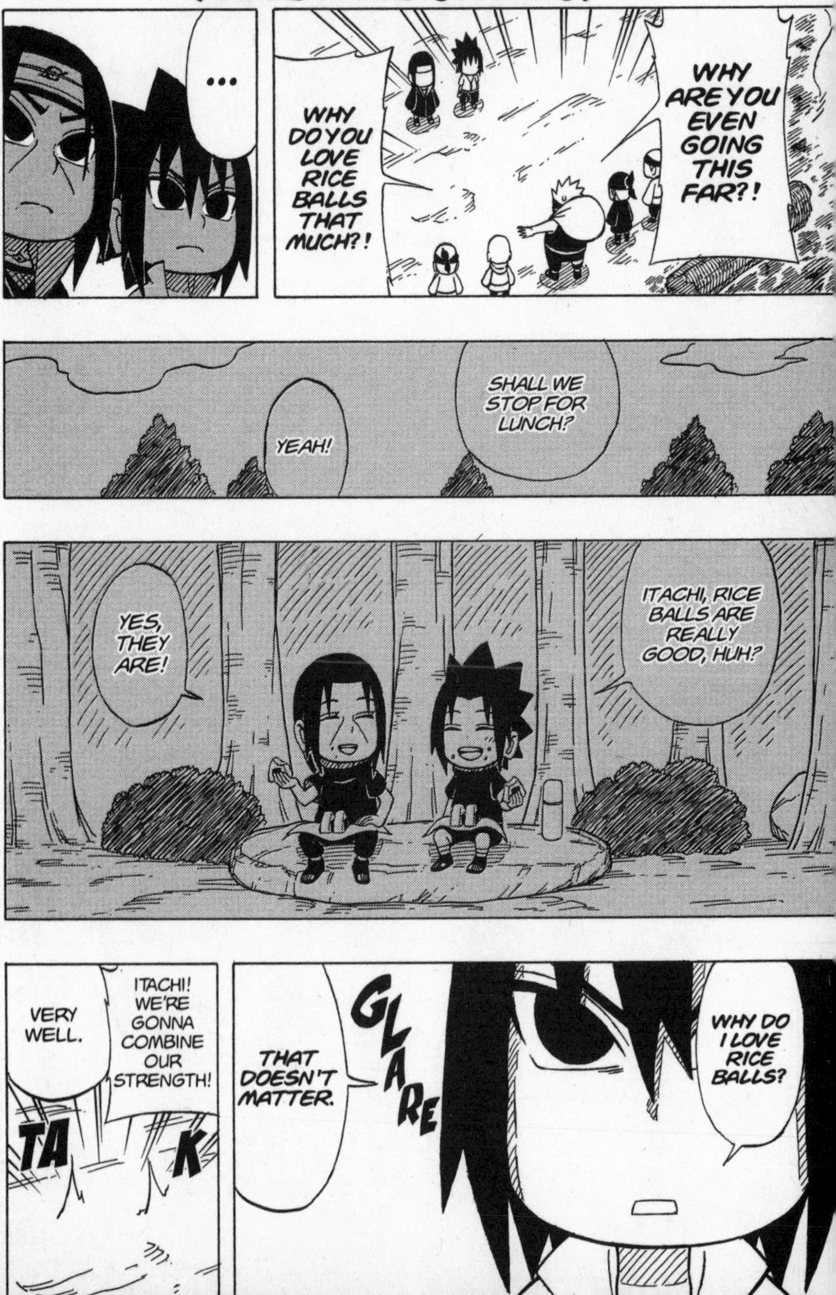
WHY ARE YOU EVEN GOING THIS FAR?!
WHY DO YOU LOVE RICE BALLS THAT MUCH?!
...
SHALL WE STOP FOR LUNCH?
YEAH!
ITACHI, RICE BALLS ARE REALLY GOOD, HUH?
YES, THEY ARE!
WHY DO I LOVE RICE BALLS?
GLARE
THAT DOESN'T MATTER.
ITACHI! WE'RE GONNA COMBINE OUR STRENGTH!
VERY WELL.
TAK

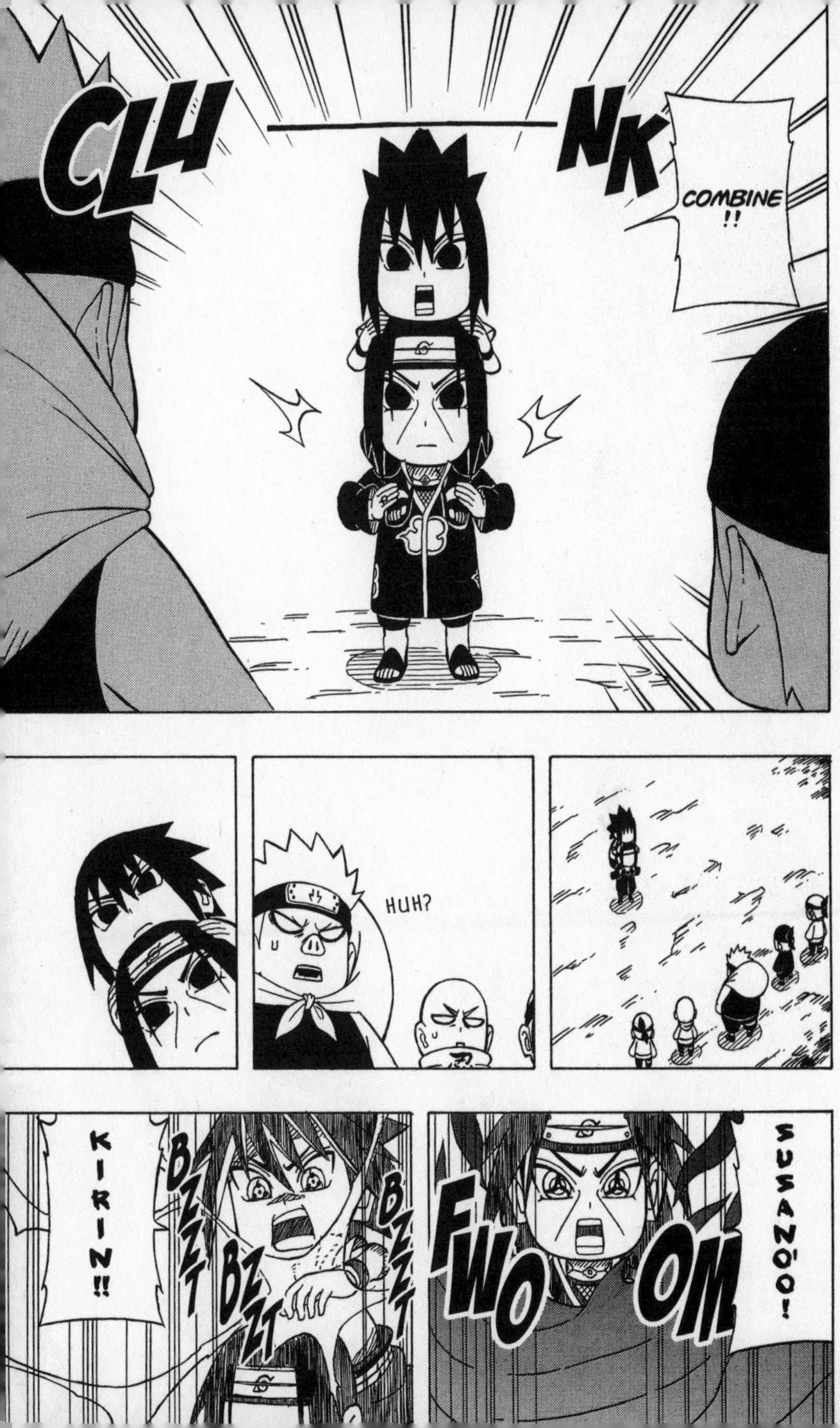

COMBINE !!
CLU—NK
HUH?
SUSANOO!
FWOOM
BZZZT BZZZT BZZZT
KIRIN!!

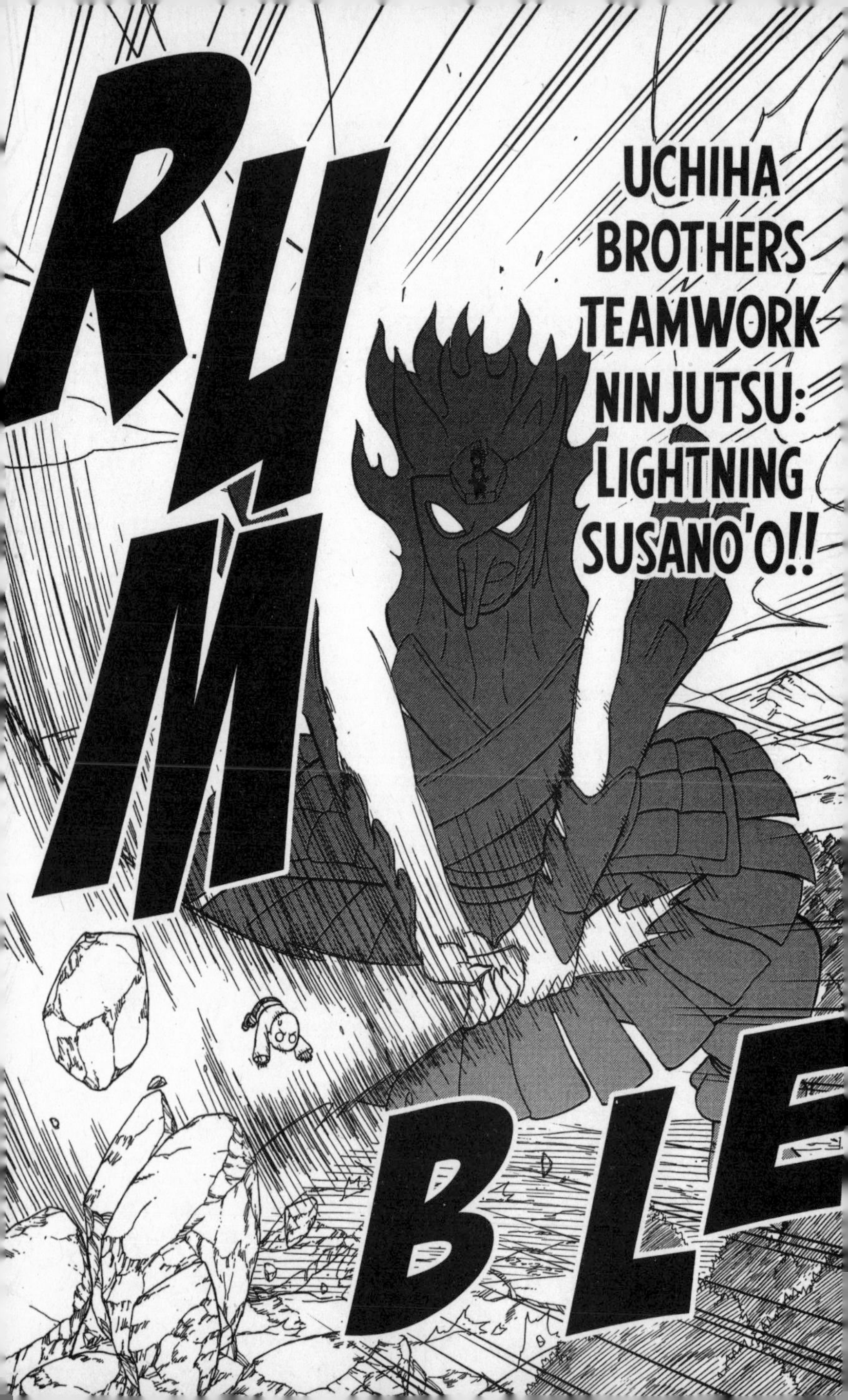
UCHIHA BROTHERS TEAMWORK NINJUTSU: LIGHTNING SUSANO'O!!
RUMBLE

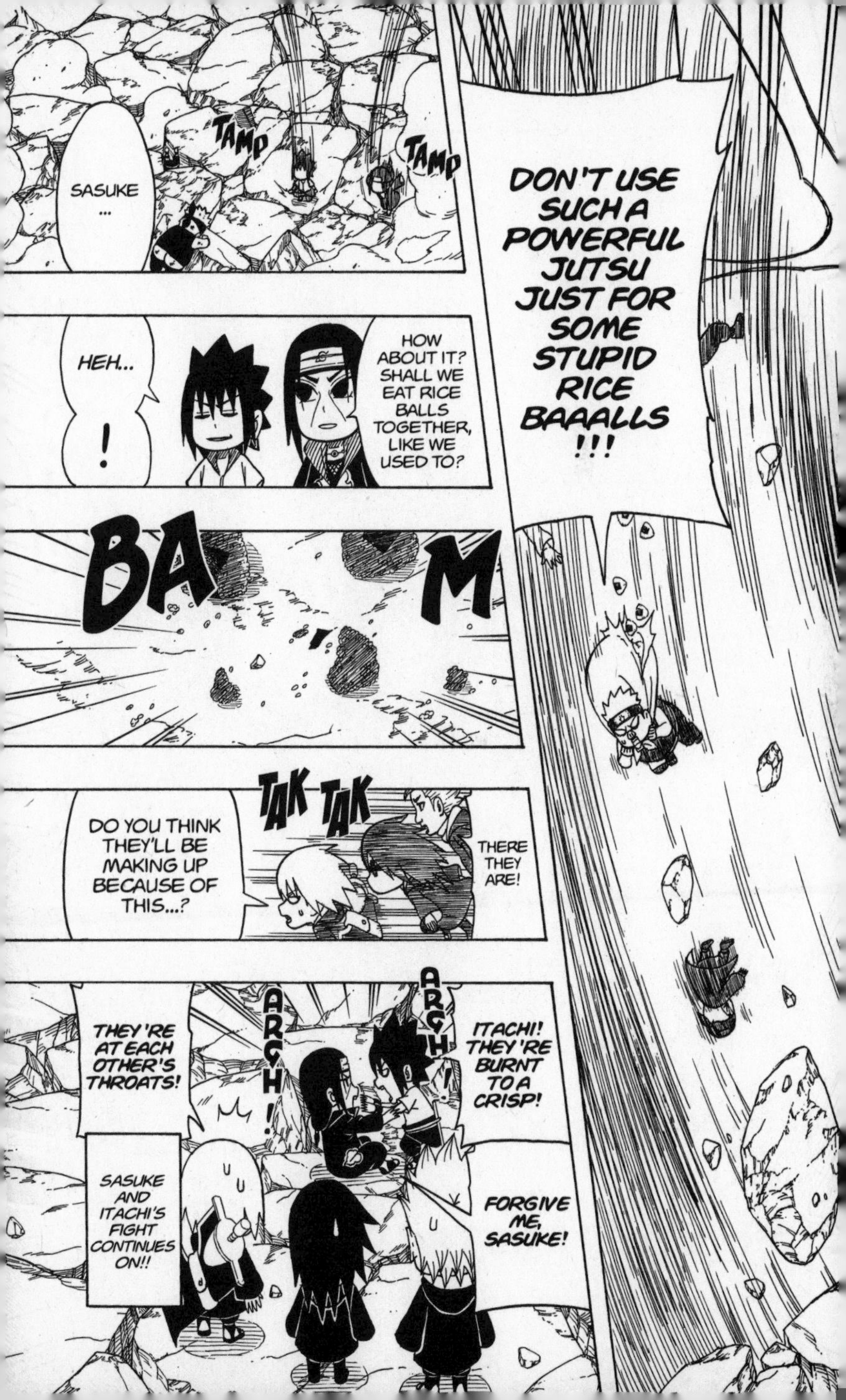
DON'T USE SUCH A POWERFUL JUTSU JUST FOR SOME STUPID RICE BAAALLS!!!
TAMP
TAMP
SASUKE...
HOW ABOUT IT? SHALL WE EAT RICE BALLS TOGETHER, LIKE WE USED TO?
HEH...
!
BAM
THERE THEY ARE!
TAK TAK
DO YOU THINK THEY'LL BE MAKING UP BECAUSE OF THIS...?
ITACHI! THEY'RE BURNT TO A CRISP!
ARGH!
ARGH!
THEY'RE AT EACH OTHER'S THROATS!
FORGIVE ME, SASUKE!
SASUKE AND ITACHI'S FIGHT CONTINUES ON!!

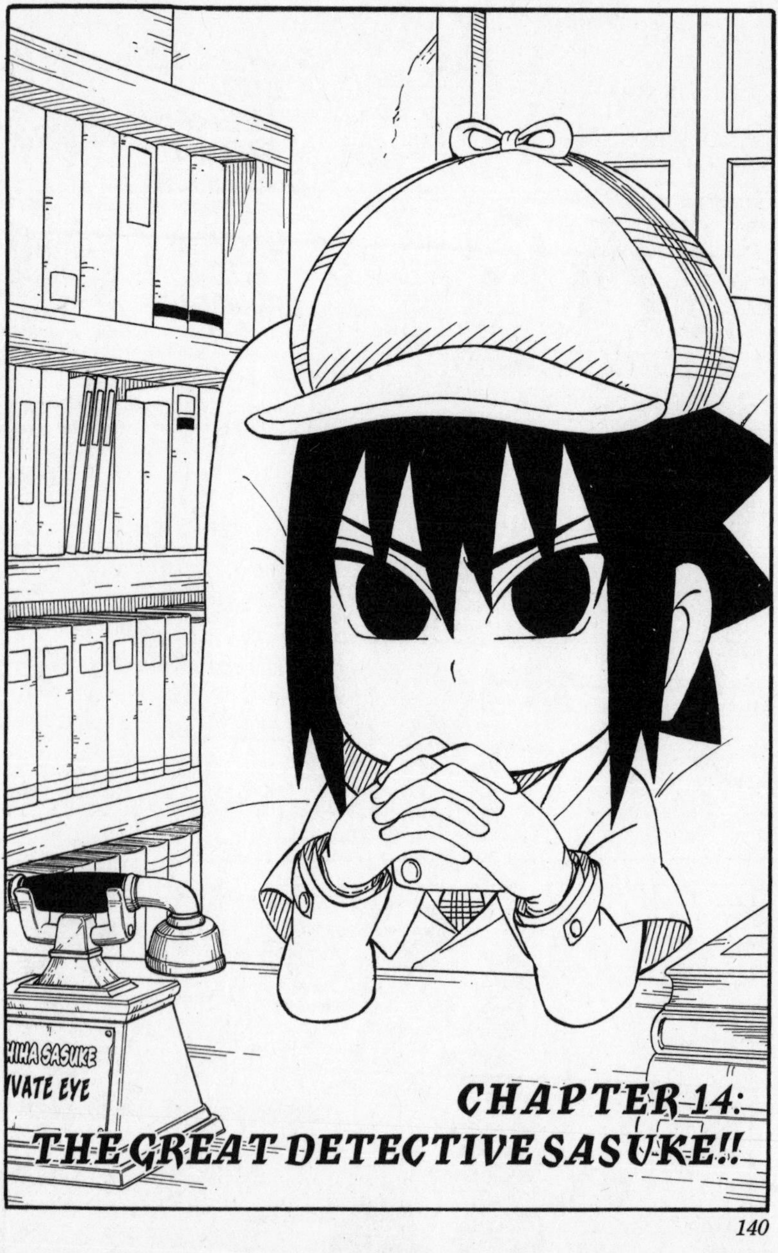
HIHA SASUKE
VATE EYE
CHAPTER 14:
THE GREAT DETECTIVE SASUKE!!

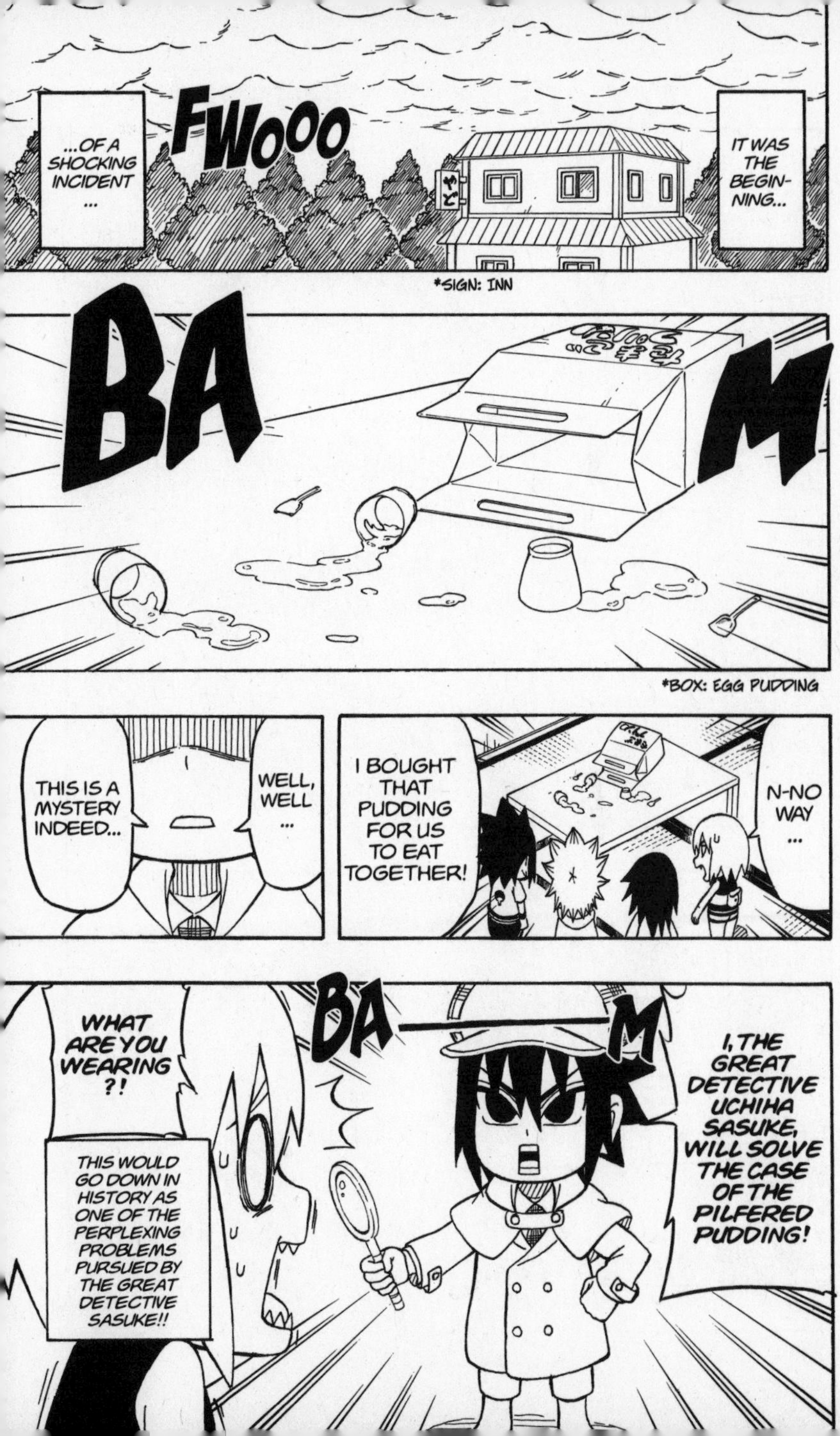
IT WAS THE BEGIN-NING...
FWOOO
...OF A SHOCKING INCIDENT...
*SIGN: INN
BAM
*BOX: EGG PUDDING
N-NO WAY...
I BOUGHT THAT PUDDING FOR US TO EAT TOGETHER!
WELL, WELL...
THIS IS A MYSTERY INDEED...
I, THE GREAT DETECTIVE UCHIHA SASUKE, WILL SOLVE THE CASE OF THE PILFERED PUDDING!
BA—M
WHAT ARE YOU WEARING?!
THIS WOULD GO DOWN IN HISTORY AS ONE OF THE PERPLEXING PROBLEMS PURSUED BY THE GREAT DETECTIVE SASUKE!!

THE GREAT DETECTIVE!

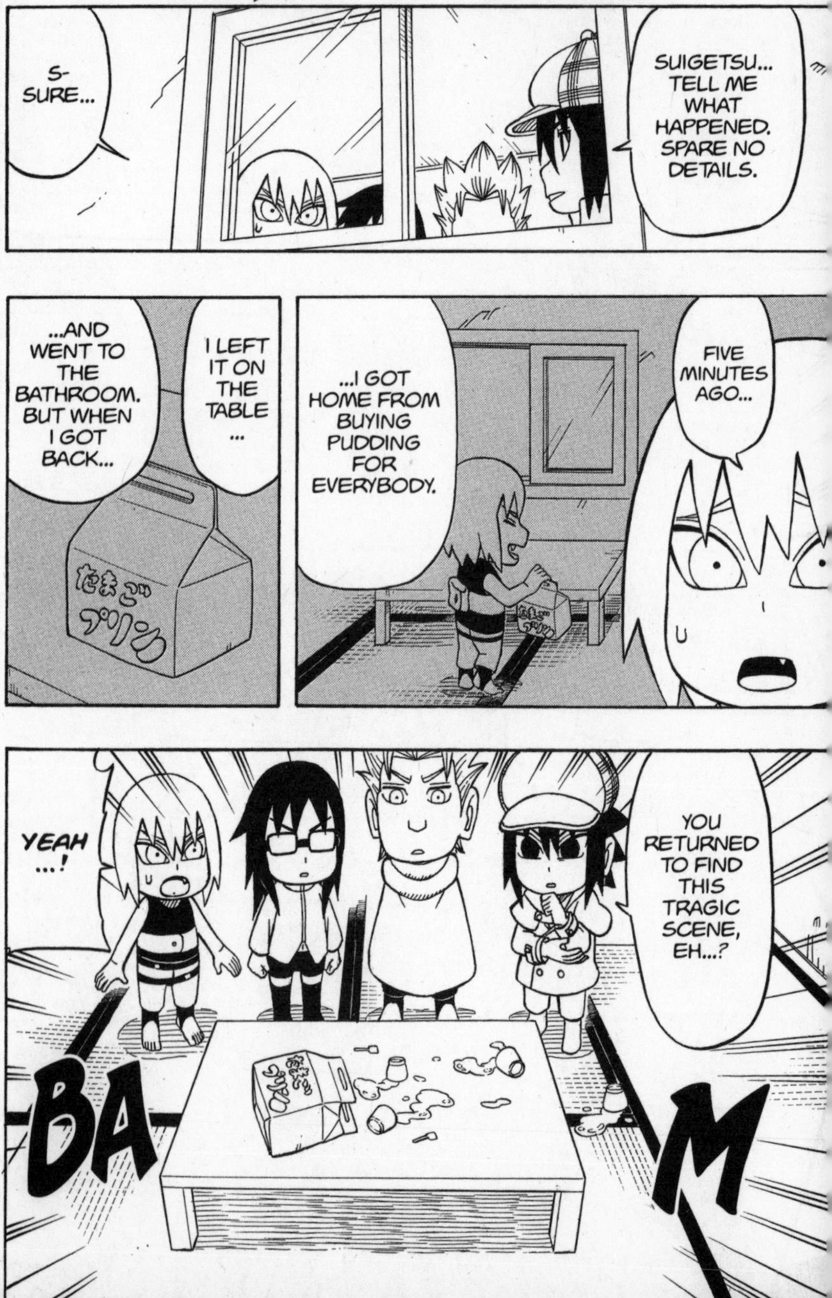
SUIGETSU... TELL ME WHAT HAPPENED. SPARE NO DETAILS.
S-SURE...
FIVE MINUTES AGO...
...I GOT HOME FROM BUYING PUDDING FOR EVERYBODY.
I LEFT IT ON THE TABLE...
...AND WENT TO THE BATHROOM. BUT WHEN I GOT BACK...
たまごプリン
YOU RETURNED TO FIND THIS TRAGIC SCENE, EH...?
YEAH...!
BAM

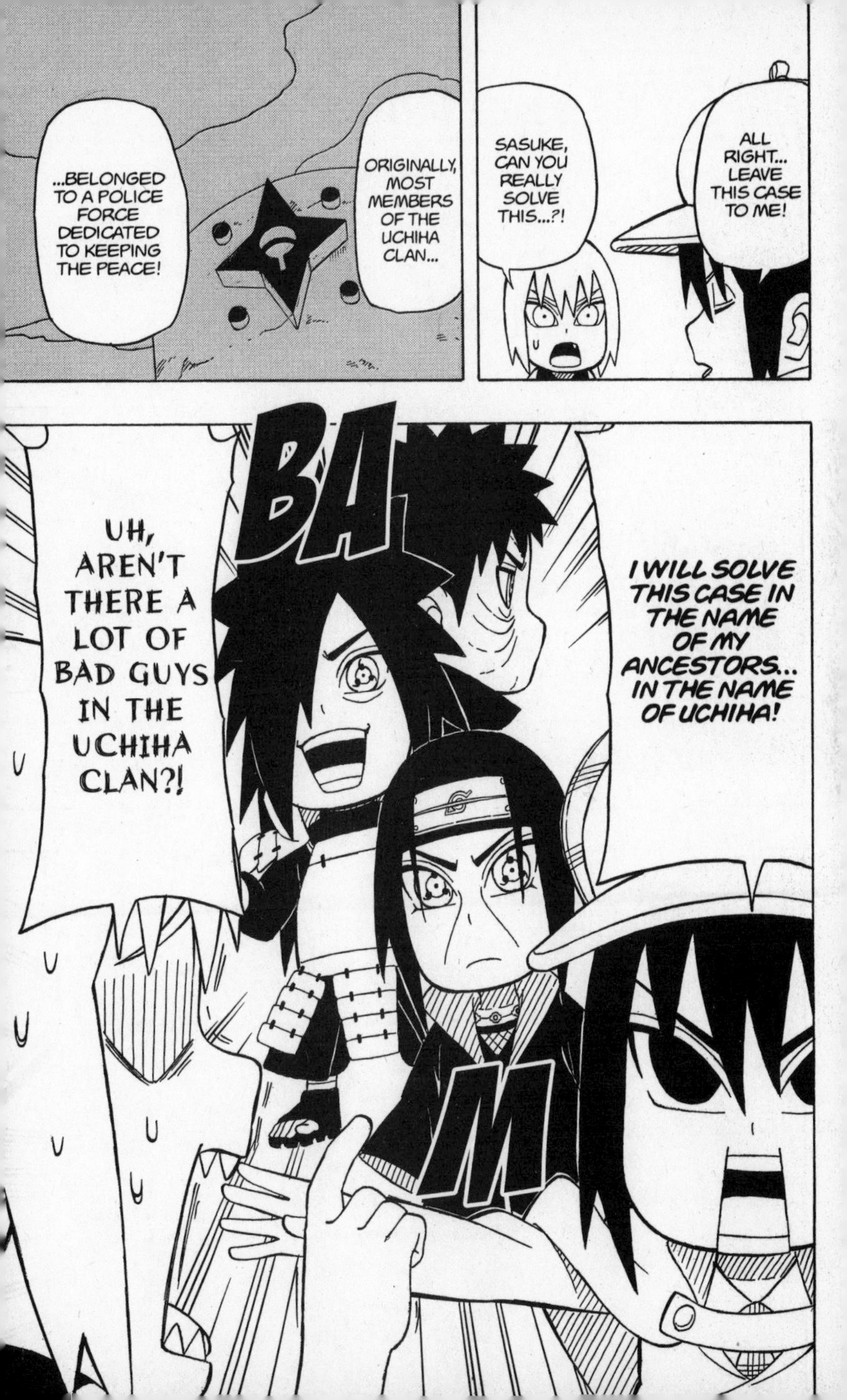
ALL RIGHT... LEAVE THIS CASE TO ME!
SASUKE, CAN YOU REALLY SOLVE THIS...?!
ORIGINALLY, MOST MEMBERS OF THE UCHIHA CLAN...
...BELONGED TO A POLICE FORCE DEDICATED TO KEEPING THE PEACE!
I WILL SOLVE THIS CASE IN THE NAME OF MY ANCESTORS... IN THE NAME OF UCHIHA!
BAM
UH, AREN'T THERE A LOT OF BAD GUYS IN THE UCHIHA CLAN?!

THE SUSPECTS

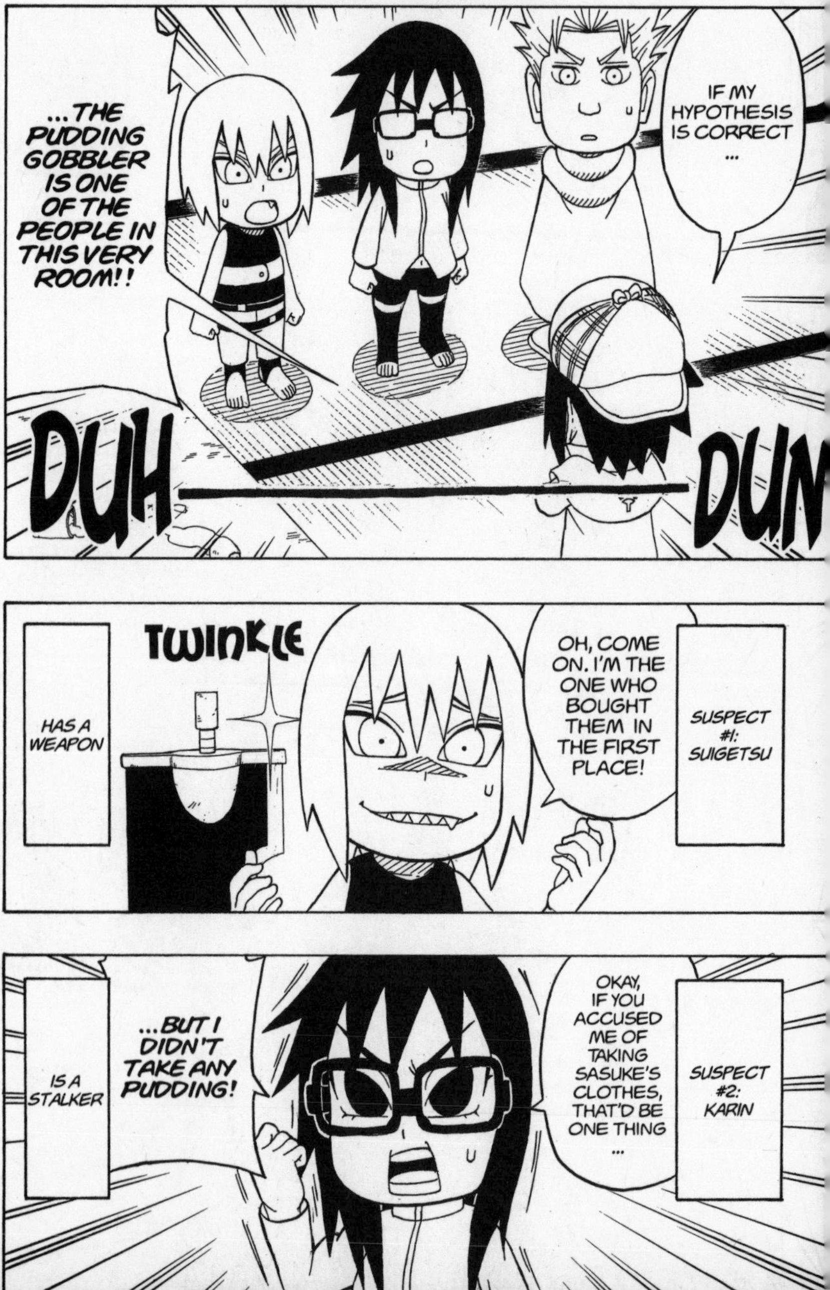
IF MY HYPOTHESIS IS CORRECT ...
...THE PUDDING GOBBLER IS ONE OF THE PEOPLE IN THIS VERY ROOM!!
DUH—DUN
SUSPECT #1: SUIGETSU
OH, COME ON. I'M THE ONE WHO BOUGHT THEM IN THE FIRST PLACE!
TWINKLE
HAS A WEAPON
SUSPECT #2: KARIN
OKAY, IF YOU ACCUSED ME OF TAKING SASUKE'S CLOTHES, THAT'D BE ONE THING ...
...BUT I DIDN'T TAKE ANY PUDDING!
IS A STALKER

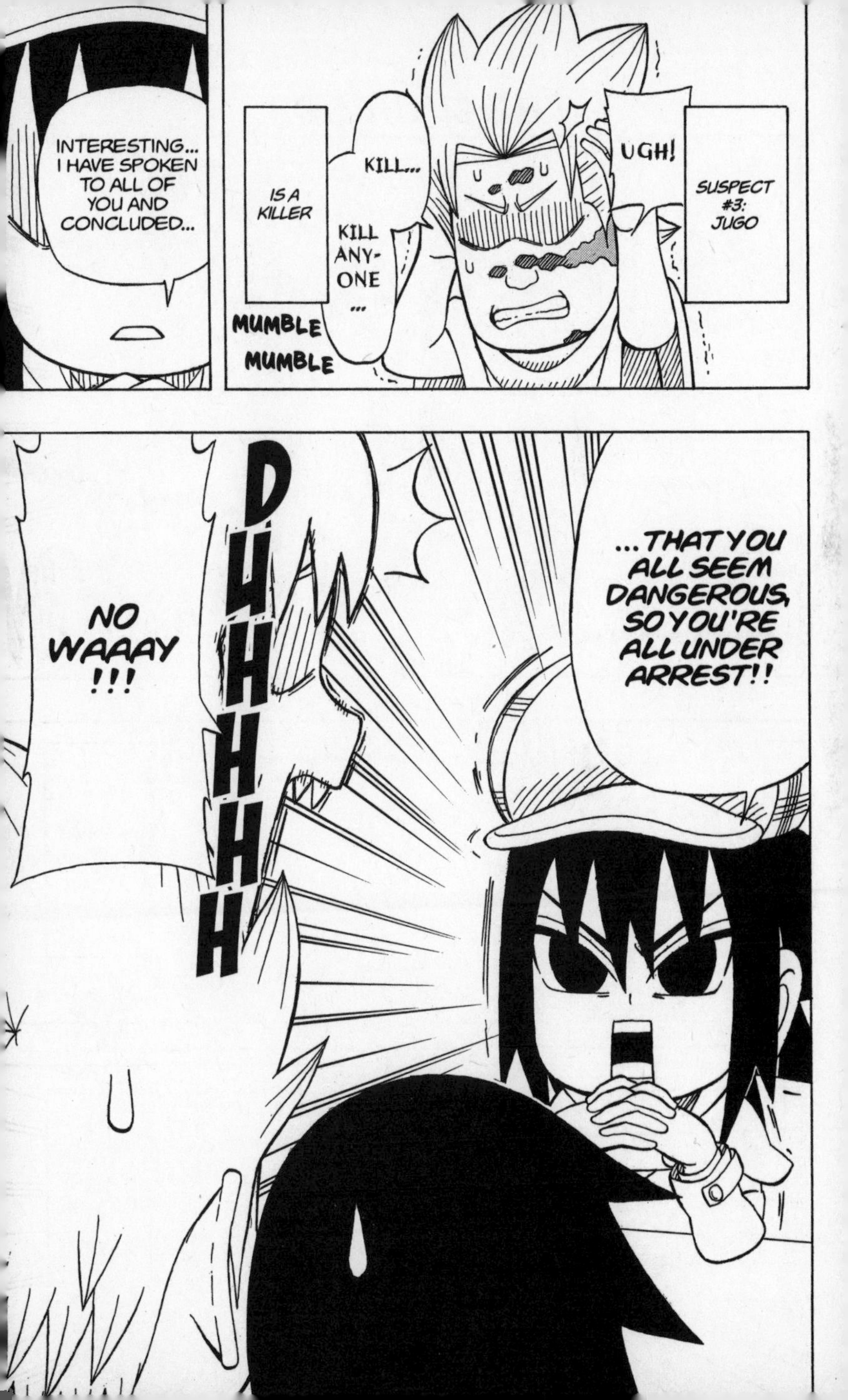
SUSPECT #3: JUGO
UGH!
KILL...
KILL ANY-ONE ...
IS A KILLER
MUMBLE MUMBLE
INTERESTING... I HAVE SPOKEN TO ALL OF YOU AND CONCLUDED...
...THAT YOU ALL SEEM DANGEROUS, SO YOU'RE ALL UNDER ARREST!!
DUHHHHHH
NO WAAAY !!!

THE EVIDENCE

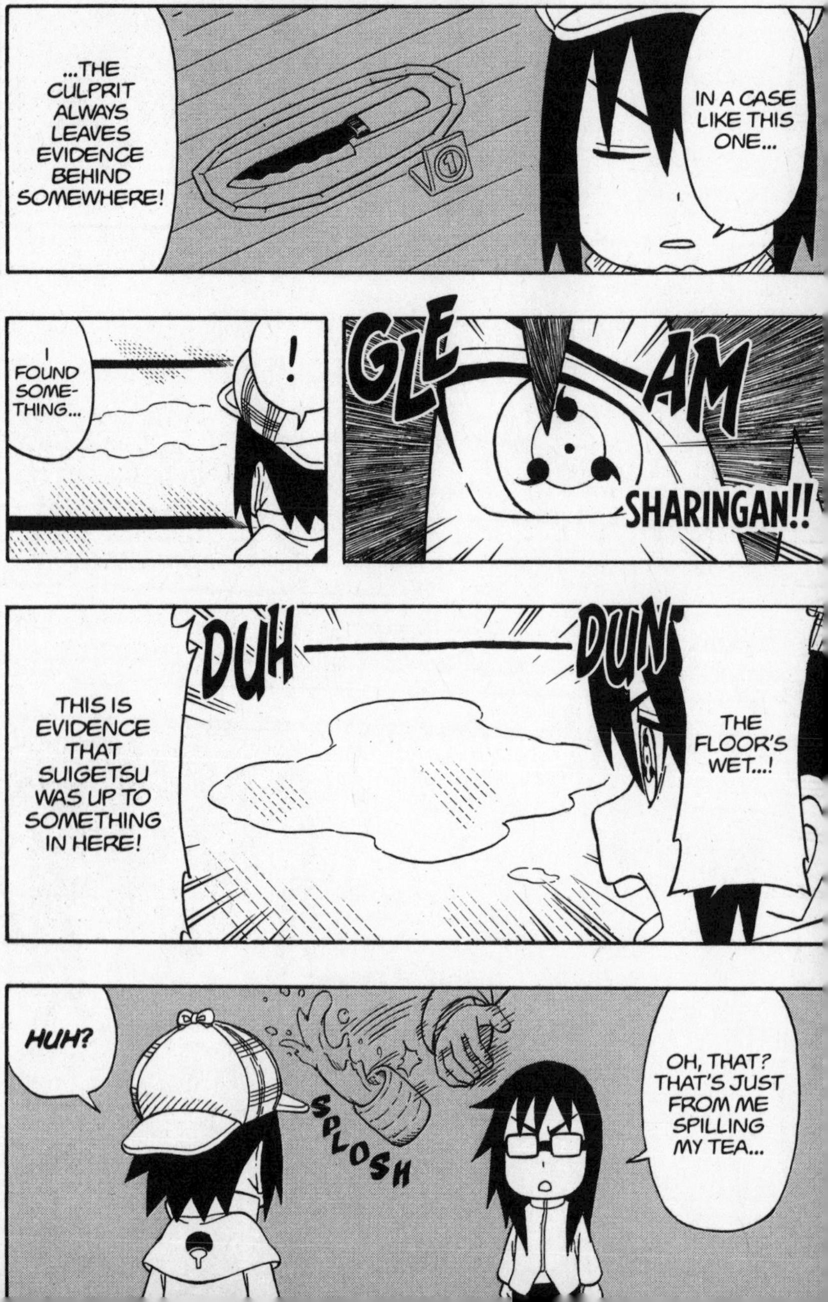

IN A CASE LIKE THIS ONE...
...THE CULPRIT ALWAYS LEAVES EVIDENCE BEHIND SOMEWHERE!
GLE—AM
SHARINGAN!!
!
I FOUND SOME-THING...
DUH—DUN
THE FLOOR'S WET...!
THIS IS EVIDENCE THAT SUIGETSU WAS UP TO SOMETHING IN HERE!
OH, THAT? THAT'S JUST FROM ME SPILLING MY TEA...
SPLOSH
HUH?

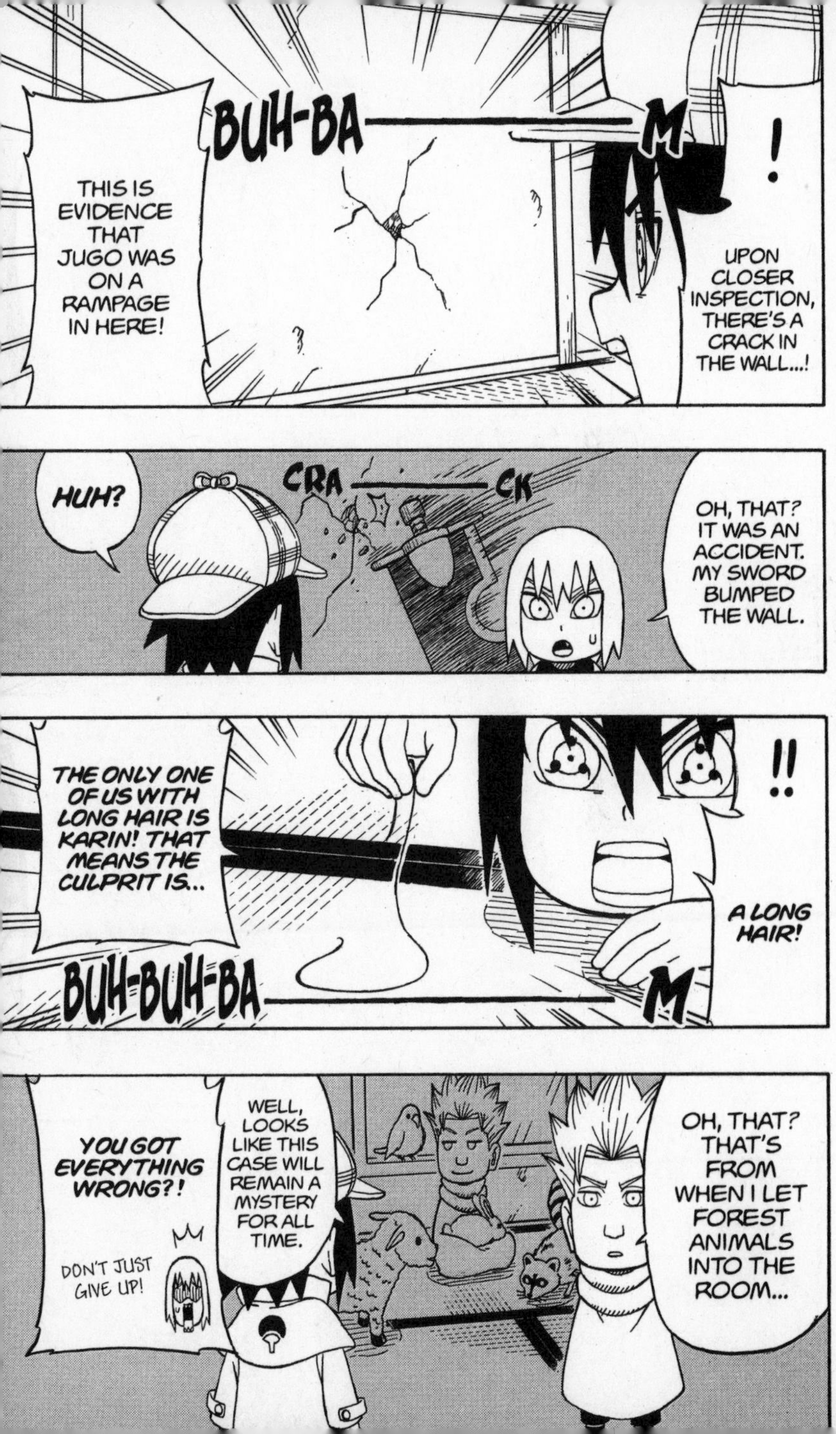
UPON CLOSER INSPECTION, THERE'S A CRACK IN THE WALL...!
!
BUH-BA——M
THIS IS EVIDENCE THAT JUGO WAS ON A RAMPAGE IN HERE!
OH, THAT? IT WAS AN ACCIDENT. MY SWORD BUMPED THE WALL.
CRA——CK
HUH?
!!
A LONG HAIR!
THE ONLY ONE OF US WITH LONG HAIR IS KARIN! THAT MEANS THE CULPRIT IS...
BUH-BUH-BA——M
OH, THAT? THAT'S FROM WHEN I LET FOREST ANIMALS INTO THE ROOM...
WELL, LOOKS LIKE THIS CASE WILL REMAIN A MYSTERY FOR ALL TIME.
YOU GOT EVERYTHING WRONG?!
DON'T JUST GIVE UP!

THE SOLUTION

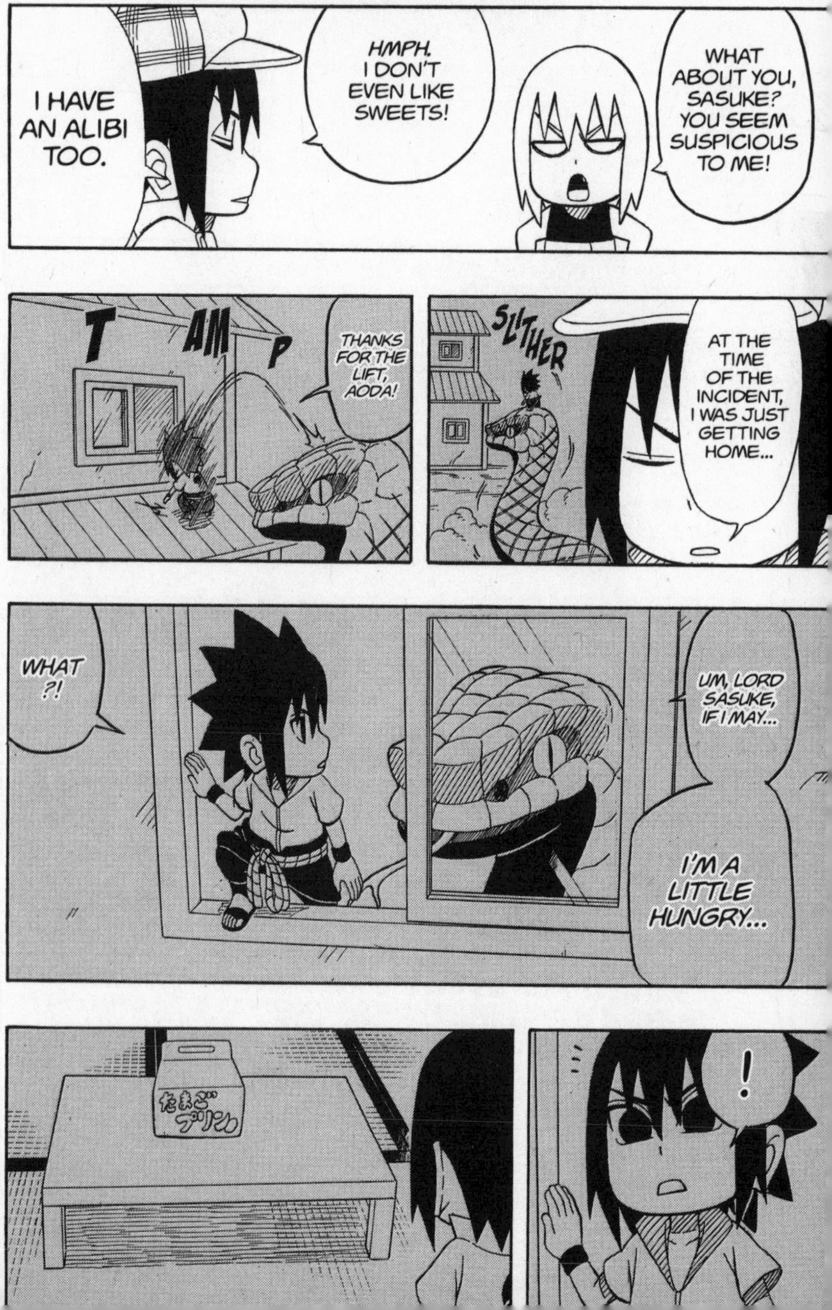
WHAT ABOUT YOU, SASUKE? YOU SEEM SUSPICIOUS TO ME!
HMPH. I DON'T EVEN LIKE SWEETS!
I HAVE AN ALIBI TOO.
AT THE TIME OF THE INCIDENT, I WAS JUST GETTING HOME...
SLITHER
THANKS FOR THE LIFT, AODA!
TAMP
UM, LORD SASUKE, IF I MAY...
I'M A LITTLE HUNGRY...
WHAT ?!
!
たまごプリン

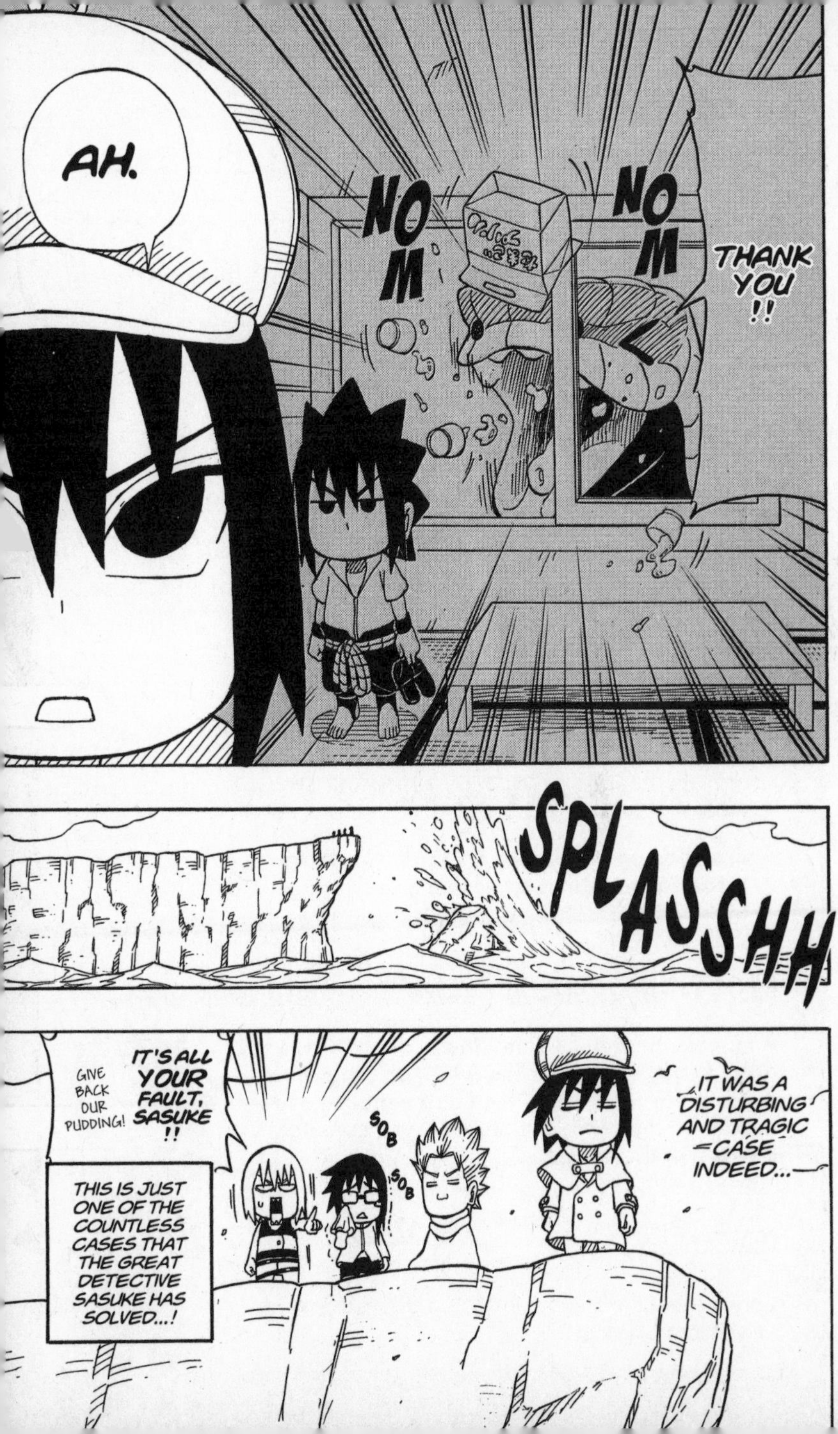
THANK YOU !!
NOM NOM
AH.
SPLASSHH
IT WAS A DISTURBING AND TRAGIC CASE INDEED...
SOB SOB
IT'S ALL YOUR FAULT, SASUKE !!
GIVE BACK OUR PUDDING!
THIS IS JUST ONE OF THE COUNTLESS CASES THAT THE GREAT DETECTIVE SASUKE HAS SOLVED...!

BONUS MATERIAL MINI MANGA CHAPTERS

MINI MANGA 1: UCHIHA SASUKE AND BORUTO (from *Saikyo Jump*, Sept. 2015)

MINI MANGA 2: *BORUTO* LAUNCH COMMEMORATION!! (from *Saikyo Jump*, May 2016)

MINI MANGA 3: BORUTO: ROAD TO BORUTO (from *Weekly Shonen Jump*, 2015 No. 36)

Mini manga for Boruto and the next generation. With things expanding even further after the original series wrapped up, you can really feel the love for the world of *Naruto*! I look forward to Boruto's coming adventures!

• •

MINI MANGA 4: SASUKE VS. THE MOSQUITO!! (from *Jump Victory Carnival 2015 Official Handbook*)

MINI MANGA 5: SASUKE VS. ONE-MAN KARAOKE!! (from *Jump Victory Carnival 2015 Official Handbook*)

MINI MANGA 6: SASUKE VS. THE BACK ITCH!! (from *Jump Festa 2016 Jump Special Comics!!*)

Records of Sasuke's frivolous and feverish battles!!

• •

MINI MANGA 7: LET'S GO TO THE *NARUTO* ART EXHIBIT! OSAKA EDITION (from *Weekly Shonen Jump*, 2015 No. 32)

Information on the *Naruto Art Exhibit* in Osaka. I got to visit not only the Tokyo exhibit but also the Osaka exhibit in person!

• •

MINI MANGA 8: HMPH... *NARUTO SHIPPUDEN: ULTIMATE NINJA STORM 4*, HUH? (from *Saikyo Jump*, March 2016)

A manga about the *Naruto Shippuden: Ultimate Ninja Storm 4* game for the PS4. You can probably guess since it's on the PS4, but the graphics are masterful! If you haven't played it yet, definitely check it out!

• •

MINI MANGA 9: NEW SERIES LAUNCH ADS!! (from *Weekly Shonen Jump*, 2014 No. 43, 46–48)

I drew these for the launch of *Chibi Sasuke's Sharingan Legend*.

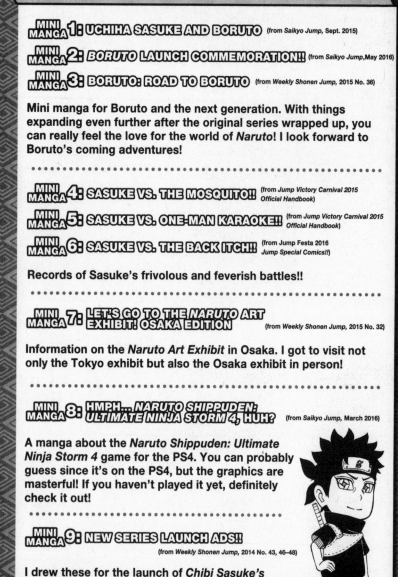

MINI MANGA 1: UCHIHA SASUKE AND BORUTO

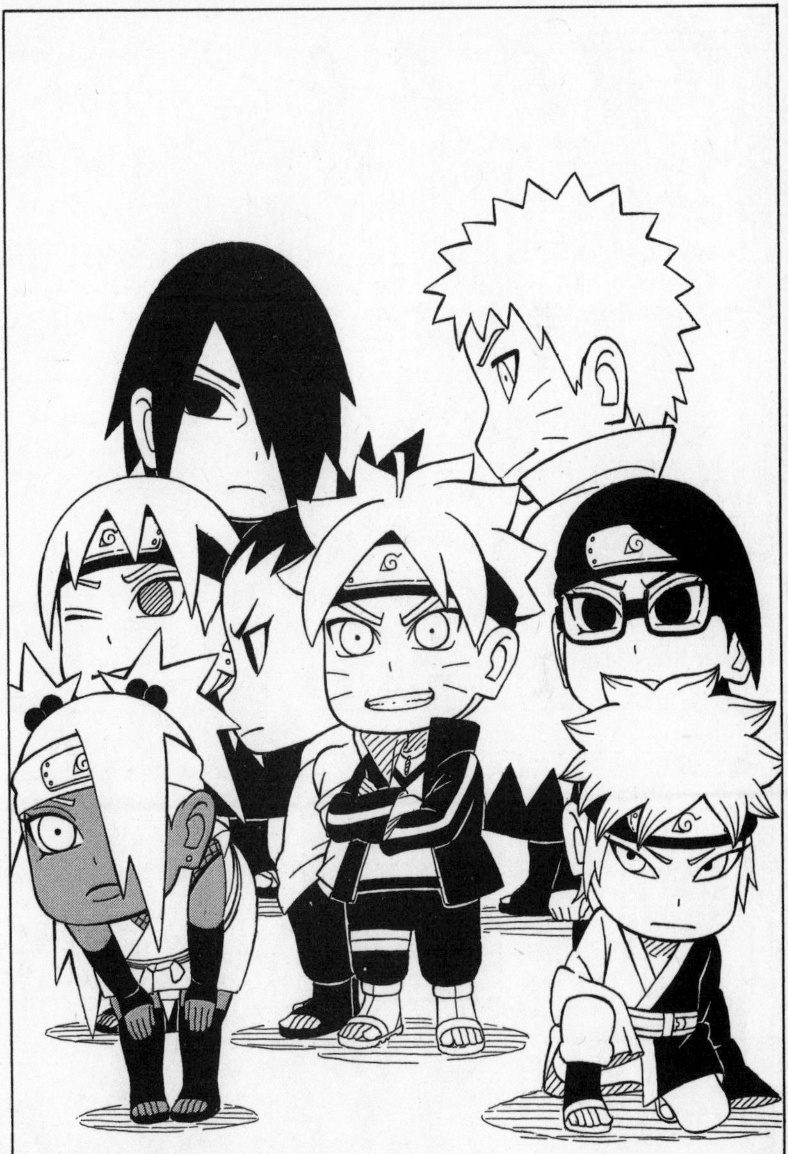

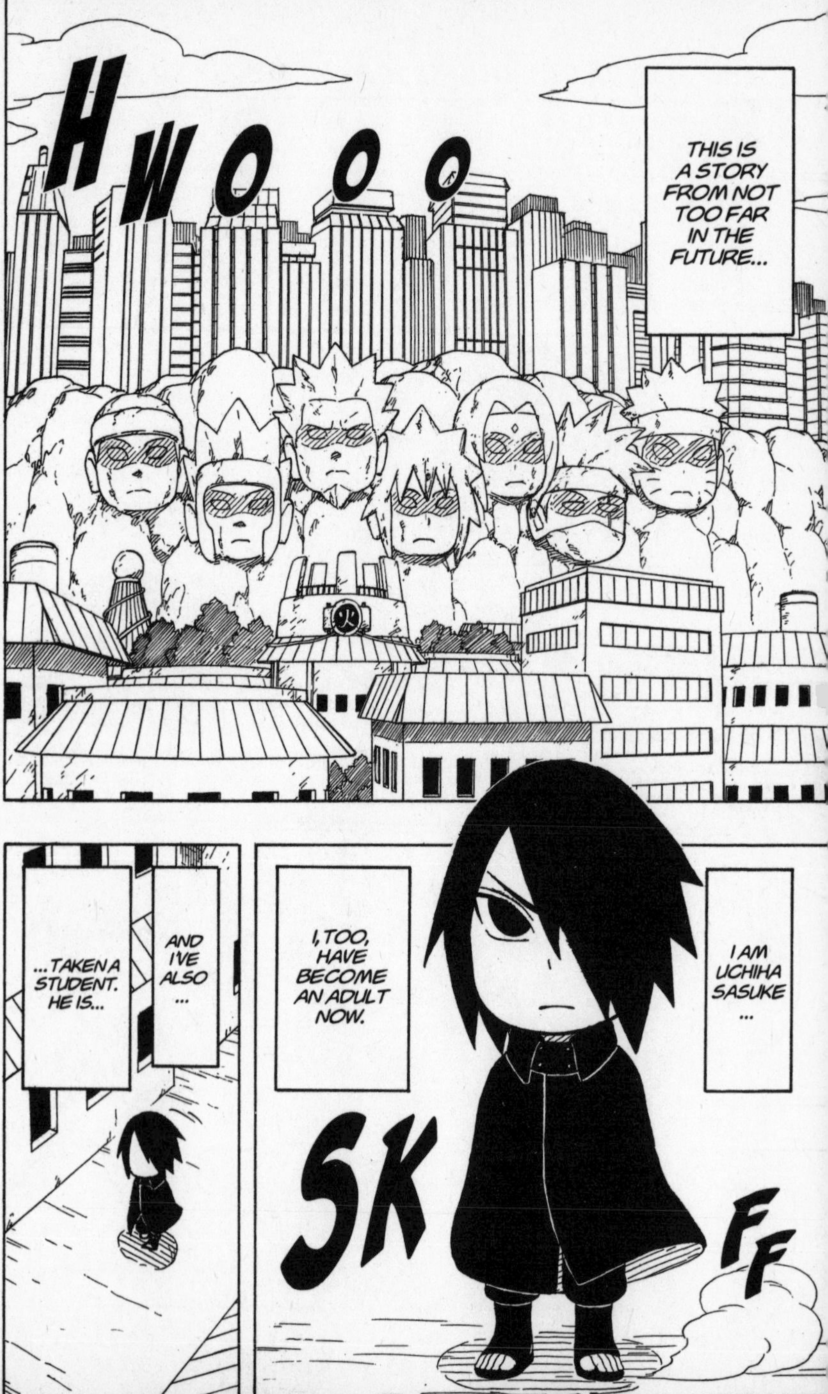
THIS IS A STORY FROM NOT TOO FAR IN THE FUTURE...
HWOOO
I AM UCHIHA SASUKE ...
I, TOO, HAVE BECOME AN ADULT NOW.
SKFF
AND I'VE ALSO ...
...TAKEN A STUDENT. HE IS...

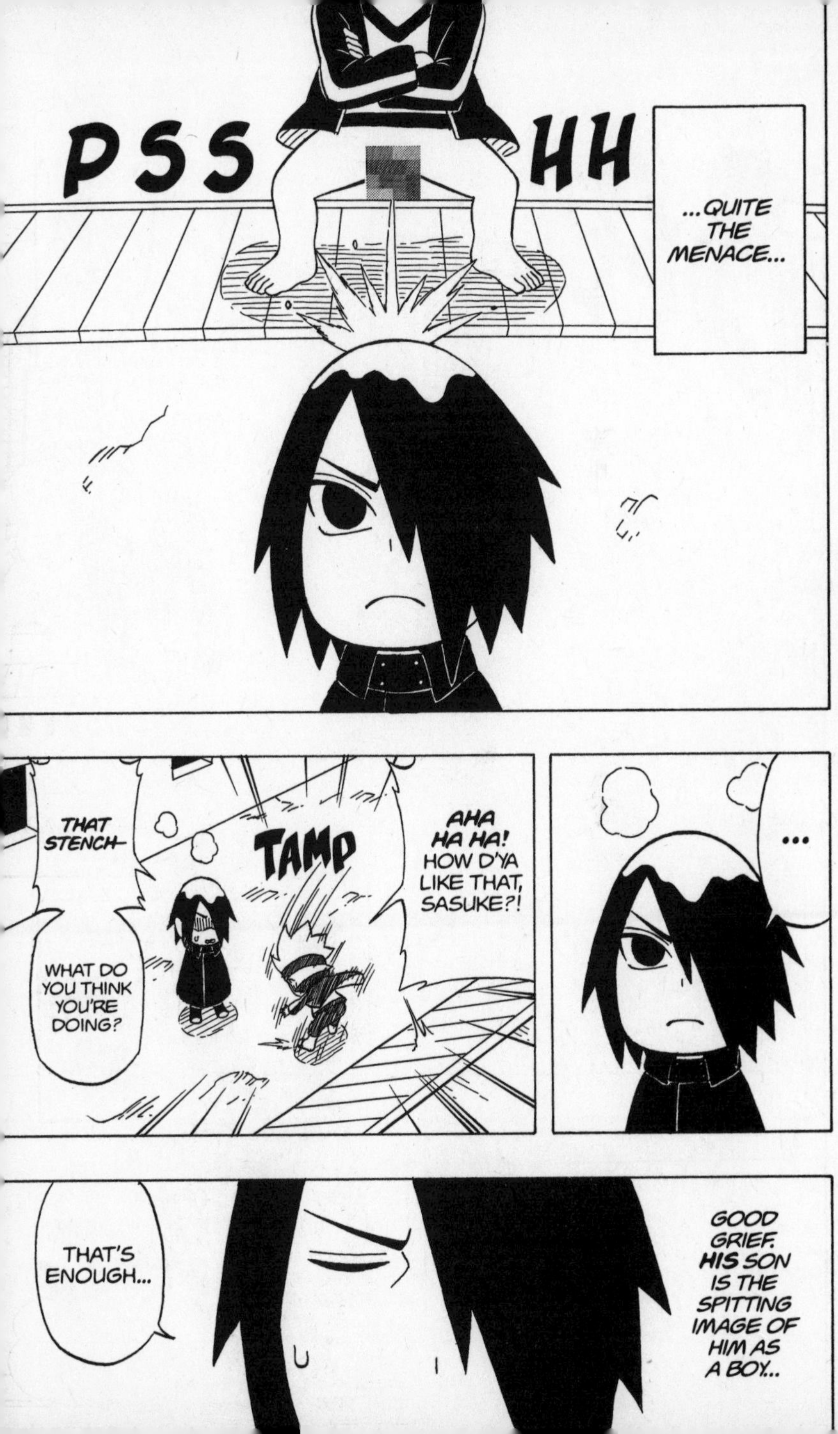
...QUITE THE MENACE...
PSSHH
...
AHA HA HA! HOW D'YA LIKE THAT, SASUKE?!
TAMP
THAT STENCH—
WHAT DO YOU THINK YOU'RE DOING?
GOOD GRIEF. **HIS** SON IS THE SPITTING IMAGE OF HIM AS A BOY...
THAT'S ENOUGH...

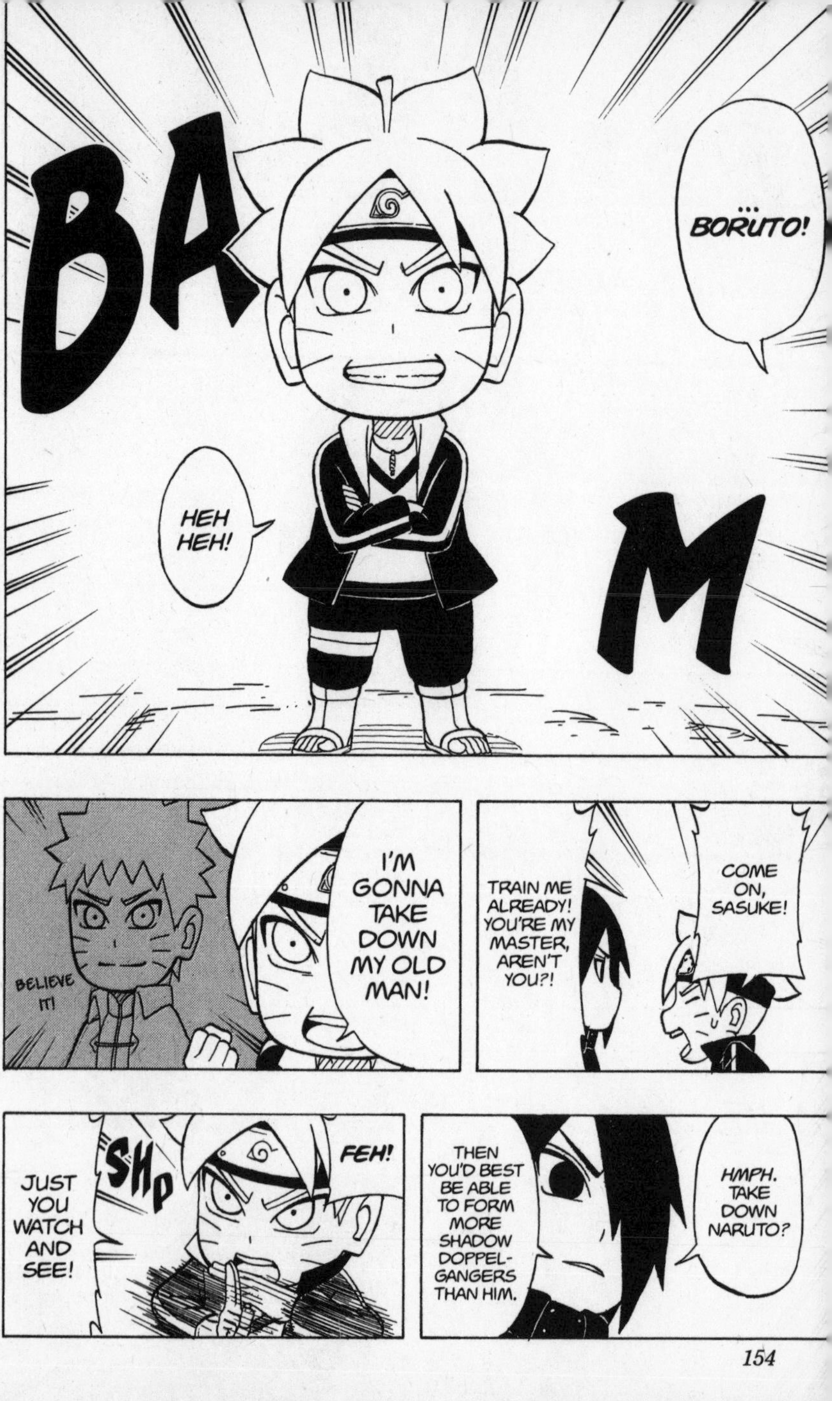
BAM
...BORUTO!
HEH HEH!
COME ON, SASUKE!
TRAIN ME ALREADY! YOU'RE MY MASTER, AREN'T YOU?!
I'M GONNA TAKE DOWN MY OLD MAN!
BELIEVE IT!
HMPH. TAKE DOWN NARUTO?
THEN YOU'D BEST BE ABLE TO FORM MORE SHADOW DOPPEL-GANGERS THAN HIM.
FEH!
SHP
JUST YOU WATCH AND SEE!

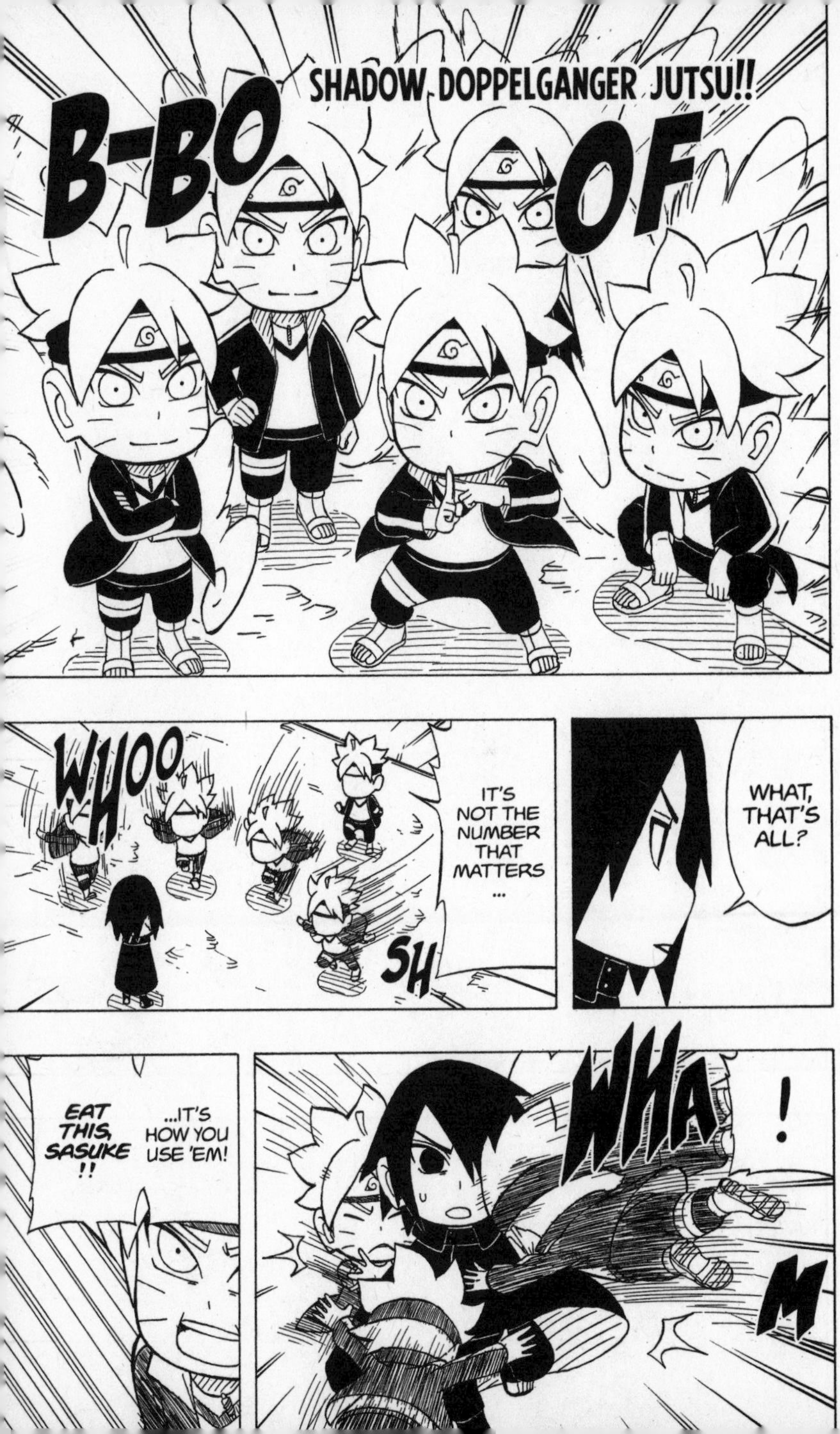
SHADOW DOPPELGANGER JUTSU!!
B-BOOF
WHAT, THAT'S ALL?
IT'S NOT THE NUMBER THAT MATTERS ...
WHOO
SH
WHAM !
...IT'S HOW YOU USE 'EM!
EAT THIS, SASUKE!!

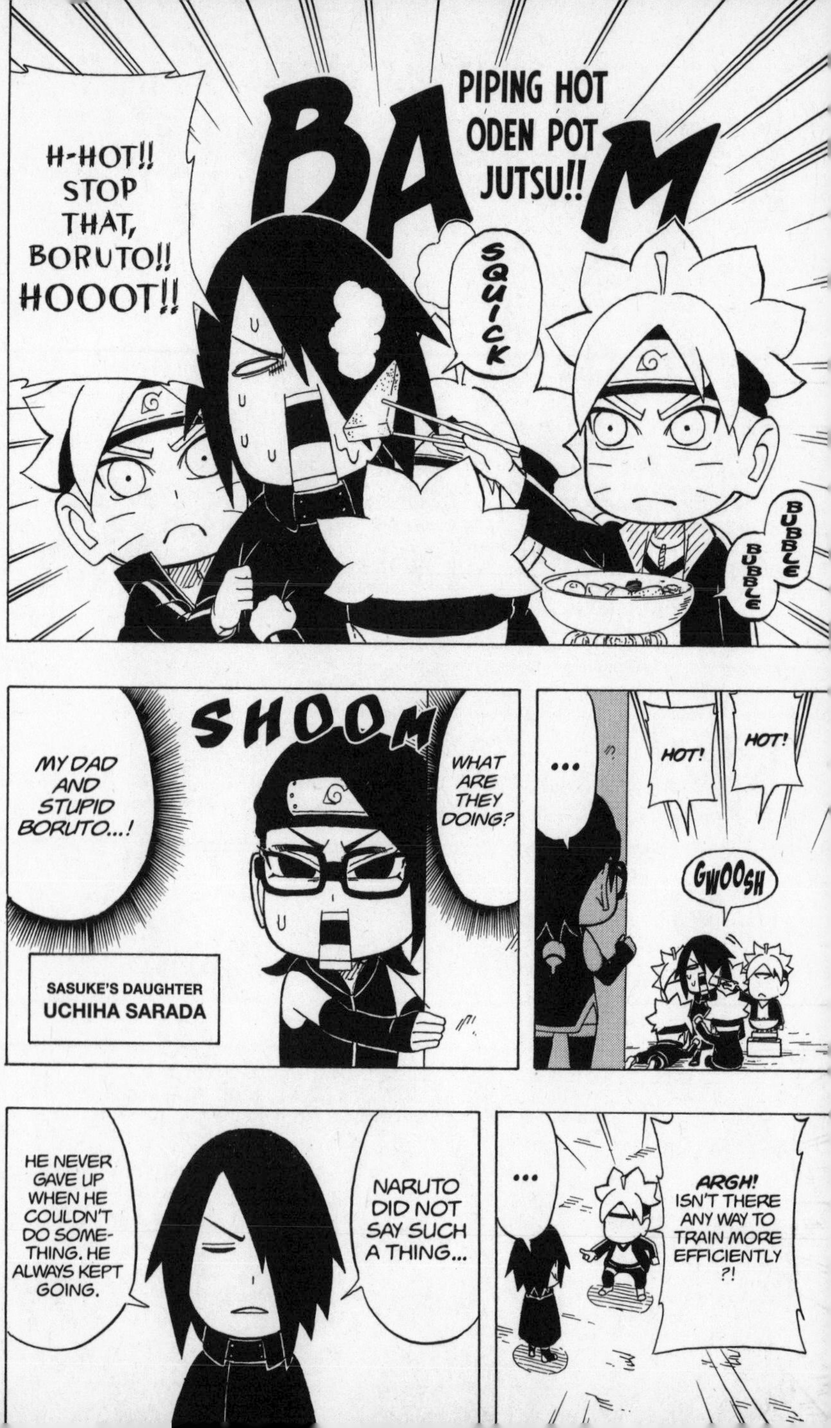
PIPING HOT ODEN POT JUTSU!!
BAM
H-HOT!! STOP THAT, BORUTO!! HOOOT!!
SQUICK
BUBBLE BUBBLE
HOT!
HOT!
...
GWOOSH
WHAT ARE THEY DOING?
SHOOM
MY DAD AND STUPID BORUTO...!
SASUKE'S DAUGHTER
UCHIHA SARADA
ARGH! ISN'T THERE ANY WAY TO TRAIN MORE EFFICIENTLY ?!
...
NARUTO DID NOT SAY SUCH A THING...
HE NEVER GAVE UP WHEN HE COULDN'T DO SOME-THING. HE ALWAYS KEPT GOING.

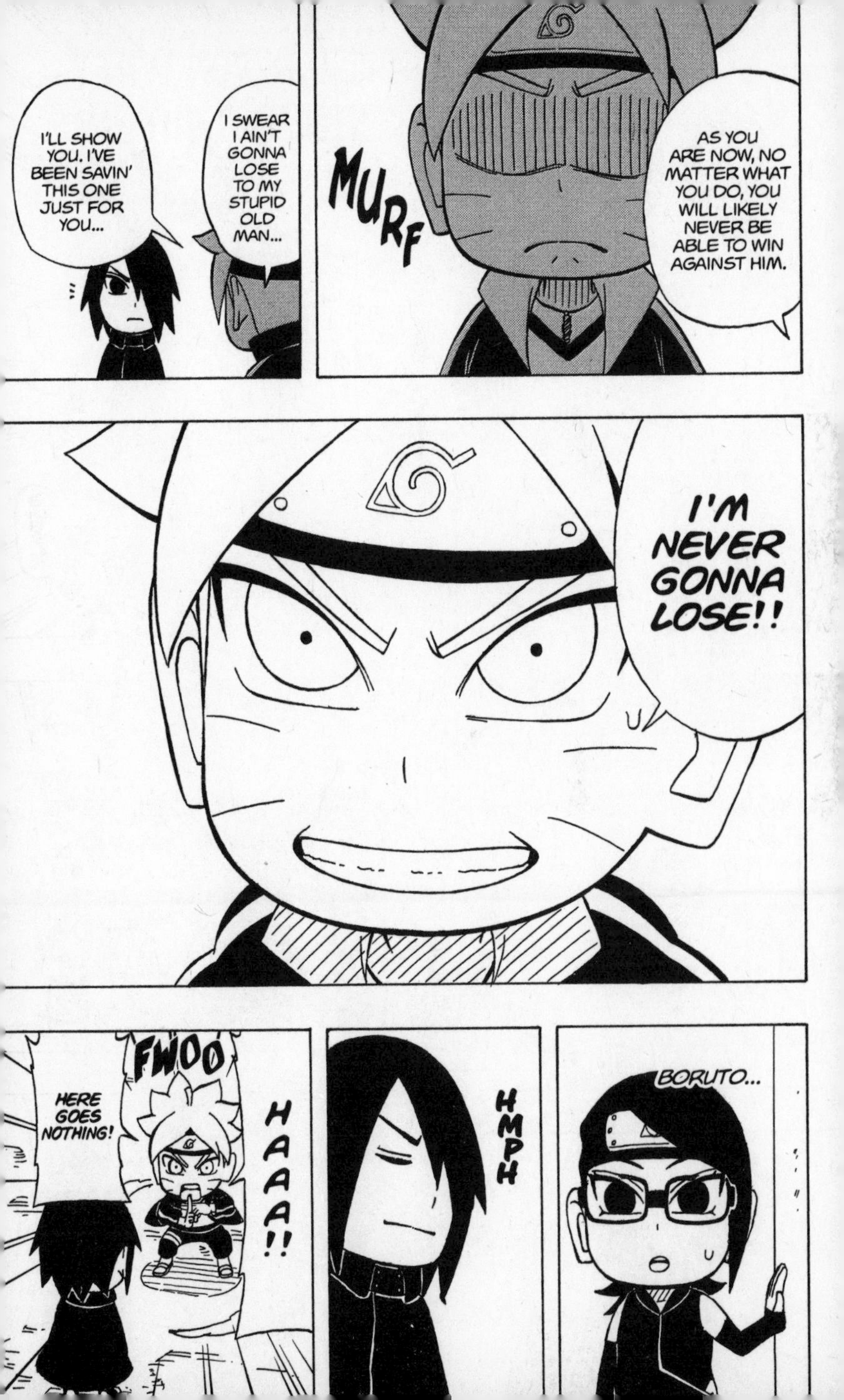
AS YOU ARE NOW, NO MATTER WHAT YOU DO, YOU WILL LIKELY NEVER BE ABLE TO WIN AGAINST HIM.
MURF
I SWEAR I AIN'T GONNA LOSE TO MY STUPID OLD MAN...
I'LL SHOW YOU. I'VE BEEN SAVIN' THIS ONE JUST FOR YOU...
I'M NEVER GONNA LOSE!!
BORUTO...
HMPH
FWOO
HAAAA!!
HERE GOES NOTHING!

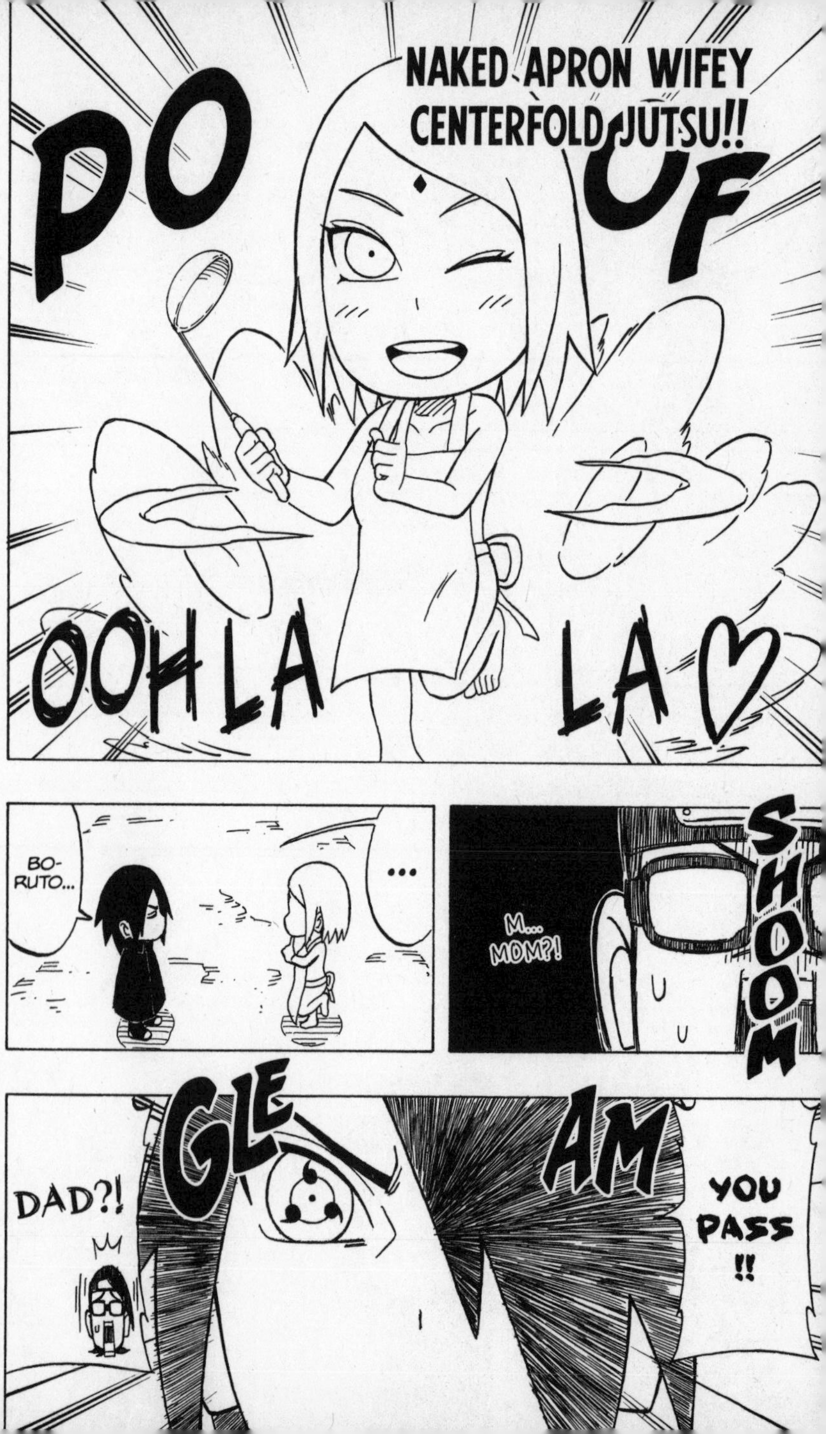

NAKED APRON WIFEY CENTERFOLD JUTSU!!
POOF
OOH LA LA ♡
SHOOM
M... MOM?!
...
BO-RUTO...
YOU PASS !!
GLEAM
DAD?!

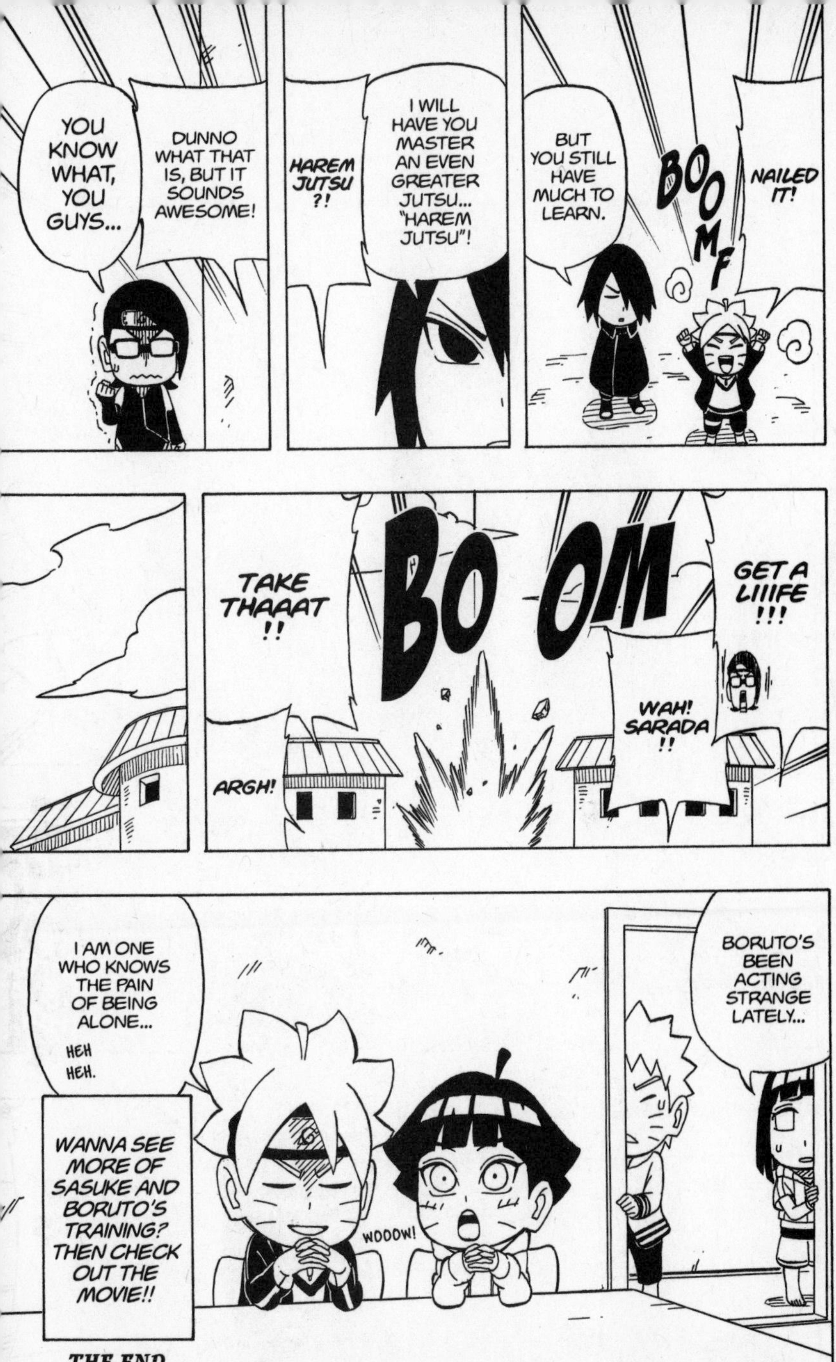
NAILED IT!
BOOOMF
BUT YOU STILL HAVE MUCH TO LEARN.
I WILL HAVE YOU MASTER AN EVEN GREATER JUTSU... "HAREM JUTSU"!
HAREM JUTSU ?!
DUNNO WHAT THAT IS, BUT IT SOUNDS AWESOME!
YOU KNOW WHAT, YOU GUYS...
GET A LIIIFE!!!
BOOM
WAH! SARADA!!
TAKE THAAAT!!
ARGH!
BORUTO'S BEEN ACTING STRANGE LATELY...
WOOOW!
I AM ONE WHO KNOWS THE PAIN OF BEING ALONE...
HEH HEH.
WANNA SEE MORE OF SASUKE AND BORUTO'S TRAINING? THEN CHECK OUT THE MOVIE!!

THE END

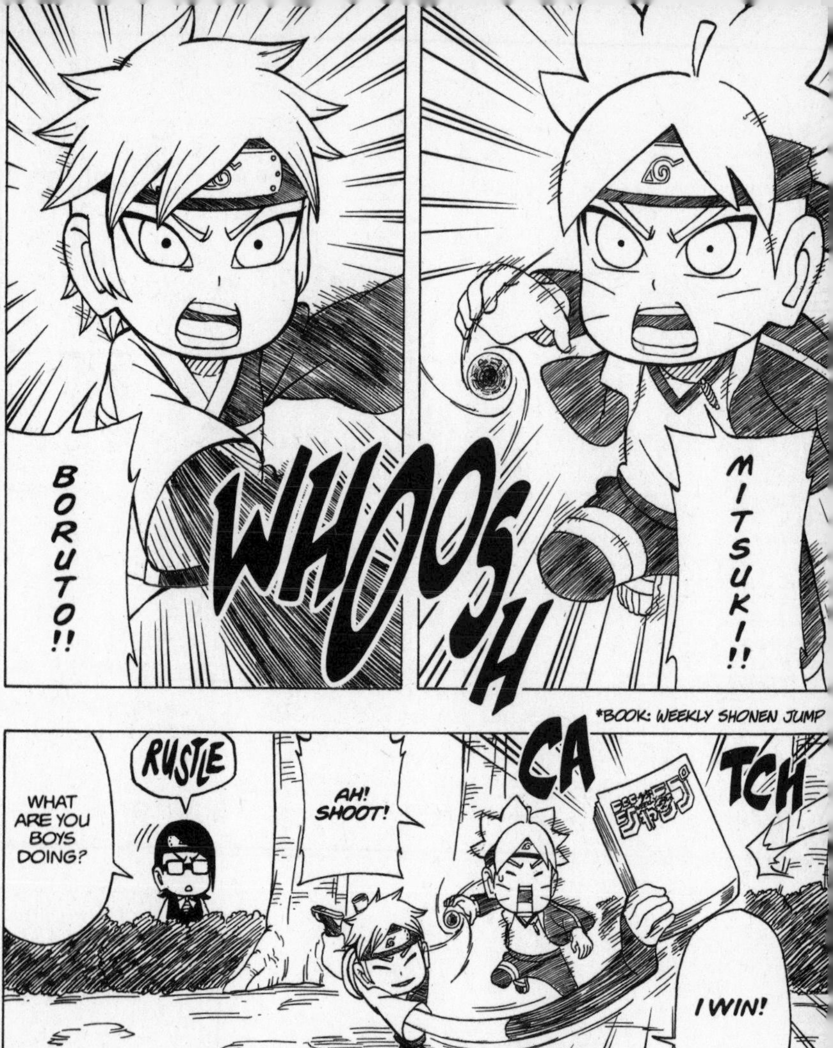
MITSUKI!!
BORUTO!!
WHOOSH
*BOOK: WEEKLY SHONEN JUMP
CATCH
I WIN!
AH! SHOOT!
RUSTLE
WHAT ARE YOU BOYS DOING?

MINI MANGA 2: BORUTO: LAUNCH COMMEMORATION!!

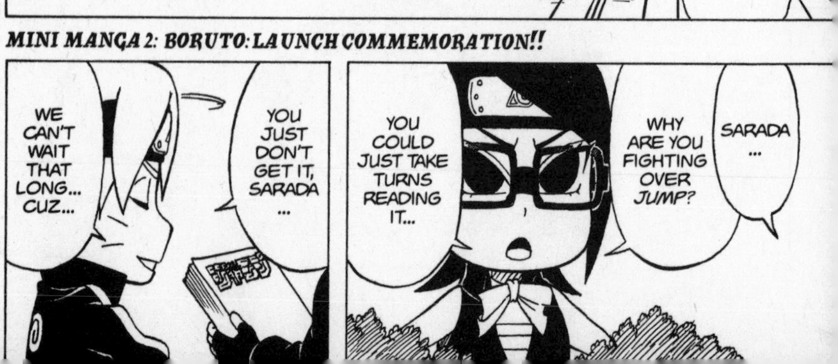
SARADA...
WHY ARE YOU FIGHTING OVER JUMP?
YOU COULD JUST TAKE TURNS READING IT...
YOU JUST DON'T GET IT, SARADA...
WE CAN'T WAIT THAT LONG... CUZ...

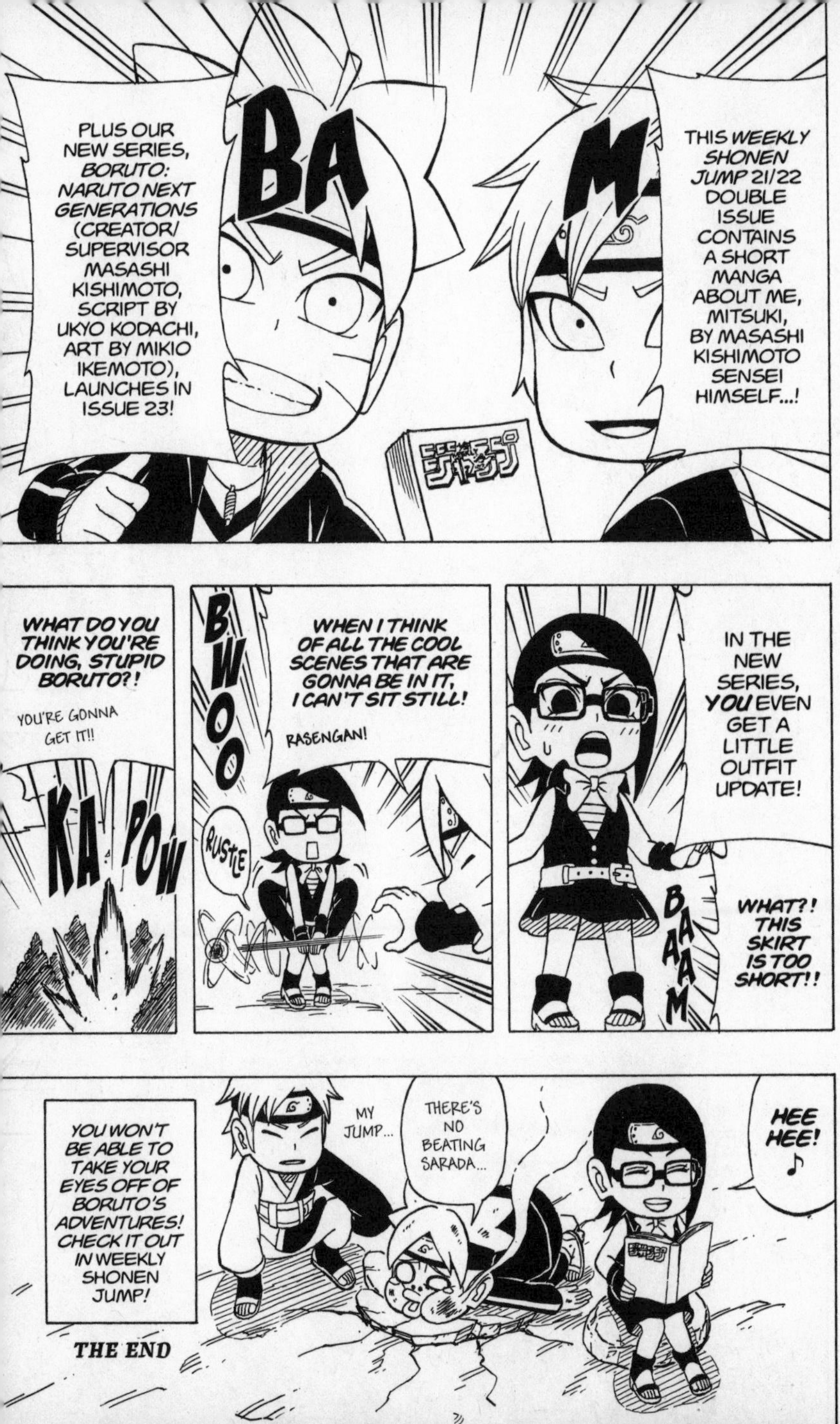
THIS WEEKLY SHONEN JUMP 21/22 DOUBLE ISSUE CONTAINS A SHORT MANGA ABOUT ME, MITSUKI, BY MASASHI KISHIMOTO SENSEI HIMSELF...!
BAM
PLUS OUR NEW SERIES, BORUTO: NARUTO NEXT GENERATIONS (CREATOR/SUPERVISOR MASASHI KISHIMOTO, SCRIPT BY UKYO KODACHI, ART BY MIKIO IKEMOTO), LAUNCHES IN ISSUE 23!
IN THE NEW SERIES, YOU EVEN GET A LITTLE OUTFIT UPDATE!
BAAAM
WHAT?! THIS SKIRT IS TOO SHORT!!
BWOOO
WHEN I THINK OF ALL THE COOL SCENES THAT ARE GONNA BE IN IT, I CAN'T SIT STILL!
RASENGAN!
RUSTLE
WHAT DO YOU THINK YOU'RE DOING, STUPID BORUTO?!
YOU'RE GONNA GET IT!!
KA POW
HEE HEE! ♪
THERE'S NO BEATING SARADA...
MY JUMP...
YOU WON'T BE ABLE TO TAKE YOUR EYES OFF OF BORUTO'S ADVENTURES! CHECK IT OUT IN WEEKLY SHONEN JUMP!
THE END

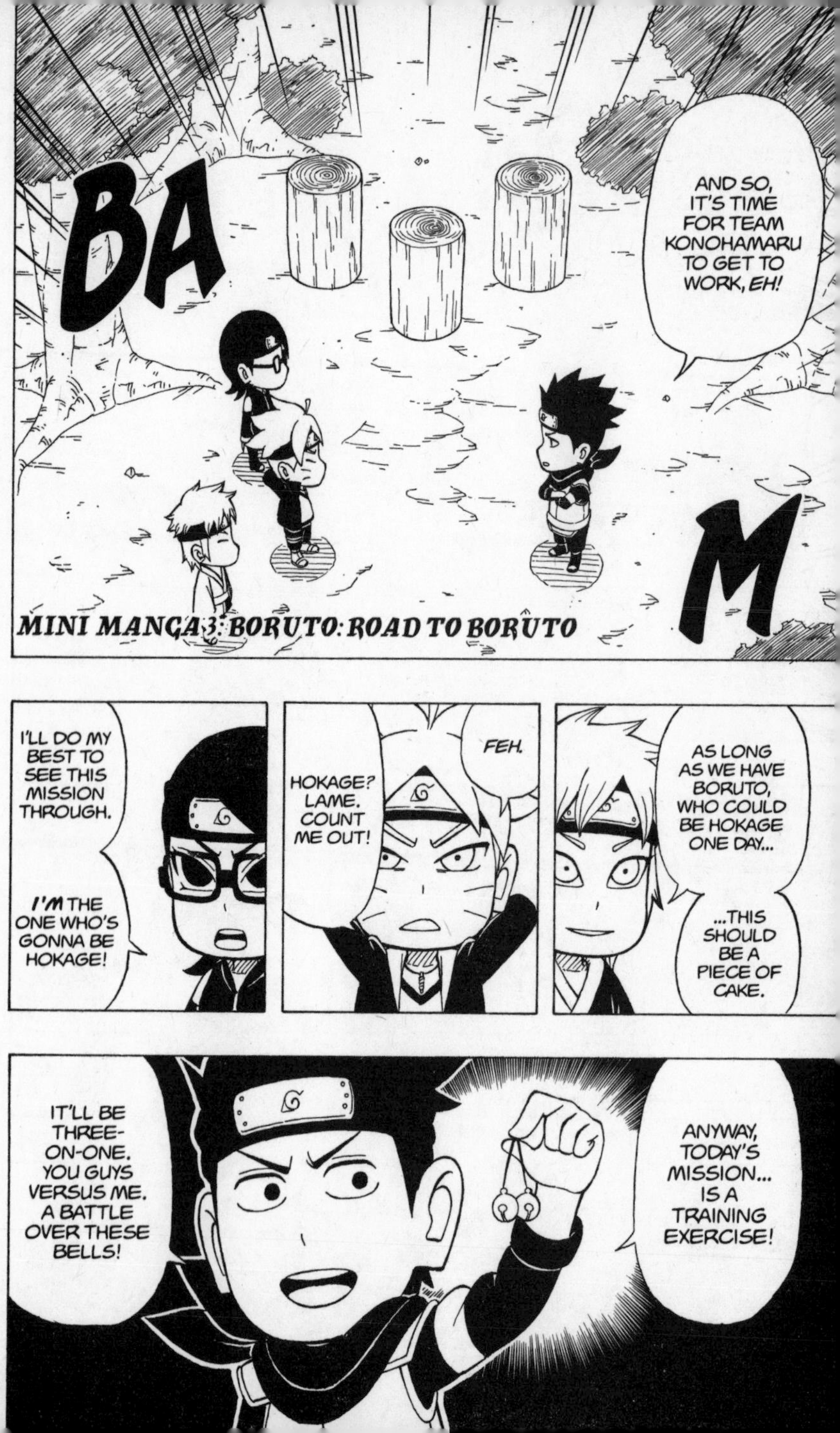
AND SO, IT'S TIME FOR TEAM KONOHAMARU TO GET TO WORK, EH!
BAM
MINI MANGA 3: BORUTO: ROAD TO BORUTO
AS LONG AS WE HAVE BORUTO, WHO COULD BE HOKAGE ONE DAY...
...THIS SHOULD BE A PIECE OF CAKE.
FEH.
HOKAGE? LAME. COUNT ME OUT!
I'LL DO MY BEST TO SEE THIS MISSION THROUGH.
I'M THE ONE WHO'S GONNA BE HOKAGE!
ANYWAY, TODAY'S MISSION... IS A TRAINING EXERCISE!
IT'LL BE THREE-ON-ONE. YOU GUYS VERSUS ME. A BATTLE OVER THESE BELLS!

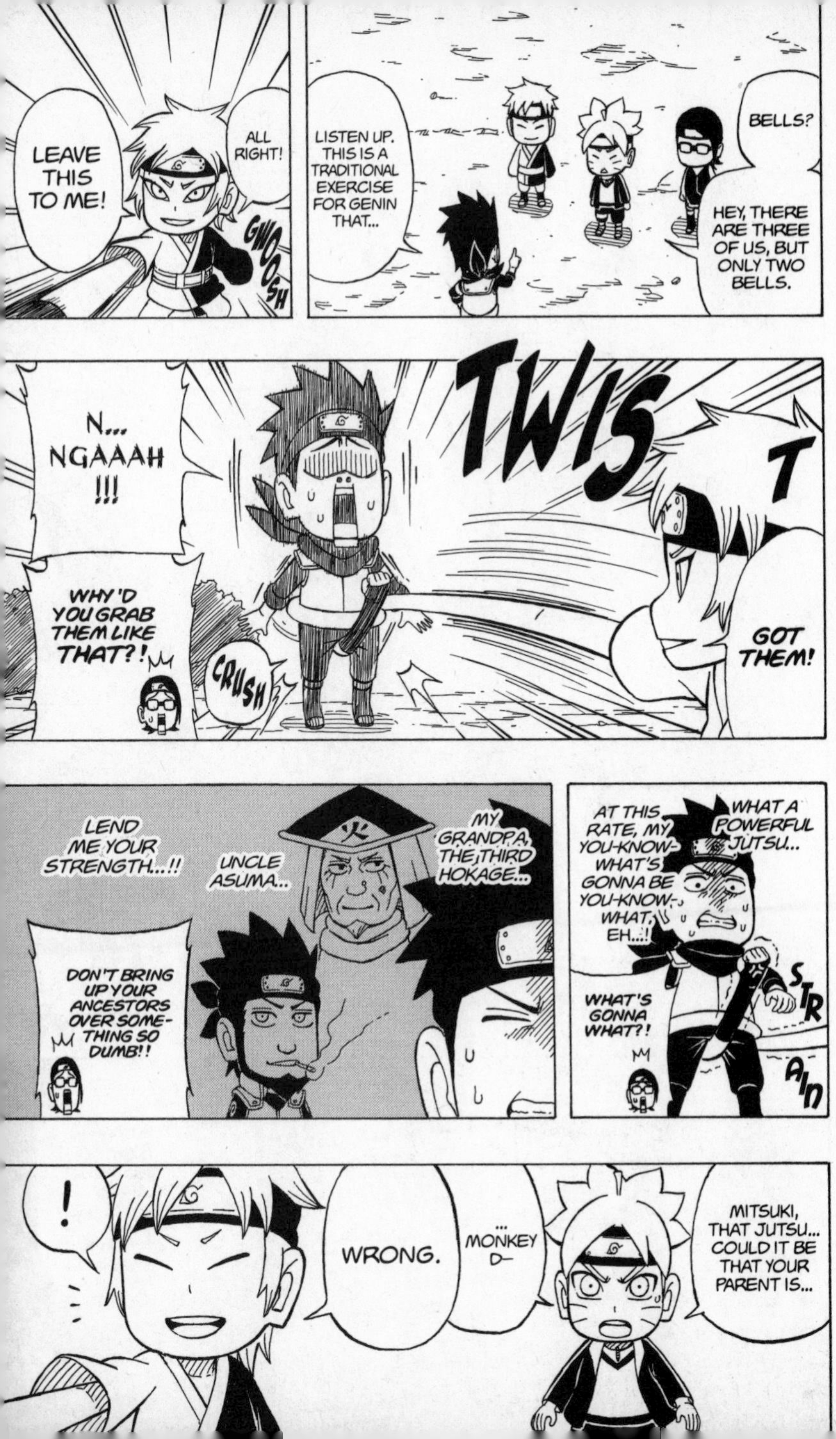
BELLS?
HEY, THERE ARE THREE OF US, BUT ONLY TWO BELLS.
LISTEN UP. THIS IS A TRADITIONAL EXERCISE FOR GENIN THAT...
ALL RIGHT!
LEAVE THIS TO ME!
GWOOSH
TWIST
GOT THEM!
N... NGAAAH!!!
CRUSH
WHY'D YOU GRAB THEM LIKE THAT?!
WHAT A POWERFUL JUTSU...
AT THIS RATE, MY YOU-KNOW-WHAT'S GONNA BE YOU-KNOW-WHAT, EH...!
STRAIN
WHAT'S GONNA WHAT?!
MY GRANDPA, THE THIRD HOKAGE...
UNCLE ASUMA...
LEND ME YOUR STRENGTH...!!
DON'T BRING UP YOUR ANCESTORS OVER SOMETHING SO DUMB!!
MITSUKI, THAT JUTSU... COULD IT BE THAT YOUR PARENT IS...
... MONKEY D—
WRONG.
!

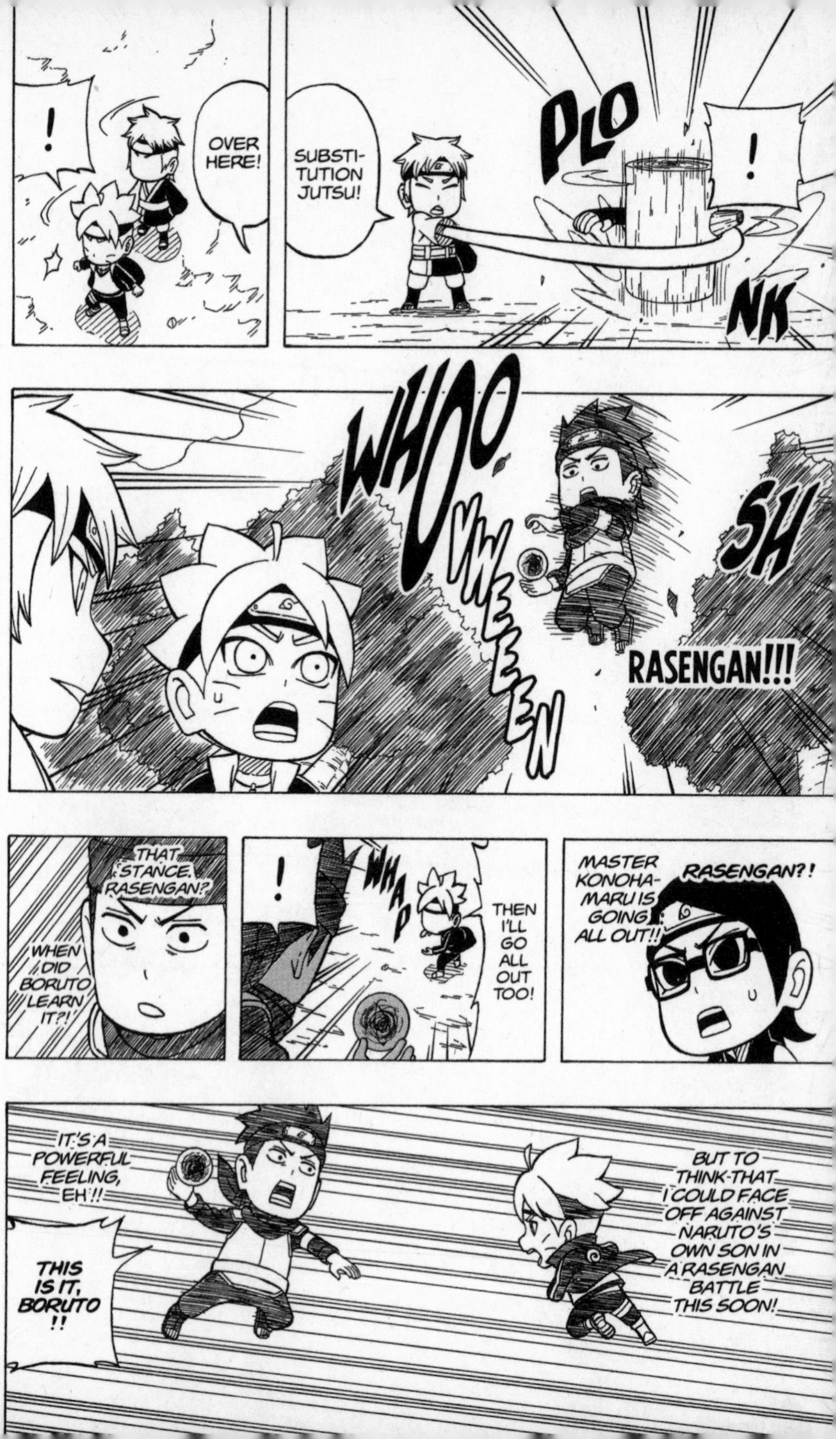
!
PLO
NK
SUBSTI-TUTION JUTSU!
OVER HERE!
!
SH
RASENGAN!!!
WHOO
VWEEEEN
RASENGAN?!
MASTER KONOHAMARU IS GOING ALL OUT!!
THEN I'LL GO ALL OUT TOO!
WHAP
!
THAT STANCE. RASENGAN?
WHEN DID BORUTO LEARN IT?!
BUT TO THINK THAT I COULD FACE OFF AGAINST NARUTO'S OWN SON IN A RASENGAN BATTLE THIS SOON!
IT'S A POWERFUL FEELING, EH!!
THIS IS IT, BORUTO!!

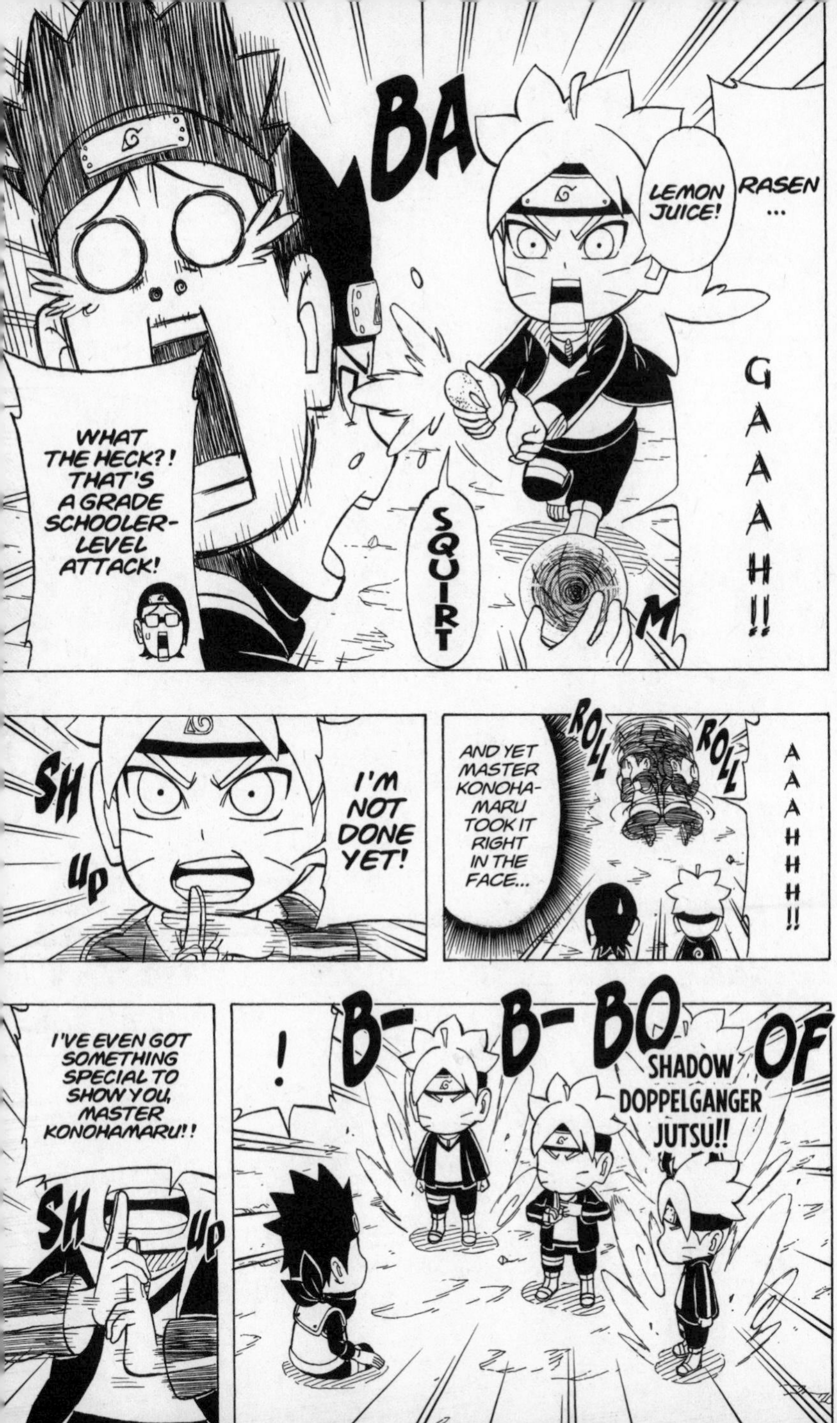
RASEN ...
LEMON JUICE!
BA
GAAAAH!!
M
SQUIRT
WHAT THE HECK?! THAT'S A GRADE SCHOOLER-LEVEL ATTACK!
AAAHHH!!
ROLL
ROLL
AND YET MASTER KONOHAMARU TOOK IT RIGHT IN THE FACE...
I'M NOT DONE YET!
SH
UP
OF
SHADOW DOPPELGANGER JUTSU!!
BO
B-
B-
!
I'VE EVEN GOT SOMETHING SPECIAL TO SHOW YOU, MASTER KONOHAMARU!!
SH
UP

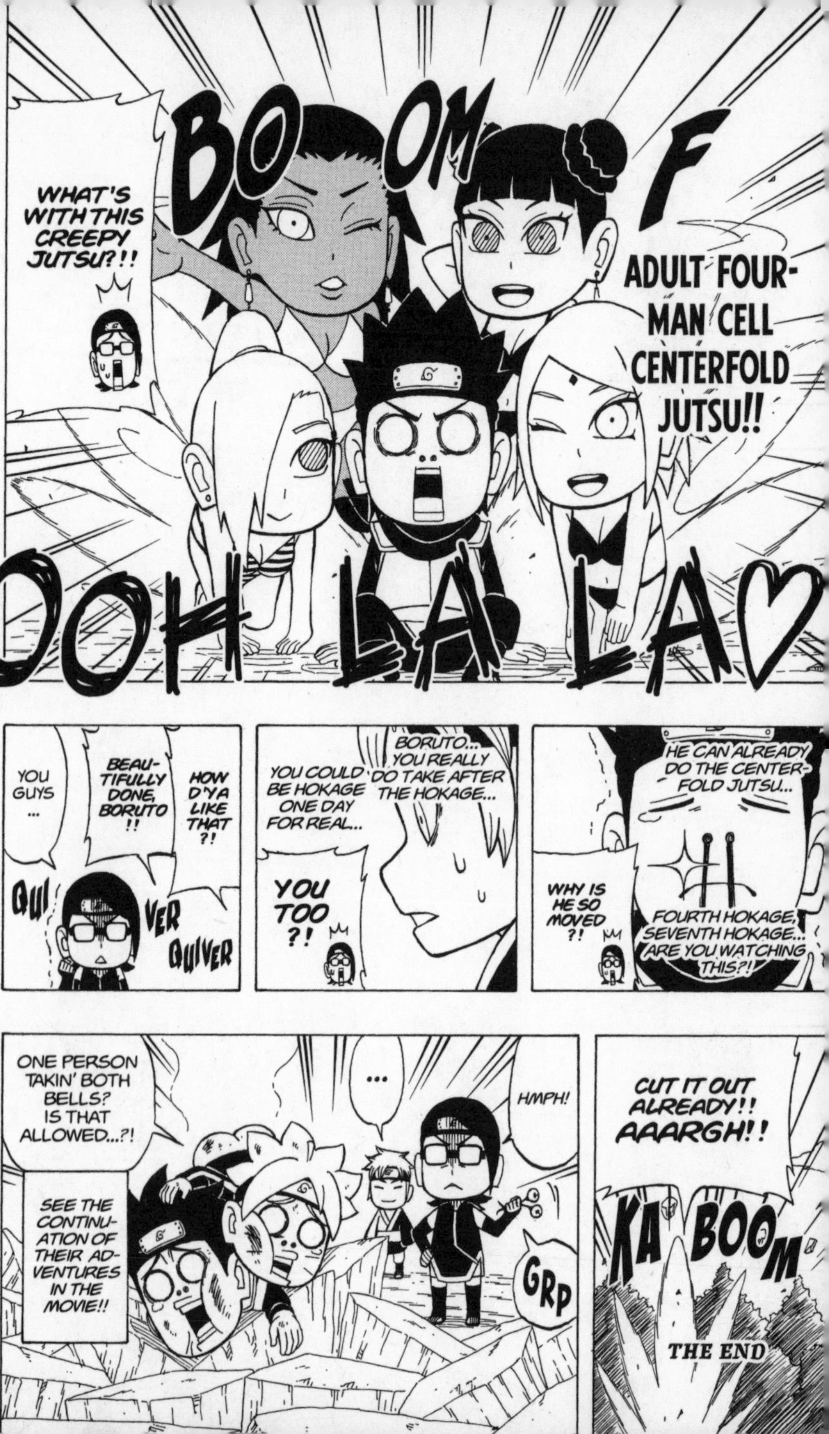
BOOMF
ADULT FOUR-MAN CELL CENTERFOLD JUTSU!!
WHAT'S WITH THIS CREEPY JUTSU?!!
OOH LA LA♡
HE CAN ALREADY DO THE CENTERFOLD JUTSU...
FOURTH HOKAGE, SEVENTH HOKAGE... ARE YOU WATCHING THIS?!
WHY IS HE SO MOVED?!
BORUTO... YOU REALLY DO TAKE AFTER THE HOKAGE...
YOU COULD BE HOKAGE ONE DAY FOR REAL...
YOU TOO?!
HOW D'YA LIKE THAT?!
BEAUTIFULLY DONE, BORUTO!!
YOU GUYS...
QUIVER QUIVER
CUT IT OUT ALREADY!! AAARGH!!
KA BOOM
THE END
HMPH!
...
ONE PERSON TAKIN' BOTH BELLS? IS THAT ALLOWED...?!
GRP
SEE THE CONTINUATION OF THEIR ADVENTURES IN THE MOVIE!!

MINI MANGA 4: SASUKE VS. THE MOSQUITO!!

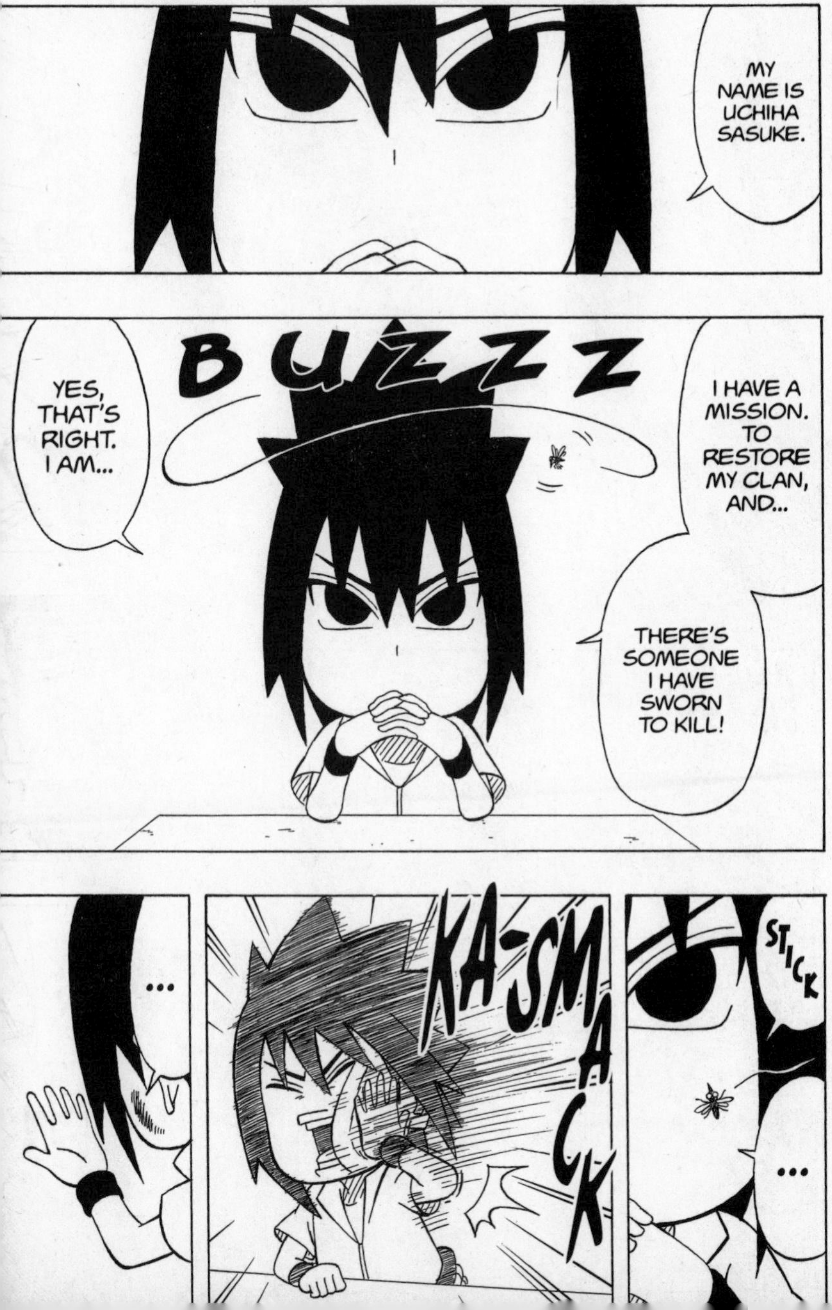
MY NAME IS UCHIHA SASUKE.
I HAVE A MISSION. TO RESTORE MY CLAN, AND...
BUZZZ
YES, THAT'S RIGHT. I AM...
THERE'S SOMEONE I HAVE SWORN TO KILL!
STICK
...
KA-SMACK
...

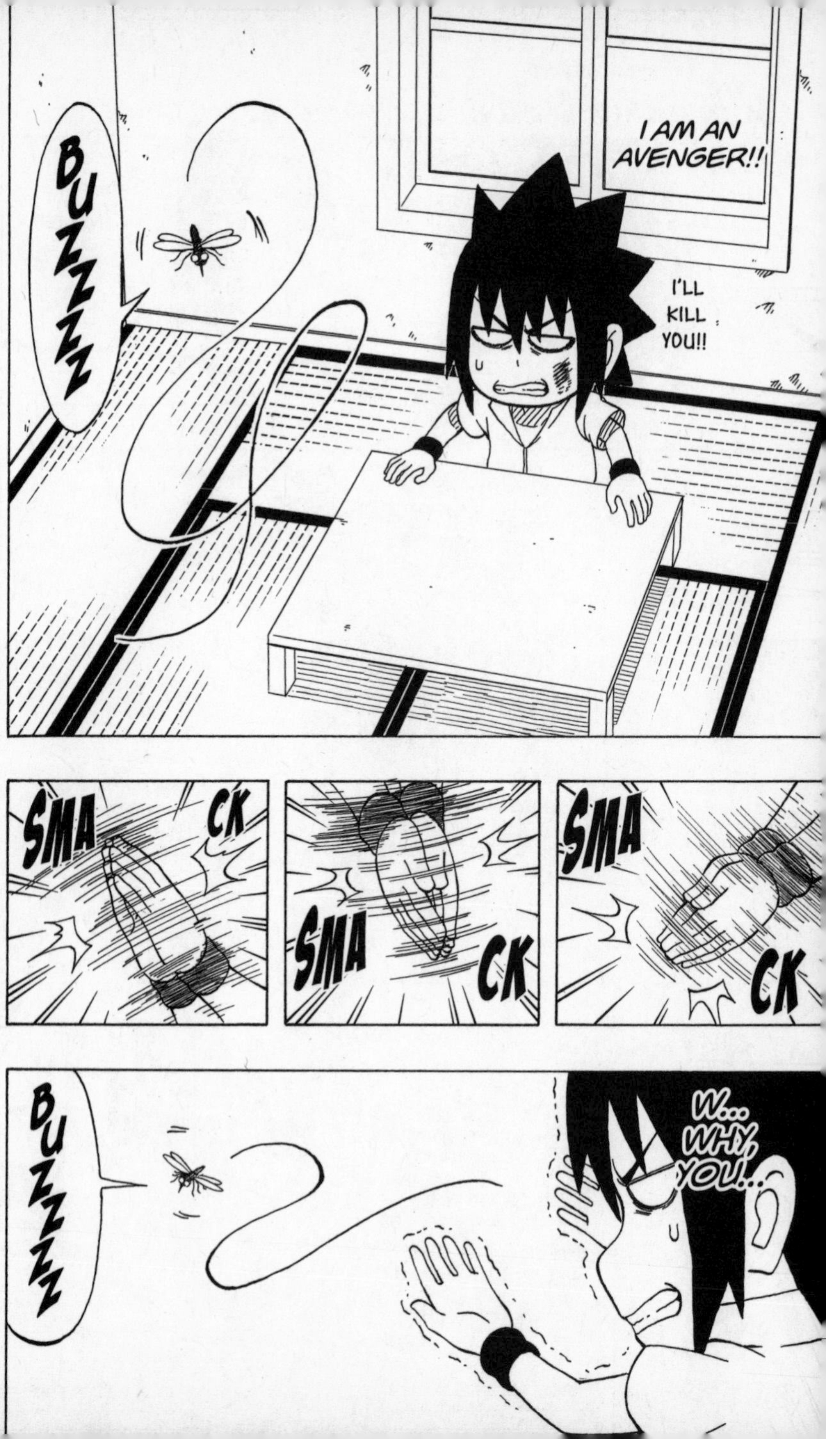
I AM AN AVENGER!!
I'LL KILL YOU!!
BUZZZZ
SMACK
SMACK
SMACK
W... WHY, YOU...
BUZZZZ

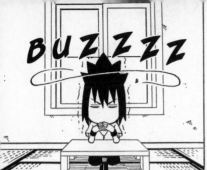

CALM DOWN! IT'S JUST A MOSQUITO.
IGNORE IT AND IT WILL FLY AWAY...
FEH
BUZZZZZ
GLEAM
SHARINGAN!!!
I HAVE THE SHARINGAN, ONE OF THE ULTIMATE OCULAR JUTSU PASSED DOWN IN THE UCHIHA CLAN.
YOU CAN'T HIDE FROM ME!!
SHP
SHP
YOU'RE A FORMIDABLE OPPONENT...
...TO HAVE MADE ME GO THIS FAR!
SHP
FWUSH
FIRE STYLE...

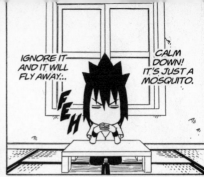

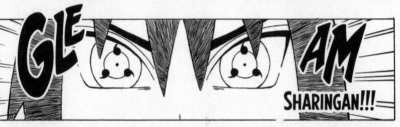

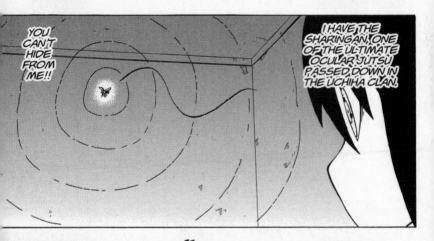

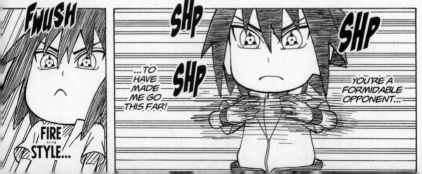

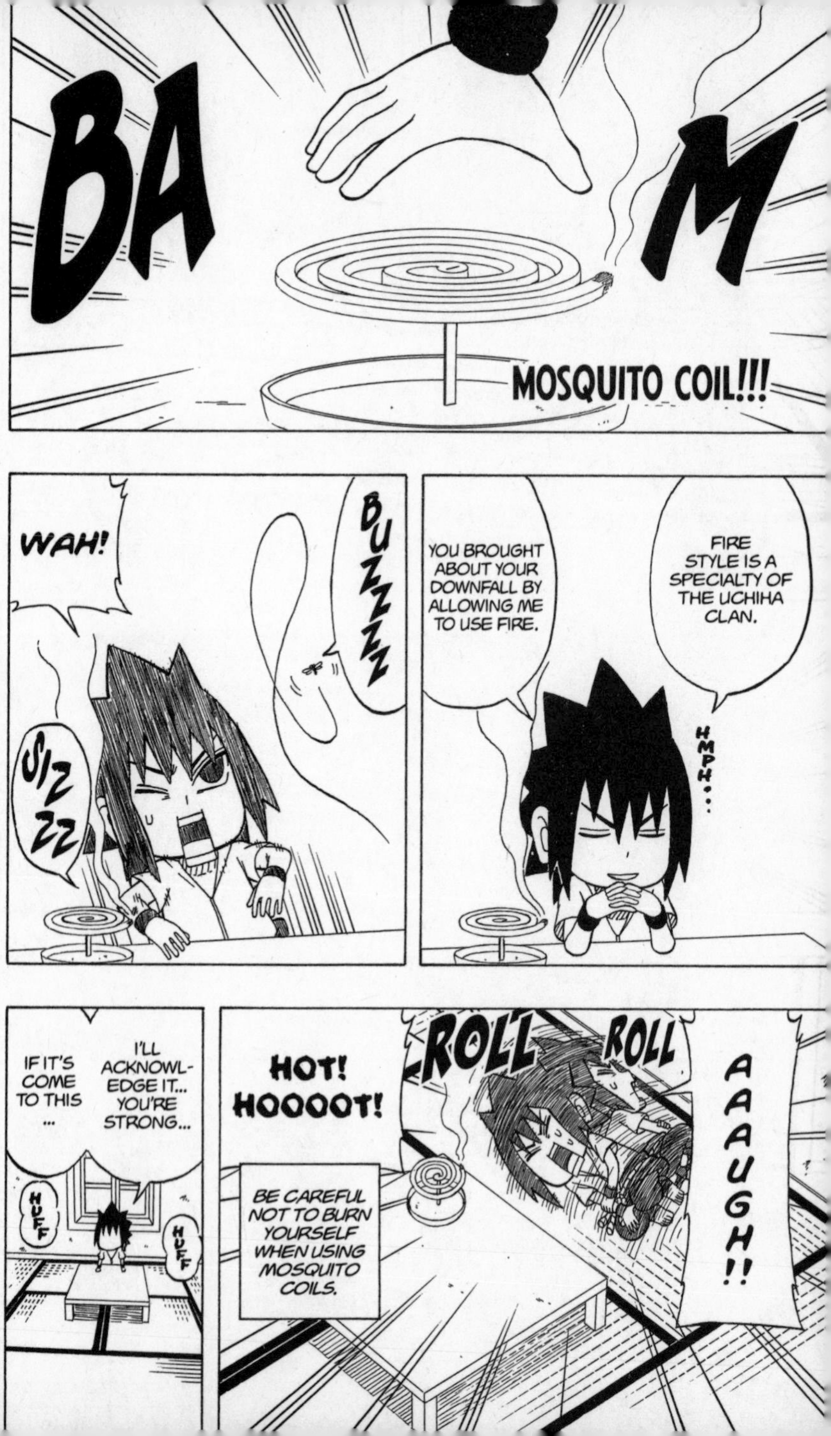
BAM
MOSQUITO COIL!!!
FIRE STYLE IS A SPECIALTY OF THE UCHIHA CLAN.
YOU BROUGHT ABOUT YOUR DOWNFALL BY ALLOWING ME TO USE FIRE.
HMPH...
BUZZZZ
WAH!
SIZZZZ
ROLL ROLL
AAAAUGH!!
HOT! HOOOOT!
BE CAREFUL NOT TO BURN YOURSELF WHEN USING MOSQUITO COILS.
I'LL ACKNOWL-EDGE IT... YOU'RE STRONG...
IF IT'S COME TO THIS ...
HUFF
HUFF

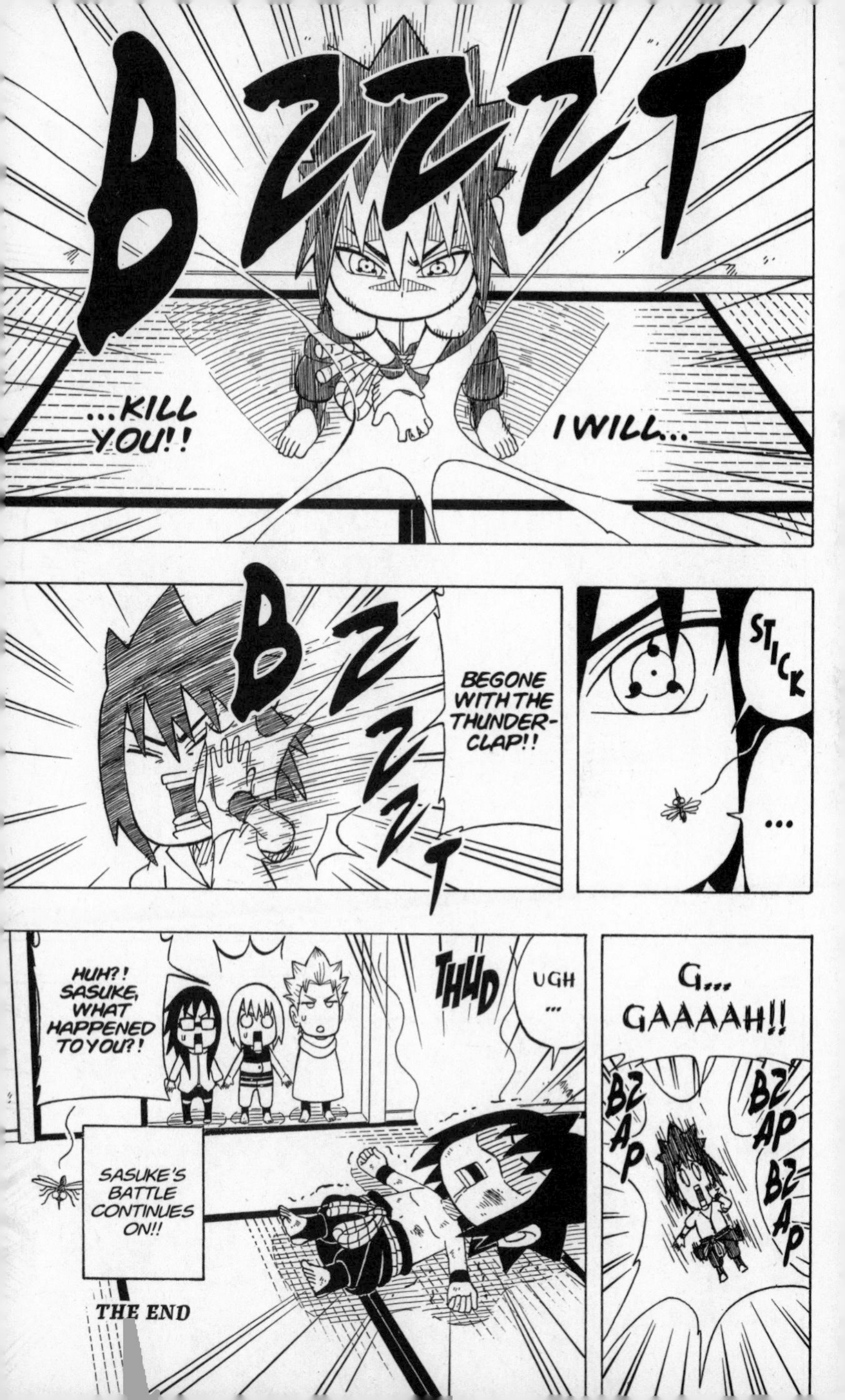
BZZZZT
I WILL...
...KILL YOU!!
STICK
...
BEGONE WITH THE THUNDER-CLAP!!
BZZZZT
G... GAAAAH!!
BZAP
BZAP
BZAP
UGH ...
THUD
HUH?! SASUKE, WHAT HAPPENED TO YOU?!
SASUKE'S BATTLE CONTINUES ON!!
THE END

MINI MANGA 5: SASUKE VS. ONE-MAN KARAOKE!!

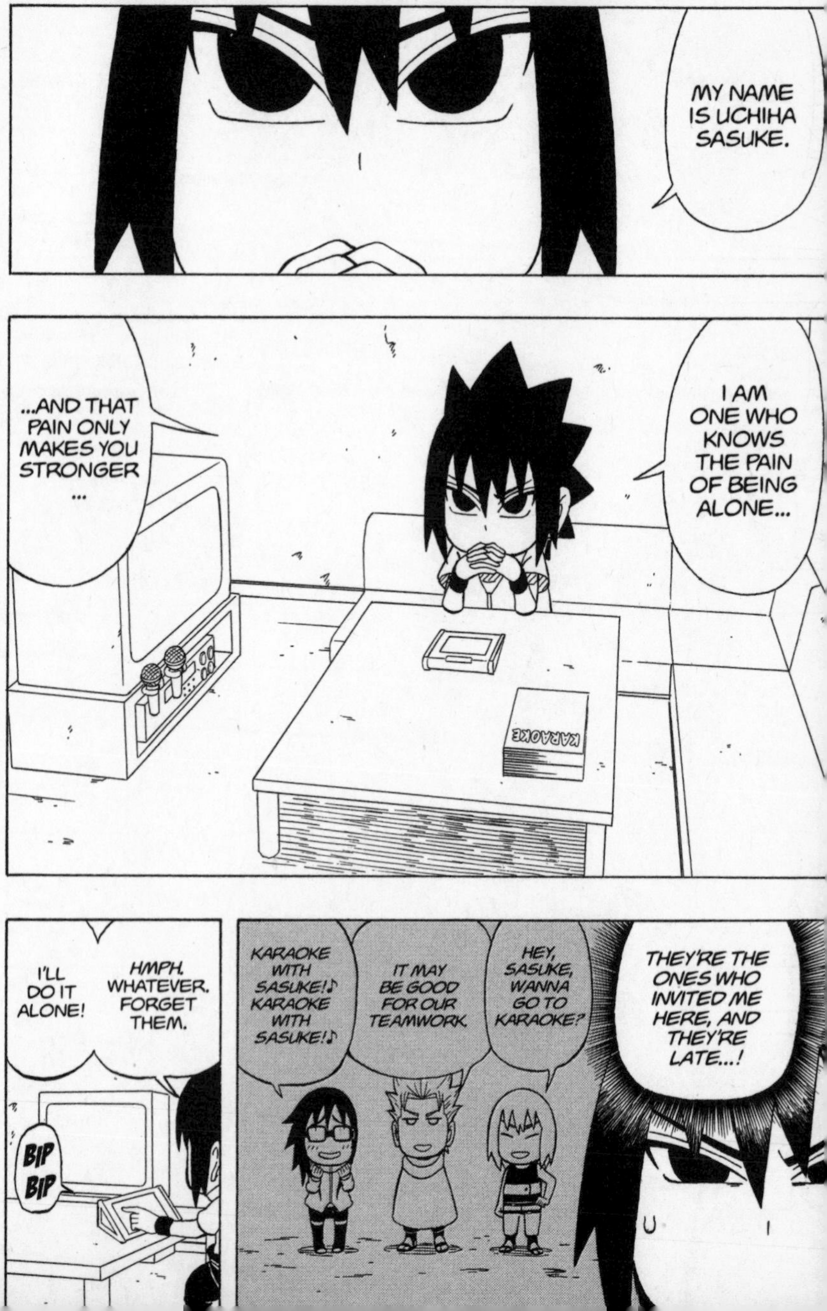

MY NAME IS UCHIHA SASUKE.
I AM ONE WHO KNOWS THE PAIN OF BEING ALONE...
...AND THAT PAIN ONLY MAKES YOU STRONGER ...
KARAOKE
THEY'RE THE ONES WHO INVITED ME HERE, AND THEY'RE LATE...!
HEY, SASUKE, WANNA GO TO KARAOKE?
IT MAY BE GOOD FOR OUR TEAMWORK.
KARAOKE WITH SASUKE!♪ KARAOKE WITH SASUKE!♪
HMPH. WHATEVER. FORGET THEM.
I'LL DO IT ALONE!
BIP BIP

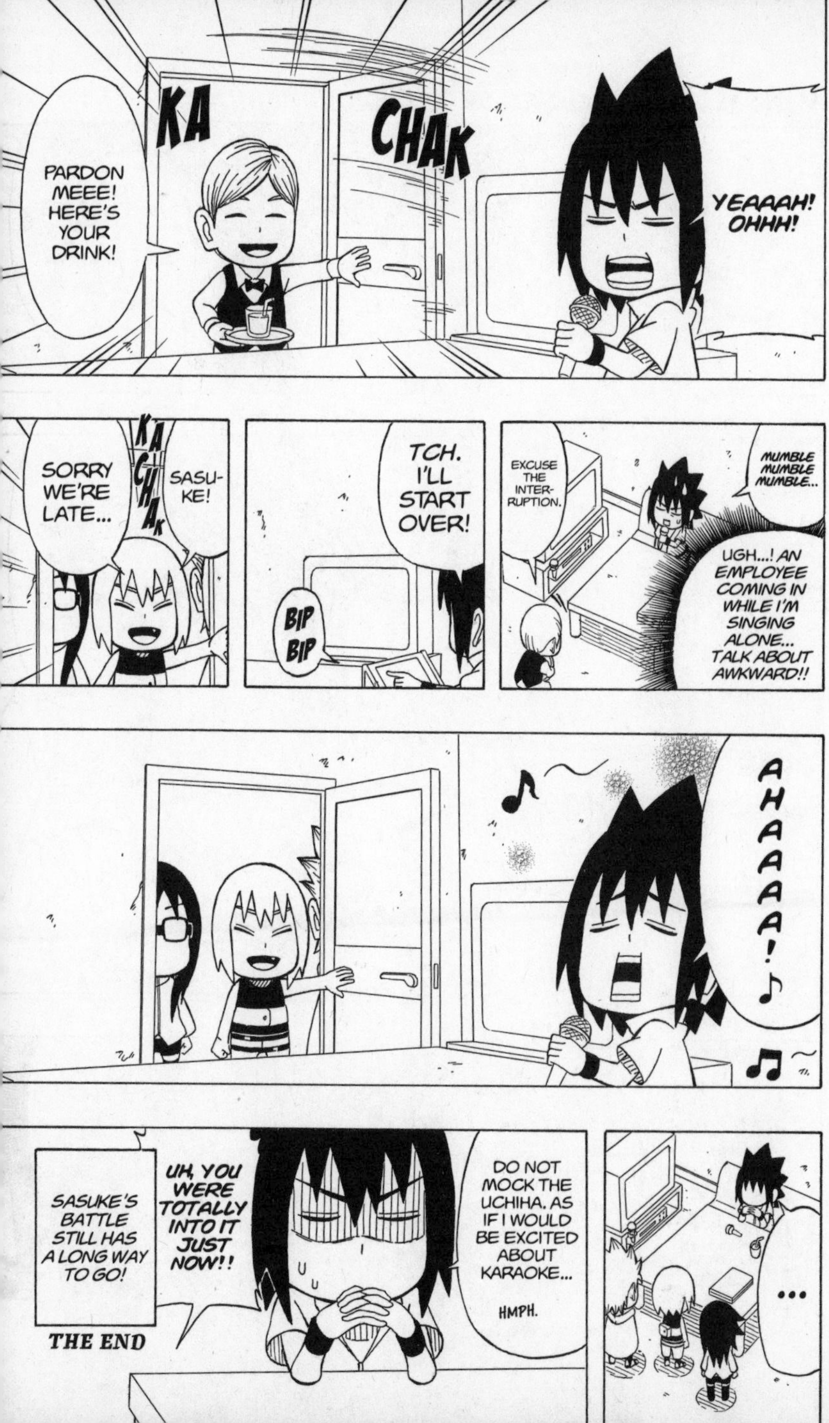
YEAAAH! OHHH!
KA CHAK
PARDON MEEE! HERE'S YOUR DRINK!
MUMBLE MUMBLE MUMBLE...
UGH...! AN EMPLOYEE COMING IN WHILE I'M SINGING ALONE... TALK ABOUT AWKWARD!!
EXCUSE THE INTER-RUPTION.
TCH. I'LL START OVER!
BIP BIP
SASU-KE!
KACHAK
SORRY WE'RE LATE...
AHAAAAA! ♪
...
DO NOT MOCK THE UCHIHA. AS IF I WOULD BE EXCITED ABOUT KARAOKE...
HMPH.
UH, YOU WERE TOTALLY INTO IT JUST NOW!!
SASUKE'S BATTLE STILL HAS A LONG WAY TO GO!
THE END

MINI MANGA 6: SASUKE VS. THE BACK ITCH!!

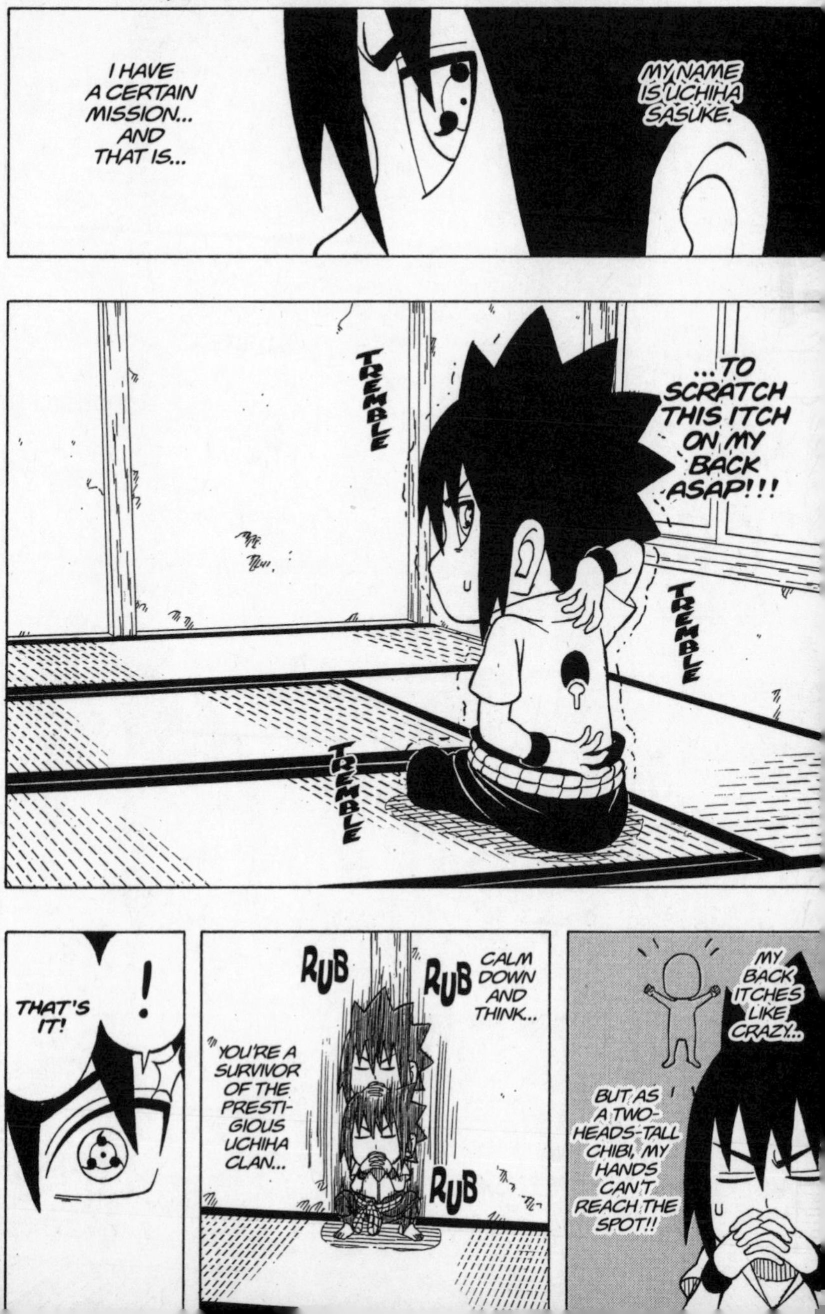
MY NAME IS UCHIHA SASUKE.
I HAVE A CERTAIN MISSION... AND THAT IS...
...TO SCRATCH THIS ITCH ON MY BACK ASAP!!!
TREMBLE
TREMBLE
TREMBLE
MY BACK ITCHES LIKE CRAZY...
BUT AS A TWO-HEADS-TALL CHIBI, MY HANDS CAN'T REACH THE SPOT!!
RUB
CALM DOWN AND THINK...
RUB
YOU'RE A SURVIVOR OF THE PRESTI-GIOUS UCHIHA CLAN...
RUB
!
THAT'S IT!

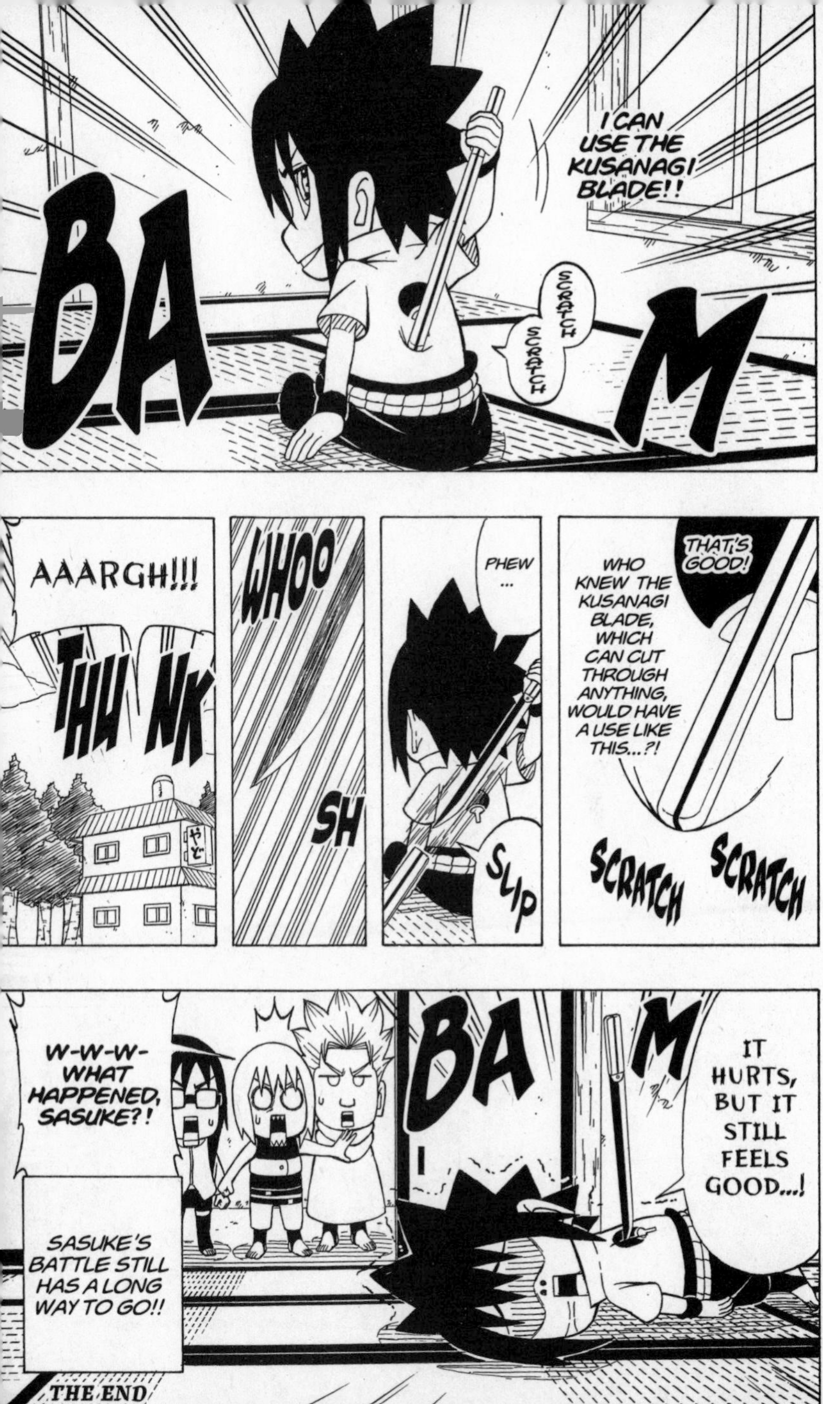
I CAN USE THE KUSANAGI BLADE!!
SCRATCH SCRATCH
BAM
THAT'S GOOD!
WHO KNEW THE KUSANAGI BLADE, WHICH CAN CUT THROUGH ANYTHING, WOULD HAVE A USE LIKE THIS...?!
SCRATCH SCRATCH
PHEW ...
SLIP
WHOOSH
AAARGH!!!
THUNK
IT HURTS, BUT IT STILL FEELS GOOD...!
BAM
W-W-W-WHAT HAPPENED, SASUKE?!
SASUKE'S BATTLE STILL HAS A LONG WAY TO GO!!

THE END

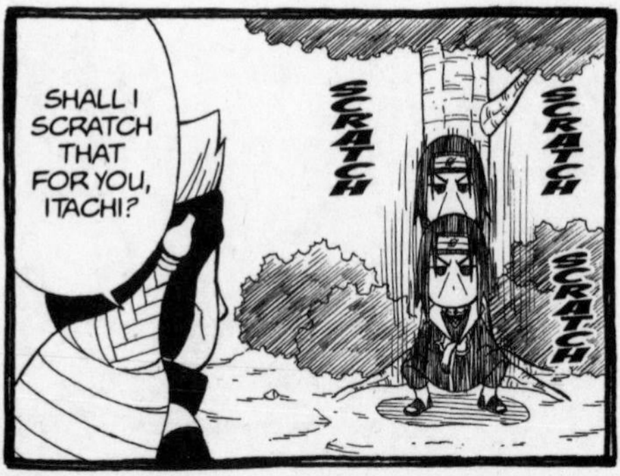
SCRATCH
SCRATCH
SCRATCH
SHALL I SCRATCH THAT FOR YOU, ITACHI?

MINI-MANGA 7: LET'S GO TO THE *NARUTO* ART EXHIBIT! OSAKA EDITION

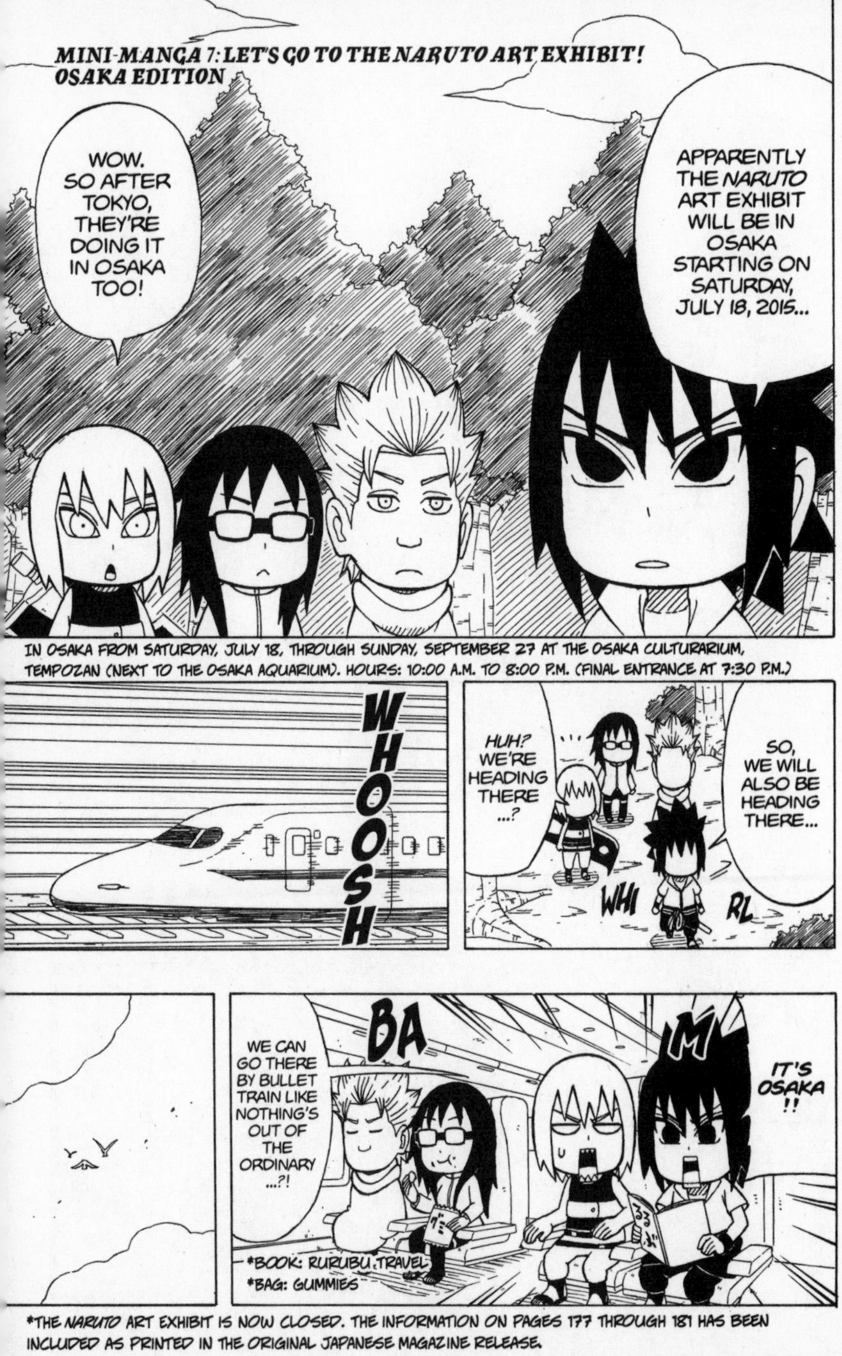
APPARENTLY THE *NARUTO* ART EXHIBIT WILL BE IN OSAKA STARTING ON SATURDAY, JULY 18, 2015...
WOW. SO AFTER TOKYO, THEY'RE DOING IT IN OSAKA TOO!
IN OSAKA FROM SATURDAY, JULY 18, THROUGH SUNDAY, SEPTEMBER 27 AT THE OSAKA CULTURARIUM, TEMPOZAN (NEXT TO THE OSAKA AQUARIUM). HOURS: 10:00 A.M. TO 8:00 P.M. (FINAL ENTRANCE AT 7:30 P.M.)
SO, WE WILL ALSO BE HEADING THERE...
HUH? WE'RE HEADING THERE ...?
WHIRL
WHOOSH
BAM
IT'S OSAKA !!
WE CAN GO THERE BY BULLET TRAIN LIKE NOTHING'S OUT OF THE ORDINARY ...?!
*BOOK: RURUBU TRAVEL
*BAG: GUMMIES

*THE *NARUTO* ART EXHIBIT IS NOW CLOSED. THE INFORMATION ON PAGES 177 THROUGH 181 HAS BEEN INCLUDED AS PRINTED IN THE ORIGINAL JAPANESE MAGAZINE RELEASE.

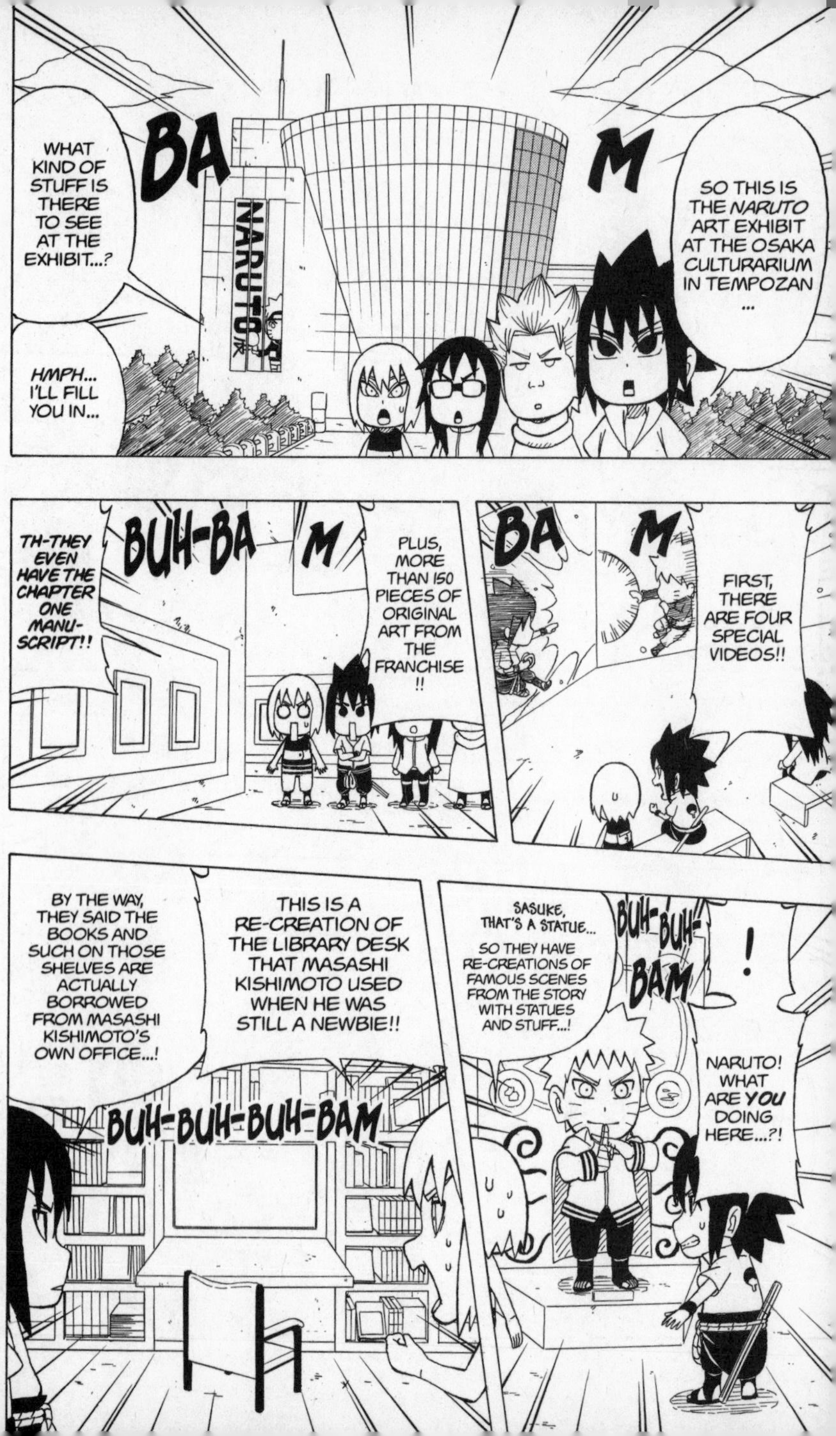
BAM
SO THIS IS THE *NARUTO* ART EXHIBIT AT THE OSAKA CULTURARIUM IN TEMPOZAN...
NARUTO
WHAT KIND OF STUFF IS THERE TO SEE AT THE EXHIBIT...?
HMPH... I'LL FILL YOU IN...
BAM
FIRST, THERE ARE FOUR SPECIAL VIDEOS!!
PLUS, MORE THAN 150 PIECES OF ORIGINAL ART FROM THE FRANCHISE!!
BUH-BAM
TH-THEY EVEN HAVE THE CHAPTER ONE MANUSCRIPT!!
!
BUH-BUH-BAM
NARUTO! WHAT ARE ***YOU*** DOING HERE...?!
SASUKE, THAT'S A STATUE...
SO THEY HAVE RE-CREATIONS OF FAMOUS SCENES FROM THE STORY WITH STATUES AND STUFF...!
THIS IS A RE-CREATION OF THE LIBRARY DESK THAT MASASHI KISHIMOTO USED WHEN HE WAS STILL A NEWBIE!!
BY THE WAY, THEY SAID THE BOOKS AND SUCH ON THOSE SHELVES ARE ACTUALLY BORROWED FROM MASASHI KISHIMOTO'S OWN OFFICE...!
BUH-BUH-BUH-BAM

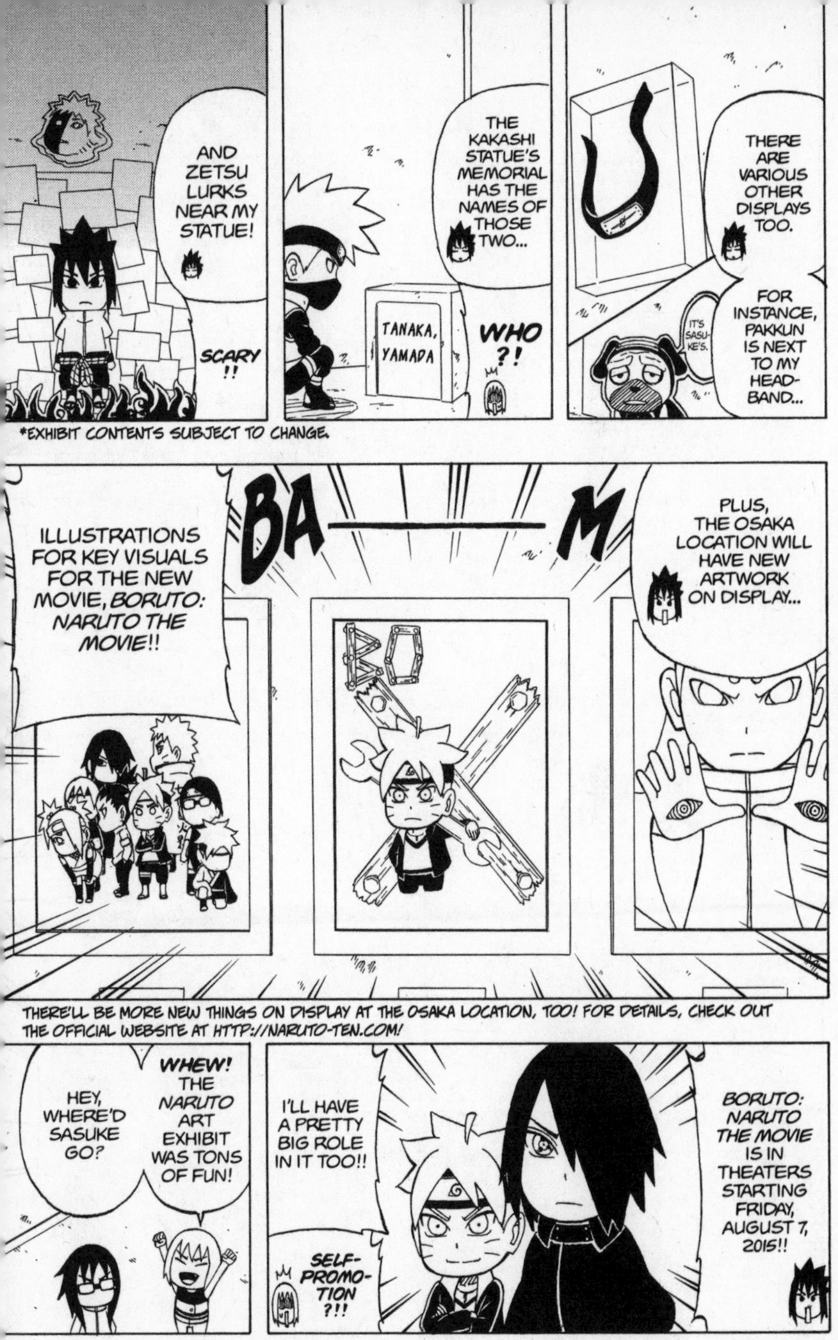
THERE ARE VARIOUS OTHER DISPLAYS TOO.
FOR INSTANCE, PAKKUN IS NEXT TO MY HEAD-BAND...
IT'S SASU-KE'S.
THE KAKASHI STATUE'S MEMORIAL HAS THE NAMES OF THOSE TWO...
TANAKA, YAMADA
WHO?!
AND ZETSU LURKS NEAR MY STATUE!
SCARY!!
*EXHIBIT CONTENTS SUBJECT TO CHANGE.
PLUS, THE OSAKA LOCATION WILL HAVE NEW ARTWORK ON DISPLAY...
BA———M
ILLUSTRATIONS FOR KEY VISUALS FOR THE NEW MOVIE, *BORUTO: NARUTO THE MOVIE*!!
BO
THERE'LL BE MORE NEW THINGS ON DISPLAY AT THE OSAKA LOCATION, TOO! FOR DETAILS, CHECK OUT THE OFFICIAL WEBSITE AT HTTP://NARUTO-TEN.COM!
BORUTO: NARUTO THE MOVIE IS IN THEATERS STARTING FRIDAY, AUGUST 7, 2015!!
I'LL HAVE A PRETTY BIG ROLE IN IT TOO!!
SELF-PROMOTION?!!
WHEW! THE *NARUTO* ART EXHIBIT WAS TONS OF FUN!
HEY, WHERE'D SASUKE GO?

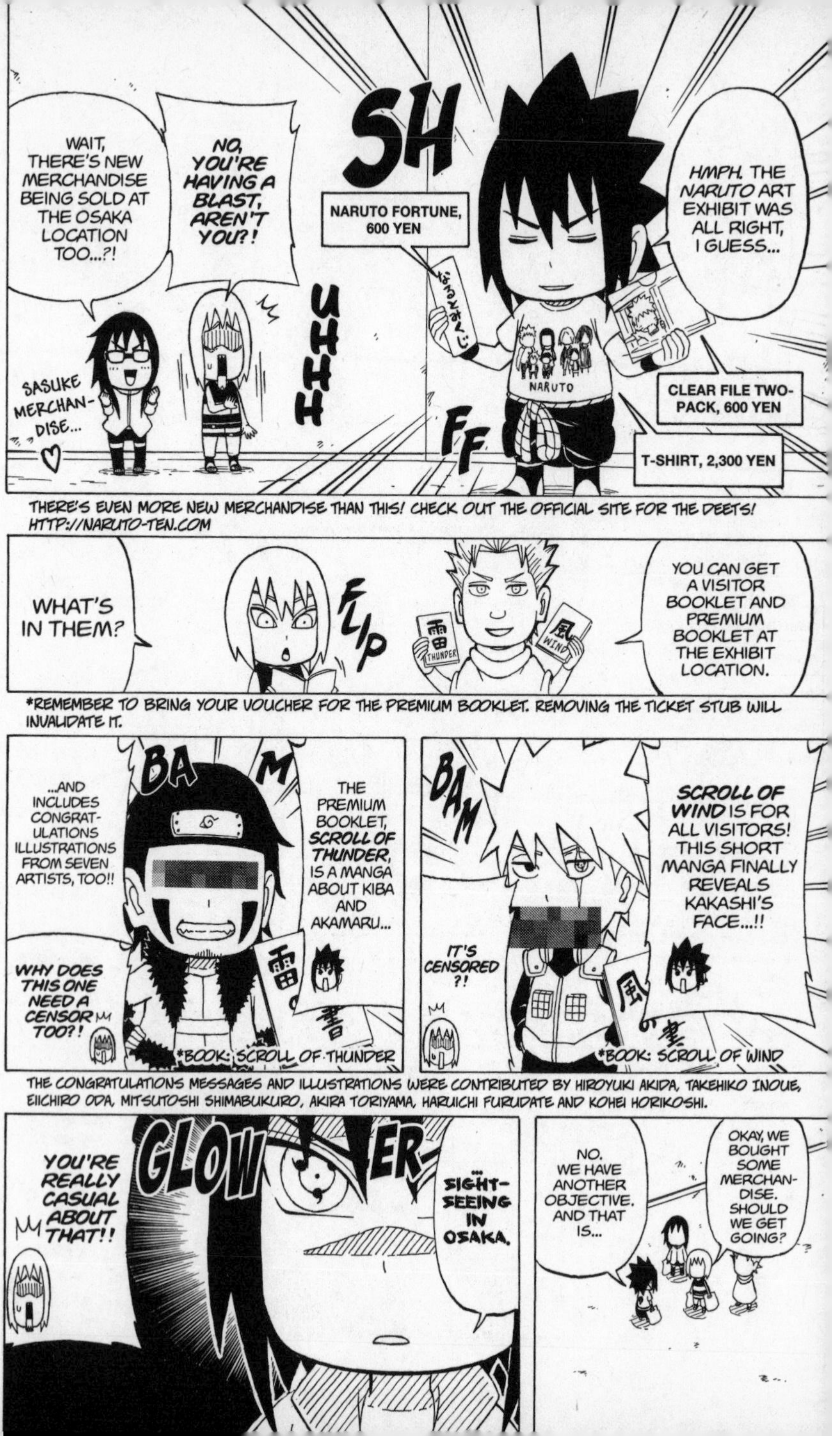
HMPH. THE NARUTO ART EXHIBIT WAS ALL RIGHT, I GUESS...
SH
FF
NARUTO FORTUNE, 600 YEN
なるとみくじ
CLEAR FILE TWO-PACK, 600 YEN
T-SHIRT, 2,300 YEN
NARUTO
NO, YOU'RE HAVING A BLAST, AREN'T YOU?!
UHHH
WAIT, THERE'S NEW MERCHANDISE BEING SOLD AT THE OSAKA LOCATION TOO...?!
SASUKE MERCHANDISE... ♡
THERE'S EVEN MORE NEW MERCHANDISE THAN THIS! CHECK OUT THE OFFICIAL SITE FOR THE DEETS! HTTP://NARUTO-TEN.COM
YOU CAN GET A VISITOR BOOKLET AND PREMIUM BOOKLET AT THE EXHIBIT LOCATION.
THUNDER
WIND
FLIP
WHAT'S IN THEM?
*REMEMBER TO BRING YOUR VOUCHER FOR THE PREMIUM BOOKLET. REMOVING THE TICKET STUB WILL INVALIDATE IT.
BAM
SCROLL OF WIND IS FOR ALL VISITORS! THIS SHORT MANGA FINALLY REVEALS KAKASHI'S FACE...!!
IT'S CENSORED?!
*BOOK: SCROLL OF WIND
BAM
THE PREMIUM BOOKLET, SCROLL OF THUNDER, IS A MANGA ABOUT KIBA AND AKAMARU...
...AND INCLUDES CONGRATULATIONS ILLUSTRATIONS FROM SEVEN ARTISTS, TOO!!
WHY DOES THIS ONE NEED A CENSOR TOO?!
*BOOK: SCROLL OF THUNDER
THE CONGRATULATIONS MESSAGES AND ILLUSTRATIONS WERE CONTRIBUTED BY HIROYUKI AKIDA, TAKEHIKO INOUE, EIICHIRO ODA, MITSUTOSHI SHIMABUKURO, AKIRA TORIYAMA, HARUICHI FURUDATE AND KOHEI HORIKOSHI.
OKAY, WE BOUGHT SOME MERCHANDISE. SHOULD WE GET GOING?
NO. WE HAVE ANOTHER OBJECTIVE. AND THAT IS...
GLOWER
...SIGHTSEEING IN OSAKA.
YOU'RE REALLY CASUAL ABOUT THAT!!

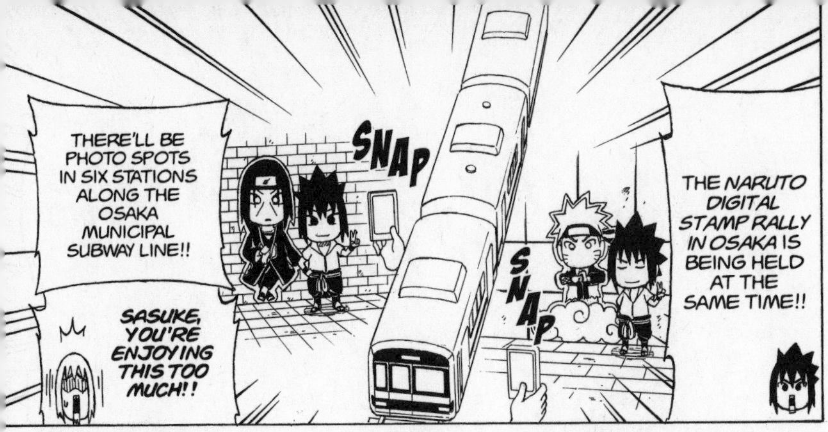
THERE'LL BE PHOTO SPOTS IN SIX STATIONS ALONG THE OSAKA MUNICIPAL SUBWAY LINE!!
SNAP
THE NARUTO DIGITAL STAMP RALLY IN OSAKA IS BEING HELD AT THE SAME TIME!!
SNAP
SASUKE, YOU'RE ENJOYING THIS TOO MUCH!!

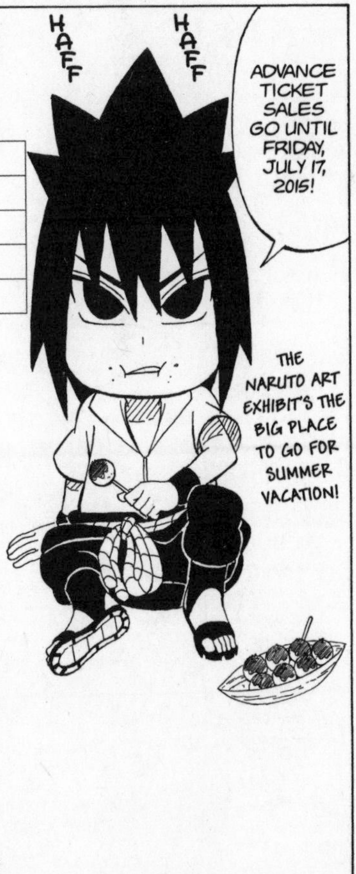
HAFF HAFF
ADVANCE TICKET SALES GO UNTIL FRIDAY, JULY 17, 2015!
THE NARUTO ART EXHIBIT'S THE BIG PLACE TO GO FOR SUMMER VACATION!

Tickets on sale at Loppi kiosks inside Lawson and Mini Stop locations nationwide, or on the Web at *http://l-tike.com/naruto-ten* !
Use the L Code "59000"!

Sales Period for Osaka	6/6 through 7/17		7/18 through 9/27
Ticket Type (includes tax)	Premium Advance Tickets	Regular Advance Tickets	At the door
Adults	¥1,900	¥1,800	¥2,000
Middle/High Schoolers	¥1,400	¥1300	¥1,500
Children over 4	¥600	¥500	¥800

Caution:
*Taxes included in the price.
*This L Code applies only to the Osaka location.
*Advance tickets sold only through Lawson Tickets.
*Please be advised that advance tickets are issued only at Loppi kiosks inside Lawson and Mini Stop locations nationwide and will not be delivered.
*At-the-door tickets are also available at the Osaka Culturarium in Tempozan, at the ticket counter in the second floor main lobby (cash only)
*Premium booklet not for sale.
*Both the Tokyo and Osaka locations will offer the same premium booklet.
*To receive your premium booklet, please present your voucher at the exhibit location during the duration of the Osaka exhibit.
*Depending on crowding, there may be a wait time or you may be unable to enter.

THE END

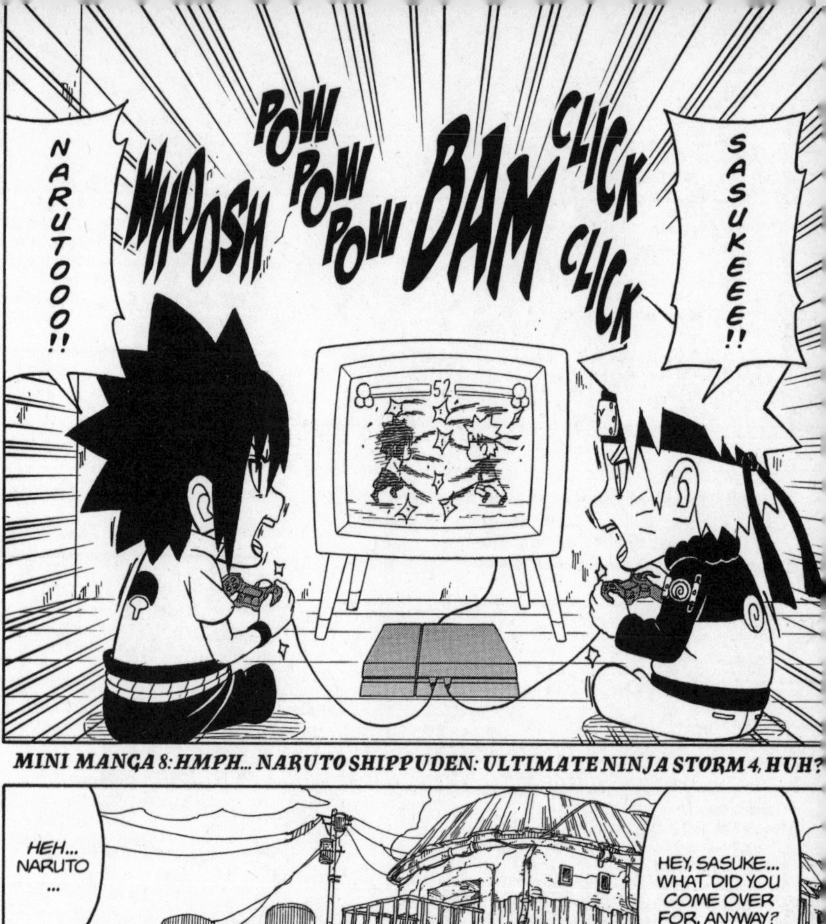
SASUKEEE!!
CLICK CLICK
BAM
POW POW POW
WHOOSH
NARUTOOOO!!

MINI MANGA 8: HMPH... NARUTO SHIPPUDEN: ULTIMATE NINJA STORM 4, HUH?

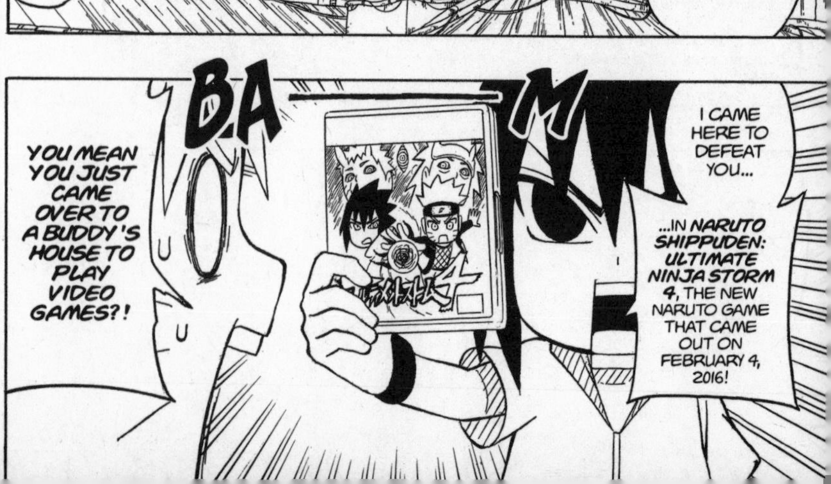
HEY, SASUKE... WHAT DID YOU COME OVER FOR, ANYWAY?
HEH... NARUTO ...
BAM
I CAME HERE TO DEFEAT YOU...
...IN NARUTO SHIPPUDEN: ULTIMATE NINJA STORM 4, THE NEW NARUTO GAME THAT CAME OUT ON FEBRUARY 4, 2016!
YOU MEAN YOU JUST CAME OVER TO A BUDDY'S HOUSE TO PLAY VIDEO GAMES?!

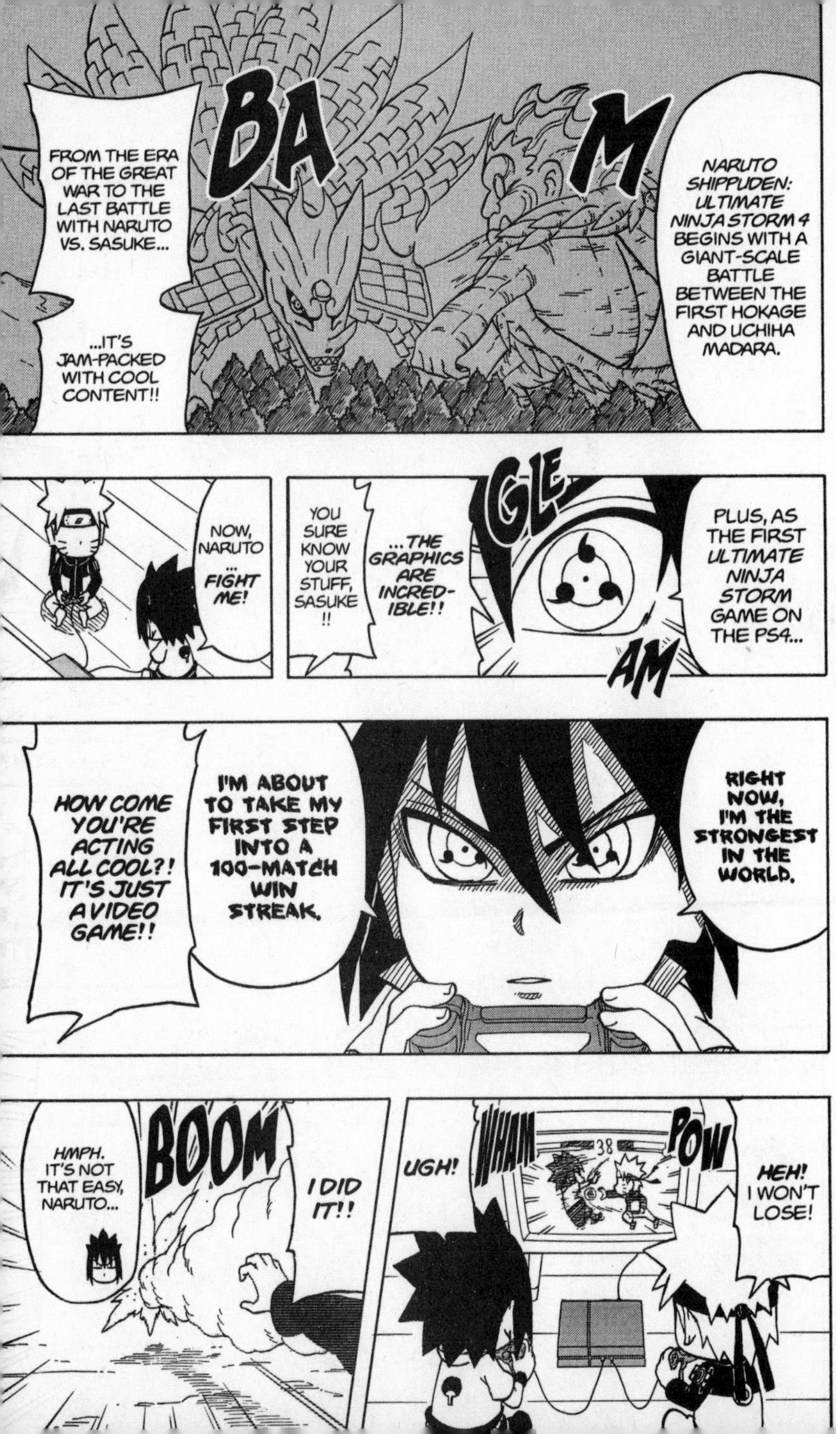
NARUTO SHIPPUDEN: ULTIMATE NINJA STORM 4 BEGINS WITH A GIANT-SCALE BATTLE BETWEEN THE FIRST HOKAGE AND UCHIHA MADARA.
BAM
FROM THE ERA OF THE GREAT WAR TO THE LAST BATTLE WITH NARUTO VS. SASUKE...
...IT'S JAM-PACKED WITH COOL CONTENT!!
PLUS, AS THE FIRST ULTIMATE NINJA STORM GAME ON THE PS4...
GLE
AM
...THE GRAPHICS ARE INCREDIBLE!!
YOU SURE KNOW YOUR STUFF, SASUKE!!
NOW, NARUTO... FIGHT ME!
RIGHT NOW, I'M THE STRONGEST IN THE WORLD.
I'M ABOUT TO TAKE MY FIRST STEP INTO A 100-MATCH WIN STREAK.
HOW COME YOU'RE ACTING ALL COOL?! IT'S JUST A VIDEO GAME!!
HEH! I WON'T LOSE!
POW
38
WHAM
UGH!
I DID IT!!
BOOM
HMPH. IT'S NOT THAT EASY, NARUTO...

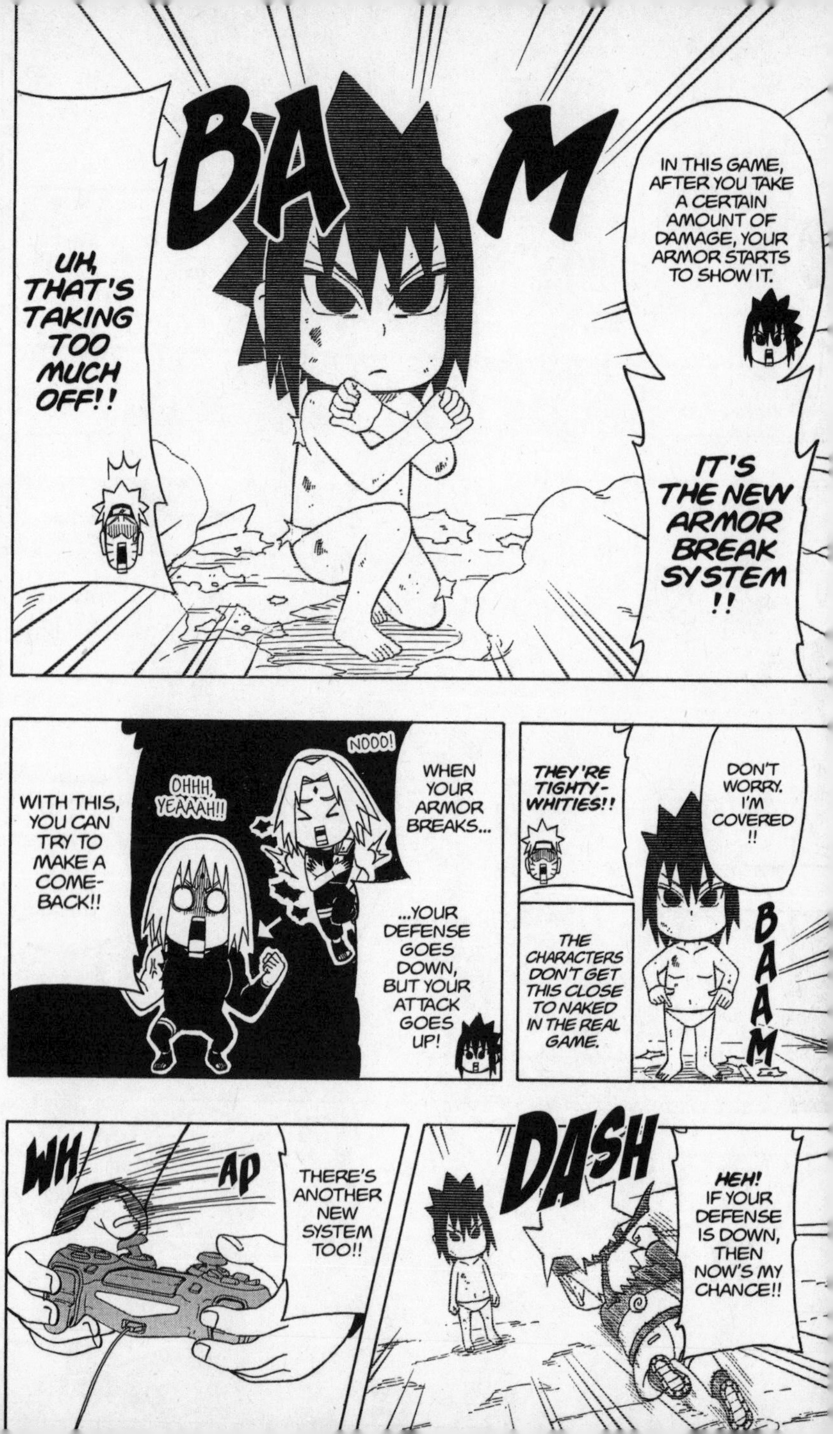
IN THIS GAME, AFTER YOU TAKE A CERTAIN AMOUNT OF DAMAGE, YOUR ARMOR STARTS TO SHOW IT.
IT'S THE NEW ARMOR BREAK SYSTEM!!
BAM
UH, THAT'S TAKING TOO MUCH OFF!!
DON'T WORRY. I'M COVERED!!
BAAM
THEY'RE TIGHTY-WHITIES!!
THE CHARACTERS DON'T GET THIS CLOSE TO NAKED IN THE REAL GAME.
WHEN YOUR ARMOR BREAKS...
...YOUR DEFENSE GOES DOWN, BUT YOUR ATTACK GOES UP!
NOOO!
OHHH, YEAAAH!!
WITH THIS, YOU CAN TRY TO MAKE A COME-BACK!!
HEH! IF YOUR DEFENSE IS DOWN, THEN NOW'S MY CHANCE!!
DASH
THERE'S ANOTHER NEW SYSTEM TOO!!
WHAP

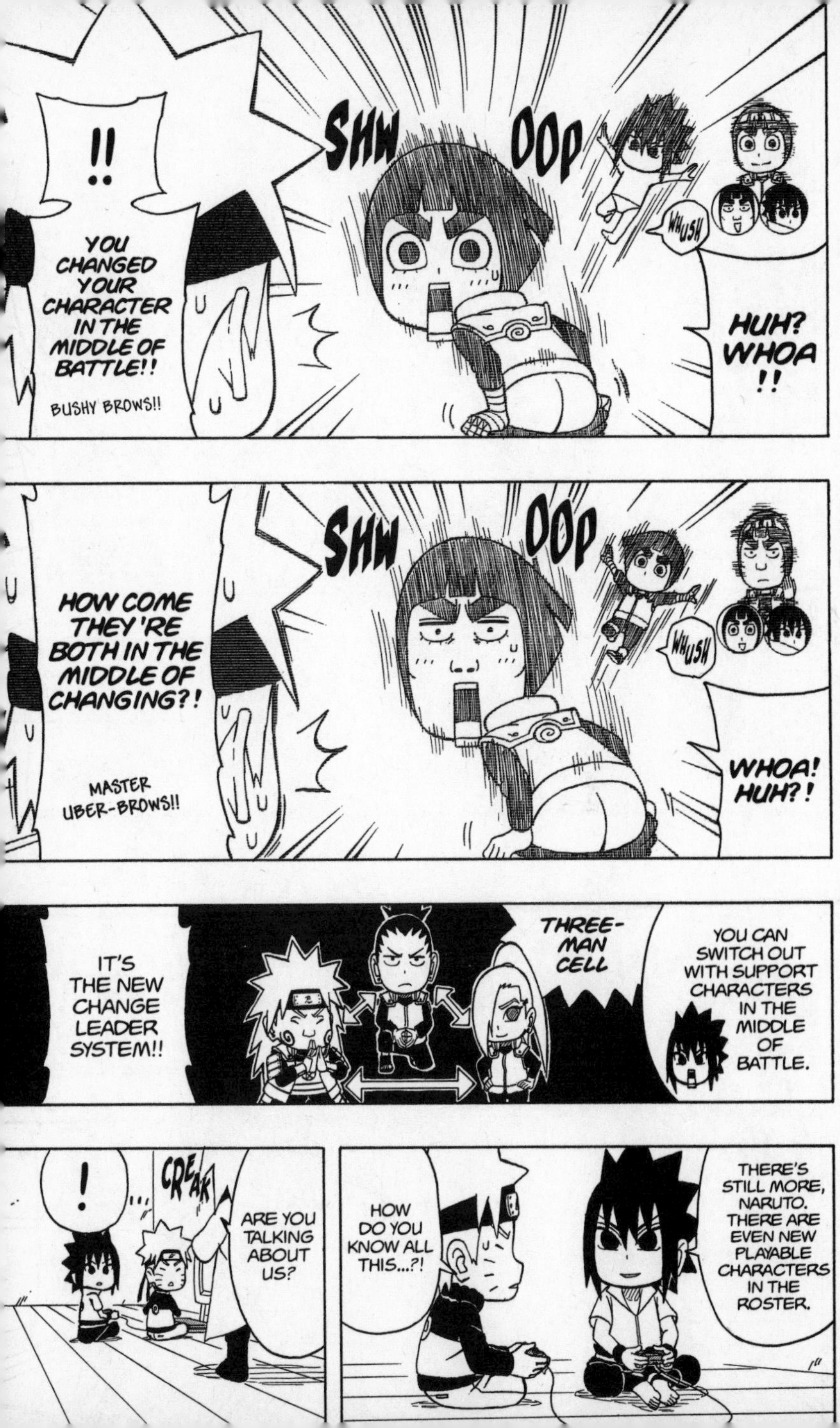
HUH? WHOA!!
WHUSH
SHW OOP
!!
YOU CHANGED YOUR CHARACTER IN THE MIDDLE OF BATTLE!!
BUSHY BROWS!!
WHOA! HUH?!
WHUSH
SHW OOP
HOW COME THEY'RE BOTH IN THE MIDDLE OF CHANGING?!
MASTER UBER-BROWS!!
YOU CAN SWITCH OUT WITH SUPPORT CHARACTERS IN THE MIDDLE OF BATTLE.
THREE-MAN CELL
IT'S THE NEW CHANGE LEADER SYSTEM!!
THERE'S STILL MORE, NARUTO. THERE ARE EVEN NEW PLAYABLE CHARACTERS IN THE ROSTER.
HOW DO YOU KNOW ALL THIS...?!
ARE YOU TALKING ABOUT US?
CREAK
...
!

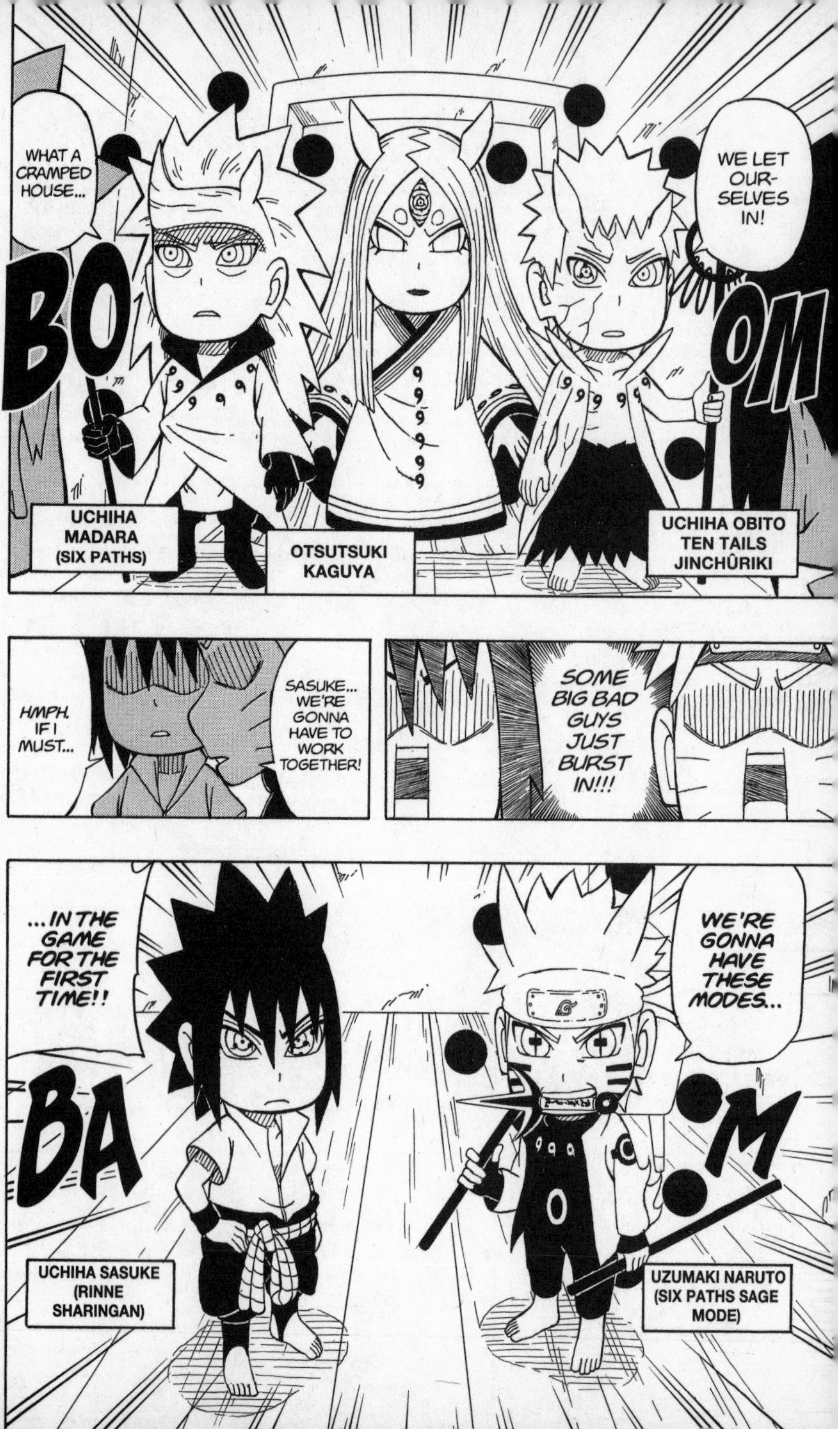
WE LET OUR-SELVES IN!
OM
UCHIHA OBITO TEN TAILS JINCHÛRIKI
OTSUTSUKI KAGUYA
WHAT A CRAMPED HOUSE...
BO
UCHIHA MADARA (SIX PATHS)
SOME BIG BAD GUYS JUST BURST IN!!!
SASUKE... WE'RE GONNA HAVE TO WORK TOGETHER!
HMPH. IF I MUST...
WE'RE GONNA HAVE THESE MODES...
M
UZUMAKI NARUTO (SIX PATHS SAGE MODE)
...IN THE GAME FOR THE FIRST TIME!!
BA
UCHIHA SASUKE (RINNE SHARINGAN)

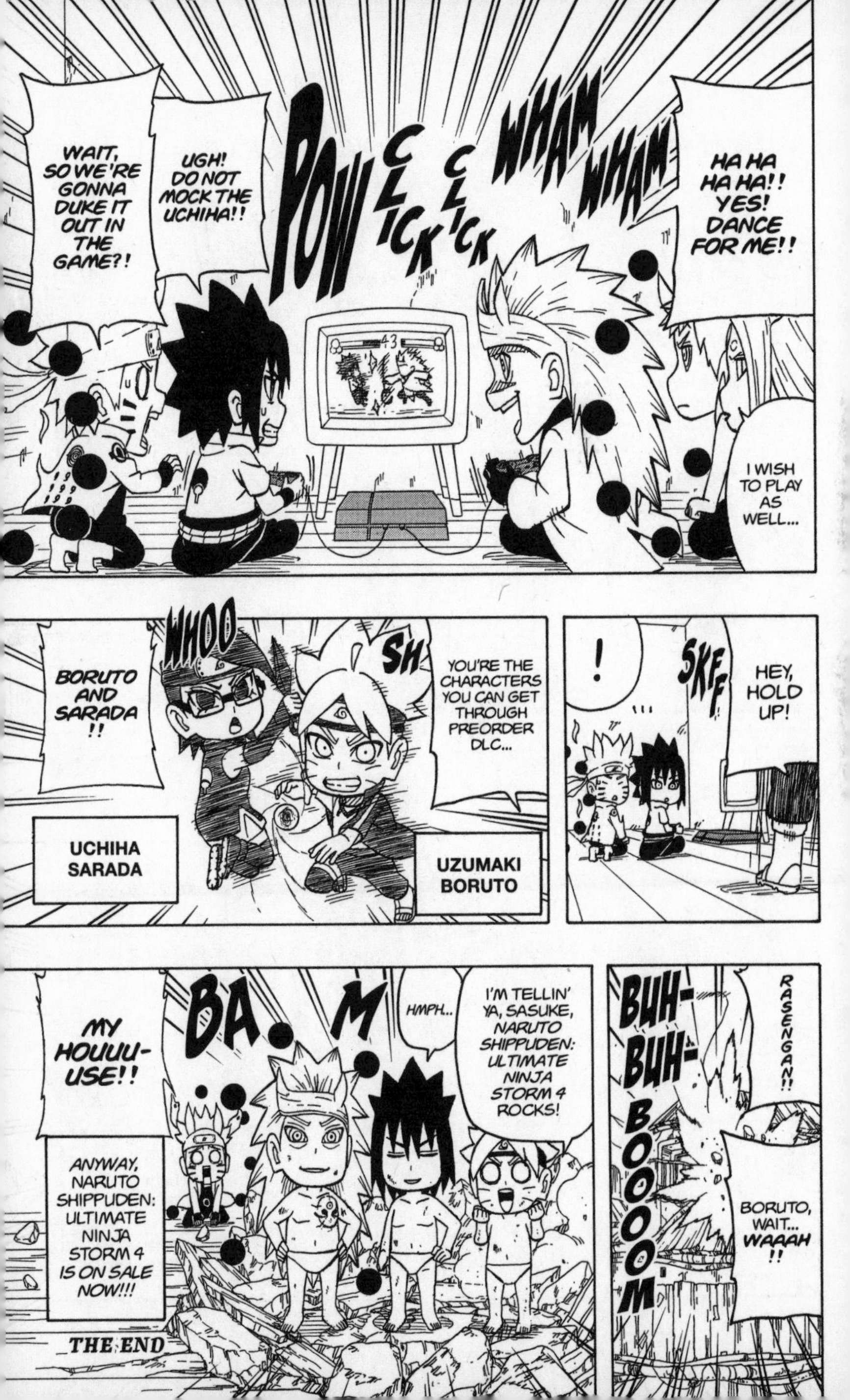
HA HA HA HA!! YES! DANCE FOR ME!!
WHAM WHAM
CLICK CLICK
POW
UGH! DO NOT MOCK THE UCHIHA!!
WAIT, SO WE'RE GONNA DUKE IT OUT IN THE GAME?!
I WISH TO PLAY AS WELL...
HEY, HOLD UP!
SKFF
!
...
YOU'RE THE CHARACTERS YOU CAN GET THROUGH PREORDER DLC...
SH
WHOO
BORUTO AND SARADA!!
UZUMAKI BORUTO
UCHIHA SARADA
RASENGAN!!
BUH-BUH-BOOOOOM
BORUTO, WAIT... WAAAH!!
I'M TELLIN' YA, SASUKE, NARUTO SHIPPUDEN: ULTIMATE NINJA STORM 4 ROCKS!
HMPH..
BA
M
MY HOUUU-USE!!
ANYWAY, NARUTO SHIPPUDEN: ULTIMATE NINJA STORM 4 IS ON SALE NOW!!!
THE END

MINI MANGA 9: NEW SERIES LAUNCH ADS!! x4

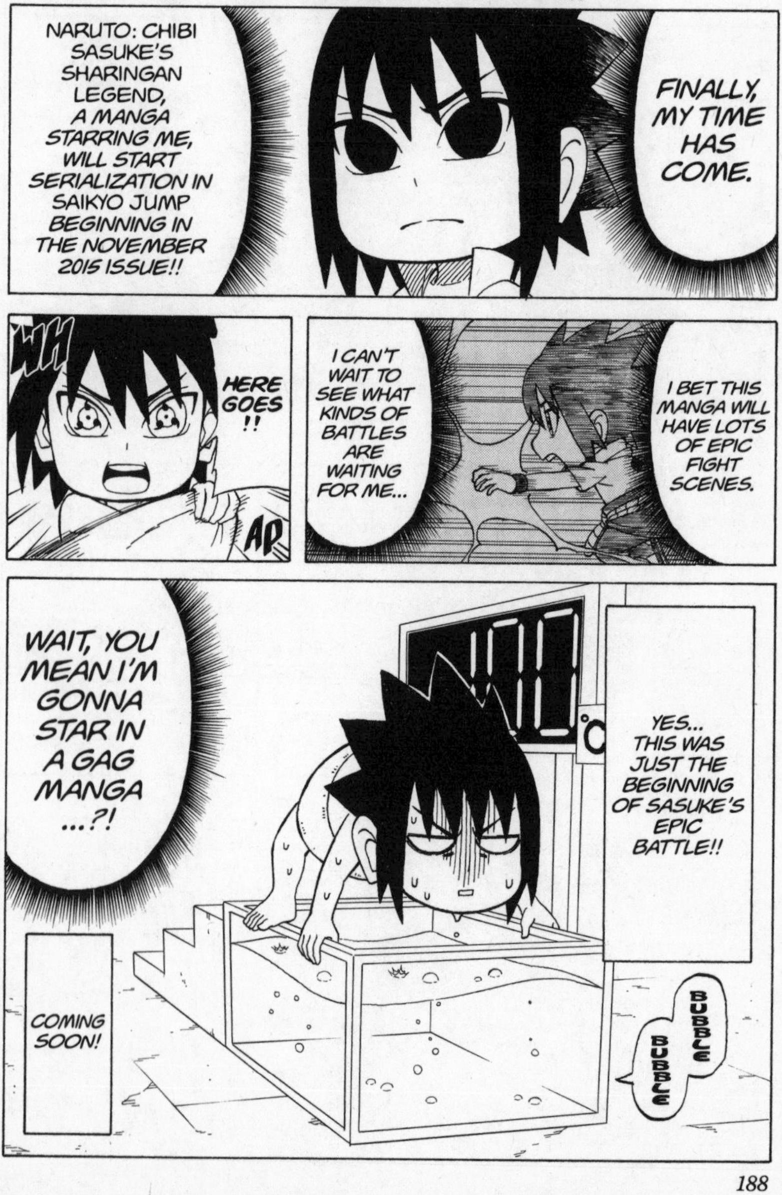
FINALLY, MY TIME HAS COME.
NARUTO: CHIBI SASUKE'S SHARINGAN LEGEND, A MANGA STARRING ME, WILL START SERIALIZATION IN SAIKYO JUMP BEGINNING IN THE NOVEMBER 2015 ISSUE!!
I BET THIS MANGA WILL HAVE LOTS OF EPIC FIGHT SCENES.
I CAN'T WAIT TO SEE WHAT KINDS OF BATTLES ARE WAITING FOR ME...
WH
HERE GOES!!
AP
YES... THIS WAS JUST THE BEGINNING OF SASUKE'S EPIC BATTLE!!
BUBBLE BUBBLE
WAIT, YOU MEAN I'M GONNA STAR IN A GAG MANGA ...?!
COMING SOON!

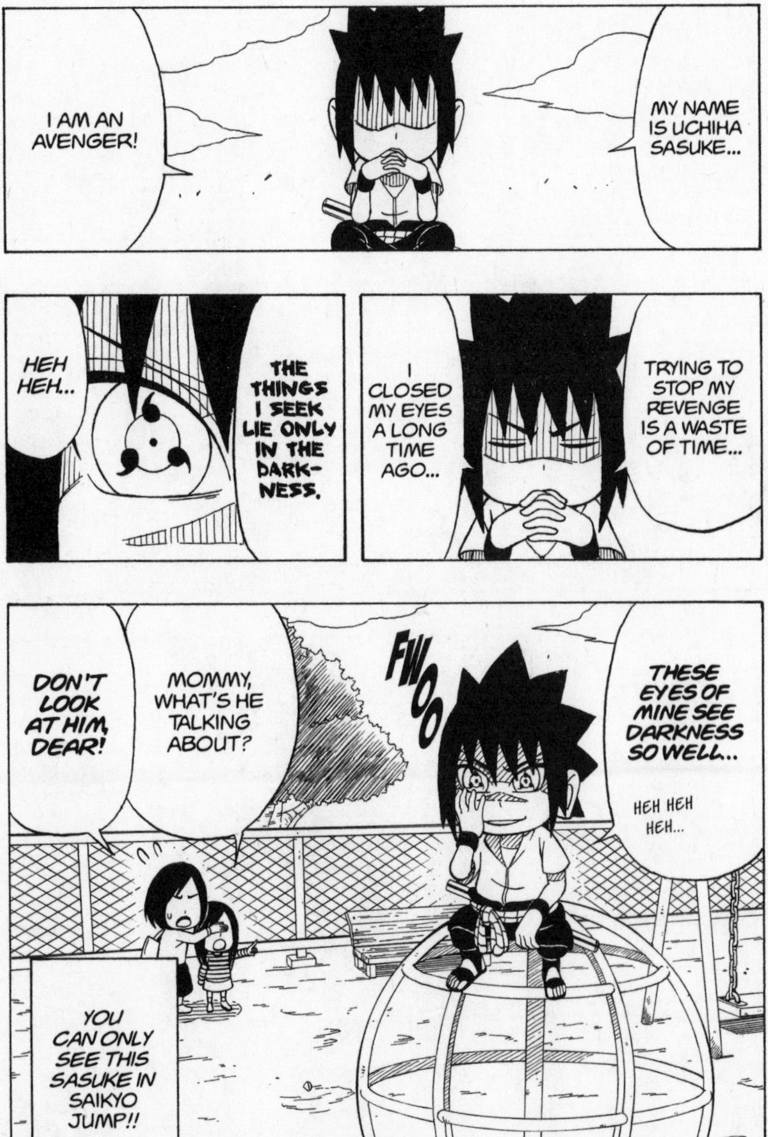
MY NAME IS UCHIHA SASUKE...
I AM AN AVENGER!
TRYING TO STOP MY REVENGE IS A WASTE OF TIME...
I CLOSED MY EYES A LONG TIME AGO...
THE THINGS I SEEK LIE ONLY IN THE DARK-NESS.
HEH HEH...
FWOO
THESE EYES OF MINE SEE DARKNESS SO WELL...
HEH HEH HEH...
MOMMY, WHAT'S HE TALKING ABOUT?
DON'T LOOK AT HIM, DEAR!
YOU CAN ONLY SEE THIS SASUKE IN SAIKYO JUMP!!

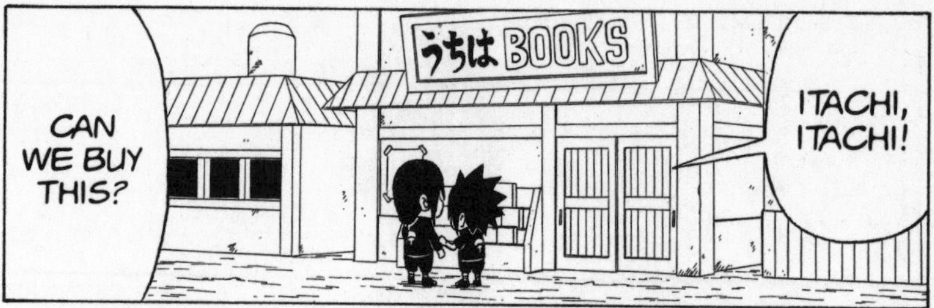
うちは BOOKS
ITACHI, ITACHI!
CAN WE BUY THIS?

*SIGN: UCHIHA BOOKS

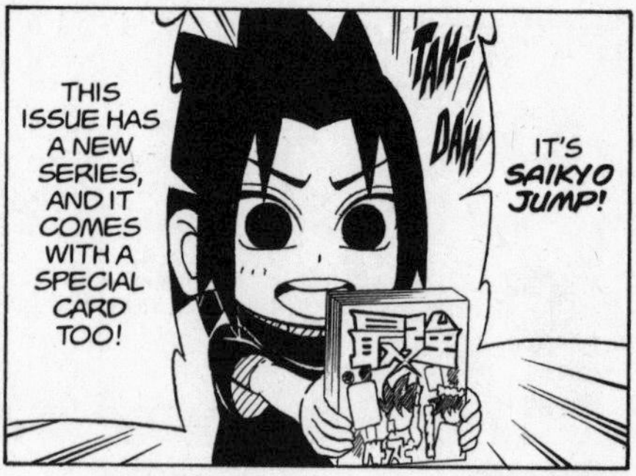
TAH-DAH
IT'S SAIKYO JUMP!
THIS ISSUE HAS A NEW SERIES, AND IT COMES WITH A SPECIAL CARD TOO!

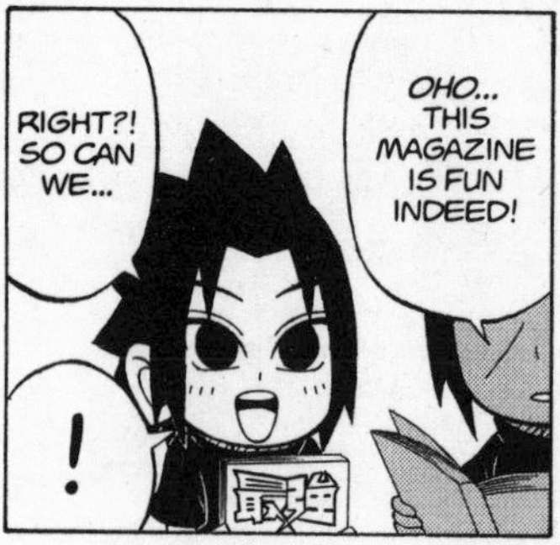
OHO... THIS MAGAZINE IS FUN INDEED!
RIGHT?! SO CAN WE...
!

*BOOK: SAIKYO

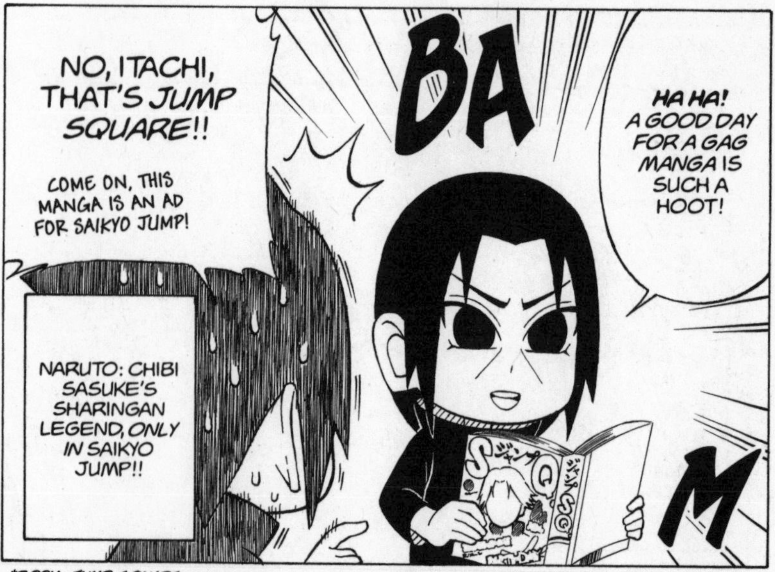
BAM
HA HA! A GOOD DAY FOR A GAG MANGA IS SUCH A HOOT!
NO, ITACHI, THAT'S JUMP SQUARE!!
COME ON, THIS MANGA IS AN AD FOR SAIKYO JUMP!
NARUTO: CHIBI SASUKE'S SHARINGAN LEGEND, ONLY IN SAIKYO JUMP!!

*BOOK: JUMP SQUARE

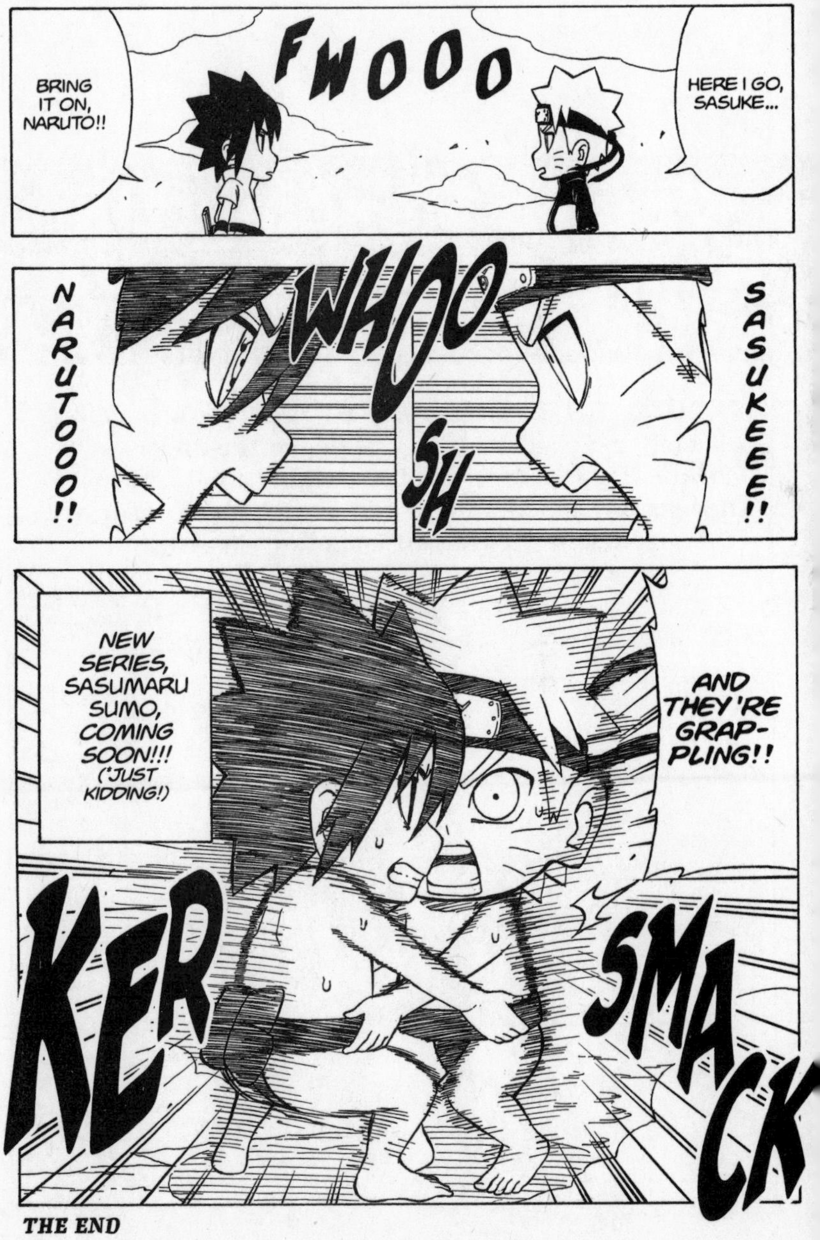
HERE I GO, SASUKE...
FWOOO
BRING IT ON, NARUTO!!
SASUKEEE!!
WHOOSH
NARUTOOOO!!
AND THEY'RE GRAPPLING!!
NEW SERIES, SASUMARU SUMO, COMING SOON!!! (*JUST KIDDING!)
KERSMACK

THE END

You're Reading the WRONG WAY!

NARUTO: CHIBI SASUKE'S SHARINGAN LEGEND reads from right to left, starting in the upper-right corner. Japanese is read from right to left, meaning that action, sound effects and word-balloon order are completely reversed from English order.

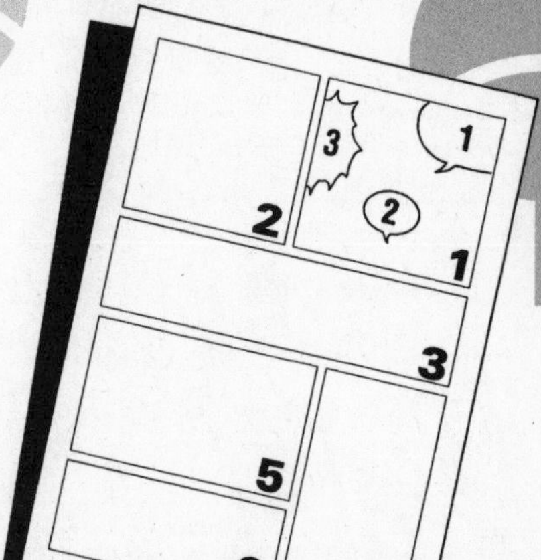

1
2
3
1
2
3
4
5
6

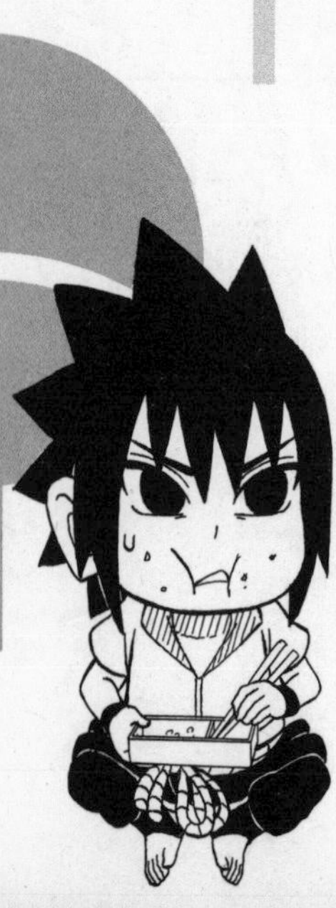

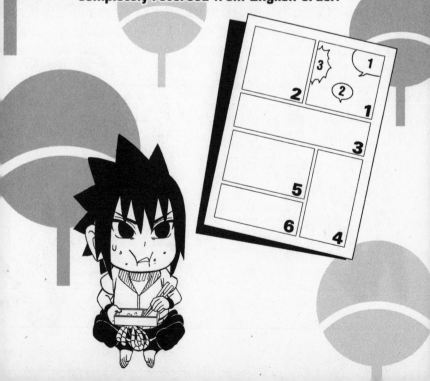